THE SOCIAL ORGANISATION AND
CUSTOMARY LAW OF THE
TOBA-BATAK OF NORTHERN SUMATRA

KONINKLIJK INSTITUUT
VOOR TAAL-, LAND- EN VOLKENKUNDE
TRANSLATION SERIES 7

&

THE SOCIAL ORGANISATION AND CUSTOMARY LAW OF THE TOBA-BATAK OF NORTHERN SUMATRA

BY

J. C. VERGOUWEN

WITH A PREFACE BY J. KEUNING

PUBLICATION COMMISSIONED AND FINANCED BY
THE NETHERLANDS INSTITUTE FOR
INTERNATIONAL CULTURAL RELATIONS

THE HAGUE - MARTINUS NIJHOFF - 1964

TRANSLATED FROM THE DUTCH BY JEUNE SCOTT-KEMBALL

PREFACE

J. C. Vergouwen's work, *Het Rechtsleven der Toba-Bataks,* here presented in an English translation, was published in the autumn of 1933, a few weeks before the author's death at the early age of 44 from tuberculosis, from which he had suffered since 1930. During the time he spent in a sanatorium in Davos and later in the Netherlands, he began and completed his monograph on the customary law of the Toba-Batak. His book immediately became one of the outstanding works of Dutch scholarship on Indonesian customary law (Adat law).

Jacob Cornelis Vergouwen began his career as an administrative officer in South Borneo (now Kalimantan) in 1913, after a brief practical training. In 1921 he was given the opportunity for further study at the University of Leiden where a five-year scientific training for a career as an administrative officer in the Dutch East Indies had just been instituted. On obtaining his Master's degree, he was appointed to the Tapanuli Residency, from of old, the homeland of the Toba, Mandailing, Angkola, and Dairi or Pakpak Batak.

As a young official, Vergouwen had already evinced great interest in the laws and customs of the Dayak people in Borneo. His studies at the University brought him into close contact with the founder of the science of Indonesian Adat law, Professor Cornelis van Vollenhoven, one of the greatest Dutch jurists of this century.

Since 1901, Van Vollenhoven had been teaching, among other things, Indonesian Adat Law at the University of Leiden. For his research he divided the Dutch East Indies into 19 law areas (*'rechtskringen'*) based on the existing diversity in the laws and customs of the peoples in the various parts of Indonesia. By 1918 he had completed the first scholarly description of the unwritten customary law in these 19 'homeonomic' groups. He found his material for it by laboriously searching through the anthropological literature of the time, in accounts of travels, in official reports, in the communications of Protestant and Roman Catholic missionaries and in adat law judgements, at that time only published sporadically. It was a masterly work; scholarly pioneering in the true sense. Van Vollenhoven worked out a fixed and specific taxonomy and introduced special terms for the qualification of the legal facts and the

legal concepts appropriate to the nature and content of the unwritten
Indonesian law. He broke away from the attempts to squeeze this law
into the straightjacket of legal taxonomy and legal terms current in
Dutch code-law, which owed their meaning and their suitability to this
Western legal system. *

With an adequate taxonomy, with a legal terminology of its own and
a specific approach, the science of adat law came to be acknowledged
as a young tree standing on its own in the park of Dutch legal science:
a yet small waringin amidst and beside the oaks and elms of the study
of Western law in the Netherlands.

Van Vollenhoven gave all his great gifts of mind and heart in the
service of the study of Indonesian adat law. A great inspiration and a
desire to study the laws and customs of Indonesian ethnic groups flowed
from him to his students, with whom he remained in constant contact
after they had begun their duties as judge or administrative officer in
the Dutch East Indies. Van Vollenhoven has had a great influence on
the striking development in the study of Indonesian adat law. During
his entire scholarly career — he died in 1933 when he was nearly 59 —
he strove for the recognition and the just appreciation of this autochthonous Indonesian law, both in the administration of justice and in the
management of internal affairs. In 1909 he wrote his booklet with the
significant title, *Miskenningen van het Adatrecht* (Four Cases of Lack
of Acknowledgement of Adat Law), and in 1919, *De Indonesiër en zijn
grond* (The Indonesian and his Land), in which, with a number of
arguments drawn from scholarship and practical experience, he took a
stand against Government plans in respect of land rights, because he saw
them as a violation of the autochthonous legal system of the Indonesian
people. In his splendid article, 'Juridisch confectiewerk; eenheidsprivaat-
recht voor Indië' (Ready-made Legislation; A Uniform Civil Code for
the Indies), written in 1925,** he exposed the artificiality, the unrealistic
nature and the practical inapplicability of a proposed uniform civil
code with a Dutch trade mark which was intended for all groups of
peoples in the Dutch East Indies — Dutch, Chinese, Arabs, Indians, etc.,
as well as for the Indonesians from all parts of the large and diversified

---

* Arthur Philips draws attention to this aspect of Van Vollenhoven's work in
Africa (Vol. XIX, 1949, p. 248): "... and the treatment of this subject (land
rights, J. K.) is marked by the use of a special terminology originally introduced by Van Vollenhoven as a remedy for the confusion caused by the
adoption of terms carrying a European legal connotation."

** Reprinted in *Het Adatrecht van Nederlandsch-Indië*, Vol. III, Leiden, 1933,
pp. 719 - 743.

archipelago. This Bill thereupon disappeared silently under the table.

The point of view, enunciated with such fervour by Van Vollenhoven and his supporters that, for the sake of justice, customary law should be acknowledged as being of at least the same ideal and practical value for the Indonesians and their social relationships as Western law is for the people in Western society, had by this time found a response among the highest policy-making Government authorities. A half-hearted taking into account of the autochthonous Indonesian law changed into a positive appraisal. As early as 1924, a Law University was established in Batavia (now Djakarta) where B. ter Haar — one of Van Vollenhoven's outstanding students — started to teach adat law, which he continued to do until 1939. *

In 1928 a commission was appointed with the object of advising the Government on the principles of agrarian legislation in the Dutch East Indies, and adat law jurists were freed to do research in various law areas. Another important feature of this new attitude towards adat law was that an investigation was ordered into the administration of justice in adat law cases, the aim being to effect a new and better regulation thereof. A pilot study was deemed necessary for that purpose and this brings us — after a perhaps overlong digression — back to Vergouwen and his work.

In May 1927, Vergouwen was relieved of his usual administrative duties and charged with the leadership of the highest Customary Courts (the so-called *Rapat na bolon*, literally, the Great Courts) in the Toba Batak country with, at the same time, instructions to embody his findings in a report and to make recommendations for reforms in the existing judicial organisation. This report appeared in 1930 (see p. 1 note 1). On its completion, Vergouwen went on leave to the Netherlands where he started, on his own initiative, the writing of his book, *Het Rechts-leven der Toba-Bataks*. That he completed this work in spite of his lingering and fatal illness, demonstrates his great interest in Toba-Batak society and its laws and customs; an interest which did not restrain him from making some rather critical observations in respect of particular facets of the culture of the Toba-Batak and their conceptions of right and wrong. In my opinion, he had a right to do so by virtue of his knowledge of their jural relationships and the disputes daily brought before him as President of the Courts, and his social intercourse with

---

* Ter Haar published a concise manual in 1939: *Beginselen en Stelsel van het Adatrecht*; translated into English and published by the Institute of Pacific Relations, New York, 1948, under the title: *Adatlaw in Indonesia*.

all levels of their society. He was no outsider dependent upon informants and enquiries; he had played an important part in deciding disputes and lawsuits of all kinds.

In a review of Vergouwen's book, Ter Haar says: "*Het Rechtsleven der Toba-Bataks* is truly a fine book. The indigenous society and its many-sided and complex relationships are studied and described 'from the inside' and customary law is shown as a pattern running through the entire social fabric." These words I readily endorse. I still remember clearly how much help this book was to me when I was a student of adat law in Leiden from 1931-34 endeavouring to grasp the inter-relationship of the Toba-Batak legal facts, and even more do I recall how, in 1935, as a young Government official, I had immediately on arrival in the Batak country the feeling that I had entered a known and understandable world. Above all, Vergouwen's study was a source, difficult to surpass, from which I acquired a knowledge and a comprehension of Toba-Batak laws and customs when I was President of the highest Customary Courts in 1940 and 1941. It made it possible for me to discuss with the chiefs, as members of the courts, on a footing of equality, as it were, the value and the meaning of the varying statements of the parties and the witnesses, and after that to establish, in collaboration with them, the rule to be applied to the case before the court. Vergouwen's exposition, moreover, showed the way to those relationships where an attempt at conciliation, or a mediatory settlement, could lead to a result satisfactory to both parties in their mutual relationships. The non-Batak President could collaborate 'from the inside' on the judicial findings and, what was also very important, could play his part in the development of the law by way of the administration of justice, under changing social conditions which modified concepts of right and wrong in social and economic life.

In my opinion rightly, Vergouwen has described Toba-Batak adat law, in its flexibility, within the framework of the social structure and forms of organisation as based on kinship and co-dwelling in village, territory and in the wider groupings. It seems to me that for this reason his book is not out-of-date and will not easily become out-of-date either, whatever changes may have taken place since 1930 in Indonesia in general and in the Toba-Batak country in particular. Vergouwen gives no hard and fast code-rules which, as such, must be upheld when they no longer correspond to the social reality. New situations and conditions can only be understood against the background of older and recent cultural and socio-economic history. On this point, one finds in Vergouwen the necessary data and their context. Naturally, his explanations of the principles and the forms of expression of particular Batak institutions are not always the only ones possible; here and there he may lay too much stress on the magico-religious element. Vergouwen did his research and wrote his book upwards of 30 years ago, and he was, moreover, not an anthropologist by profession.* But, it seems to me, that this does not alter the fact that from his book one can become acquainted with the Toba-Batak people and understand their social and juridical life in diachronic perspective. This establishes the value of this book for the present day. Dutch cultural anthropologists esteem highly *Het Rechtsleven der Toba-Bataks*. In it they have found much important material for theoretical studies in the field of kinship and affinal relationships in a patrilineal society with an asymmetrical connubium.

I am pleased that funds have been made available for the translation of Vergouwen's book into English. One of the best Dutch works on Indonesian adat law can now be made accessible to the international world of students of social anthropology and customary law.

The translation of a scholarly work of this nature is always a hazardous undertaking, particularly when the author can neither supervise it nor influence it. In translating Vergouwen's book into English a number of problems presented themselves. He wrote in a rather old-fashioned style of Dutch in which long sentences, built up of subordinate clauses which were meant to explain the main theme, were frequent. These have been broken down for the sake of readability. He also refers to Government measures or plans for reforms which are not relevant to the present day and I have taken the liberty of either deleting these passages from the translation or, in some cases, have given a shortened version. But, these minor alterations apart, Vergouwen's disquisition has not been altered: the present translation is *his* book in substance and in spirit. And the translator, in reproducing the essentials and the details of his work has succeeded, in my view, in achieving, as far as such is possible in a translation, conformity with the style in which the original is written.

Such minor, or perhaps major, errors as occur in the English syntax must be attributed to last-minute alterations in the final draft. For these I accept responsibility.

J. KEUNING
University of Leiden

---

* For this reason his theoretical digression on the possibility that a matrilineal kinship system preceded the present patrilineal organisation was omitted from the translation. It is no longer accepted in social-anthropological theory.

CONTENTS

The nature and extent of the Batak's knowledge of their descent 17. The main lines of the genealogical structure: general distribution 21. *A.* THE LONTUNG MOIETY 21; Limbong, Sagala and Malau 22; the Lontung group 22; the Borbor complex 24. *B.* THE SUMBA MOIETY 25; the Nai Ambaton division 25; the Nai Rasaon division 25; the Nai Suanon division 26; the Pohan group 27; the Sipaettua group 27; the Silahisabungan group 27; the Radja Oloan group 28; Sihombing and Simamora 28; the Sobu (Hasibuan) group 29; the Naipospos group 29. The age of the tribal groups and *marga* 30. The meaning of "*marga*" 30. The lineage, *saompu* 32. The lineage as a ceremonial and sacrificial community 34. *Sapanganan* 34. The larger genealogical communities 35. Connection with the giving of women in marriage 36. The kinship group in village and territory 37. The agnatic kinship system 37. The *uaris* concept 40. Disputes about descent 41. Changing one's *marga* 42. The significance of the patrilineal structure 42.

Establishment and consolidation of the affinal relationship 44. The affinal relationship in the wider context 47. The affines as a group 48. The in-dwelling *marga boru* 50. Marriage frequency 53. The magico-religious character of the affinal relationship 54. The *mangupa boru* 56. Adoption of a *hula-hula* 57. Participation in ceremonies 57. Gifts between affines 58. *Ulos* gifts 58. *Ulos* gifts other than cloths 59. Motives for giving gifts 60. The *piso* gifts 61. *Tulang-ibebere,* brother-sister 63. The affinity relationship and the administration of justice 64. A kinship and affinity relationship system 66.

The gods 67. The spirits 69. The *sumangot* 70. The *sombaon* 71. The *bius* sacrificial community 73. The *parbaringin*-organisation 75. Some

judgement: *uhum* 412. Content of the judgement 413. The administration of justice by the chiefs and customary law 417. The long-
neglected complaint 418. The *Porang Tangga Batu* limitation 419.
Implementation 421.

INTRODUCTION

During the years 1927-30 the Government ordered an inquiry into the operation of the native administration of justice in the Residency of Tapanuli, and in 1930 my report was published in the *Mededeelingen der afdeeling Bestuurszaken der Buitengewesten, Serie A, No. 10.*[1] This Report dealt mainly with the manner in which the administration of justice was at that time organised, directed and prosecuted. Some mention was also made of legal proceedings and criminal law.

This inquiry was responsible for my further investigation into the principles of Toba Batak customary law and the whole of their law and customs. The material I obtained in the course of it is presented in this book.

The territory I cover includes: the Toba Batak Country (excluding Lower Barus) and the sub-division Padang Lawas, division Padang Sidimpuan. I will only pay a little attention to the latter[2] and will make only passing reference to the rest of South Tapanuli; nevertheless, I hope that it may be sufficient to awaken a desire for further study for there is more similarity between the laws of the north and south than one would suppose after upward of half a century of Government administration of justice in the latter.

I did not visit the region inhabited by the Pakpak Batak, the Dairi Country, and it is not discussed since Ypes has provided much infor-

---

[1] Communications of the Section for Administrative Affairs of the Outer Provinces, Department of Internal Affairs.
[2] The reader is referred to the important contributions, which are still valuable, of J. B. Neumann "Het Pane- en Bilastroomgebied" (The Basin of the Pane and Bila Rivers) in *Tijdschrift Koninklijk Aardrijkskundig Genootschap* (Journal of the Royal Geographical Society), 1885—1887, and to the accurate information in Willer: "Verzameling van Battahsche wetten en instellingen in Mandheling en Pertibi" (Compilation of Batak Laws and Institutions in Mandailing and Portibi), *Tijdschrift voor Neêrland's Indië* (Journal for the Netherlands Indies), 1846, Part II.

mation about the area [3]. I did not visit Habinsaran and Upper Barus
either. The first displays hardly any individual characteristics. The latter
is the region where Dr. H. Neubronner van der Tuuk collected his
linguistic data. His dictionary [4] gives many particulars about law and
customs of this region which has much in common with the benzoin
region of West Humbáng: the organisation of the corporate groups and
land tenure being some of the individual aspects they share.

I obtained many data from the Toba Country on a number of
different subjects but no attempt has been made to present them all
here. Rather have I endeavoured to trace the general outline and have
used particularities as illustrations with the object of giving the whole
work the character of an introduction and manual.

The whole of the Toba Country can be divided into three regions [5]
each of which has well-defined legal features of its own:

1. The whole southerly part comprising Humbáng, South Habinsaran,
Silindung and Pahae to which should be reckoned Upper Barus and
Hurlang.

2. Toba Holbung, North Habinsaran and Uluan.

3. Muara, Samosir and the westerly shores of Lake Toba.

Within these three regions the laws and customs differ, the differences,
in the main, distinguishing the large tribal group areas from one another.
Each of the Batak tribal groups has, generally speaking, its own dwelling
place in these areas where the group or a division of it lived and still
lives together as of old, closely knit and with its interests confined within
that area. As a result, each group has tended to go its own way so that
many of the legal institutions have developed in a distinct manner.
As a rule such a group accommodates one or two enclaves of alien
groups, and the tribal groups always have some of the so-called 'in-
dwelling' *marga* (members of another tribal group) living among them.

---

[3] W. K. H. Ypes, *Bijdrage tot de kennis van de stamverwantschap, de in-
heemsche rechtsgemeenschappen en het grondenrecht der Toba- en Dairi-
Bataks* (Contribution to the Knowledge of the Kinship structure, the Corporate
Communities and the Land Law of the Toba- and Dairi-Batak), 1932, and
"Nota omtrent Singkel en de Pakpak-landen" (Memorandum concerning
Singkel and the country of the Pakpak Batak), *Tijdschrift voor de Indische
Taal-, Land- en Volkenkunde* uitg. door het Bataviaasch Genootschap van
Kunsten en Wetenschappen (Journal of Linguistics, Geography and Anthro-
pology of the Indies publ. by the Batavia Society of Arts and Sciences, Vol. 49,
1907.

[4] H. N. van der Tuuk, *Bataksch-Nederduitsch Woordenboek* (Batak-Dutch
Dictionary), 1861, in the Batak script.

[5] vide map.

In many respects the way of life of the present-day Batak does not differ greatly from that of his forebears: there is still mutual marriage between the tribal groups — even more than formerly; they still visit each other's great markets; and for the greater part still live their daily lives within the closed circle of lineage, *marga* and tribal group (a circumstance dictated in former times by the many mutual wars). Each tribal group has its own territory and views a tribal group in an adjoining area to some extent as an alien one. Yet these are all Batak territories, inhabited by Batak, perhaps related, but each, nevertheless, with a distinct history, organisation and local customary law. Ypes has given abundant evidence of these differences in his work.

It has not been possible to state on every point how far old laws have been eroded and superseded by new ones, for such a process never takes place uniformly, either in regions or branches of the law. There are many strong stimuli that have influenced it and affected it differently: there has been Christianity which has been spreading further afield and penetrating deeper; Government measures have been more intensified; there has been contact with international trade; and education of the young. One finds old ideas surviving where one would not expect them, and where one would presume there would be a tenacious adherence to old customs and beliefs, resistance to new influences is weak. Thus I use the past tense only where the facts are such as to present no difficulty, but when I use the present tense it does not always mean that the facts are today applicable everywhere.

It is hardly necessary to mention that great instability and disruption have been observed in many an area. In this respect, in a country such as this with its wealth of laws and customs, directing the administration of justice is a delicate and important task.

There has been no attempt in this work to incorporate everything that has been written on the Batak people. The material presented is for the greater part the result of my own investigation and observation and it speaks for itself that both have been insufficient. Therefore it is possible that there are interpretations that are not correct and explanations that do not touch the core of the matter, but I have written as I have found and have refrained, I hope, from empty conjectures. But if these data help to clarify some of the already known facts then I think much will have been gained.

Chapters III and VII, which deal with the corporate groups and land law, could be considerably shortened since the appearance of Ypes' work on these subjects, and in general my material benefits in many ways from the elucidation he provides.

The reader will readily appreciate that when working on my notes I found gaps in the material which I could have perhaps filled had I still been in the country. Thus there will not be an answer to every question, but it must be borne in mind that the Batak himself would not always have an answer to hand.

It will help if a brief description of the country is given.

Lake Toba was formed when the crest of a volcano collapsed. Part of the crest protrudes above the surface of the lake: this is the island of Samosir. The north and west walls of the cauldron are steep and high, up to 1,500 feet, as is also part of the south wall (Muara). Small, secluded territories lie between the ridges of the wall on the shores of the lake and along the base of the cliffs. The south-east and east sides of the declivity form the walls of the Habinsaran and Simanuk-manuk mountain ranges which separate Uluan from Sumatra's East Coast. Uluan is a rather high hilly region; Toba Holbung (lower Toba, usually abbreviated to 'Toba') is a broad, fertile, thickly populated lake shore plain between Balige and Porsea: eastward the land rises gradually. Habinsaran is a sparsely populated region.

Humbáng is a large high plateau looking rather like a steppe and the tuff grit is cut in many places by very deep watercourses along which wet rice-fields, *hauma saba*, have been laid out. There is only one large river, the Aek Sigeaung, which traverses the Plain of Sipoholon, the adjacent broad Silindung Valley and the low Plain of Pahae ultimately falling into the sea as the Batangtoru. Between these densely populated plains and the narrow coastal strip lies a disintegrated mountain country, Hurlang, with few conspicuous peaks but a great many fantastic ravines and declivities. The northern part of Hurlang, particularly, is typical benzoin country where the *sidjamapolang* = benzoin tappers live.

The whole country is between 2,100 and 5,400 feet above sea level, Mt. Pusuk Buhit, about 1,000 feet higher being the only outstanding mountain peak.

With regard to the language: the stress on a Batak word falls on the penultimate syllable whatever the length of the word, for example, *dábu, dabu-dábu, dabu-dabúan, pardabu-dabuánon*. There are a few exceptions and where these occur in the text the stressed syllable has been accented. The "*e*" in words such as *bere, dege, lehan* etc., is pronounced as the vowel in break or eight.

THE GENEALOGY OF THE BATAK PEOPLE

(particularly the divisions living in the Tapanuli Residency)

OBSERVATIONS

The following genealogy agrees in the main with that incorporated in the *Poestaha taringot toe tarombo ni bangso Batak* (Outline of the Genealogy of the Batak People) by W. M. Hoeta Galoeng (1926), as well as with that given by Ypes. The clan and lineage lists that I give are not, however, so elaborately detailed.

A great number of data could be controlled on the spot and some could de amended, but here and there, in particular in North Samosir, the statements made on the mutual connection of the *marga* (clans) and their devisions were contradictory and it was clear that there was no longer a high degree of accuracy in this matter. Where a difference of opinion about the classification of this or that *marga*, or about which was the first to come into being was encountered, the classification and sequence given here favours neither side: the most plausible conclusions have been drawn from the data obtained.

The Roman figures on pages 6 - 16 refer to the genealogical chart on which the regions occupied by the tribal groups, of which the Batak people consists, are indicated in rough outline. The ordinary numerals between brackets refer to the pages in the text where the divisions and groups are given in detail, and where the distribution of the *marga* within and outside the ancestral areas proper is also indicated, though by no means fully, and then only with regard to the *marga* inhabiting a territory as the so-called ruling *marga* and not to the *marga* in-dwelling with another.

The population figures in the genealogical chart are (approximately) those of the 1930 census. The names in the lists are not all the proper names of *marga*; some of them are the names of the ancestors from whom the *marga* originated.

The main division is dual:

SI RADJA BATAK $\left\{\begin{array}{l}\text{Guru Tateabulan}\\\text{Radja Isumbaon}\end{array}\right.$

The so-called LONTUNG moiety, which contains the Lontung tribal group proper, the closely related B o r b o r Complex, as well as a couple of smaller *marga*, sprang from Guru Tateabulan.

The so-called SUMBA moiety, to which all the remaining tribal groups and *marga* belong, sprang from Radja Isumbaon.

THE LONTUNG MOIETY

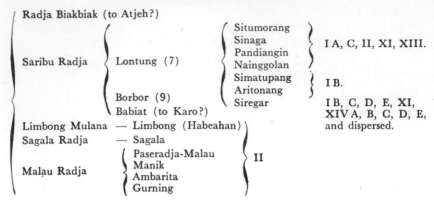

Radja Biakbiak (to Atjeh?)

Saribu Radja — Lontung (7) — Situmorang, Sinaga, Pandiangin, Nainggolan { I A, C, II, XI, XIII.

Simatupang, Aritonang { I B.

Borbor (9), Babiat (to Karo?) — Siregar I B, C, D, E, XI, XIV A, B, C, D, E, and dispersed.

Limbong Mulana — Limbong (Habeahan)
Sagala Radja — Sagala

Malau Radja { Paseradja-Malau, Manik, Ambarita, Gurning } II

Radja Biakbiak apparently went to Atjeh. There is no mention of any descendants.

Limbong inhabits in the main a valley to the south of the ridge that connects Mt. Pusuk Buhit with the tableland, and Sagala Radja one to the north of the ridge.

Malau Radja is distributed over the region around Pangururan (the island and the mainland) and, under the name Damanik, is the ruling *marga* of the self-governing Siantar territory in Eastern Sumatra.

THE SUMBA MOIETY

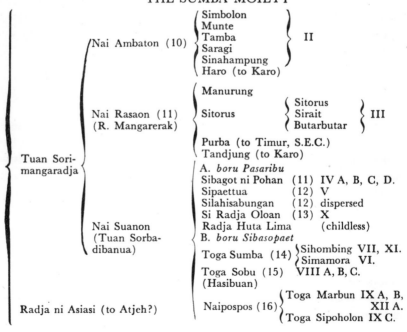

Tuan Sorimangaradja

Nai Ambaton (10) { Simbolon, Munte, Tamba, Saragi, Sinahampung, Haro (to Karo) } II

Nai Rasaon (11) (R. Mangarerak) { Manurung

Sitorus { Sitorus, Sirait, Butarbutar } III

Purba (to Timur, S.E.C.), Tandjung (to Karo)

Nai Suanon (Tuan Sorbadibanua)

A. *boru Pasaribu*
Sibagot ni Pohan (11) IV A, B, C, D.
Sipaettua (12) V
Silahisabungan (12) dispersed
Si Radja Oloan (13) X
Radja Huta Lima (childless)

B. *boru Sibasopaet*
Toga Sumba (14) { Sihombing VII, XI. Simamora VI.
Toga Sobu (15) VIII A, B, C. (Hasibuan)
Naipospos (16) { Toga Marbun IX A, B, XII A. Toga Sipoholon IX C.

Radja ni Asiasi (to Atjeh?)

The Lontung Group

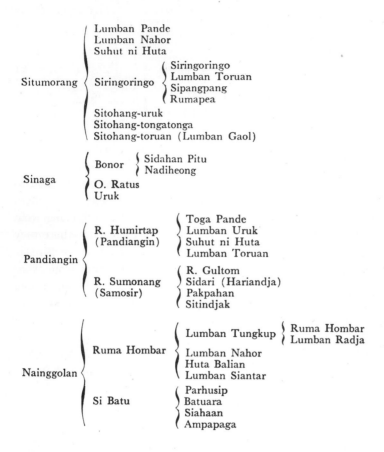

The first four 'head' *marga* of Lontung are established in South Samosir (IA) as well as in the Sabulán and Djandjiradja territories which lie opposite on the mainland (II). Part of Situmorang inhabits the Lintong and Parbuluan (XIV) territories both of which are on the tableland to the west of Mt. Pusuk Buhit. From the Pandiangin, part of all four *marga* of R. Sumonang (Samosir) have migrated to South Habinsaran round about Pangaribuan (IC) and from there a part went to East Pahae (XI). A branch of Nainggolan is also to be found there. A combination of parts of Situmorang and Nainggolan is to be found in Pusuk (Upper Barus, XIIA).

Simatupang	{ Sitoga Torop (Siborutorop) { Sianturi { Siburian				
Aritonang	{ Ompu Sunggu { Radja Gukguk { Simaremare				
Siregar	{ Silo { Dongoran { Silali { Siagian	{ Ritonga { Sormin	{ in Angkola, { Sipirok, { Lumut { & { Hadjoran:	{ Siregar Ri { Siregar Salak { Siregar Baumi	

The last three 'head' *marga* of Lontung are established in the coastal lake region near Muara (IB) where each occupies its own territory, and also on the small island of Pulo which lies opposite. Siregar went to Muara from the small Siregar territory in Sigaol: the others went there direct from Urat on Samosir. Parts of Simatupang and Aritonang went to the margin of the Humbáng Plateau adjacent to Muara where they occupy the Paranginan and Huta Gindjang territories. Parts of Siregar travelled through Humbáng to South Habinsaran (Ic) and from there went to Sipirok (ID) and Dolok (IF, where there are the *marga* Ritonga and Sormin), and East Pahae (XI, the Onan Hasang and Simangumban territories). From Sipirok Siregar spread further to the *luat* Hadjoran in Padang Bolak (IE) and to the *kuria* Marantjar in North Angkola (XIVc) and the *kuria* Lumut in South Sibolga (XV). A small Siregar group is also to be found between Laguboti and Porsea (IVc).

The Borbor Complex

The Borbor Complex is to be found distributed over the whole of Tapanuli. The statements regarding the genealogical tree and those concerning the manner of the distribution of the Complex deviate here and there considerably from each other.

Pasaribu and Lubis are to be found in Haunatas (near Laguboti V) and in the Pasaribu and Lubis territories in Central Habinsaran (IC) and, as far as I know, Lubis is also in South Mandailing (XIVE) and Pasaribu in Simanosor (South Sibolga, XV) and Upper Barus (XIIA).

The *marga* which, so it is said, together form the Daulae group are found in Padang Lawas, South Angkola (XIVD), South Sibolga (XV, *kuria* Pinangsori) and, among other places, in Mandailing as in-dwelling *marga*.

Sipahutar originally occupied the small territory of that name in East Humbáng (IVB) from which it was driven by the *marga* Silitonga (Pohan): it then spread into Pagar Batu (in IXC), Silindung (VIIA) and Habinsaran (IC).

Harahap is the ruling *marga* of Central Angkola (XIVC) and of Padang Bolak (XIVB); Pulungan that of the *kuria* Batang Toru in North Angkola and the *kuria* Sayur Matinggi in South Angkola.

Rambe is the ruling *marga* of a couple of territories in East Dolok (XIVA).

THE SUMBA MOIETY

Nai Ambaton

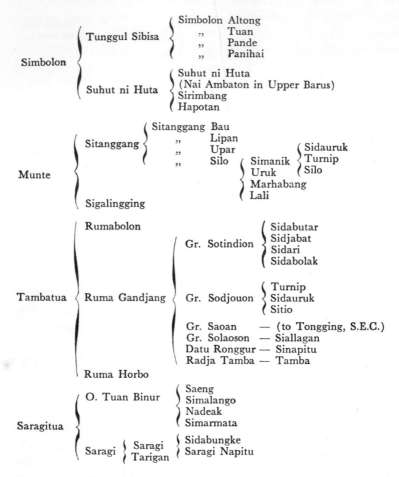

Sinahampung (to Dairi)

This sequence and classification is, in the main, that given in W. M. Hoeta Galoeng's *Poestaha*. On Samosir, however, other renderings were frequently heard.

The *marga* Simbolon and Munte, combined with Saragitua, have spread over the territories of West Samosir (II). Parts of Simbolon and Sigalingging have also made their way to Si Onom Hudon and Siambaton in Upper Barus (XIIA); Sigalingging have also gone to Salak (XIII) where some of them have formed separate *marga*.

Tambatua went originally to the Tamba territory on the mainland
(II). Radja Tamba stayed there, but the rest of the *marga* went to
North-East Samosir (II) and spread over the territories there.

Saragi became the ruling *marga* in the self-governing Raya territory
on Sumatra's East Coast where it split up independently: it also occupies
a small area within the self-governing Siantar territory.

Nai Rasaon

Of this tribal group the *marga* Manurung, Sitorus, Sirait and Butar-
butar occupy the whole of Uluan in small groups (III).

A part of Sitorus occupied the small Sitorus territory in the middle
of the Pohan group (IVc): from there branches went to the environs
of Parsoburan being known there by the name Pane, among others.

The *marga* Purba and Tandjung are to be found on Sumatra's East
Coast in the Timur states and the Karo Country respectively.

Nai Suanon (Tuan Sorbadibanua)

A.   Sibagot ni Pohan

Sibagot ni Pohan	Tuan Sihubil	Tampubolon
		Silaen
		Baringbing
	Tuan Somanimbil	Siahaan (Nasution?)
		Simandjuntak { Nasution? / Dalimunte?
		Huta Gaol
	Tuan Dibangarna	Pandjaitan (Dairi)
		Silitonga
		Siagian (Pardosi)
		Sianipar
	Sonak Malela	Simangungsung
		Marpaung
		Napitupulu (Pardede)

The whole Pohan group is spread over Toba Holbung (IVA), Eastern Humbáng (IVB) and the region near the Bight of Porsea, as well as over the northern part of Habinsaran (IVc)). Parts of most of the *marga* occur in these areas either in separate territories or in combinations.

Small parts, under the name Pohan, also rule in the *kuria* Barus Mudik (XIIB) and in the *kuria* Anggoli (XV). Nasution is the ruling *marga* in North Mandailing and Batang Natal (IVD). Dalimunte occurs in South Angkola (XIVD). Both of these *marga* are said to belong to this tribal group.

Sipaettua

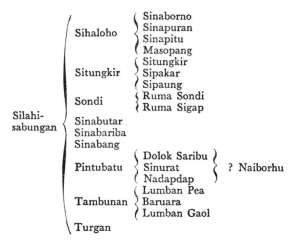

This tribal group occupies the region around Laguboti (V), the *marga* either being separate or living in combinations. As far as I know there have been no dispersals elsewhere.

Silahisabungan

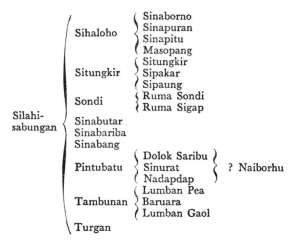

This genealogy is taken from W. M. Hoeta Galoeng's *Poestaha*, though other renderings were also heard.

This tribal group does not have its own region where its parts have remained together. It has spread over the whole of North Tapanuli, while large branches are also to be found on the East Coast (particularly in the Karo Country), sometimes under other names.

Divisions of this group are found mainly in: the Silalahi and Paropo territories on the shores of Lake Toba (XIII, its country of origin); the Parbaba and Tolping territories in North Samosir (II); the Tinambun, Dolok Saribu territories and in many other places in Uluan (III), where they are sometimes the in-dwelling *marga*; the Naiborhu territory near Porsea (IVc); the Tambunan and Pagar Batu territories near Balige (IVA); the Sigotom territory near Sipahutar (IVB); and also in Tuka, North Sibolga (VIIIc).

Si Radja Oloan

Nai Baho occupies, among others, a small territory near Pangururan (II); Sihotang occupies the territory of that name on the mainland (II). Both these *marga* have spread to the Dairi Country; Sihotang also to Upper Barus.

Bakkara, Sinambela, Sihite and Simanullang are established in their ancestral area, Bakkara; the last two are also found in Humbáng and Upper Barus (X). Sihite also forms part of the small Si Ualu Ompu territory near Tarutung.

B.   Toga Sumba

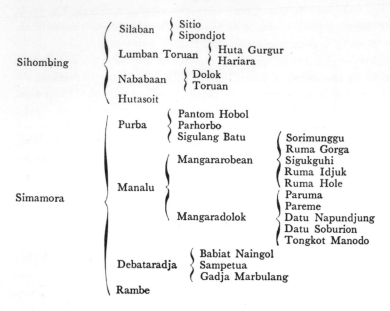

The Sihombing group occupies area VII. Each of the four *marga* (their branches are not yet separate *marga*) occupies either its own territory or lives in combination with parts of the others. A part of this group has dispersed to South-West Pahae (XI).

The Simamora group occupies area VI. Divisions of the three *marga*, Purba, Manalu and Debataradja (their branches are not yet separate *marga*) either occupy territories of their own or live in combination with parts of the others. The Rambe *marga* occupies a territory of the same name in Upper Barus (XII) with parts of the other three *marga*.

Nearly all the divisions of Simamora and Sihombing (except Rambe) occupy the small Tipang territory near Bakkara, while Simamora also occurs in Bakkara itself from which place it went to the Humbáng plateau. It is also one of the parts of the Si Ualu Ompu territory near Tarutung.

Toga Sobu (Hasibuan)

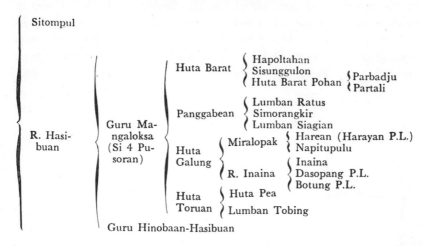

The ancestral area of the Sobu *marga* is the Silindung Valley (VIIIA); the exception being the descendants of Guru Hinobaan who are only to be found in the Hasibuan territory on the Sigaol promontory, Uluan (III).

Their distribution over the Silindung Valley and its environs is indicated in the chart on p. 16 of Dr. J. B. Haga's "Nota omtrent de Inl. Rechtsgemeenschappen in het gewest Tapanoeli" (*Mededeelingen van de afdeeling Bestuurszaken der Buitengewesten*, Serie B, No. 6) [6] from which it appears that parts of the *marga* Sitompul, Huta Barat, Panggabean (of which the division Simorangkir is now a *marga*), Huta Galung and Huta Toruan (of which the divisions Huta Pea and Lumban Tobing are now *marga*) occupy their own territories. They are combined only in the recently formed Pagar Batu territory dating from ± 1880 and situated on the edge of the area of the Naipospos tribal group. A couple of the *marga* have also become part of the Si Ualu Ompu territory near Tarutung.

Each of the *kuria* in the northern part of Sibolga (VIIIc) belongs to one of the Sobu *marga*.

Huta Galung has also dispersed to Padang Lawas, particularly to the region of the Barumun and Sosa Rivers (VIIIB), where it occupies the entire south under the name Hasibuan of which the divisions Harayan

---

[6] "Memorandum Concerning the Indigenous Corporate Communities in the Tapanuli Residency"; Communications of the Section for Administrative Affairs of the Outer Provinces, Department of Internal Affairs.

and Botung have not yet become separate *marga*. Dasopang is found in the territories in the middle of the Borbor area (XIVA and B, hatched on the chart). It cannot be said with certainty whether the division Hasibuan-Handang Kopo in the Huristak territory originates from Huta Galung or Huta Barat. A small group of the Huta Barat *marga* is to be found there under the name of its branch, Hapoltahan.

Naipospos

The greater part of the Marbun *marga* is established in the area marked IXA on the chart, as well as in the Bakkara territory, while the Sanggaran and Sihikkit territories to the west of Parmonangan are occupied by parts of Bandjar Nahor and Lumban Gaol (IXB). The four *marga* originating from Lumban Batu, occupy territories named after them in the Kelasan area of Upper Barus (XIIA). Each of the four Sipoholon *marga* occupies its own territory in the vicinity of Sipoholon (IXc). Both the Naipospos territories in the western part of this area are mainly occupied by Situmeang.

CHAPTER I

GENEALOGICAL STRUCTURE:
THE KINSHIP SYSTEM

A. Kinship

The kinship system of the Batak is patrilineal. It is true that a Batak calls members of his *marga* his *dongan-sabutuha* = those who have sprung from the same womb, but matrilineal descent is not known at present, from known history or from legend. A man's lineage is continued by the men born into it and becomes extinct if no sons are born to them. This patrilineal kinship system is the backbone of Batak society which is built up of lineages, *marga* and tribal groups all connected with each other in the male line. Men form the kinship groups: the women create the affinal relationships because they have to marry into other patrilineal groups.

THE NATURE AND EXTENT OF THE BATAK'S KNOWLEDGE
OF THEIR DESCENT

The historical knowledge that the Batak have of their descent goes far back into their past. This applies to individuals as well as to groups. Anyone whose forefather was not snatched from the bond of his kinship group (by being kidnapped, taken into slavery because of a debt, or because he fled following an offence) during the turbulent *Pidari* time that preceded the coming of the Dutch Government, and who knows something of the facts, can enumerate without fault six, eight, or even ten or more generations of the ascending line of his agnates. Within the narrower kinship group (*sasuhu* = belonging to one group, *saompu* = coming from one ancestor) everyone knows precisely the relationship of its members. The mutual connection of the lineages is generally well known to all though the particularities may not be known to everyone. No man has any difficulty in stating the position in the *marga* or *marga*-branch of the lineage to which he belongs. Each child knows to which *marga* he belongs, that his mother came from a different *marga* and that his sister will go to a different *marga* again on her marriage.

2

A man's *marga* probably ascends for 15 to 20 generations, that is, to at least four centuries ago. The meeting point of a man's *marga* with its companion *marga* in one tribal group lies some generations earlier and then the connections go further back still to the earliest known times until they are lost in legend.

The knowledge regarding these genealogical relationships is not, however, everywhere equally extensive or well-preserved. If people have been concentrated in one region and have always lived there together, and if at the same time the parts of the *marga* have not spread everywhere over the region, but have continued to associate with each other and have consequently been in regular communication, there is usually in existence a sound knowledge regarding the connections in the genealogical tree of the *marga* rising to and including the ancestor who first occupied the region. The mutual relationships between the *marga* and the lineages is then known to all and people will diverge in little more than in points of precedence on account of earlier birth. Thus in the Sumba moiety (see genealogy p. 10), generally speaking, less difference of opinion and less divergence in the facts is to be found than in the Lontung moiety which has occupied larger and more widely dispersed areas. Within the great complex of Tuan Sorbadibanua (see p. 11) the classification of the tribal groups is not only clearly established but a number of historical details are also known about them. However, of all the groups that belong to it, Silahisabungan is the least in a position to boast that the facts relating to the kinship relation between its divisions are indisputable since, unlike its brethren, the divisions of this group have not been confined to a single ancestral area comprising them all but have dispersed over the whole of North Tapanuli. In former times when small groups split off from a *marga* and went a long way off in order to begin a new life and to found new lineages, the knowledge of the relationship with those who remained behind in the ancestral area could be lost in the ensuing centuries of isolation and precarious existence. Thus room was made for legend.

The most noteworthy example of the growth of such a legend is to be found in Padang Lawas. For a century or two after the departure of the Hindus — who built the temples the remains of which are to be seen here and there today — the south of Padang Lawas was occupied by Hasibuan (see p. 15) and the north by Harahap and Siregar (see pp. 8, 9). Now, in the eighties of the last century, thus immediately following the breaking of the centuries-long isolation in which they had lived, the Hasibuan served up a story to the Controleur = District

Officer Neumann of their descent from one of the distinguished families in the retinue of Alexander the Great. They probably borrowed this story from Mandailing. They believe in it no longer. In 1929, under the leadership of the *luat* chiefs, they participated with zest in the great *marga* festival of Huta Galung at which, for the first time in history, the entire Huta Galung *marga* assembled in the *bona ni pinasa*, the small territory of its origin in the middle of the Silindung Valley; a gathering that made all the other Batak envious. Harahap, on the other hand, stood by a legendary cyclops, *Parmatasapiak*, who, according to them, went to Padang Bolak from somewhere in Toba. In Sipirok, however, people are better informed about their connection with their land of origin, Muara, and W. M. Hoeta Galoeng's *"Poestaha taringot toe tarombo ni halak Batak"* tells of an emigration from Muara first to Lobu Siregar (now abandoned) in Humbáng and afterwards to Sibatang-kayu from which place Sipirok and Padang Bolak were occupied.

However, the gradual decrease of precise knowledge regarding origin and descent does not necessarily lead to an irreparable loss of the historical links with the ancestral land. If people on both sides retell the communal tales about events of old that have been preserved, then the genealogical connections that were missing or had become doubtful are frequently made clear again. There were also the 'tokens of recognition', articles given to the emigrating group — along with good wishes and provisions — by those who were staying behind. These articles were to be preserved and used as recognition tokens in the event of the descendants of either side encountering each other later on. To give an example: the lineage of the *kuria* chiefs of Sipirok is the custodian of some spears of which the sheaths have remained in the land of origin, Muara. And again, one of the lineages of the *marga* Samosir (see p. 7) in East Pahae (see chart XI) has in its possession, among other things, half a bead necklace that is said to fit onto the other half which is still to be found in the land of origin, Samosir, and so on.

It is, however, remarkable that in a group of *marga* such as, for example, those of the Tambatua in North-East Samosir (see pp. 10, 11), so much confusion can sometimes prevail regarding the facts of the mutual connection of the divisions that have always continued to live close together even though they have spread over the various areas of North-East Samosir. The people themselves attribute this to the fact that no *datu*-class (*datu* = priest - medicine man in one) has developed among them. Elsewhere it is said that the *datu* have contributed much to the preservation of historical stories and the knowledge of the relationships within the *marga* and tribal groups. In the Silahisabungan group of North-East Samosir the keeper of old of such knowledge was the *boru silaon*, the representative of the oldest branch of the oldest in-dwelling *marga*, who directed the territory's communal sacrifices as well as the collection of the contributions to them and the dividing up of the sacrificial animal, all according to the *marga* branches that inhabited the territory. Each of these *marga* branches was *sada somba* = one unit for worship; *sada raga-raga* = having one and the same sacred rack as the dwelling of the ancestor; *sada guguan* = one collecting unit for the contributions to the offering-ceremonies of the community; *sada djambar* = one unit entitled to a portion of the sacrificial animal. As will become evident, this was everywhere the case in pagan times.

Naturally only a few Batak have a knowledge of the entire social structure of their society. In the *Pidari* time the facts could not be obtained because of the dangers and difficulties of travelling through the whole country where one was not safe outside one's own ancestral area. And even at the present time it is difficult, in a country with so many out-of-the-way places, to get to know more than the main genealogical outlines. In these circumstances, therefore, one should have sincere appreciation for the care and attention that the Assistant-Demang (= Batak sub-district officer), W. M. Hoeta Galoeng has given to his book on the genealogy of the whole Batak people. He gives the lineage lists of each tribal group and *marga* in considerable detail, the regions to which the descendants of the ancestors mentioned in the genealogical tree went are always enumerated, and there are numerous ancient tales that are important for the history of the tribal groups and *marga*.

The ordinary Batak has a marked partiality to '*martutur-tutur*' = trace the family links (*partuturan*) when he meets another Batak; to establish whether one is the kinsman of the other; whether they have later become affines by some marriage; and how they should address each other as a consequence. These ever-present relationships of kinship or affinity provide the Batak with a ready motive for mutual demonstrations of cordiality. They can also be profitable sometimes. The interest that every Batak feels in the ancestry of his people is expressed in the following *umpama* [7] = maxim:

----

[7] An *umpama* might be called a literary device. It consists of two lines. The second line is the "rule" line. The function of the first line is only to provide words which rhyme with those of the "rule" line.

tiniptip sanggar bahen huru-huruan,
djolo sinungkun marga asa binoto partuturan;
To make a bird cage you must first cut the cane.
A man must first inquire about the *marga* so that he may learn
what the mutual kinship connection is.

And there is nobody who gives more thought to the genealogical list
of Matthew I or to the relationships of the tribes in the Old Testament
than the Christian Batak.

THE MAIN LINES OF THE GENEALOGICAL STRUCTURE: GENERAL DISTRIBUTION

The whole of the Batak people derive their origin from Si Radja
Batak. According to legend he sprang from a descendant of a god. The
child's mother, Si Borudeakparudjar, had been commanded by the High
God, Debatá Muladjadi Nabolon, to create the earth. Having done so
she went to live at Siandjurmulamula. This village, which later became
the dwelling place of Si Radja Batak also, was situated on the slopes
of Mt. Pusuk Buhit.[8] The Toba Batak regard it as the place of origin
of the whole of the Batak people, including the Karo Batak.

The oldest history tells of forest spirits, cyclops, encounters with the
daughters of gods and other supernatural beings, and of miraculous
happenings, as well as events and episodes that could have taken place
at the present time. Many of these stories contain a kernel of historical
truth, others are only the local versions of Indonesian tales. And the
more recent the stories are the more likely they are to have some truth
in them. In many of these tales much is ascribed to individuals that
should undoubtedly cover whole periods, particularly where very ancient
history is concerned, and the reducing of 'head' *marga* and tribal groups
back to one person is often founded on a naive tendency to give things
a concrete basis.

So, Si Radja Batak is said to have had two sons, Guru Tateabulan
and Radja Isumbaon, who have become the ancestors of the two
moieties into which the Batak people are divided: LONTUNG and
SUMBA.

A. THE LONTUNG MOIETY

Guru Tateabulan had five sons and four daughters. The eldest son,
Radja Biakbiak, is said to have gone to Atjeh and to have left no
descendants.

---

[8] Samosir has been made into an island by the cutting of a canal through the
ridge connecting it with Mt. Pusuk Buhit.

LIMBONG, SAGALA AND MALAU

The three younger sons (see p. 6) Limbongmulana, Sagalaradja
and Malauradja became the ancestors of the *marga* Limbong, Sagala
and Malau. In size and importance these three *marga* are far behind
those that sprang from the second son as well as those which belong to
the Sumba moiety. The area in which these three *marga* live is limited
to the immediate environs of Siandjurmulamula. Limbong inhabits a
territory to the south of the ridge that connects Mt. Pusuk Buhit with
the tableland, and Sagala lives in one to the north of it: Malau has
spread over some territories round about Pangururan.

However, neither all the parts of Limbong nor all those of Sagala
remained together in the territories just mentioned. In olden times
emigrants from the one *marga* as well as the other went to Parbuluan,
the Pakpak region and the Karo Country where they formed their own
marga, to which they either gave new names or names recalling the
originals. Here and there one also finds very small groups of Limbong
and Sagala in-dwelling in the territory of another *marga* — Sagala even
in the Sipirok area. Of the many *marga*-branches that are also found
with Limbong and Sagala, only one of the former has become known
in the Toba Batak Country as a *marga* under a name of its own: this
is the *marga* Habeahan.

The *marga* Malau is one of the few genealogical units of some extent
in the Toba Batak Country that has not acquired its own well-rounded
regional core where a great part of it has stayed together. The oldest
part of the *marga*, that stemming from Paseradja and still called Malau,
has become the affine and firm associate of the *marga* Simbolon and
Sitanggang which, with Saragi, occupy the territories in the North-West
corner of Samosir. The other parts, from a different mother, have
formed the *marga* Manik, Ambarita and Gurning which have spread in
small groups on and around Samosir. On the East Coast of Sumatra
Malau, under the name Damanik, is the ruling *marga* in the self-
governing Siantar territory.

The second son of Guru Tateabulan, Sariburadja, has become the
ancestor of the two great groups within the Lontung moiety: the
LONTUNG *marga* proper and the BORBOR Complex.

THE LONTUNG GROUP

According to the universally known legend, Si Radja Lontung, the
ancestor of the Lontung group, was born as a result of incest, *marsumbang*, committed by Sariburadja with his sister Borupareme, one of the

daughters of Guru Tateabulan. Because of this they were driven from Siandjurmulamula. They then made their way to Sabulán on the shores of Lake Toba where Si Radja Lontung was born and where he lived all his life. He in turn committed incest with his mother, though initially unwittingly, and begat seven sons by her. These seven sons have become the ancestors of the seven 'head' *marga* that form the Lontung group. He also begat two daughters. His descendants were driven out of Sabulán by a heavy flood that almost completely devastated the whole territory and they settled down in Urat (on Samosir) which lies opposite Sabulán. From Urat, which henceforth became reckoned as the place of dispersal, *parserahan*, one part of his descendants spread, *marserak*, over South Samosir and another part over the southern and western coastal regions of Lake Toba.

The first part, which went to South Samosir, consisted of the descendants of the four elder sons, Situmorang, Toga Sinaga, Toga Pandiangin and Toga Nainggolan (see p. 7). In the first instance they went to North Samosir but were driven from there by the *marga* Simbolon and Sitanggang to an imaginary line which, on the making of peace between them, was drawn from a rivulet on the west coast to a large boulder on a promontory on the east coast, southward of the Tomok territory. This line is still the accepted boundary between the Lontung and Sumba territories on the island (see chart IA and II).

In the course of time these four 'head' *marga* Situmorang, Sinaga, Pandiangin and Nainggolan, have split into 30 *marga* all of which are to be found in South Samosir, many of them only there. Their distribution over this part of the island, including the territories on the mainland, Sabulán and the adjacent Djandjiradja territory, has in the main been effected by small groups from a couple of *marga* of the four 'head' *marga* linking up in a territory in which each usually formed its own small cluster of villages. Some other small territories, Nainggolan, Samosir and Gultom, have been almost exclusively settled by *marga* of the same name, with in-dwelling *marga* of other tribal groups.

Outside the island, dispersals of Situmorang are to be found in the small Lintong territory on the edge of the Humbáng Plateau and round about Parbuluan (XIII) and in Upper Barus (XIIA). Of the *marga* from Pandiangin, those stemming from Toga Samosir went partly to South Habinsaran (Ic) and afterwards to East Pahae (XI) where a small Nainggolan territory is to be found occupied by a *marga* of that name. All three branches of Sinaga rule in the self-governing Tanah Djawa territory (East Coast of Sumatra) where the *marga* split up separately into the different small territories that make up that region.

Of the three younger sons of Si Radja Lontung (see p. 8) who neither stayed on Samosir nor left their descendants there, Simatupang and Aritonang went to the mainland via the small island of Pulo where they took possession of the territories of the same name eastward of Muara (Iв). Siregar went from Urat first to Sigaol, where a small fragment has remained in a territory called Siregar, and then to Muara. Parts of Simatupang and Aritonang climbed the Humbáng Plateau, populated the Huta Gindjang and Paranginan territories on its margin (Iв) and did not extend further except as in-dwelling *marga* accepted by other tribal groups.

A part of Siregar, however, went first to Humbáng where the deserted village of Lobu Siregar (in the Pohan area IVв) still recalls its passage, then to the now vanished village of Sibatangkayu (in South Habinsaran, or southward of Sipahutar) and from there to Sipirok (Id). There it occupied the extensive region of the *kuria* Sipirok, the *kuria* Parau Sorat and the *kuria* Baringin, which were founded by three brothers. From Sipirok a section broke away and went to Padang Bolak where it founded the *luat* Hadjoran (Iᴇ). Other sub-branches occupied the *kuria* Marantjar in North Angkola (XIVc) and the *kuria* Lumut in South Sibolga (XV). Individual groups, namely, the *marga* Dongoran and Ritonga went from South Habinsaran (Ic) to Dolok where they occupied separate territories. As a result of these dispersals Siregar forms an almost unbroken belt in the middle of Tapanuli which divides the Sumba area in the central Batak Country from South Tapanuli.

THE BORBOR COMPLEX

The Borbor Complex (see p. 9), which also springs from Saribu-radja, has not acquired its own ancestral region in the environs of Lake Toba and its *marga* have maintained themselves with difficulty in the regions of the Sumba tribal groups. One hears of many expulsions such as, for example, that of the Sipahutar *marga* from the territory of the same name by the Pohan *marga*, Silitonga, which still lives there (IVв), and of the *marga* Pasaribu which had villages in Silindung from which it was driven by the ancestors of the Hasibuan group that inhabits the whole valley to the present day. Apparently the only fixed base has been Haunatas (in V) from which place some territories in Central Habinsaran were occupied and from where Harahap went to the Angkola region (XIVc). This Harahap *marga*, which occupies Central

Angkola, has also settled in Central Padang Lawas (Padang Bolak, XIVʙ). Other *marga* belonging to the Borbor Complex are to be found in South Angkola (XIVᴅ), Dolok (XIVᴀ), South Sibolga (XV) and Upper Barus (XIIᴀ). And, as far as I know, the *marga* Lubis, the large ruling *marga* in South Mandailing (XIVᴇ), is reckoned as belonging to it.

There is much divergence in the statements concerning the genealogy and the dispersals of this Complex.

B. THE SUMBA MOIETY

This moiety stems from Radja Isumbaon the founder of Pangururan. His only son, Tuan Sorimangaradja, is said to have had three wives — all Lontung women — each of whom has become the ancestress of an important division of this extensive moiety.

THE NAI AMBATON DIVISION

From the first of these wives, Nai Ambaton, sprang the *marga* (see p. 10) of which the ancestral area is the whole northern part of Samosir (II) and the southerly part of the area along the western shore of Lake Toba (II in the chart).

The 'head' *marga*, Simbolon and Munte (Sitanggang and Sigalingging), have spread direct from Pangururan over the territories along the west and north coasts of the island. The 'head' *marga* Saragi, which must initially have gone to Simelungun, north-east coast of Lake Toba, apparently later returned in part and settled down in different parts of the same region. Tamba occupied the territory of the same name on the mainland where the youngest of the branches has remained, while the other branches went to the north-east corner of the island, round about Ambarita.

Younger and older settlements of all these 'head' *marga* are to be found on Sumatra's East Coast where Saragi is the ruling *marga* of the self-governing Raya territory, and a small territory within the self-governing Siantar territory. Small branches of Simbolon went to Upper Barus (XIIᴀ) where they are to be found in the Siambaton, Sionomhudon, Pusuk and Simataniari territories. A small part of Sigalingging also went to Upper Barus but the greater part went to Salak in the Dairi Country (XIII).

Members of this division are rarely found southward of Lake Toba.

THE NAI RASAON DIVISION

From Nai Rasaon, the second wife of Tuan Sorimangaradja, sprang Radja Mangarerak (see p. 11) who went to Sibisa in the north of

Uluan (III) and became the founder of the tribal group comprising the *marga* Manurung, Sitorus, Sirait and Butarbutar which together inhabit nearly the whole of Uluan. Parts — branches and lineages — of each of the four *marga* are encountered in almost all of the territories in this area. These territories, as in many parts of Samosir, are therefore nearly all combinations of parts or small fragments of two or more of the four *marga* each of which, as a rule, lives together in its own cluster of villages. Between them some smaller territories of other *marga* and tribal groups are distributed — mainly Silahisabungan — which stand in an alliance-relationship to the main inhabitants or are in-dwelling *marga*. Sometimes they had already occupied their small territory before the Nai Rasaon, spreading from the north, had penetrated so far and were not then driven out.

The region is a high and hilly country enclosed on its north-east side by the Simanukmanuk and Pangulubau mountain chains so that its only communication with the East Coast is along the northern corner and by the Asahan River in the south. Consequently, only some branches of the four *marga* are to be found on the East Coast. A branch of Sitorus set itself up in the small Sitorus territory that lies in the middle of the Pohan region (IVc) and from there some further parts, under the name Pane, have dispersed to Habinsaran and even to Angkola. In Central and South Tapanuli people belonging to this division are as scarce as those belonging to the Nai Ambaton division.

THE NAI SUANON DIVISION

From Nai Suanon, the third wife of Tuan Sorimangaradja, sprang Tuan Sorbadibanua the ancestor of the great complex of eight tribal groups (see pp. 11-16). These occupy the entire central part of the Toba Batak Country, the broad thickly populated lake shore plain of Toba Holbung along the southern shore of Lake Toba (IVA, V, IVc, westerly part), the northern part of the sparsely populated mountainous region of Habinsaran (IVc easterly part), the whole Humbáng Plateau (IVB, VII, IXA), the region of the *sidjamapolang* = benzoin tappers (X, IXB, VI), the Sipoholon (IXc), Silindung (VIIIA) and West Pahae (XI) Valleys and also the mountainous Hurlang between these valleys and the Indian Ocean. Parts of two of the eight groups also occupy the whole of South Padang Lawas (VIIB) and North Mandailing, with Batang Natal (IVD).

This dispersal took place from a village near Mt. Dolok Tolong (near Balige) where Tuan Sorimangaradja apparently lived. He had two wives, *boru* Pasaribu and *boru* Sibasopaet. The first presented him with four sons — not counting a young one who died — each of whom became the ancestor of a great line, namely, the groups Sibagot ni Pohan, Sipaettua, Silahisabungan and Radja Oloan. The second bore him three sons from one of whom originated both the Sihombing and Simamora groups, while the other two became the ancestors of the Sobu (Hasibuan) and Naipospos groups.

THE POHAN GROUP

The Pohan group has spread over the regions marked IVA, B and C on the chart. In these regions nearly all the *marga* that form part of this group (see p. 11) are represented by branches or lineages with the exception of a couple of *marga* like Silaen, which only occurs in Parsambilan (in IVc), or Silitonga which only occurs in and around Sipahutar (IVB, see also Appendix II). In addition, a small Pohan group went to Barus where it rules in the *kuria* Barus Mudik (in XIIB) under the name Pohan. Another group established itself in Anggoli, South Sibolga (XV), while by a route unknown to me, a branch dispersed to North Mandailing and Batang Natal (IVB) where it has formed the large ruling *marga* Nasution.

THE SIPAETTUA GROUP

This group (see p. 12) established itself round about Laguboti (V). It has continued to live there in its entirety in a number of territories that comprise either a single *marga* or *marga* branch, or a combination of two or more branches of the different *marga* of which this group consists. Together they form an unbroken whole. Members of the *marga* of this group are only found in very small numbers outside this ancestral area.

THE SILAHISABUNGAN GROUP

The Silahisabungan group (see p. 12), in complete contrast to Sipaettua, has spread over a great part of the Batak Country. Only the small Silalahi territory (with Paropo) in the northern corner of Lake Toba consisting of only a few thousand people, can be regarded as its ancestral region where its ancestor settled originally and where he begat a great number of sons by a number of wives. Most of the descendants of these sons have forsaken their small ancestral area (the *bona ni pinasa*) and have dispersed in many directions. As a result, small Silahisabungan communities are to be found in a number of places, usually consisting of a single genealogical group, but sometimes also containing a combination of lineages of different *marga*-branches. Most of these are enumerated in the genealogical tree on page 12. Quite a number of *marga* which must belong to this group are also to be found in the Dairi Country and on the East Coast of Sumatra.

THE RADJA OLOAN GROUP

This group (see p. 13) is also dispersed though to a somewhat lesser degree. The ancestor, Si Radja Oloan, was originally married to a *boru* Limbong and continued to live in the neighbourhood of his father-in-law. The firstborn son, Baho, saw the light of day at Pangururan where the *marga* that sprang from him, Nai Baho, forms a territory of its own within the larger territory of the *bius* Sitoluhae. From there dispersals from this *marga* went to the Dairi Country (the *marga* Bako). A second son, born of the same mother as the first and called Si Godang Ulu, became the ancestor of the *marga* Sihotang in the territory of the same name on the shores of Lake Toba (II). There it split into branches: some went to Dairi (XIII, the Pegagan territory) and to Karo and there formed new *marga*. The younger branches went to Upper Barus (XIIA, the Sihotang-Hasugian territory), and parts of them went to the Dairi- and Karo areas as well.

The four youngest *marga* of this group came into being in the Bakkara territory where Si Radja Oloan had established himself with a second wife, *boru* Pasaribu. His descendants have partly remained there, the *marga* Bakkara and Sinambela almost in their entirety, but some, principally from the *marga* Simanullang, went to the nearby western part of Humbáng and to Upper Barus (X) where they live in their own territories. Sihite, which has occupied its own territory in Humbáng, also forms part of the small Si Ualu Ompu Confederacy in the Silindung Valley near Tarutung. A few small parts of this group are to be found in the vicinity of Porsea (IVc) under the name Dairi.

SIHOMBING AND SIMAMORA

Of the two groups that sprang from Toga Sumba, Sihombing and Simamora (see p. 14), the first inhabits a well-defined area on the Humbáng Plateau (see chart VII) which was occupied from the village of Sipagabu. Each of the four component *marga* of this group, Silaban, Lumban Toruan, Nababaan and Hutasoit, occupies, in the main, its own corner of the ancestral region, though the boundaries are not everywhere distinct. Small dispersals went to West Pahae, while a combination of the *marga* of Sihombing and Simamora inhabit the small Tipang territory near Bakkara.

The Simamora group is established in the so-called *sidjamapolang* region, the region of the benzoin tappers, where it occupies a linked area, and also in a small territory, Rambe, in Upper Barus. This group has occupied its area in such a way that each of the *marga*, Purba, Manalu and Debataradja, has its own corner of it. Outside this area Simamora is found in Bakkara and in the aforementioned Tipang and Si Ualu Ompu territories.

THE SOBU (HASIBUAN) GROUP

This group, which sprang from Toga Sobu (see p. 15), has as its oldest branch the *marga* Sitompul which occupies a small territory of the same name in the Silindung Valley. From there branches went to West Pahae, occupying a more extensive area. Of the numerous groups that form the main part of the Sobu tribal group, a younger branch has remained small and is to be found in Sigaol, Uluan (III) where it has continued to live together in the small Hasibuan territory. The oldest division, however, Guru Mangaloksa, has brought into being the four large *marga* which collectively bear the name Si Opat Pusoran, namely, Huta Barat, Panggabean (from which has sprung Simorangkir), Huta Galung and Huta Toruan (from which have come Huta Pea and Lumban Tobing). This division occupied the rest of Silindung after driving out the *marga* Pasaribu: each of the four *marga* occupies its own corner. Branches of some of them, principally of Huta Galung and Huta Barat, have dispersed to Pahae and Hurlang. And all four have occupied their own territories in the coastal region of North Sibolga. A very important dispersal took place to Padang Lawas (VIIIB) where the river basin of the Barumun and Sosa Rivers (the last extends outside the boundaries of Tapanuli) has almost completely been taken over by branches of the *marga* Huta Galung which are there called Harayan and Botung. A small group called Handangkopo inhabits the Huristak territory. Its members say they are of Huta Barat origin, but the rest of the Hasibuan reckon them to be Botung. Two groups of the *marga* Dasopang, established in the Pangirkiran territory in Padang Bolak, and Silangge in Dolok, must also be of Huta Galung origin and must have reached their dwelling place along their own route.

THE NAIPOSPOS GROUP

This group split in half. The older half, that arising from Toga Marbun, inhabits a rather large area in North Humbáng (IXᴀ) and also has a branch in Bakkara. Single branches of the component *marga,* Lumban Batu and Bandjar Nahor, occupy the Sanggaran and Sihingkit territories in the benzoin region (IXʙ). Some small groups of Marbun are also encountered in a few small territories on the Humbáng Plateau, among others, Si Pitu Huta, while in the Kelasan district in Upper Barus, a quartette of *marga,* Marbun, Sehun, Meha and Mungkur, lie together. These *marga* must also belong to this tribal group and are said to have sprung from Lumban Batu. The Martua Same half went to the Sipoholon Valley and the adjacent part of the Humbáng Plateau (IXc) in which region each of the four component *marga,* Sinaga-bariang, Huta Uruk, Simanungkalit and Situmeang, occupies its own territory. Some parts of all four *marga* went westward to the mountainous Hurlang region and to the coastal area of Lower Barus.

THE AGE OF THE TRIBAL GROUPS AND MARGA

No endeavour has been made in the foregoing general outline to suggest the probable age of the tribal groups and *marga.* Only a detailed investigation, in which the data of the Batak themselves could be controlled, would make it possible to draw conclusions with regard to this point with some measure of probability. One usually hears the age of the *marga* given as about 15-20 generations by the persons concerned. Frequently, however, it can be assumed that it is upward of this figure.

One gets the impression that the Lontung moiety, as a more differentiated moiety, is older than the Sumba moiety.

THE MEANING OF "MARGA"

The words 'tribal group' and 'head' *marga* have already been used frequently as well as the word '*marga*'. This usage does not conform to the Batak idiom in which the meaning of the word *marga* is indefinite. The Batak use it to indicate the smaller units as well as the larger ones and the largest groups. Limbong (see p. 6) with only a few thousand people, which forms one of the oldest separate units, is as much a *marga* as Lontung, the moiety that has split up into seven "*marga*" each of which has again split once or twice into *marga.* A Nababaan (see p. 14) when asked what his *marga* is can give this name as well as Sihombing. And one can see announcements of births signed 'Ompu Sumurung' by persons who are also spoken of as Hasibuan but who belong to one of the branches of the *marga* Lumban Tobing (this is not indicated in the genealogical tree on page 15 because such a branch is outside its scope; it is given in Appendix I). There are no specific words to indicate the large complex of groups. If one wishes to know to which complex a particular *marga* belongs one will simply be told: "It belongs to Sumba, or Borbor", *"masuk Sumba do"* or *"masuk Borbor"*.

Whether a man reckons himself as belonging to a greater or smaller unit depends on whether a further distinction is pertinent at the time in question. In the coastal areas of Sibolga, where the *marga* name Pohan (see p. 11) is well-known but where people are not very well informed with regard to the divisions of the Pohan tribal group in Toba, a Pardede man will sometimes call himself Pohan for convenience and will allow others to address him as such. On the other hand, among the Lumban Tobing, who are considered to be enlightened, who are great in number and frequently in foreign parts, there is an increasing need for distinguishing proper names within a limited compass, and for this purpose a Lumban Tobing will choose the name of a division like Ompu Sumurung although this lineage, strictly speaking, is not yet a *marga, ndang marga dope.*

In the Hasibuan group, to which the Lumban Tobing belong, it is a fixed custom that a division is only called a *marga* when the marriage prohibition has been lifted between it and the remaining parts. An example is Simorangkir, a division of Panggabean, which became a *marga* after a marriage was allowed between a man of Simorangkir and a woman of Lumban Siagian, but, Lumban Ratus and Lumban Siagian are still called *marga* Panggabean (see p. 15).

In other regions, however, this criterion does not apply. For example, mutual marriage, *masibuatan* = recriprocal taking of women, is not permitted any of the Nai Ambaton *marga* of North Samosir, though the splitting up into 'head' *marga* (see p. 10) is nearly as old as the group itself, and the separation into *marga* goes back some centuries. And within the Pohan group the marriage prohibition has been broken in a different way between the parts of the Pohan *marga* living in East Humbáng (IVʙ) and those of the same *marga* that have settled elsewhere (IVA and c). In respect of tribal groups such as these, one can only say that within them a unit which has acquired its own commonly used name has become a *marga*.

There are tribal groups, such as we have already met with, which, if they occur in more than one place, have in one region split up and have given the new divisions numerous new names, while elsewhere they have remained an undivided whole. As a rule, this relates to separations that took place in very early times. For instance, as already mentioned, the Guru Hinobaan branch of Hasibuan went to Sigaol, Uluan, and has continued to live as a small Hasibuan *marga*, only a couple of hundred people strong, in the small territory of the same name and its nearby environs. On the other hand, however, before the descendants of Guru Mangaloksa had divided into four separate *marga*, a couple of small groups of descendants from Radja Huta Galung went to Padang Lawas where, as we saw, they have retained the *marga* name of Hasibuan. They have never known the name Huta Galung as a *marga* name and have given names to their own divisions that are unknown in Silindung. A similar thing occurs among the old Pohan emigrations on the west coast (Barus and Anggoli): these have not taken up the *marga* division of the ancestral area, have not split up into *marga* either, and have thus continued to live under the name Pohan. It is thus quite understandable that later refugees and emigrants from the Pohan group who joined their relatives, relinquished their own *marga* names and took the general name of Pohan.

It is obvious from the foregoing that the only object in introducing new terms such as 'tribal groups' and 'head *marga*' is to help the imaginative faculties of the outsider who would have difficulty in forming a clear picture of the somewhat intricate structure of Batak society from terms of which the purport is elastic. The term 'tribal group' is thus applied to the *marga* groups which are shown individually on pages 7-16 of the genealogical tree: 'head *marga*' is a serviceable term for the main divisions into which most tribal groups have split up. That leaves the term '*marga*' for the separate parts of the 'head' *marga*. The term '*marga* branch' is used to indicate the largest, but still not separate, divisions of the *marga*, and 'lineage' defines the smaller agnate groups which build up the *marga* branch.

THE LINEAGE, SAOMPU

The term *marga* branch defines quite clearly the two or three or more equivalent divisions (branches of the *marga*-tree) of which a *marga* consists. The term lineage, in common with its Batak equivalent, *saompu*, suffers from the same drawback as the term *marga* in that it is difficult to circumscribe its limits. Such is its nature. Such close attention is given to relationships resulting from descent and so much importance is attached to them because, in the sequence of the generations, every father who has had more than one son becomes a sharply defined joint in the genealogy of his patrilineal group. From him two or more groups of descendants have sprung, each of which has its own identity. But, if they unite, they will find in him the *ompu parsadaan* (*sada* = one), their meeting point, *pardomuan*. In the same manner each of his sons again forms the core of a smaller lineage.

Ompu means: grandfather, great-grandfather, forefather, and ancestor. Those who are of one and the same lineage, *na saompu*, thus represent the lineage stemming from a common forefather four generations back, as well as the lineage that is already 12 *sundut* = generations, old and is on the way to becoming a *marga*. Thus each individual belongs to a system of ever widening lineages, to a number of ever extending groups of which the unifying connection is always to be found further back in time. This is most important, because a man who belongs to a lineage that is strongly branched and has numerous members, *na balga partubu* = he who belongs to a great descent group, is differently placed in life and may reckon himself more fortunate than a man who can only show a slender lineage, *na metmet partubu*, and he again is different from the man who is alone and who must pursue his existence far from the kin-group to which he belongs. Hence the saying:

> *molo otik saompu, sori-ni-arina ma i,*
> *molo godáng saompu, godang ni tuana ma i;*
> The small lineage is the victim of its ill fortune,
> The great lineage owes its existence to great blessings.

The meaning of the term *suhu* = corner, group, is close to that of *ompu* in the expression *suhu ni partubu* = corners of the lineage, descent groups within one lineage. The word *suhu*, however, usually embraces less than *ompu*: to quote the saying:

> *dung sansimu marsambola, dung marsuhu-suhu marsaompu,*
> The half comes after the slice; the large lineages (*saompu*) come after the smaller ones (*sasuhu*).

The term *saompu* defines units of about the extent of a *marga* branch but each genealogical *suhu* is also an *ompu*. The terms are interchangeable.

Ripe = a separate unit, a family unit, in the narrowest sense means immediate family; the *dongan saripe* = member of the family, is the husband. But it extends beyond these limits and can even indicate a separate *marga* branch, as can be seen from the story of the settlement of the dispute in the Sipahutar territory given in Appendix II: *hita na saripe pinompar ni Si Radja Silitonga* = we the descendants of Si Radja Silitonga, who are of one family. In Mandailing the word has come to mean 'village ward', 'kinship ward', which is nearer to the original meaning of the word *ripe* than one who is not acquainted with the connection between the genealogical groups and the territorial distribution would think.

THE LINEAGE AS A CEREMONIAL AND SACRIFICIAL COMMUNITY

The terms relating to drum playing, *gondang*, banquets, *panganan*, and feasts, *hordja*, apply in a totally different manner.

The *gondang* is a set of drums and gongs. It is played when the spirits of the ancestors, the *sumangot ni ompu*, are summoned at ceremonial occasions of all kinds when the presence, benediction and assistance of the revered ancestors are invoked. It is played on the adoption of a name; when a house is consecrated; when sickness and calamities have to be warded off; when the bones of one of the ancestors are reburied, etc. The terms *sagondang* = belonging to one *gondang*, and *sapargondangan* = belonging to one *gondang* playing unit, apply to a drum-community that assembles at ceremonies for the veneration of the ancestor common to all its members. And, since offerings are made at these ceremonies, *dipele*, one can also speak of an offering-community, *sapelean*.

The identification of *sagondang* with lineage is obvious: *sagondang* means precisely the same as *saompu*, and like it, is vague, though to a lesser degree.

It is less vague because at these ceremonies an animal is slaughtered, a small part of it being set aside as the offering, while the remainder is eaten, *dipangan*, by the community.

SAPANGANAN

The *sapanganan* = those who partake of the same meal, are thus the members of the group of agnates who assemble for a ceremony and who, to further distinguish themselves use the name of the animal they eat at the ceremony.

The smallest group is the *sapanganan manuk*: its members partake of a chicken at its gatherings. Its extent is about that of a group of cousins who stem from a great- or great-great-grandfather, thus a group that cannot usually be called a lineage, but should rather be termed an extended family. It is roughly the group living together in or belonging to a recent *huta* i.e., a village that was only founded one or two generations ago. The Batak description of customary law, *Patik dohot*

Uhum ni halak Batak [9] speaks of four *sundut* = generations, at the
most as comprising a *sapanganan manuk* (in Chapter VI under A).
However, too much weight should not be attached to such a figure: if
there was only one son somewhere in the sequence of forefathers the
unit easily becomes a generation deeper, and the participation of
children, fathers and grandfathers at the meal is prejudicial to the
accuracy of the figure. One must also bear in mind that local usages
in this respect are rather divergent.

After the *sapanganan manuk* comes the *sapanganan babi* or *sapanganan dalu-dalu* (*babi* = pig, *dalu-dalu* = boar) (also called *sagondang
dalu-dalu* or *sapelean dalu-dalu*, here again the words merge in their
meanings), which takes its name from the pig that is killed and eaten
when this agnatic group assembles. The *Patik dohot Uhum* says that
it contains six generations, but it can be more or less, for various factors
can have influenced its extent: the numerical strength of the descendants
of each generation; whether they have remained together or have dispersed; the relationship to the more comprehensive group. It can be
called a 'lineage' and to define it somewhat more precisely, it inhabits
or belongs to a small cluster of villages that have arisen from a single
huta, the mother village, in the course of the last two or three centuries.

The next is the *sapanganan lombu*, the group of agnates who partake
of a cow and which comprises some lineages stemming from one forefather: it can again be larger or smaller according to the circumstances.

The small Silahisabungan territory of Tolping in North Samosir is
of old, with its kinsmen in the Silalahi territory on the north-west shore
of the lake, a *sapanganan lombu* and the present-day members of the
group are already 12-15 *sundut* removed from the common ancestor.
Elsewhere, in areas where the branchings of a *marga* have stayed together, this agnate group will have above it the larger patrilineal group
which, in its turn, will have joints above it before the ancestor of the
marga is reached. The *Patik dohot Uhum* mentions eight generations
for a *sapanganan lombu*: elsewhere five or six are given.

THE LARGER GENEALOGICAL COMMUNITIES

The *sahordja horbo* is the small or large *marga* branch, or even the
marga itself, which gathers together over a buffalo. It goes back not less
than three centuries and, if it has stayed together, occupies a territory
of some extent.

---

[9] "Rules and Laws of the Batak People", 1899; translated into Dutch in *Adatrechtbundel* (Collection of Descriptions of Adat Law), Vol. XXXV,
pp. 1-109.

More extensive again than the *sapanganan lombu* and the *sahordja horbo* was the *hordja rea*, or *santi rea*, both names for the very large sacrificial ceremonies and for the sacrificing communities, and the *sapanganan horbo sombaon*, the group which partook of a buffalo when the spirit of the highest revered ancestor, the *sombaon*, was to be worshipped, receive homage and offerings. The *hordja rea* and the *sapanganan horbo sombaon* comprise an entire 'head' *marga* or tribal group and have their focal points in the *raga-raga* of these kinship complexes. This *raga-raga* is a square rack, carefully cared for, that hangs in the *ruma parsantian* = House of the Tribal Group. The ancestral spirit was presumed to descend into it when he lowered himself amidst his descendants at the ceremonies arranged for his veneration.

The collection of the festival contributions and the division of the offering-animal at these larger ceremonies by the component lineages, which can also be called *saguguan* = one collecting unit, or *sadjambar* = one sharing unit, has already been referred to and will again be dealt with in Chapter II, where a description of the religious character of the genealogical groups will be given.

CONNECTION WITH THE GIVING OF WOMEN IN MARRIAGE

Within the framework under consideration the terms *hordja* and *panganan* have another meaning again, namely, referring to the giving of daughters in marriage.

One of the principal ceremonies of the marriage contract is the *mangan djuhut* = eating meat, also called *mangan tuhor ni boru*, literally, to partake of the marriage payment received for a daughter, which means that the bride's father and his kinsmen participate in the formal transfer, *parundjuhan*, of the marriage payment by the bridegroom's father. This transfer is coupled with the ceremonial presentation of cooked meat. The *sapanganan djuhut* = those who eat meat together, is in one place the wider agnate group, in another the narrower which participates in the ceremony of giving a daughter in marriage or receives a *djambar* = portion. In its most extended form it can be called the *sahordja mangan tuhor ni boru*. It is the group entitled to be heard when one of its female members is 'surrendered', a recognition which is expressed by its being invited to the ceremony or receiving a portion of the meat. And henceforth it reckons the married couple and their offspring as its *boru*. An example is the Huta Barat branch which went from the original seat of the *marga* in the north-west of Silindung to the Lumban Garaga territory in North Pahae and there became a separate *hordja* for giving its daughters in marriage.

THE KINSHIP GROUP IN VILLAGE AND TERRITORY

The lineages have not split up into villages and village groups according to a fixed rule and there are always members of other *marga* living in the villages as co-inhabitants. Nevertheless, as a general rule, it is fairly safe to say that the villages lying round a mother-village (inhabited or deserted) and which sprang from it, are of one *ompu* and that when the village chiefs go to a gathering of the chiefs of the territory, they go according to lineage, *marsuhu-suhu* or *marompu-ompu*: in Humbáng one finds some of the chiefs called *radja suhu-suhu*; they are the elders of the lineages. So, the term *hordja* can also be used to indicate a territory of unmixed composition. There are also, however, a number of terms that have a geographical meaning, for example *ladang* = complex of fields for agriculture and *luat* = land area. Others relate to the administration of justice and government, like *saharung-guan* = those who meet at one gathering place, or indicate an assembly of mixed composition, *sapartahian* = those who deliberate. Yet others are connected with the general offering-ceremonies, the *bius*.

Frequently, however, such a territorial community acquired the name which is the actual name of the tribal group, *marga* or smaller kinship group that prevails there. Thus the territory on the shore of Lake Toba where the youngest of the Tambatua *marga*, which retained the name Tamba, stayed after the other companion *marga* went away, is called Tamba. The territory lying between Balige and Laguboti, where the Silahisabungan *marga* Tambunan is established, is called Tambunan. And there are many more such. Villages can be counted by the hundred which bear the names of the *marga* to which they belong, such as Lumban Manurung, Sosor Nadapdap, Huta Sipordabuan. They are mainly to be found in the territories that are not homogeneous in composition or where the in-dwelling *marga* have been allowed to establish their own villages.

Conversely, a number of *marga* and *marga* branches bear the name of the village (*huta, lumban*) that was founded by one of the forefathers or was inhabited by them and from which the later villages have arisen (see pp. 7-16).

THE AGNATIC KINSHIP SYSTEM

The kinship system, *ruhut ni pardonganon*, relating to agnatic kinsmen is rather simple. On the one hand it counts generations, considered in respect of the common ancestor, in horizontal layers in the genealogical tree: on the other hand, it reckons according to first and later birth, thus with vertical divisions.

Brothers from one father, *ama*, are of one generation; they are the *ampara* of each other, they are *marampara*. This applies throughout the male line to all grandsons, *pahompu*, from one grandfather, *ompu*, to all great-grandsons, *nini*, from one great-grandfather, *ompu*, and so on until the knowledge of the mutual kinship relationship is lost.

The eldest son is the *sihahaan*, the youngest the *siampudan* or *sianggian*. Those between are the *silitonga*. This *partording ni partubu* = order of birth, is maintained for sons and all of their descendants.

With regard to the use of some of these terms in relation to *marga*: a couple of *marga* which are the oldest in their group are called Siahaan, and there is also a *marga* called Silitonga (see pp. 11, 13). In the case of the twin *marga* of the Nai Rasaon tribal group, Manurung and Sitorus, it is not known which came into existence first. The custom has therefore been established that a Manurung who visits a Sitorus, Sirait or Butarbutar will always be regarded as the youngest, and in this tribal group the first born of twins is always provided immediately with a distinguishing mark.

For various reasons that will become clear later on, it is very important that when people address each other no wrong inference should be created by the way in which they do so. Only one example will be given at the moment. There is a speech ban between an elder brother and the wife of his younger brother and were they to break the prohibition they would be confusing the kinship relationship, *imbar ni partuturan*. Here it can also be remarked that popular usage demands that people generally avoid using proper names when they address each other and use instead a word that indicates their family connection, *partuturan*, which means, literally, addressee-addressor relationship.

When brothers are speaking to each other the word *haha* indicates the elder (*dahahang* = my elder brother) and *anggi*, the younger (*anggikku* = my younger brother). This also applies to other kinsmen in one generation irrespective of their ages: the sons of an elder brother call those of a younger, *anggi*, as their father calls his brother. And the term *marhaha-maranggi* means "those who are the elder and younger brother of each other". This applies not only to actual brothers (of the same father) but also to cousins (sons of brothers) etc. From every ancestor who had more than one son there is an older branch of descendants, the *haha ni partubu*, and a younger, the *anggi ni partubu*. Brothers who are born after each other are called *martinodohon* =

those who denote each other as being born in succession: a man refers
to his brother who was born after him as *na hutodohon*.

The generations who follow each other never lose sight of their
partording. Father's brothers are also regarded and addressed as fathers.
Damang means 'my father' and if it is necessary to emphasise the fact
that a man is referring to his own actual father, then *na tumubuhon
ahu* = he who begat me, or some similar term is added. A man's father's
eldest brother is the *damang sihahaan*, to whom he himself is *marama tu*.
He also calls 'father' all those of his lineage who are of the same
generation as his actual father, to them also he is *marama tu*. Similarly,
he regards as his grandfather and his great-grandfather, *ompu*, all those
who are of the same layer in the genealogy as his own grandfather and
great-grandfather respectively. Persons of the preceding generations refer
to him as their *anak* and *pahompu*. For example, *na maranak ahu tu
N.* = I regard N ... as my son, that is, he is of the generation following
mine. This applies irrespective of the age of the persons concerned, thus
a boy can call an adult his *anak* = son.

In reckoning kinship relations each generation starts with itself and
works back to the ancestor, and includes him. Thus two *sundut* equals
son-father; three *sundut* equals son-father-grandfather, and so on. The
uncle-nephew relationship is thus determined through a double reckoning. The following chart clarifies these points.

The A branch is the *sihahaan* or *haha ni
partubu*, the oldest by birth in relation to B
and C. A, B, and C, on one line are each other's
ampara; A 5 is the *haha* of B 5 who is *maranggi
tu* C 5. The three together are *marhaha-
maranggi* in the narrower sense and so are the
branches in their entirety.

A 5 as well as C 5 are *maranak tu* B 6 who
is *marama tu* both of them, while B 6 is
marompu tu A 4 and C 4; A 3 and C 3 and
so on upwards.

A 6 to the ancestor 0 is reckoned as 7 *sundut*;
C 4 as 5 *sundut* and so on. All kinship relations,
therefore, trace back to the common ancestor,
the *ompu parsadaan*.

	0	
A 1	B 1	C 1
A 2	B 2	C 2
A 3	B 3	C 3
A 4	B 4	C 4
A 5	B 5	C 5
A 6	B 6	
	B 7	

The entire group that sprang from this ancestor forms a *saompu*, a
lineage; a *sasuhu*, a group standing opposite the next related lineages;
a *sapanganan*, a sacrificing community of about the extent of the

sapanganan dalu-dalu. The members of the group, of any layer, can also be called *marhaha-maranggi* when it is not necessary to determine the exact mutual relation.

In the chart, A 5, B 5, and C 5 are *ditoru ni tutur* in relation to A 4, B 4 and C 4. A 3, B 3 and C 3 are *digindjang ni tutur* in relation to A 4, B 4, and C 4. These terms mean respectively "those who are below" and "those who are above".

The members of a *marga* are the *dongan-samarga* = members of the same *marga*, or *dongan-sabutuha* = those who have sprung from the same womb: the term is usually shortened to *dongan*. The terms *pardonganon, parsabutuhaon,* or in full *pardongan-sabutuhaon,* define the consanguinity of the agnates.

As the lineages diverge from each other the individuals also lose sight of the order of their mutual relationship more and more and the modes of address make the disparity in age more pronounced, but on formal occasions the genealogical connection comes to the fore again. Then one can truly say of the genealogical tree, *tarombo*:

> *djodjor bona songon boras ni taem,*
> *martording mardjodjoran songon tangga ni balatuk;*
> Its heart is like the many-lobed indigo seed,
> It has a regular graduated sequence like the steps of a ladder to a house.

THE UARIS CONCEPT

The *uaris* concept is connected with the foregoing relationships and is of particular importance in respect of family law and the law of land tenure. It has no connection with the law of inheritance since this provides that the next of kin, either direct of collateral, are entitled to inherit. The *uaris* of a living person is the person or group most closely related to him who live in the same region as the man himself and can act on his behalf in his absence. If a man has left his village and before doing so pledged his fields, then his *uaris*, who remained in the village, can redeem them and use them as his own until the return of their owner. If a man dies and leaves a child and his brothers are not in a position to care for it, then the *uaris*, who lives in the neighbourhood, will take care of the orphan and the property or goods left to it.

The *uaris* is entitled to redeem land that has been given by a bridegroom's father who is closely related to him, as a pledge for part of the marriage payment to the bride's father, etc.

The extent of the *uaris*-relationship is not always easy to define but as a rule it is limited to, say, 5 or 7 *sundut*. It depends on the nature of the matter to be settled; on the breadth of the kinship group around the person concerned; on the character of the conflicting interests; and also on local circumstances and ideas. If there are but a few members of a *marga* living in an area of another *marga*, then it may refer to a far-removed kinsman.

DISPUTES ABOUT DESCENT

From time to time a dispute will arise about someone's descent; usually from circumstances resulting from war and the slavery of the *Pidari* time. This is especially the case in those regions where villages were looted, where the people were driven from house and field or were captured and became slaves, for then many a man lost almost all contact with his kinship group.

It was, therefore, a sound measure of the first Dutch District Officer of Samosir to order every person, freeborn or emancipated slave, to return to the region of his origin, the *bona ni pinasa* = foot of the nangka tree, or *bona ni pasogit* = the place of the first small offering-shrine of the *marga* or tribal group. The object was that the threads of normal relations with the people among whom they originally belonged should be taken up again, and it placed the groups concerned under an obligation to see that the transfer went smoothly, thus diminishing the chance of disputes about descent arising in the future.

Sometimes it was necessary for a person or persons to flee and seek refuge with their *marga* members who were living in another area. When they settled among them there was then a gradual absorption of the descendants of the new arrivals into the lineage in the place where they had found refuge. After a number of years, however, disputes might arise for one reason or another, or the lost ones might be traced by their real kinsmen. The quarrels that arose, usually about the rights to land, resulted from the difficulty of determining descent.

Disputes are produced by a variety of circumstances. If a woman recently widowed quickly remarries another man who is not related to her deceased husband and shortly afterwards bears a son, he will endeavour to pass himself off as the child of his mother's deceased husband if the latter's kinsmen are more prosperous and have more influence than her second husband's kinsmen. Small daughters whose parents have died and who are without near kinsmen are sometimes the victims of spurious kinship relationships concocted in order to obtain their possessions, and later to acquire the marriage payment for them. The area for disputes of this kind is Toba where there are lawsuits in abundance instigated by the less scrupulous. Disputes can also arise in connection with a ceremony. It is one of the main concerns of the giver of a feast that each of his guests shall receive the portion of the slaughtered feast-animal, the *djambar*, to which he is entitled according to the *partubu*, and if there is dancing a long-slumbering quarrel may break out suddenly between the groups participating as to which stems from an older group and therefore has precedence over the other. I once saw such a dispute on Samosir settled by a statement by the *boru silaon* (see p. 20).

It is easy to understand that where the genuine facts about descent are in doubt it is not difficult to frame a fictitious genealogy and to surround it with fine fantasies.

CHANGING ONE'S MARGA

Besides the reasons already given, changing from one *marga* to another can also be the result of expulsion or banishment, *ambolonghon, pabalihon*. It is rare for a father to curse his son and disown him, but should it happen, then the son will depart and try to find someone in another *marga*, for example, a childless man, who is disposed to adopt him, *mangain*. This will be discussed later in Chapter V.

It can also be done for purely practical reasons. It is common knowledge that some generations ago one of the *marga* in the Silindung Valley more than once transferred some of its families to another *marga* in order to achieve a better balance in numerical strength in the matter of the contributions, *guguan*, given towards the *bius*-feast in which both *marga* participated. They were also mindful of the tussle, which always took place between both parties, over the stabbed buffalo which each side desired to drop on the opposite side. This change from one *marga* to another was final.

THE SIGNIFICANCE OF THE PATRILINEAL STRUCTURE

The entire life of the Batak is governed by the patrilineal structure of his society. It is far from being limited to the sphere of the law of inheritance. Government and land tenure, marriage and spirit worship, the administration of justice, dwelling place and cultivating the land are all directly connected with the genealogical relationships. Even the Christian Church is affected.[10] Of old, the circle of agnates was defined as: *sisada sipanganon* = eating together as one; *sisada sinamot* = one in prosperity; *sisada hasangapon* = one in prestige; *sisada hailaon* = one in humiliation.

The terms that are drawn from spirit worship and sacrificial cere-monies would suggest that the bonds of the patrilineal system will loosen with the gradual disappearance of paganism. However, the direct con-nection between genealogical grouping and geographical distribution has allowed the patrilineal structure to penetrate deeply into all spheres of life and it is therefore to be expected that the forms that this society has developed will be preserved for a long time to come. There are various reasons for this: the ground on which a village stands, the walls surrounding it, the trees on its land are the exclusive domain and property of the patrilineal descendants of the founder and this will continue to be so as long as there is a public authority strong enough to prevent wars between village and village, territory and territory. A cluster of villages around a mother-village is inhabited by a lineage that in former times kept to itself for reasons of solidarity and safety, and now is still a small territory with its own identity. The groups of these territories which occupy the *marga-* and tribal territory, together form a larger genealogical unit which has its own area in which no other *marga* are permitted to establish a village, and its forests, waters and uncultivated ground are only at the free disposal of members of these groups. They alone have the prerogative of ruling over others in these territories.

It is factors like these that from olden times have cultivated in all patrilineal divisions, large and small, a strong sense of belonging together, a strong feeling of solidarity in *marga* and tribal group with, at the same time, a keen awareness of the separation of interests according to genealogical lines, and a strong instinct of self-preservation.

The exogamous marriage form leaves intact the patrilineally distinct groups with their internal relations on the one hand, while on the other, as soon as an affinal relationship is commenced it creates a kind of link that so deviates from that among the agnates that it delineates the latter the more clearly. Moreover, the history of a man's lineage, the renown of great ancestors, the wealth that one group possesses above that

---

[10] The parishes generally follow the genealogical boundaries much closer than do the districts and sub-districts created by the Government.

of another, the offices and the influence deriving from them all bear on the durability of the structural forms within which a man lives.

Not the least factor in this respect is the festivals which, by their procedure, repeatedly motivate the tracing of the genealogical relationships and stimulate their preservation.

And that this sense of solidarity is capable of finding new outlets is proved by the Study Fund Movement of recent times which, like the *santi rea* of former times, brings together those descending from one ancestor, not as formerly for his ritual veneration, but to promote their own welfare and glory.

B. The Affines

It is often said that the Batak 'buys' his wife. With this idea in mind it is rather difficult to understand that relations can still be maintained between the two parties after this transaction. Such an idea is manifestly not consistent with the facts. When a woman marries neither her father's love for her nor the bond between her and her brothers nor her relations with her lineage kinsmen suddenly cease. When a woman leaves the circle of her lineage to marry she creates the affinity-relationship, the *partondongan*, which continues to bind her, her husband, his agnatic group, her children and her future male descendants to the lineage from which she came. The agnatically independent parts of the people are thus brought into association with each other in a variety of ways and this is maintained in the succeeding generations. The *pardongansabutuhaon* can be thought of as a system of lines radiating from the junctions of the people, the tribal group, *marga* and lineage, from top to bottom (a usual way of representing the genealogical tree). The threads of the *partondongan* are woven through these lines from left to right and vice versa at varying angles, thus producing a very intricate pattern. This *partondongan* considerably tempers the unilateral characteristics of the agnatic structure and softens its sharp edges, and it permeates the whole social life of the Batak.

The woman, as the link between the men and the men's groups, creates a specific bond totally different from that enjoyed by the agnates by virtue of their relationship within the agnatic circle.

First we will consider the various relations that a marriage creates.

ESTABLISHMENT AND CONSOLIDATION OF THE AFFINAL RELATIONSHIP

When a man gives his daughter, his *boru*, in marriage he acquires in her husband his son-in-law, his *hela*, who is also called his *boru*. The descendants of the woman, the *ianakhon*, or *tubu ni boru i*, will therefore become the *anak boru*, abbreviated to *boru*, of her father and his kinsmen. These latter are the *hula-hula* = relatives-in-law, of the *boru*, and are also regarded as such by the woman immediately she marries. They are each other's affines, *tondong*; they are *martondong* = affines of each other.

The creation of the *boru—hula-hula* relationship by a marriage is termed *umpungka partondongan*. It affects not only the newly married couple and the first generation stemming from them, but it also establishes the position which, irrespective of later events, will continue to exist between the succeeding generations of the men who descend from the woman on the one hand, and from her father and his agnatic group on the other.

In order to strengthen the *boru—hula-hula* relation there will be initially a tendency for a man to take his wife from the circle of his mother's *hula-hula*. This preference of a young man to marry the daughter of his mother's brother, his *tulang*, is called *manunduti*. The girl is thus his *boru ni tulang*. This girl, born in the same agnatic circle from which the young man's mother comes, connects her husband, who is the *ibebere* (or *bere*) of his *tulang* (the girl calls him among other things, *ibebere ni damang*), once again as *hela* and also as *boru*, with her father, consequently doubling the strength of the existing affinity bond. His brothers, however, will then seek their wives in another circle, either one belonging to the same *marga* as the mother's *hula-hula*, or one belonging to another *marga* or tribal group. In doing so, each forms his own new *hula-hula* group.

Daughters are never married into the nearest *hula-hula* from which their mother or their father's mother came. This would reverse the affinity-relationship, *marsungsang partuturan*, which is out of the question. It conflicts with the whole structure. The direction in which the women go is followed repeatedly, but marriages do not go in the opposite direction, at least not initially. After some generations, and if the link has not been continually strengthened by repeated *manunduti*, it is permissible to take a woman as wife from the circle of the *boru* of the bridegroom. In other words, a girl can be given in marriage to a man of her father's *hula-hula*. In the first instance, however, daughters go in another direction and they again form *boru* groups for the agnatic circle of their fathers. In this manner every Batak has his very diversified two-directional conjoined affinal relationships. On the one side is his *hula-hula*, the different groups of agnates from which have originated his mother, his father's brother's wife, his paternal grandmother, the mother of his paternal grandfather and the female ancestor of his lineage, his *marga* branch, his *marga* and tribal group. On the other side is his *boru* or *ianakhon*, that is, the men who took as wives his daughter, his sister, his father's sister, his grandfather's sister, the daughters of his lineage and the men who sprang from these various marriages. With his agnatic descent in the male line, the man stands, as it were, between these *hula-hula* and *boru* groups.

This is illustrated in the following chart in which the men are indicated by crosses, the women by dots and the marriages by dotted lines.

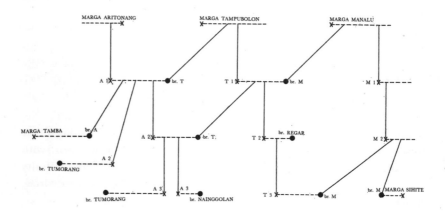

Man A 1 is the first Aritonang to take a *boru* Tampubolon as wife. Thus the first thing is that the lineage of Tampubolon within which the wife was born, and in a broader sense the whole branch of the Tampubolon *marga* to which the lineage belongs, acquires its *boru* in A 1 and his descendants A 2, A 3, etc.

If A 2, one of the sons of A 1, takes as wife one of the daughters of his *tulang*, T 1 (he is called her *anak ni namboru* = son of her father's sister), then the connection already established is strengthened by *manunduti* = repetition. The relationship continues even if the sons A 3, their sons or grandsons take their wives from another *marga*, and it will be renewed again, *mangaratai*, if at a later date a young man A takes his wife from the lineage from which came his great-great-grandmother and her mother who were the two *boru* T. When this happens the woman then becomes the *boru ni tutur* = daughter from the "address", since, although the regular and very important affinal relationships may not have been maintained in daily life with the group from which she comes, it is nevertheless proper to regard this group as relatives-in-law in the matter of address.

Similarly, the T group has its *hula-hula* in the M group in which there was at first no *manunduti*, this being effected later in the case of T 3 . . . br. M.

It is also *manunduti* if a son of one of the A 2's takes as wife br. Tumorang from the same group as did the other A 2.

A 1 and T 1 are *lae* = each other's brother-in-law. But it is important to note that T 1 is the *tunggane* (also meaning elder) of A 1 who may not speak with the wife of T 1. He refers to her as his *bao*, and he cannot marry her if she is widowed.

Brother T 1 and sister br. T are mutually *iboto*.

Two sisters, such as the daughters of M 2 are each other's *pariban*, they are *marpariban*, and call each other *haha* and *anggi* and not *iboto*. Each sister is also *marpariban* to the husband of the other and both their husbands are *marpariban* to each other also. Sisters are always very attached to each other, and, as a rule, the same is true of their husbands.

Surprisingly enough, the two A 2 and their *boru ni tulang*, br. T are also the *pariban* of each other. As already mentioned, they are the *anak ni namboru* of br. T. Their marriage is the one most desired, though it is decreasing more and more at the present day.

In complete contrast to this *pariban* relationship between cousin A 2 and cousin br. T is that between cousin T 2 and cousin br. A, thus between an *anak ni tulang* and a *boru ni namboru*. In fact, both regard themselves as brother and sister, *iboto,* as do the young man's father and the girl's mother. Marriage between them is out of the question. It would be the worst form of *marsungsang* possible and, consequently, as far as I know, never happens.

For the remainder of the affinal relations and the terms used to define them see the chart on p. 66.

THE AFFINAL RELATIONSHIP IN THE WIDER CONTEXT

It is worthy of special mention that as in the case of the agnates the affinal relationships embrace a wider circle than only those directly concerned. This is shown in the following diagram

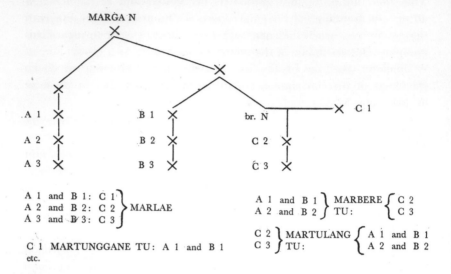

A 1 and B 1: C 1 ⎤
A 2 and B 2: C 2 ⎬ MARLAE
A 3 and B 3: C 3 ⎦

A 1 and B 1 ⎤ MARBERE ⎰ C 2
A 2 and B 2 ⎦ TU: ⎱ C 3

C 1 MARTUNGGANE TU: A 1 and B 1
etc.

C 2 ⎤ MARTULANG ⎰ A 1 and B 1
C 3 ⎦ TU: ⎱ A 2 and B 2

The terms *marbere tu* etc., here also mean: to regard as *bere*.

If the brother of C 1 takes his wife from a lineage other than that of the As or Bs, he is related to the As and Bs only in an indirect way; he is not regarded as their *boru*.

Daughters born to br. N and their male descendants are called the *boru ni boru* or, the *boru ibebere,* of the As and the Bs. This is not, strictly speaking, an affinal relationship.

The accurate determination of the kinship between two individuals is, understandably, only necessary in daily intercourse between those of a comparatively small circle who are in frequent association with each other. As soon as the relation is farther removed and if mutual intercourse is slight, no one unravels its precise details if there is no immediate need to do so. Then the difference in age is the determining factor; adult males from different *marga* call each other *lae*, or in the case of an older woman of the *marga boru* she is called the *namboru* and so forth.

THE AFFINES AS A GROUP

If, after a number of generations, a great lineage has arisen from a woman she becomes, as the ancestress, the established link between her descendants and those of the agnatic group within which she was born.

This *hula-hula* group is regarded by her descendants as the *bona ni ari* = 'The Beginning of the Days' and is always accorded the reverence that is its prerogative. People will never neglect inviting this 'first' *hula-hula* to participate in important feasts of their own circle. For, as we shall see later, the Batak — as does the kinship group to which he belongs — owes a considerable part of his position in life to the blessings he has received from his *hula-hula*.

The groups that follow this 'first' *hula-hula,* both in importance and chronologically, are the *hula-hula* groups from which the later fore-fathers of the lineage have taken their wives. These groups are also entitled to be treated with respect by the descendants of these women.

Sometimes, however, human nature overrules what should be observed as being right and just. Keen as a Batak is on honour and respect, *hasangapon,* being shown to him and also to his affines, he is apt to neglect a group that has diminished in numerical strength, wealth, power and influence even though it is important from the genealogical standpoint, and to attach himself to another group that has become of more consequence in society. The old cooking pot is thrown on the ash-heap and a new one appears on the rack above the hearth fire, as the saying goes. In fact, a *parhula-hulaon* which could no longer shed lustre and glory on those connected with it or provide them with profit, has been known to be rejected completely.

I recollect a lawsuit in which an ancestor ten *sundut* removed had had four sons. Only from the youngest had a powerful lineage sprung from which, in recent times, the *djaihutan* and *negeri* chiefs of the territory where the whole of his descendants lived, had been drawn. The other three branches had not done so well for themselves in the world. The second had even shrunk to a very small humble group that could barely provide its own village chief, despite the fact that a *boru* group, which had acquired a prominent position in its own territory and which had furnished the principal chiefs of that community, had arisen from this second son. So, one day the announcement was made that the ancestress was not a daughter of the second son but of the fourth and that henceforth the direct affinity relation was to be regarded as having commenced with the male descendants of this fourth son.

In such a case proof can be found in the history of the feasts of the group concerned since people invite each other to the feasts that con-cern the whole group, or to those given by the most important people (see Appendix I).

4

Further evidence can be provided by the *marebat-ebat* = the periodical paying of visits to each other, that is regularly done by the affinal groups. They announce their intention to pay a visit previously and travel in great numbers, sometimes by the hundred, and from great distances, to the territory of their affines, taking with them the customary gifts. There they are received and entertained liberally and, if possible, if the *hula-hula* is receiving the party, in the house where the ancestress of the group was born and brought up. If the *boru* is host, then the guests will be entertained in the house where the ancestress started her married life. For a further discussion, see Appendices II and III.

Such visits, naturally, are only made if both the groups concerned are living in different territories.

In order to maintain the type of affinity relationship of which the particular aim is to keep alive the basic connections between two groups, it is necessary that a direct descent from a *boru* of the visited or visiting group is demonstrable. Thus, such mutual visiting is only done between such groups.

For the more general aims, it is not, however, strictly necessary that the forefather of the one had a sister who became the ancestress of the lineage of the other. It is sufficient if the *marga* or *marga* branches, in certain circumstances even the tribal groups — when two Batak meet in foreign parts — are related as affines through one or more of their principal divisions. Hence the saying: *sada tumoktok hite, luhút marhitehonsa, sada do martondong, luhút martondonghonsa* = one person builds a bridge and everyone can go over it: one person enters an affinal relationship and everyone likewise becomes an affine.

The Batak uses his affinity connection advantageously when he travels. In olden times he could safely journey through areas over which his affines ruled, and even today it makes it easier for him to go on a visit to people who are unknown to him personally. It also means that if two Batak, who come from areas that are not too far apart, such as Silindung and North Samosir, meet and proceed to *martutur* = trace the family relationship, they can nearly always discover some way or other in which they are related to each other through a marriage in earlier times.

THE IN-DWELLING MARGA BORU

A particular phenomenon of the affinity relation is the *boru* 'living-in' in the territory of its *hula-hula*. In early times it often happened that an enterprising man broke away from his kinship group and went elsewhere to seek a new place to live where he could found a new lineage, and took with him a prosperous *boru* to help him clear and cultivate the land, *rap manombang tano i*. This *boru* continued to live with him and his descendants became the in-dwelling *marga* of the territory, the *boru gomgoman* = the *boru* that is ruled, since it was ruled by the descendants of the principal emigrant who were called the *marga radja* = ruling *marga*.

Sometimes the emigrant did not take such a *boru* with him but later on some other man married among the first settlers of the region (was taken as a son-in-law, *hinela*) and, if he became prosperous and the union was fruitful, then an in-dwelling *marga boru* came into being.

If the in-dwelling group began such an affinal relationship with the ancestor of the whole circle of agnates which ruled in the territory, then one speaks of the *boru parsadaan* or the *boru hatopan*, the *boru* common to the whole circle. If the relation only affected one of the branches that had sprung from the common ancestor, then this branch — which usually lives in a particular corner of the territory — calls its *boru* its *hapundjungan* = its own individual affines. Naturally, one finds a number of different phenomena in this matter, for history does not always repeat itself. Here we will only remark that there are regions, such as Silindung, where a great number of members from a number of different tribal groups are in-dwelling in the territories of the *marga* and *marga* branches of the Hasibuan group which rules there. These are the older *marga boru*, but others live with the lineages and extended families of which these *marga* branches consist: these are the younger *marga boru*. By contrast, elsewhere, especially on Samosir and in Toba, the number of people who belong to the in-dwelling *marga* is rather small. Then again, there are regions, such as Pahae, where one does not come across a *boru* group common to a territory; they can only be regarded as villages affines. It is often the younger areas of emigration which were split up when they were occupied and where the choice of marriage partners has always been considerable that provide examples of such a situation.

The oldest in-dwelling *marga* has different names in different regions and each name defines one of its characteristics.

In Silindung and Humbáng it is called the *boru na godjong* = the very old *boru* group; on Samosir one speaks of the *boru silaon*, which means the same thing; in Toba it is called the *boru sihabolonan* = the great, common *boru* group; in Barus it is the *boru ni ladang* = the *boru* group of the complex of cultivated fields = the territory; in the Dairi

Country this group is the *boru tano* = the *boru* group to which land rights have been granted.

It is distinguished from the *boru* groups which came to dwell in the territory later on by having had some particular rights granted to it and these vary according to place and area. For instance, it has the right to found its own villages and to live together there on land assigned to it; it can receive other *marga* as in-dwellers and can give them the use of land for cultivation; it has the right to give land which it has developed as a marriage gift, *pauseang*, to its daughters; the right to perform important functions in the communal sacrifices and in the administration of justice; and to take part in general deliberations. Mostly these latter privileges are exercised by the representative of the oldest branch, the *radja ni boru*, of such a first in-dwelling *marga*.

In many regions, besides this *marga* in-dwelling in a territory, individual *huta* = villages can have their own *boru ni huta*. If, for instance, a member of the ruling *marga* left his village in order to found his own village within the confines of the territory, he made sure, in this as a rule costly undertaking, of the collaboration of a well-to-do person, chosen from among his next related affines, who could contribute to the cost of the construction of the new village. This man then continued to live in the new village as the *boru* particularly connected with it and, as compared with members of other *marga* which later married into the village, acquired a position of considerable influence. In the more southerly parts of the Batak Country such a *boru*, and his descendants, who brought prosperity to the village, is called the *namora boru* = the rich *boru*.

It is a mistake to think that this in-dwelling of the *marga boru* with its ruling *hula-hula* indicates an inferior or second rate position. Were this the case, every man who is not chained by sheer poverty to his dwelling place would return to the territory of his own *marga* or tribal group where he would be cordially received by his lineage. But it is not so. It is true that only the members of the oldest *boru* groups, to whom was granted the right to have their own villages and fields by their *hula-hula*, have unrestricted control over the land they have cultivated, but, members of the younger *marga boru* too, through their fathers-in-law, or broadly, the families-in-law, can acquire land rights that are almost absolute in the form of gifts (*ulos, pauseang*, etc., which will be discussed later in Chapter V) that are frequently made by the *hula-hula* to the *boru*. In addition, they have the opportunity of temporarily using land given to them by the chief of a village or of a cluster of villages so long as they are in-dwellers in the village itself. In general, it can be said that the relations between the affines when one of the groups is the ruler, the *panggomgom* and the other the *ginomgom* = the ruled, are of a totally different character than these terms would suggest.

Before dealing with its noteworthy features, we will devote a little space to the marriage frequency between the ruling and the in-dwelling *marga*.

MARRIAGE FREQUENCY

It speaks for itself that the marriage frequency is very great between the *marga* ruling in a territory, or village and the in-dwelling *boru* group that has lived there since olden times. As observed earlier, the is the ruler, the *panggomgom* and the other the *ginomgom* = the ruled, *marga* after some generations (*marsungsang*). In doing so it becomes the *hula-hula* of the ruling marga. Nevertheless, it is the first marriages in olden times which determine the general relationship of affinity.

In the *Pidari* time, when one could not move freely about the country, the marriage frequency between ruling and in-dwelling *marga* was naturally greater than it is at present, and it was then further stimulated by the preference for a *boru ni tulang* (m.b.d.) or a *boru* from the *tulang*'s lineage. A preference that has declined in more recent times. The ancient in-dwelling *marga* has therefore rightly been termed the 'marriage *marga*'. This term, however, suggests too strongly that marriage with this *marga* was the rule and with others the exception. This is not the case and never has been. Other in-dwelling *marga* came into a territory or village after the *boru na godjong*. And many a young man also sought his bride outside the territory, among the closely related *marga* in the same tribal group into which a man could marry, or in the region of an adjacent tribal group, and thus often established a new affinal relationship. One factor that contributed to the development of all kinds of such marriages was the gatherings at the regular four-day markets. In the Silindung Valley, for instance, after the four descendants of Guru Mangaloksa (see p. 15) had mutually broken the marriage ban existing between them, Panggabean became the *radja boru* of Huta Toruan and the *radja hula-hula* (also called *radja ni tutur*) of Huta Galung and so on. The terms indicate the direction in which the first marriages went. But rarely, if ever, did these Hasibuan marry into the neighbouring Naipospos group since they were hostile to them.

For similar reasons the marriage frequency between groups which were the first to have affinal relations could be and can be very limited.

ERRATUM

Page 53, line 12 read:
in-dwelling *marga* can also give its daughters in marriage to the ruling

Radja Lontung, for example, who had no *hula-hula* because he married his sister, became the *radja hula-hula* of Sihombing and Simamora since both his daughters married the ancestors of Sihombing and Simamora. Hence the standing expression: *Lontung sisia marina, pasia boruna Sihombing, Simamora* = Lontung has nine children by one mother, the nine being made up by the daughters from whom originated the groups just mentioned. Radja Lontung's sons-in-law occupied their own territories on the Humbáng Plateau rather far removed from South Samosir. As a consequence, later on, young girls from Lontung were not willing to marry and live there and the young men of Sihombing and Simamora seldom wanted to go to live in the Lontung area of their *hula-hula*. Thus no part of Simamora has ever lived there and Sihombing is only represented here and there as an in-dwelling *marga*: there is a small fragment of the *marga* Lumban Toruan in the Hatoguan territory. Besides that, the marriage ban between most of the Lontung *marga*, about 30, which occur in South Samosir, has long been lifted. It is thus understandable that the *mangaratai* = renewal, of the affinity link with Sihombing and Simamora has, in practice, not often taken place and it has tended to become more and more platonic in character.

THE MAGICO-RELIGIOUS CHARACTER OF THE AFFINAL RELATIONSHIP

The affinity system that the Batak have envolved and which they still maintain has such ramifications, extends so far back in time, and is so dispersed geographically, that neither love, reverence nor interest could have sustained it had there not been a contributory condition of a magico-religious nature. This aspect will only be touched upon here sufficiently for an understanding of the discussion that follows.

It is not enough to say that the *boru* should have an attitude of reverence towards its *hula-hula*, that it should treat it with respect, or that a *hula-hula* can reflect lustre and glory on its *boru*. The *hula-hula* is a source of supernatural power, of individual vitality for its *boru*. The *boru* sees the members of its *hula-hula* as being endowed with *sahala*, that special power which can be regarded as a rich, more than usually potent force of the *tondi* = soul. A beneficial and salutary influence for the *boru* can emanate from this *sahala*; at the same time, however, its power creates fear and respect for it. This means that the *boru* should avoid doing anything that would be harmful or offensive to its *hula-hula* and the *boru* never omits to show gratitude for favours received from its *hula-hula*. A person should not quarrel with the near related *hula-hula,* he should fear its *tondi* = soul force: *hula-hula so djadi badaan, habiaran ma tondina i.*

Should a *boru* have cause for complaint about its family-in-law it will not stand too much on its rights and, if, as can so easily happen, angry words are spoken accidentally on both sides, then the upshot will be an admission by the *boru* that it was in the wrong and it will endeavour to restore harmony by offering an atonement meal.

Certainly the *parhula-hulaon* is a source of no trifling gifts. If a *boru* does not fare as well in life as it would wish to, if no children are born, if a disaster like continual sickness strikes it, if there is a death in the family, if there is a fire, if, to put it in a nutshell, it is pursued by the evil powers of its fate, *sori ni arina,* then it turns to its *hula-hula* with its urgent entreaties, *elek-elek,* and its reverential obeisances, *somba-somba,* in order that some of the *hula-hula's sahala* may be reflected upon it and thereby reinforce its defence against the powers of evil that assail it. To express it in the Batak language: *asa manumpak tondi ni parhula-hulaon, manuai sahalana* = so that the *tondi* of the family-in-law will give help, *tumpak,* and its *sahala* pour forth its benevolent felicity, *tua.*

It is sometimes said that in the mortal world the *hula-hula* is the *wakil ni Debatá* = deputy of the High God, for the issue of its daughters, the *ianakhon.* It is the *pangidoan dohot pandjaloan pasu-pasu di boruna* = the group of people to whom the *boru* specially addresses itself for blessings, *pasu-pasu,* if it is in need and from whom it does indeed obtain them.

The following is an example of a request to a *hula-hula* which a woman's husband will respectfully address to his family-in-law if she is childless, the greatest misfortune that can befall her. Before trying any other expedients they will turn to her kinsmen, her brothers or parents, who are her husband's family-in-law:

Umbahen na ro hami tu djolomuna tung naung ngolngolan do rohanami na laos so mardakdanak * borumuna on; djadi ia tung adóng hasala-salaannami, ba na manopoti ma hami nuaeng tu hamú radjanami ba, manumpak ma sahalamuna dohot tondimuna, sai dilehon Debatá ma hagabeon di hami ianakhonmón, ninna:

"The reason that we have come to you is because we have waited for a long time and now we are distressed because your daughter has not had any children. Perhaps we have offended you and so we

---

* The original has *marnidakdanak,* but this cannot be correct. We have also slightly altered the translation of this sentence. (Transl.)

have come now to acknowledge our guilt, *manopoti,* to you Our Lord. Let your *sahala* and your *tondi* grant us their help and may God give us, your children-in-law, the children for whom we long".

Entreaties such as this, to reinforce the individual life-giving power by which children and other fortune can be obtained, are made in the first instance to the actual family of the barren wife, the *boru na hol.* If they are of no avail the wife, her parents and brothers, turn to the *hula-hula* of her mother. However, should the *datu* see from his oracular signs that it is necessary to resort to the *hula-hula* on her father's mother's side, or to affines still further removed, then this will be done. If the misfortune affects not only the wife but another member of the family, or the entire family then, for preference, all will offer their respectful obeisances, *somba-somba,* to the *hula-hula* of the husband's mother, or to that of his father's mother if there should be good reason for doing so, if, for example, the mother's kinship group is small or poor.

THE MANGUPA BORU

The *hula-hula* responds to these pleadings with the *mangupa boru* = the ceremonial transfer of its own greater spiritual power to the *boru.* Here the *hula-hula* can also take the initiative since it can perform the *mangupa* ceremony of its own accord if it observes that its *boru* is in distress or in any particular danger, e.g., if a married daughter is pregnant. The ritual by which this enrichment and strengthening of the *tondi* of another person takes place will be dealt with in the following chapter. For the present, some idea of its character can be gained from an address relating to a pregnancy which was delivered by a *hula-hula.* The *hula-hula* offered the pregnant woman an *ulos,* an upper garment (this is sometimes accompanied by a present) during the opening stage of the address.

"We now present this garment which is the enrichment, *upa-upa,* of the soul force of our daughter. It brings coolness, *upa dingin;* it strengthens the stability of the soul, *upa horas.* It is a garment in which sons and daughters may be carried by her. With the help of our *tondi* may the foetus come forth easily. May the fear that disturbs the soul disappear and the bad dreams also. May the birth of the child be as light as the sun, as serene as the moon and as limpid as a spring, for this our daughter, O My Soul. May the fate of our daughter be as clear as the sound of this dish on which we offer her a meal, so that sons and daughters may be born to her."

ADOPTION OF A HULA-HULA

It is so necessary to the life of a Batak that he receives benedictions from the side of his *hula-hula* that a female slave — in a region such as Samosir, for instance, where there was much kidnapping and slavery during the *Pidari* time — who was later unable to find her kinsmen, adopted a father on her marriage in order to acquire a *hula-hula*. It was necessary for her busband to have some measure of prosperity since he had to slaughter at least a pig on this occasion, and had to make a gift of money to his new father-in-law and to the chiefs. The adopted father was thereafter at the disposal of his daughter and son-in-law for all the 'services' that a family can expect of its *hula-hula*.

PARTICIPATION IN CEREMONIES

The most distantly related *hula-hula* do not usually come into contact with the less important family events of the members of the *boru* group. These larger groups attend the more important ceremonies that concern the *boru* group as a whole or its principal families, such as the reburial of the bones of a forefather or an ancestress, the giving in marriage of a son or daughter, the consecration of a new dwelling and formerly, the celebrating of a *hordja santi* because of continued childlessness in the lineage.

Great ceremonies such as these, to which the distantly related *hula-hula* are 'fetched' *marnialap*, (they are also termed *na nialap* = those who are fetched; *marnialap* is also the term used for the ceremony itself), thus bring together the *bona ni ari* as well as the younger *hula-hula* groups with their *boru* right down to the family-in-law of those living at the present day. (See Appendix I). In attending the ceremonies all of them contribute their dances, their gifts and their benedictions in order to achieve the aim for which the ceremony is held, i.e., to obtain blessing for the event for which they have been called together. When their turn comes to dance, the melody *somba-somba* = reverential obeisances, is played on the *gondang* and the dancers express their relationship to the giver of the feast by making a bene-dictory gesture with their fingers. In many regions the *djambar*, the part of the feast-animal, to which they are entitled, is also called the *somba-somba*. These *hula-hula* are accorded particular attention and respect throughout the whole ceremony.

When, however, the *boru* attends the feasts of its *hula-hula*, then it has to be deferential and evince a respectful interest in what is done

by the venerated group. The *boru* is well aware that in the circumstances so much good can emanate from the *sahala* of the giver of the
feast, that it is inclined to lighten its burden by making substantial
contributions towards the cost of the feast in the hope that something
may accrue to it. When the *boru* dances it is accompanied by the melody
called *parmeme* = the chewer, which refers to the time when the
mother was feeding her infant and chewed its food. Hence the saying:
tungkap marmeme anak, tungkap marmeme boru = the mother bends
forward to chew the rice for her infant sons as well as for her infant
daughters. This saying has no relevance to the adult sons since, upon
marriage, according to law and custom, they have the right to be set
up in their own households, *mandjae,* and to succeed automatically to
their father's property after his death, *mangihut-ihut.* For the daughters,
however, it always has significance, because everything they receive in
their maturity from their parents and brothers can only be given out of
affection and good will. Consequently in their dances the gesture made
with the fingers is one of questioning helplessness. Their *djambar* is
almost everywhere the neckpiece, *rungkung.*

GIFTS BETWEEN AFFINES

The gifts and counter-gifts that pass between affines on numerous
occasions have a particular character. Their general names are *ulos-ulos*
or *ulos* when the presents are given by the *hula-hula* to its *boru*; when
the gifts go from the *boru* to its *hula-hula* they are called *piso-piso* or
piso. But in addition to these general terms the gifts can have specific
names according to the particular occasion on which they are given.
Only the general character of both kinds of gifts will be outlined here;
they will be dealt with in greater detail in Chapter V.

ULOS GIFTS

The *ulos* gifts go from the *hula-hula* to the *boru.* An *ulos* is a kind
of garment. The cloth is woven by the Batak women in a variety of
patterns and is sold in the market place. The weaving of such a cloth,
the ingenious co-ordination of the great number of threads into a whole
cloth to protect the body is, according to pagan concepts, an act imbued
with a magico-religious quality and therefore one surrounded with
many prohibitions that must not be disregarded during the weaving.
The cloth can therefore be regarded as being permeated with sacred
powers. It must be of a specific length otherwise it will bring death and
destruction to the *tondi* of the wearer instead of luck and good fortune:
when it is of a particular pattern it can be used as an oracle, and so

on. The *ulos* has become one of the means by which the *hula-hula* transfers its *sahala* to its *boru* when the latter is in need of its protection.
This can be attributed to the fact that in covering the body of the
person concerned it exerts a protective influence not only on the body
but on the *tondi* as well. The word *ulos* has also become the term used
for gifts *in natura*, other than cloths, that can be given by the *hula-hula*.

If an unfolded cloth, *ulos herbang*, is given then it is wrapped round
the body of the recipient (see photo I B) to the accompaniment of some
appropriate words such as: *sai horás ma helanamí maruloshon ulos on,
tumpahon ni Ompunta martua Debatá dohot tumpahon ni sahala-
nami* = hail to you our son-in-law, may good fortune be yours in
wearing this cloth and may the benediction of the Beneficial Lord and
of our *sahala* be yours. If an *ulos* is given during a greater ceremony,
such as that mentioned in Appendix III, the presentation takes place
during the dancing.

An *ulos* pre-eminent is the *ulos ni tondi* = cloth of her soul, that
parents present to their daughter when she is expecting her first child
and they come to bless her, *mangupa*. The address with which this
presentation is coupled was given on p. 56.

The special character of this cloth relates to the magically dangerous
situation in which a pregnant woman is considered to be and from
which its peculiar properties aim to protect her. The woman regards it
in her future life as one of her sacred objects, the so-called *homitan ni
tondi* = that which is subjected to the *tondi*, and by preserving it and
using it she links herself to the benediction embodied within it. This
special cloth will serve to protect her when she is in labour, or if she
is sick at any time. Should her children be in a similar danger they
will likewise be protected by the beneficial qualities of this talisman.

The cloths given to a woman or a family stricken by various kinds
of calamities have a similar purpose. These cloths may have to be woven
by a remote *hula-hula* if the *datu* specially advises is. When such cloths
have brought about the desired benediction they become henceforth
specially sacred objects, *pusako*, for their owners and their descendants.

ULOS GIFTS OTHER THAN CLOTHS

Of the things that are given as *ulos* presents *in natura* to the *boru*,
land is the most important. As with the cloth, land cannot be given in
the reverse direction, that is, from the *boru* to the *hula-hula*. For the
boru that receives such a piece of land it is a garment that never wears
out, *ulos na so ra buruk*, since, in general, the purport of such a transfer

of land is that it is given permanently, *sipate-pate*, to the *boru*, unless it is expressly stipulated otherwise or if the special conditions are clear from the nature of the contract.

The reason that land assumes such an important place among the gifts must, in the first place, stem from the fact that a ruling *marga* living in its own ancestral territory is the only group that, collectively, has the ultimate right of disposal over land, although the members who have cleared and cultivated part of it have, by doing so, appropriated the land and bound it to them. This is a point that will be discussed in Chapter III.

The in-dwelling *marga*, which is usually the *marga boru* of the ruling *marga*, had, in the earlier generations of its sojourn at least, still nothing but a right of usufruct, a temporary right to use the land so long as it kept the land under cultivation. This then is the reason, generally speaking, why the *hula-hula* is the group that can use land as a present to its *boru* affines if it wishes to give them something that stands in a particular and personal relationship to it. The idea associated with this giving of land as a present is that the blessing that the land and its fruitfulness can bring to its cultivator will be transferred to the needy *boru* and thus improve its possibilities for a better life.

The same idea applies when cattle are given as *ulos*, the term then used being *andor ni ansimun* = tendrils of the cucumber, the hope being that, like the cucumber, they will increase in number and that the recipient will do likewise. Money, rice, houses, trees, etc., can also be used as *ulos* gifts, and formerly male and female slaves were so used as a sign of the prominence of the donor.

MOTIVES FOR GIVING GIFTS

Although the occasions on which gift-giving takes place and the circumstances that motivate it will be dealt with more fully in due course, some cursory attention will be given to this subject here with a few illustrative examples.

In Toba a young girl may wheedle a small piece of land out of her father in order to carefully store up its produce year after year until she marries; such a gift is called a *hauma bangunan* = field given out of affection. Such a course will be especially adopted by a girl who is ugly or deformed since otherwise no man might want to marry her. Usually, however, a girl will wait until she marries, then she will receive the marriage gift from her father, the *pauseang*, which can be regarded as the *ulos ni sinamot*, the counter-part of the marriage payment. This *pauseang* is given to her so that she will be more respected by her husband, *asa sangap ibana,* and for her offspring to enjoy its fruits. When her first son is born, then her father, mother and more distant kinsmen will visit her in order to enrich and strengthen the soul, *marupa-upa,* of the infant scion, and the child's grandfather will present him with a piece of land, the *indahan arian* = the daily meal of rice. When the mother takes her son a few months after his birth on a visit to her parents or, if they are dead, to her eldest brother, she will then receive an *ulos parompa* = a cloth in which to carry her son on her back.

Should a married daughter be very ill, her father comes to *mangupa* her. He wraps the *ulos ni tondi* that she received during her pregnancy round her and presents her with an *ulos na so ra buruk,* so that her *tondi* will again live strongly in her body by virtue of the beneficial effect of both the cloth and the piece of land. If the woman's husband dies and he has a younger brother who can marry the widow in levirate, then her father, who has a preference for such a marriage, will give the suitor an encouragement cloth, *ulos pangapo.* The same idea underlies a father's giving his daughter an *upa mangunung* (usually a wet rice-field) as an inducement to her to marry a man who is acceptable to him but for whom she has no particular fancy.

An *ulos* gift in a wider context is the land on which the *boru* group in a territory may found a village and the strip of land that is put at its disposal for cultivation, the *talian.* This can be regarded as an *ulos* gift from the *hula-hula* group in which was initially vested the right to the land in the territory. Another right that can be regarded as an *ulos* gift is the right to cut down trees in the territory of the ruling affines. The counter-present to this gift being money or something else. Hence the saying: *tua ni na mortua sitorop hula-hula* = fortunate is he who has an extended group of *hula-hula,* is not without point. There is another pertinent maxim: *durung do boru, tomburan hula-hula* = the *boru* is the landing net, the *hula-hula* is the well.

THE PISO GIFTS

The *piso* or *piso-piso* gifts are the opposite of the *ulos* gifts and go from the *boru* to the *hula-hula.*

The word *piso* means a knife or a sword. Such a knife can be given *in natura,* but so far as I know this is never done. It is always money, cattle, rice, and similar commodities that serve as *piso* gifts. A more specific and elaborate term for such gifts from the *boru* to the *hula-hula* is, *piso hadjodjahan* = a knife with which to support oneself. It was

not particularly expected of the *boru* in the *Pidari* time to render assistance by way of arms in times of war, but help in general was expected
from the *boru* who had become wealthy. In this connection the case can
be cited of the emigrant who departed for a distant region and often
took with him a well-to-do *boru*, or that of the founder of a village who
sought the co-operation of a wealthy affine who would become the
namora boru of the village. And members of the in-dwelling *marga* who
often cannot call the land they cultivate their own, having only the right
of temporary use, readily seek employment in trade, cattle rearing, and
business and frequently become more prosperous than the sometimes
prodigal and spendthrift notables of the group that has the absolute right
to the land. The character of the *piso* gift, therefore, is as much that of
a counter-present for *ulos* gifts, either received or promised, as that of
a contribution in a case where the *hula-hula* is economically in need of
support. So, for example, if the *hula-hula* has offered a piece of land
as a present at the *mangupa,* the son-in-law recipient will hand over a
counter-present in money with the following address:

"*nunga diupahon hamú, alé amáng, ulos tondi ni borumuna i, sai pir
ma tondinta, ndión ma pisonami djalo hamú ma, sai saur matua hamú
paihut-ihutonnami* = You have now enriched your daughter's soul,
tondi, with a cloth of her soul. Here now is our *piso* gift so that our
souls may always remain strong, *pir.* Take it, and may you keep us
among your followers until your old age". These counter-presents are,
consequently, as numerous as are the occasions on which the *hula-hula*
gives its benedictions, *pasu-pasu,* to its *boru.* The *boru* pays its debt
of gratitude for the many blessings that it receives from its affines by
always being ready with a contribution, *tumpak,* should its *hula-hula* be
beset with difficulties: on the marriage of a son, or to the many other
ceremonies that cost it money. By so doing the *boru* augments the
hasangapon = glory of its affines, and at the same time enhances its
own respectability. The counterpart of the sayings just quoted illustrating
the richness of the gifts that may come from the *hula-hula* runs as
follows:

> *tinapu* * *salaon, salaon ni situa-tua*
> *martua do halak molo gabe boruna*
> *ia dipangido hepeng ndang olo mandjua.*
> The indigo is gathered, the indigo of the elders.
> Fortunate is he whose *boru* is prosperous;
> If he asks for money the *boru* will never refuse it.

---

* The original has *tinapa,* probably a printing error. (Transl.)

An expression in which gross materialism and magico-religious beliefs are bed-fellows.

Here it can be noted that the terms *ulos* and *piso* are sometimes used to denote the money gifts that are exchanged between members of the same *marga,* as, for example, after intercession in a dispute. Another term used in the latter instance is *batu ni sulang-sulang* (if a meal is to be served) or *tali-tali.*

It will be clear from the foregoing that nothing definite can be said about the size of the .gifts that pass to and fro since everything depends on the circumstances and the existing relations.

One or two aspects of the affinal relationship will also be dealt with here.

TULANG-IBEBERE, BROTHER-SISTER

A father is always a bulwark for his daughter and on his death the mantle falls on his eldest son, her *iboto,* who is the *tulang* of her children. This is expressed in the maxim that is the counterpart of that relating to the chewing of food for infants:

dangka do dumpang, amak rere,
ama do tulang, anak ibebere;
A branch is a fork, a mat is a mat.
As a father is the *tulang*; as his sons are his nephews.

This maxim demonstrates the affection that exists between affines. It also marks the impartiality with which the interests of sons and daughters, brothers' sons and sisters' children have to be weighed up. It does not, however, mean that there is equality between the two categories, since only the agnatic line has distinct rights; the daughters and their offspring have none. It is particularly the *tulang* who is the mother's own brother who always extends his protective influence over her family when there is need for it. At such an important event as the first hair cutting of a small child, an opportunity for evil forces to become active, it is often the *tulang* who performs the operation. He is present at the name-giving and, formerly, at the tooth-filing, and his blessing is constantly with his *bere.* Consequently, when the relationship is a good one the sisters' children particularly are frequently pampered, especially if the *tulang* has a daughter who it is hoped will become the wife of his *ibebere.* This latter knows the circumstances and is thus in a position to take advantage of it. If, for example, he has a gambling debt and payment is pressed for, *pondjot dabu-dabuan,* he will sometimes take something from his *tulang* without permission and pledge it confident that his *tulang* will not make any objections. Should he quarrel with his father, then his *tulang* is his friendly counsellor. At the same time the *tulang* can mete out a more serious punishment where necessary than the actual father would usually give. I once saw a young girl, an orphan, given into the custody of her *tulang* — by a judgement of a court — because her first guardian, her father's younger brother, the *amang uda,* from whose supervision she was withdrawn, had made it apparent in a disgraceful manner that he had no interest in his 'small daughter' at all. His only interest was the marriage payment he would receive for her. It was for this reason that her *tulang* had made a stand on her behalf.

There is likewise a great measure of helpfulness and a willingness to oblige in a wider context. If a man has borrowed money from an affine, then in all probability the recovery of the loan will be slower than would be the case among strangers, and if the debtor is willing but unable to repay the money his affined creditor is quite ready to waive it in part.

THE AFFINITY RELATIONSHIP AND THE ADMINISTRATION OF JUSTICE

Disputes between the *hula-hula* and the *boru* are usually dealt with amicably when they are brought before the judge. There is often an opportunity, by referring to the particular affinal relations between the parties, to make an appeal for mutual leniency and when the judge knows to place the emphasis in the case before him and shows an appreciation of the legal position of both parties, he will often be successful in prevailing upon them to accept a solution that is mutually agreeable and that restores harmony again.

The judge's solution will then often be that the plaintiff, if he loses the case, must be given an *ulos* or *piso* gift by the defendant, to satisfy him as a kind of compensation for his defeat. Should the plaintiff's claim be allowed, then he will be ordered to make a similar present. Which of the two the judge decides upon depends entirely on the nature of the case, the character of the persons concerned, and their relations. An answer to difficulties that have arisen can also be found by suggesting a renewal, *pangarataion,* of the existing affinity link by a new betrothal or a new marriage by virtue of which all claims are foresworn by either side.

With regard to disputes between the agnates, the obvious peace-makers are the affines. They are as a rule the most suitable intermediaries between parties who stand in equal relationship to them. This is expressed in a well-known maxim:

sinabi laitu binahen tu harang ni hoda,
molo gulut boruna, amana do martola,
molo gulut amana, boruna do martola.

The grass is mown and goes into the horse's fodder bag.
If the daughters, the *boru,* quarrel their father settles the dispute.
If the fathers quarrel the *boru* settles the dispute.

The suitability of the affines to act as mediators is directly related to the features that typify the affinity relations. The fear and respect with which the *parboruan* regard their *hula-hula* prohibits their flouting its advice or opposing its wishes, and, conversely, they will not lightly give preference to the one above the other when they have to weigh up the interests of the quarrelling members of their *hula-hula.* The saying: *ndang heá naeng mago hula-hula di roha ni ianakhonna* = the *ianakhon* never desire to harm their *hula-hula,* has a moral as well as a practical purport. For their *hula-hula* they are the *parhata siat* = the ones whose word is accepted, and were the *hula-hula* to reject obstinately its *boru*'s just proposals, the latter's *tondi* might work in an adverse way. Confidence in its *boru*'s fairness and honesty is strengthened by the knowledge that it will naturally be impartial and disinterested when confronted with matters relating to its *hula-hula,* and that it is interested in restoring harmony.

For a *boru* group, a dispute in the bosom of its *hula-hula* over land will always be for it a quarrel over something that lies completely outside its control so long as it continues. And there will be no chance of its members receiving the 'keepsake' *daon sihol,* from a deceased father-in-law's property so long as the brothers-in-law are in mutual disagreement about their individual portions. And so, if one man quarrels with another and will not give way even though the proposals for a solution are reasonable, his *boru* will often accept them if it is possible to do so, or, if it is not possible, will give an assurance that satisfaction will be forthcoming from the obdurate one. The *boru* acts in this way secure in the knowledge that its affine is quite convinced that it only has his welfare at heart.

5

A KINSHIP- AND AFFINITY RELATIONSHIP SYSTEM

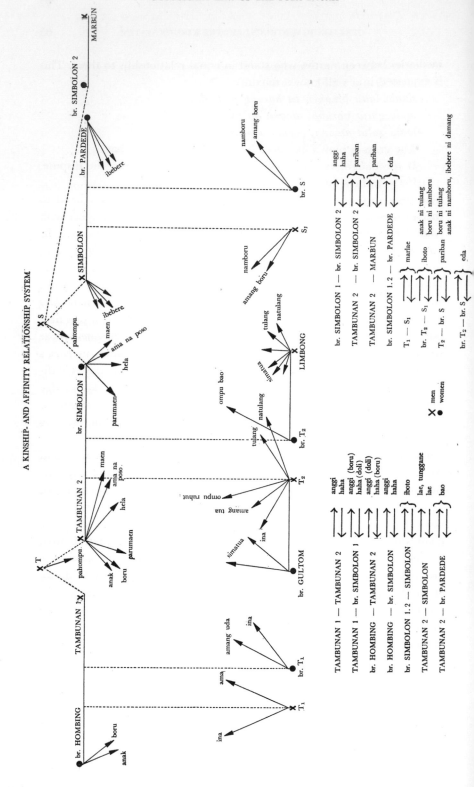

CHAPTER II

RELIGIOUS CONCEPTS

It will be apparent from the previous chapter that further consideration of the religious beliefs of the Batak will throw light on many points of the subject matter of this work. The whole of the personal and social life of the pagan Batak is permeated with their religious conceptions and there is scarcely a sphere of life in which their behaviour is not guided by religious motives and their thoughts dominated by concepts of the supernatural. These pagan ideas continue to live on for a long time after conversion to Christianity — as is the case the world over. A number of usages and customs, that are of a demonstrably pagan character, have been preserved either as a result of habitual use or as by-products of old fears. They may have been modified by Christian beliefs and by admission into the Christian sphere, or absorbed into the neutral zone of ancient usages, tradition, reverential practices, symbolism, obligatory ritual and the requirements of juridical forms, etc., where, for that matter, some of them existed earlier.

The paganism of the Batak is a mixture of theistical belief in gods, animistic veneration of the souls of the deceased, and dynamism. In many procedures and customs these three forms of religious thought are still inseparably interwoven, and, in applying them, neither the ordinary man nor the leaders of the established cult or of magico-religious practices distinguish these elements sharply from each other. On the contrary, they have only confused ideas about them. Thus the description and explanation of many a phenomenon can provide elucidation in two different ways according to whether the emphasis is laid in one direction or in the other. In the following observations I have limited myself as much as possible to drawing on those of my notes that relate to the legal relationships. I have also borrowed some data from Dr. J. Warneck's "Die Religion der Batak" (1909) and Dr. J. Winkler's "Die Toba-Batak auf Sumatra in gesunden und kranken Tagen" (1925), and from the work of Ypes.

THE GODS

In the whole of the pagan religious life of the Batak the least important role is that played by the five deities which the Batak acknowledge: *Batara Guru, Soripada, Mangalabulan* (the *Debatá na tolu*), *Muladjadinabolon* and *Debataasiasi*. The first three appear to have been borrowed from the Hindu Trimurti, while *Muladjadi*, "The Beginning of Existence", is probably an old Batak deity. The Batak do not make a clear distinction between the characters of these gods and their functions. They are rather overshadowed by the more general concept of God, *Debatá*, who, in their consciousness, is regarded as the embodiment of the Supreme Force. The veneration of these gods was principally concentrated in the great religious ceremonies, such as the public offering feasts for warding off catastrophes and plagues that took place in the *bius*, the communities that existed for that purpose; and in the ceremonies of the great tribal groups for the veneration or the spiritualistic conjuring up of the oldest ancestors. They were also venerated at the annual agricultural offerings, *asean taon* = the cleansing of the rice year, which took place at the expiry of the rice year, *partaonan*, when the benedictions of the higher powers were invoked for the coming year, so that the fields would be fruitful and the cattle multiply: *asa gabe na niula, asa sinur na pinahan*, which summarises all the material desires of the Batak.

The name of one or more of the five deities just named always occurred in the *tonggo-tonggo* = reverential (public) invocations, that were made on ceremonial occasions either by the *datu*, by the *parbaringin* = the offering priest of the *bius*, or by the principal chief of the *marga*. They were also invoked when a great oath was taken, when an oracle was consulted, when calamitous spells and similar things were concocted. The Batak do not, however, ascribe to these deities activities that react generally on all aspects of their lives.

In addition to these main deities there are the important personified natural forces: the *Boraspati ni tano*, and the *Boru saniang naga*. The first is a god having the form of a lizard. He lives under the earth and to him is due the fruitfulness of the land. For this reason he frequently occupied a principal place in the *tonggo-tonggo*. He was invoked on such occasions as the founding of a village, the building of a new house, when the offering-pole was driven into the earth, because all these acts brought people intensively into contact with the earth and it was therefore felt necessary that the greatest protection should be obtained by means of his benedictions. The *Boru saniang naga* is a female water deity in the form of a snake. She rules the forces of water and is a dangerous and threatening force for fishermen and others who have to come into contact with streams of water. She can give benediction after offerings have been made to her.

THE SPIRITS

The mind of the animistic Batak is more susceptible to the activities of spirits, *begu* — he calls himself a *sipelebegu* = venerator of spirits — than it is to all the deities just referred to. The term *begu* embraces the spirits of the deceased as much as nature spirits, and includes all those spirits exclusively devoted to inflicting harm on people, the *begu na djahat*, as well as those which, by worship and sacrifice, can be induced to give earthly blessings. It is these spirits that he encounters in his daily life, and on them a great part of his fate depends, for they can cause bad harvests, death of children, sickness in man and cattle, death in childbed and a multitude of other calamities.

The particular *begu* to be feared are those of people who have died suddenly, those who have had no children, those of women who died in childbed — these last named are extraordinarily malign — of lepers, suicides, etc. No offerings are made to them. The spirits called *homang*, which live in the forests and try to kidnap children are also malignant as are the water spirits, *solobean*, which make navigation dangerous, and the *begu antuk* which bring cholera, and so on.

Antidotes, *pagar*, such as carved images, *gana-ganaan*, and amulets, *porsimboraan*, of which the magical ingredients are prescribed by the *datu* and strengthened by his ritual, are made to ward them off.

If it is thought that a sick person's soul is held fast by a *begu* then, among other things, a small image, *porsili*, is made out of a banana stem or a sugar palm and the sickness is transferred into it. It is then offered to the spirit as a substitute. If the spirit of a deceased person is thought to be the cause of a sickness, then a close kinsman will make an offering of food so that the *begu* will release the sick person from its power.

The more benign *begu* associate with people in their dreams and give them good advice, but the danger in this association is that the person may be carried off by the *begu* and will sicken and die. Criminals seek to enter into an agreement with a feared *begu* so that no man will dare to oppose them. It is thought that the *begu* are united in a *begu-community* which is very similar to the human community. The *begu* do everything that humans do but in reverse: what human beings do by day the *begu* do by night; what *begu* do from top to bottom, humans do the other way round. The *begu* live in places as old trees and large stones, in solitary places, in impenetrable forests, on sharp mountain peaks, in deep chasms thus in places shunned by man.

They also live in small springs, *homban*, that are venerated by men. Such small revered springs are found everywhere in the country. They are usually under the care of a larger or smaller group of agnates who think an ancestral spirit lives there. Sometimes these springs are in the territory in which an agnate group dwells, sometimes in one it occupied formerly, but they can also be found in any other place. The *datu* determines by an oracle whether a new spring must be found or an old one must be better looked after. In the latter case the ceremonial *patiur homban* takes place during which the water goddess *Boru saniang naga*, who is also associated with springs, is invoked.

THE SUMANGOT

Among the *begu*, the spirits of deceased ancestors occupy a particular place especially the spirits of those who, in their lifetime, became rich, had power and material goods and whose descendants are many. These spirits, the *sumangot ni ompu* = the revered spirits of the ancestors, desire to be worshipped and honoured with offerings in order to continue to be active in promoting the welfare of the descendants of these ancestors. Then they will be able to make the harvests thrive, increase the wealth, multiply the cattle, grant many children and protect from disasters. But, if they are neglected they can cause the children to die, the harvest to fail, the cattle to fall sick and similar catastrophes. The *datu* determines from an oracle whether a particular disaster emanates from a wrathful ancestral spirit, a *sumangot na tarrimas*, and, receiving confirmation, he then decides on the nature of the sacrifice that must be made. Sometimes the spirit reveals its wishes and desires through a medium, the *sibaso*, who is 'possessed' by the spirit on a special occasion. In the larger and smaller lineages people regularly made sacrifices to the common ancestor when they partook of a meal and the *gondang* was played. The offering, *tibal-tibal*, was customarily placed on one of the large side rafters, *pangumbari*, of the house in which the ancestor formerly lived and where the head of the group probably still dwells.

If these ancestors were powerful and important people during their lives, then their *begu* are also powerful and important in the spirit world and respect for them increases as the ancestors' descendants and their influence grow and *vice versa*. For the childless, *na mate punu*, the position is totally different. They enter the spirit world as solitary ones. They can never be remembered with offerings so, as a small compensation, their next of kin give them a large funeral to cover the cost of which a great part of their assets are used. In Toba Holbung a fine small house, *djoro*, was built for such people as a last dwelling place.

The *ompu parsadaan* of a great lineage, however, is held in as great esteem in the spirit world as he is in the mortal world. Each time his bones are reburied in a new grave it is with greater splendour, and a handsome tomb — at the present time made of cement, *simen* — is erected on his final resting place. All the members of the lineage assemble at such a *hordja* or *turun* ceremony, the *tondong* are invited and the *bona ni ari* are *nialap* = fetched from afar. The ceremony can go on for days — in olden times it could continue for months — for it is an important event for a lineage with numerous members, and a large number of buffaloes and cattle are slaughtered. The exhumation of the bones of the deceased ancestor, *mangongkal holi-holi*, must be accompanied by the *gondang* and a salvo of guns. The *bona ni ari* provide the cloth in which the bones will be wrapped before they are carried away and the oldest *boru* supplies the food that will be offered to the bones; it also carries the bier to the new grave. Offerings are made; there is dancing and eating and a great number of spectators flock to the ceremony and enhance its glory. The *hula-hula* groups bring their *ulos* gifts; the *boru* groups make their *piso* contributions and finally, the chiefs, kinsmen and affines receive the portion, *djambar*, to which they are entitled of the animal that was specially slaughtered for the occasion.

THE SOMBAON

In the ceremony just described the great ancestor is accorded the respect that is his due. But, greater honour still was given to the *sumangot* if his line had grown to a great *marga* or tribal group. (Here one must speak in the past tense since Christianity has spread everywhere.) He was then elevated to the highest rank of spirits approaching the status of the gods; he became the *sombaon* = he who is revered. Formerly this elevation took place at a great sacrificial ceremony that was specially arranged for the purpose, the *santi rea*, at which all his descendants and their affines assembled. Henceforth the *sombaon* would dwell in a holy place, on the summit of a mountain, in a primeval forest, or in a great river. In the Nai Rasaon group, for instance, the dwelling place of the spirit of the tribal ancestor is the Simanukmanuk mountain range that separates Uluan from the East Coast. The *sombaon* was always invoked at all important religious ceremonies as the principal and most powerful of all the spirits of the patrilineal community. As a rule, his veneration took place at a place permanently assigned for the purpose: sometimes it was the market place of the whole community, sometimes it was elsewhere. The principal chiefs of the lineage met and made the necessary arrangements. On the evening before the feast day a slaughtering pole, *borotan,* was brought from the forest and was stripped and adorned with leaves. On the following day, after much preparation, the pole, by then strongly permeated with supernatural strength as a result of the ceremonial performance conducted under the direction of the *datu,* was driven into the ground by a member of the oldest *boru* of the genealogical group concerned. The *datu* brought his rice offering, *parbue santi-santi* and danced to the earth spirits, the gods and the ancestors. After that the decorated sacrificial-animal was brought up and amidst great rejoicing was tied to the pole. Then people began to dance, first the *datu* and then the wives of the leaders of the ceremony. This was the *tanda hasahatan,* the sign that all the groups who were eligible were participating in the ceremony and that they were one festival group under one head, *sisada gondang, sisada hasahatan.* Then it was the turn of the kinsmen to dance, then the affines, and following them the chiefs of the *parboruan,* the in-dwelling groups of the territory. The *datu* then danced again before the animal was stabbed. He carried the offering-cake, *sagu-sagu sitompion,* that was to be offered to the ancestral spirit, wrapped in a cloth on his back. Once again he performed a number of ritual acts. Then the slaughterer, *panamboli,* came forward, asked the feast leader's permission to slaughter the animal, and stabbed it. The animal was then flayed and cut up, an operation usually done by the *anggi ni partubu,* the younger branch of the genealogical group concerned. The vital parts of the animal, the heart and kidneys, were cooked and set aside as offering; the remainder was divided into the *djambar* and distributed among the rightful claimants. The *boru* group pulled the slaughtering pole out of the ground and received an *ulos* from the leader of the feast. Contributions, *guguan,* to the cost of the feast were made, *margugu,* by all the lineages concerned, each household supplying the same quantity of rice and other necessities. The collection of all these contributions was arranged by the *boru* group.

A particular motive for invoking a highly revered ancestor is the presence of many childless families among his descendants who want to beg the ancestor to grant them a 'quiver full of children'. A dwelling rack, *raga-raga* or *sibaso na bolon,* for the ancestral spirit is always kept in the *djoro,* the small house, also called *ruma parsantian, pasogit* or *parsibasoan*, in the village which was the cradle of the entire *marga* branch, *marga* or tribal group. The rack is square, decorated with leaves and cloths and has a rattan rope attached to its centre. It is hung high up in a large house, from which act the ceremony is called *mamampe raga-raga* from *dipampe* = to be hung up. The barren women *boru na hol* then dance round it carrying offering cakes wrapped in a cloth on their backs and allow themselves to be sprinkled with lemon juice. Sometimes a cow or a buffalo is offered. Then follows the ceremony of shaking the spirit's rack, *manghuntal raga-raga*, when all the childless women and men try to grasp the hanging rattan rope in the hope that by touching it they will receive some of the benediction-bringing fortune, *tua*, that descends from the ancestral spirit.

THE BIUS SACRIFICIAL-COMMUNITY

The sacrificial feast that was arranged by the *bius*, or *bus* ('was' because the Dutch Government forbade these ceremonies many years ago) showed great conformity in its aims and forms with the big *sombaon* offering-ceremonies. The *bius* was distinguished from the latter in that it did not embrace a genealogically pure group of agnates (to whose feasts the affines and the chiefs of the neighbourhood were invited as guests), but a larger or smaller geographical area and all its inhabitants. Nevertheless, the genealogical divisions of the groups living within that area were not lost sight of. These factors played a role in the *bius* as a matter of course. To give one or two examples: the small Nai Baho *marga* of the Radja Oloan tribal group (see p. 13) near Pangururan, was one of the three components of the *bius* Pangururan (also called Si Tolu Hae) that appeared at ceremonies as a separate unit and received its own quarter of the buffalo: the other two parts were divisions of the 'head' *marga* Simbolon and Sitanggang. Hard by this Nai Baho territory lies the Rianiate (= collection of hearts) territory which comprises eight *marga* branches, namely four divisions of the 'head' *marga* Simbolon as well as four divisions of Sitanggang, Sigalingging, Nai Baho, and Malau. The territory is therefore called Si Ualu Tali = the eight strips. Each of these parts participated in the *bius* feast as a separate group. It was the same in Uluan where there are many detached parts of the Silahisabungan group among the dispersed divisions of the Nai Rasaon group. Thus a number of *bius* were composed of these elements.

The *bius* and its cult had the least significance in areas where the *marga*, in occupying their ancestral territory, continued to live together as a whole with their separate branches and lineages, each *marga* having its own corner of the territory. These *marga*, apart from dispersals, there formed genealogically as well as geographically wellrounded kinship groups. Each could conduct its own *hordja*, feasts, as occasion demanded for its own territory and if they united, they still always formed a higher group of patrilineally linked kinsmen in one area. Only if, for example, an epidemic ravaged the entire ancestral area or if drought threatened the fields of the inhabitants, would there be recourse to a general assembly of the inhabitants of the very large territory which embraced the tribal group as well as its in-dwelling groups and enclaves. The *bius* connection there did not have more far-reaching consequences than those resulting from the periodical sacrificial-feasts. Politically people were adequately organised through the convergence of the genealogical and geographical main dividing lines within the great area of the *bius*. If, for example, the divisions of the Naipospos group (see p. 16) round about Sipoholon (see IXc on the chart) assembled as a *bius*, the oldest *marga*, Sinagabariang and Huta Uruk, in the north and south corners respectively of the ancestral areas, and the youngest, Simanungkalit and Situmeang in the central area, would meet. When they did so they represented the higher all-embracing genealogical group. Only in the Simamora area (see chart VI) did I find the *bius* connection completely unknown.

In other regions, however, such as Samosir and Uluan, where the *marga* did not so often occupy their own homogeneous area but where, on the contrary, their divisions were usually dispersed over the whole of the tribal area in large or small groups, the formation of religious groups had acquired a secular significance too. There was not, as elsewhere, the opportunity to assemble for religious purposes in the ascending chain of the agnatically closed circles. The fragments of a *marga* were sometimes small, dispersed and without direct contact with each other and often they were from parts which were not directly connected genealogically. However, here too, co-operation was felt to be necessary if the harvest failed, *molo mago partaonan*, or if too many *begu* played havoc with their sicknesses, *molo mararathú begu*. When it thus became necessary to invoke the favour and benediction of the ancestral spirits and the gods, people sought affiliation with the groups of other *marga* living in the neighbourhood which belong to the same tribal group or which consisted of friends or affines.

Thus *bius* were formed which had a mixed religious and secular character. Each *bius* usually comprised a not too large geographical area and formed a political community of a couple of thousand people in which a common feeling of solidarity outside the sphere of the sacrificial-feasts proper had also developed. The objects of veneration in these *bius* were generally the ancestor common to all, the *sombaon*, as well as the gods and the nature spirits, and all the forefathers who had lived previously, the *ompu sidjolo-djolo tubu*. And there was a tendency to gather up these 'small' *bius* into a very large one which embraced the whole tribal group, or a very large part of it, with the sole object of celebrating the very large and communal sacrificial-ceremonies; for example, the *bius* 'Hariara maranak' for the whole of South Samosir, or the *bius* 'Onan na godang' for the whole of South Uluan and 'Pansur na pitu' for North Uluan.

It is worthy of note that in areas where the *bius* acquired this political character paganism has held out the longest. This is not attributable to the fact that worldly and spiritual power were under one control because this has not been the case, except in one or two areas, and then only temporarily. In part it can be ascribed to the influence of Singamangaradja whose most active representatives were always the *parbaringin*, the priests of the *bius* feasts. This applied only in the Sumba territory around the south-westerly parts of Lake Toba and not to the Lontung territory of Samosir and its environs where Singamangaradja met nothing but opposition. However, in these Lontung territories, the extensive organisation of officials which the *bius* brought into existence, and who conducted the more or less important rituals in the offering-ceremonies, was also a powerful stronghold of paganism.

THE PARBARINGIN-ORGANISATION

The *parbaringin*-organisation has become the carrier of pagan concepts. In the region where it is operative it almost entirely controls the regular worship and the agricultural ceremonies connected with it, and it has a powerful hold on the thoughts of the ordinary man such as is not to be found elsewhere. Such an organisation does not exist in the south of the Toba Country where the periodical *bius* feasts were directed by the principal chiefs of the tribal group. The *datu* co-operated where necessary and the *paung na opat*, as the representatives of Singamangaradja were sometimes called there, took part, but they remained in the background. Moreover, the annual agricultural offering, the *mamele taon* or *mangase taon*, was there the concern of the villages and the smaller circle of agnates. But in areas where the *bius* was a powerful institution the *parbaringin* were important people. It was the secular chiefs who decided to hold a *bius* ceremony, but in most of the *bius* it was the *parbaringin*-organisation, which could be very extensive, that almost completely controlled the procedure of the ceremony. An example of this organisation is the small Djandjiradja territory south-ward of Sabulán and consisting of only 1,500 people. Eight Lontung *marga* live there together. Each *marga* has a *radja na ualu* as its leader; each leader has four assistants, the *radja na tolupuludua,* and there are also a still larger number of *radja parhara* who attend to the summons to participate. The Sihotang territory which lies a little more to the north and consists of less than 3,000 people, is inhabited by the five oldest *marga* of the Sigodang Ulu (see p. 13). The oldest and fore-most of these five *marga* has a *pande bolon* as chief *parbaringin*; the two following it in importance have as their leaders a *suhut ni huta* and a *pollung na bolon.* Under these three officials are the five *radja lima,* one for each *marga,* who act as their assistants. Below the *radja lima* are the *sidjalo paningkiran,* two or three to each *marga,* whose function is to examine the offering-buffalo. Under these functionaries are the *pangulu radja,* eight or ten per marga, who attend to even more insig-nificant tasks, and finally there are the *parhara* = the callers: all together, about a hundred men. Some of these functions are hereditary either in the direct agnatic line or changing alternately from one lineage to another. Official perquisites in fields, *upa radja,* (*upa pande, upa parhara, indahan ni baringin,* etc.), are attached to some of these duties. The clothing of these officials has its own characteristics: as a rule their head cloth is the *tali-tali birong* which is made of blue yarn. It is clear that the desire for distinction which is natural to primitive people is here given full rein. It is also understandable that this small army of officials is a powerful force in the service of traditional religion.

It is not necessary here to go into all the particular details concerning usages common to the sacrificial-ceremonies of the *bius.* Many of them are mentioned in Ypes' work, and many points of difference, large and small, will be found from region to region.

SOME FURTHER DETAILS CONCERNING THE BIUS

I have already observed that the main motives for holding the sacrificial-ceremonies were great drought and the fear of a bad harvest to follow, epidemics, particularly smallpox, and cholera, and the annual agricultural-offering, the *mangase.* The decision to hold such a ceremony was either taken by the chiefs or by the *datu,* after a pronouncement by the oracle. It was also sometimes taken on the instruction, *tona,* of Singamangaradja. In addition to venerating the gods and the *Sombaon* offerings were made to the water spirits of the *homban* and to the 'Soul of the Rice'. The *parbaringin* do not usually indulge in divination or practice medicine, but by virtue of the nature of many of their ritual acts during the ceremonial of the sacrificial-feast, they are regarded as people who have great magico-religious power. The *parbaringin* will not allow their hair to be cut; they do not as a rule smoke and are some-times subjected to other restrictions. During the time they are exercising their functions they wear a branch of the waringin tree on their heads and for this reason they can also be called *parsanggul baringin* or *na mandjudjung baringin*. They occupy a somewhat indefinable position in their small world. In the neighbourhood of Pangururan their offi-ciating at the agricultural ritual — it is they who give the signal to commence work in the rice-fields — entitles them to have a say in the control of the land within the *talian*, the well-defined agricultural area of their own *marga*. In the Sumba areas many of them were appointed by Singamangaradja. Christians are often disposed to revert to pa-ganism for the sake of obtaining the office of *parbaringin* and the honour and respect, *hasangapon*, associated with it. The head of the officials enforces discipline in the corps, but for want of secular power they must be supported therein by the secular chiefs. As a rule the head of the corps is from the *sihahaan* branch of the ruling group and the succession always goes from father to son: thus a child can be head of the corps. The office of *parbaringin*, as well as the lesser offices, can, however, also alternate between two or more lineages, either according to a fixed plan or by selection by the chiefs or the people. In Uluan the office of *parbaringin* can coincide with the secular chieftaincy, just as elsewhere an influential chief can sometimes be an able *datu* at the same time.

The contributions, *guguan*, to the cost, *harugian*, of the ceremonies were not as a rule made per family but per participating *marga*, each *marga* in its turn asking for a contribution from the lineages. This, as we have already seen, could give rise to a change of *marga* in exceptional cases. The size of the contributions was determined in one place by the oldest in-dwelling *marga*, in another by the *parbaringin*. Usually the contributions that everyone made consisted of rice, but sometimes special obligations were laid upon some participants as, for example, in the *bius* Rianiate, where one branch of the *marga* Manalu attended to the *ogung* = gongs, while the other provided the rice flour for the small offering-cakes.

The animal that had to be slaughtered was usually a buffalo and for this reason the ceremony was also termed *mangan horbo bius* = partaking of the *bius* buffalo. Due observance was always made to the genealogical relationships when the animal was divided up, but the cutting up specifications varied. The most usual division was lengthwise, in half, *bariba*, for two combinations of participating groups, each of which was given a half. This was followed by dividing the halves into quarters, *hae-hae*, or into as many parts as was necessary. If there were three participants as, for example, in the *bius* Si 3 hae, then a *hae* was sometimes allocated to the musicians. The *boru na godjong* of the territory often received a portion, usually the neckpiece, *rungkung*, for which reason it could be called the *sidjalo rungkung* = the recipient of the neckpiece: in this way it was distinguished from the other indwelling *marga* in the territory. Where there were no *parbaringin*, the *boru na godjong* usually attended to the offering-pole, the collection of the contributions, and the division of the meat among the rightful claimants. If there was no *boru* common to the *bius*, then the *marga* which were the *boru* of the constituent parts usually received their separate portions from their own *hula-hula*. In some cases *marga* which belonged to those ruling in the *bius*, could not take their portions directly from the hand of the person who divided the animal. They had to take them from another ruling *marga* acting as an intermediary, as a token that they came into the area later and were received by the *marga* already there. This could be of consequence in the matter of the right to the principal chieftaincy. The way in which the meat was divided is usually of great importance for a knowledge of the internal relationships within the *bius*.

Sometimes one or more of the component parts of the *bius* formed small *bius* of their own which then offered a cow or a pig, not a buffalo. If they were entitled to their own system of officials, then they were said to be *mandjae* = set up on their own. The composition of such a small *bius* and what its relation was to the *bius* of the territory, depended entirely on the local relationships. The same applied to the latter with regard to the very large *bius* above it.

PARTICIPATION IN SACRIFICIAL CEREMONIES

In the complete genealogical sacrificial-communities as well as in the mixed genealogical-territorial ones, there was a natural solidarity. Once it had been decided that a ceremony would take place it was fitting that everybody who belonged to the community should participate.

Any disinclination to do so would not be tolerated, an attitude expressed in the following saying:

hata mamundjung hata lalaen;
hata na torop sabungan ni hata:
The word of one man is the word of a fool.
The words of many are the deciding words.

The obstinate one was expelled, *dipabali, dipaduru,* put outside, and had to brave the wrath of the spirits. Deep seated disputes with other members did not absolve one from participating, any more than the planners of the ceremony could pass over a member who had a private quarrel with one of them. They would be punished as being "those who tore apart the kinship ties and separated the crowns of hair belonging together: *sisirang partubu, sipadao pusoran*", and would be obliged to set a meal before the person whom they had thus offended. The conflicts which arose for the first Christians when they abstained from participation, necessitated the pioneer of the Batak Mission, Nommensen, gathering them together in a separate village. But, because Christianity was spreading so rapidly, this only happened once. Later on the Government and the Mission forbade all playing on the *gondang* and also the *bius* feasts.

During a *gondang* or *bius* ceremony no debts could be collected, and in the *Pidari* times no one could be fettered or put in the block, and no disturbance or quarrels were permitted. A festival peace prevailed for all the participants and spectators. Only murderers, abductors and other dangerous criminals were not protected by this peace and they were not allowed to participate in the feast. They were *di balian ni patik, di balian ni hordja* = outside the protection which the law gave to people at the ceremony.

So much for the public veneration of the gods and spirits. The Batak ideas about the nature and personality of man are related to it.

THE HUMAN BEING'S TONDI

A human being is considered to be in possession of a *tondi,* an invisible essence which is usually translated by the word 'soul'. This *tondi* is with people during their lifetime but if they are sick it leaves them for the duration of the sickness. It departs from their bodies for good when they die and then becomes the *tondi ni na mate* = the spirit of the deceased.

The Batak conception of the *tondi* has engaged the attention of many writers and it has frequently served as evidence for certain views on the primitive forms of religion. The question then, is this: does the Batak think of his *tondi* in an animistic sense, as being an independent, individual personality which exists in, and on behalf of, one particular person, or does he interpret it in a more dynamistic sense as an impersonal force or substance which is found not only in human beings but, to a certain degree, in animals, plants and even objects and which is susceptible to augmentation, diminution and transference? This is the more general concept, for which the Melanesian word '*mana*' is often used.

In my opinion, neither of these points of view can be chosen with certainty. One's approach should be cautious, but not only because the concepts are obscure to the Batak. I think the truth must lie somewhere between these views. The Batak finds in his spirit-peopled world the best starting point for the consideration of his 'spiritual life' as a personified soul with its own independent life. But, on the other hand, he also regards his *tondi* as being possessed of a power which in certain circumstances and in a particular relationship can exercise an influence on the *tondi* and the life of another person. The discussion that follows will throw some light on both these sides of the matter.

THE TONDI PERSONIFIED

There are numerous phenomena from which it can be deduced that the *tondi* is regarded as being an independent entity.

The material I give here can be considered as an addition to that found in the works of Warneck and Winkler in which special attention is given to this aspect.

The *tondi* is thought to be able to move outside the body during sleep. It can then have experiences, can meet, among other things, *begu*, and it is in a position to receive communications. When any of these things happen to the *tondi*, the sleeper can recall everything when he awakes and understands the significance of what has befallen his *tondi*. He can also invite the *tondi* to make known its wishes in a dream. If a man wants to know whether or not he should undertake an important commitment, for example, which piece of forest land he should select for clearing, or whether he should ask for a girl he desires in marriage, he goes to sleep with the specific intention of invoking a vision in his sleep, *marmangmang nipina*. He separates his sleeping mat from those of the other members of the household, wraps himself in a special over-garment, places rice and magical plants or objects under his pillow to the accompaniment of appropriate invocations and directs a prayer, *tonggo-tonggo*, to the gods and spirits, particularly to those of his deceased ancestors, that he may have a dream which his mind, *roha*, will understand and which will be accepted by his *tondi, sipeopon ni roha, sidjanghonon ni tondi*. He also requests that no one will disturb him suddenly in his sleep since it would make him ill. If such a thing happens when the *tondi* is outside the body and cannot return to it in time, then a *begu* can gain control of it and hold it fast.

It is always dangerous if the *tondi* leaves the body of a person who is awake. A sudden fright or contact with a strong supernatural power can cause it to do so, or the *tondi* can be capricious and leave of its own accord. It is therefore very important that the *tondi* is always firmly attached to the body so that it can resist shock and temptation. Thus a common part of an address is: *sai pir ma tondim* = may your *tondi* be always firmly attached to you. This much-desired situation is also expressed in the word *horas* (Mal. *keras*, firm, fixed). In many addresses such elegant compositions occur as: *pir ma tondi madingin, horas tondi matogu* = may the *tondi* be firm and cool, may the *tondi* be firm and strong. A customary farewell is *horas be ma* = may both of us be strong, and *horas* = hail, will be the cry of a joyful multitude. Coolness, *dingin*, promotes this stability of the *tondi*; heat (anger, excitement) is prejudical.

Since fright also creates the dangerous situation that the *tondi* may take leave of the body, people often express the wish, *dao songgot* = may fright stay away from you. If someone suffers such a fright, then it is expedient to mollify the *tondi* and bring it to a state of tranquility so that it does not withdraw from the body or, if it is already outside the body, returns to it. This is effected by the *mangari-ari tondi* = recalling the *tondi* to reassure it. For this the *gondang* is played, the frightened person is fed and is addressed, and usually he is given a present. One or two examples of such a *mangari-ari* are given in the *Ruhut Parsaoran di Habatahon*.[11] One of them presumes the intervention of a judge ordering that a ceremony should be arranged on behalf of the *tondi* of a person who had been frightened as a result of a quarrel, or who had fallen into a ravine, both of which produce the same effect. If some-one becomes seriously ill after being frightened, then a *datu* can order the more elaborate procedure of the *mangalap tondi* = bringing back the *tondi*; this is also called *manghirap tondi*. A procession goes to the

---

[11] "Customs of Batak Society", 1898, translated into Dutch in *Adatrechtbundel* Vol. XXXV, p. 110 et seq. (For the *mangari-ari tondi* see pp. 118, 134.)

place where the sick person was overcome with fright, since it is thought that the *tondi* might still be there or lingering in the neighbourhood. The gods and spirits are invoked and offerings are made in an endeavour to persuade the sick person's *tondi* to return to him.

The ceremony of the *padiruma tondi* = binding the *tondi* to its dwelling, which takes place when someone has been able to withstand a great danger to which his soul has been exposed but nevertheless, feels that he will benefit from a 'reviver', has a similar purport. It is done, for instance, when a husband returns safely after a long journey when his wife will scatter a few grains of rice over his head.

All these procedures — more of which could be mentioned — form at the same time the more or less fixed rites of the *mangupa tondi* = the enrichment, strengthening and binding of the *tondi* by magicoreligious means. This relates to the other aspect of the *tondi* as a seat of supernatural power. All human beings are thought to possess it. It finds particular expression in certain people, or in particular relationships and then it can have an influence on other people.

THE TONDI AS THE SOURCE OF SUPERNATURAL POWER

The transference of *tondi*-power has already been touched upon with regard to the relations between the affines. In that instance it was in connection with the great potency which the *tondi* of the *hula-hula* exhibits and makes manifest when the *hula-hula* enters into a ceremonial relation with its *boru*. This great supernatural power is not, however, confined to this relationship. Other people have *sahala* also.

Particular attention has been devoted to this *sahala* by Dr. H. Th. Fischer in his article "Het begrip *mana* bij de Toba Batak" [12] in which he points to a correspondence with the Melanesian *mana*-concept. Dr. Fischer regards the *tondi* and the *sahala* as being distinct from each other, although in his opinion the *sahala* often closely approaches the concept of the 'soul'. He thinks the best definition of the *sahala* is that given by Warneck: "Sahala ist eine besondere Eigenschaft des Tondi". I think myself it would be more accurate to make the connection between *sahala* and *tondi* still closer by calling the *sahala* the particular and often clearly perceptible potency of the *tondi*. Probably the address of the son-in-law to his father-in-law given earlier creates the impression that *sahala* and *tond*i are to be regarded as distinct qualities since help

---

[12] "The Conception of Mana among the Toba-Batak", *Koloniaal Tijdschrift* (Colonial Journal), 1931, p. 604.

was expected from each, but this can hardly be more than a figure of speech and it could have been omitted. The *sahala* of a person is his *tondi*-power in its most active and most perceptible form. If one accepts this idea then Winkler's belief — frequently denounced, and by Fischer too — that the *tondi* is a kind of material substance that is divisible and capable of transference without diminishing in quantity in the person from whom it comes, can be definitely set aside.

Though the *tondi*-potential is present in everybody, its supernatural force is neither apparent to everybody nor conspicuously active until a man displays particular qualities. Then its existence comes to light. A man who becomes wealthy, one who has a host of sons and daughters and grandsons, a man who carries on authoritatively the chieftaincy obtained by his forefathers, a courageous man, an eloquent man, all bear witness that their *tondi* has abundant power of which these desired qualities are a manifestation and, as a result, they have their share of courage, wealth, temporal power, etc., the *sahala habeguon, hamoraon, haradjaon,* etc. Of particular note are the 'potent ones', people like the *datu* or the *parbaringin*: they have been specially initiated into the secrets of magico-religious practices, they know how to arouse this power and how to make it efficacious. For this reason their supernatural power is very potent. This attribute was most marked in the supreme magician, Singamangaradja, who had complete control over these forces and knew how to direct them. The influential chiefs also display it to a remarkable degree. All who exhibit a particular 'power' are always honoured and respected by people as those deserving of respect, *na sangap*. Honour and respect, *hasangapon,* are the desirable results of possessing *sahala*.

Before the Batak came into contact with the West they thus acknowledged in their own way that the acquisition of wealth brought respect and honour from which 'power' could accrue. The Batak *sahala* and our 'success' thus overlap to a great extent.

But there is a difference, because, besides the *tondi*-power which is discernible by all and respected by everybody, there is a special distinction between the soul-condition of men who stand in a particular relationship to each other. A father has *sahala* over and above his children; a grandfather over his grandchildren; a teacher over his pupils; the *hula-hula* over its *boru*. There is something striking about this. The distinction in soul-condition only operates as far as the circle of agnates is concerned, between members of the direct descending line with, at most, a deviation to father's or grandfather's brother. No difference is thought to exist in the soul-condition between other agnates. In the affinity relationship, however, this difference, which starts primarily with the relations between father-in-law and son-in-law, is afterwards also manifest in the descendants on both sides for many generations.

All these people's *sahala* can actively influence others, and in many different ways: if they touch people, spit on them, cast their shadow on them, a favourable effect can be produced on the fortune of persons whose *tondi*-power is weak. By these means those rich in *sahala* can bestow their *tua* = benediction. A comparable power is attributed to words that express a blessing and also to presents such as woven cloths given to the *boru*. And the remains of a meal of a respected chief can cure a sick person who eats them. So, when Singamangaradja passed by, mothers turned their infants' faces towards him. Conversely, a man who hurts, offends or angers a person or persons who are rich in *sahala* will earn the displeasure of their *sahala* and in serious cases such a person will be struck by a curse, *sapata*.

A person whose *tondi* has been subjected to an appreciable degree to malevolent magical influences is not only unfavourably affected himself, but his condition will react on those around him. A poor man, *na pogos*, and a wretched man, *na dangol*, will be spurned; a man who is continually sick will be avoided; a widow will not be permitted to enter a newly consecrated house. In Toba a great ceremony is held when a childless person dies so that the curse that rests on him may be exorcised from the land (see photo III).

THE MANGUPA TONDI

One of the most common ways by which the stronger power of the *na morsahala* can be transferred to another person whose *tondi* needs enriching is the *mangupa*, a particular form of which has already been mentioned in connection with the affinity relations. The word is often translated as 'to reward' which refers to the present-day meaning of the word *upa*, namely, reward. The *mangupa* is thus regarded as the granting of a mark of gratitude to the *tondi* which has escaped a hazard, or as an encouragement to it to resist any approaching dangers or to behave differently. In my opinion, however, the purpose of the *mangupa* is essentially the enrichment of the *tondi*, the augmenting of the power that resides within it, and the strengthening of the link between it and its dwelling place. If, for example, the *mangupa* takes place for a woman who has been barren for a long time and a piece of land is given to her as an *ulos na so ra buruk,* the object is to increase the resistance of her *tondi* to the animistic and malevolent powers which obviously lay in wait for her. Similarly, the *pangupaon,* which is held after a danger has been averted, cannot be seen simply as an expression of gratitude towards the *tondi* for its good offices (though the idea of a thanksgiving will probably come to prevail among Christian Batak). Above all it is a means of disposing of the threat to which a person in a dangerous situation has been subjected; a means of restoring the temporarily disturbed balance of the agitated *tondi*; and of creating a state of tranquility for the *tondi* and its powers by a beneficial influence.

The strengthening of the *tondi* is, therefore, not exclusively effected by transference from a person rich in *sahala.* The means applied by such a person are magical and also have to themselves the quality of automatically exercising their influence as soon as they are brought into action. And though the possession of greater *tondi*-power provides a greater measure of capability of invoking this activity, nevertheless, the means used have of themselves an efficacy. A woman can '*mangupa*' her husband by performing the appropriate ritual, and a man can '*mangupa*' another man who is his equal, and he can even '*mangupa*' himself.

There are numerous circumstances in which the *mangupa tondi* is regarded as needful. If, for example, the *tondi* has been subjected to a great fright it must be strengthened. It may have been frightened as a result of its owner being bitten by a dog or by a quarrel that led to a fight in which someone was wounded, and so forth. The owner of the dog or the injured person's assailant must then '*mangupa*' the frightened *tondi* — if need be after a judicial decision. In such cases, the *mangupa* has the same effect as the *mangari-ari tondi.*

When a person has had bad dreams he will ask to be *niupa* by the head of the family to which he belongs. This must also be done when someone has accidentally witnessed anything that is regarded as being supernaturally dangerous to his well-being, such as the mating of certain animals like snakes and lizards.

Participation in rites of which the aim is to invoke strong supernatural activity, also requires the *pangupaion,* the ritual of the *mangupa.* For instance, if an image, *porsili,* is made and offered with all kinds of ritual acts to an angry *begu* as a substitute for a sick person so that it will release the sick one from its power, the *mangupa* must be performed for him afterwards: this can be done within his own family. The same applies after such ceremonies as the *mangase taon,* the *mamampe raga-*

raga and the *mangalap tondi* and the *papurpur sapata* (see photo III) etc.

If danger threatens, then the *mangupa* has the character of enriching and strengthening the *tondi* so that it can the better resist it. The meal called the *pangulahon* must be given to a traveller just before he departs to ensure his safe return, and if the journey will be long and full of danger, then kinsmen and affines bring provisions and give their blessings. The particular danger to which a pregnant woman is exposed and which necessitates the use of all kinds of *pagar* = antidotes, makes her parents resort to the *mangupa boru*, either at her request or on their own initiative, so that the beneficial influence of their *sahala* will pass over to their daughter. On this occasion she is presented with the *ulos ni tondi*, cloth of her soul, which will protect her in childbed and will also shield her and her infant from sickness.

A sick person is surrounded by danger. Such a one must receive the *upa saem* = the enricher of a soul in need, to which contributions are made not only by his parents and grandparents, but by his father's *hula-hula* and his grandfather's *hula-hula*, and, if the sickness is a serious one, by such persons who are rich in *sahala* as chiefs and other influential people.

If a person is afflicted with persistent misfortune, if a man becomes poor and is beset with debts, if all his children die in succession, *martilaha*, if a member of his family is perpetually ill, then he will turn to his *hula-hula*, sometimes on the advice of a *datu*, and ask for its benediction. His request will sometimes be made to very far removed affines, because the cause of the sickness or misfortune may lie in earlier generations. These affines then present as their *pangupaon* a piece of valuable cloth or a plot of land, the *tano na niupahon,* which is given permanently and will always carry the desired benediction.

After danger has been averted the meal called *upa sita-sita* = the enricher of the soul's happiness, must be given. Its aim being the promotion of a tranquil and balanced state in the *tondi* of the man to whom it is offered. It is given after a person returns from a long journey, and when an emigrant returns to the village of his birth. It is the rule after recovery from a serious illness and it is never neglected after the felicitous birth of a son.

In this last case it has the more definite name of *marupa-upa,* and is as much a thanks-offering as an enrichment of the mother's *tondi* and the child's, both of which are thereby strengthened and protected from the dangers of life. Particular interest is aroused at the birth of the first child if it is a son since this promises the continuance of the lineage. The family from all sides will then show their interest: kinsmen as well as the *hula-hula* and the *boru* come with their *ampang* = rice baskets, in which their benedictory gifts of rice and money for the new-born child are carried. The father of the young mother sets aside a wet rice-field as the *indahan arian* = daily meal of rice, for his grandson, while others give him cattle as the *andor ni ansimun* = tendrils of the cucumber, etc. When they have all assembled, the meal is piled up in a high dome shape on a fine dish and is set before the happy mother. One of those present, the husband, the *tulang*, or someone else who is respected in the family, takes hold of the dish, makes smacking noises with his mouth and the dedication, *manghatahon*, of the benediction-bringing pile of food begins. The address appropriate to such an occasion is included here not only to enliven the description, but also because it demonstrates so well the mixed magico-animistic character of the ceremony. "Thou, food, which will now enrich the *tondi*. Thy aim is to promote coolness, *upa dingin*, and stability, *upa horas*, so that the *tondi* will be firm and cool, strong and powerful; so that the malicious plans of men and evil spirits, those spirits that always lie in wait, the spirits of the solitary places, will remain far distant. So that everything that can be a hindrance, such as obstacles on the road and evil omens, remain far distant. Thy concern now is the mother's *tondi*, the cool *tondi*, the stable *tondi*. Thy concern now is the *tondi* of this dwelling, the powerful ruler which has the whole of the contents of the dwelling under its control, which beckons good fortune from the south and the south-east and from the regions between the eight points of the compass. Thy concern now is the *tondi* of the hearth, this warm, dry corner from which may everything that is evil remain far distant. This is what the *tondi* always desires and what the sons and daughters desire also", and so forth.

The principal elements of the *mangupa* are eating together or serving a meal, making addresses, giving presents, and counter-presents. These last and their supernatural significance have been dealt with sufficiently in connection with the discussion on the affines. They will also be discussed in Chapter VIII. We will here deal with food and addresses.

FOOD AND MEALS

Eating is an important matter for the Batak. His mealtime is the highlight of the day. His food is rich in *tondi*-power and he must therefore eat it in peace and quiet. No Batak will disturb another while he is eating. The only people who have no right to such a privilege are murderers, abductors, and other malefactors: *hundul di pontas pe i mangan di pinggan puti, boi do buaton* = should they sit in the place of honour and eat out of the consecrated dish, they will be seized.

In ordinary life the preparation of a meal does not entail much work. This applies particularly to the meat, *djuhut*, which is bought on market days and cut up in small pieces before it is eaten. It is a different matter, however, when the meat is part of a meal which is to be the main element in some ceremonial. The meat is not then bought in pieces in the market but, if possible, one of one's own fat beasts is selected. Before the knife is plunged into it it is dedicated, *dihatahon* = talked to, if it is to be slaughtered for an important occasion such as a *mangupa*; the rice, *indahan*, is also 'talked to': the meal is then considered to be consecrated, *na tinabean*. Such a meal will be efficacious in creating the anticipated fortune-bringing activity. The beneficial power that it contains will be transferred to the person for whom it has been consecrated and the *tondi*-power of the one person will pass on to the other. When food is ceremonially conducted from one village to another, homage must be paid to it by passers-by. In the *Pidari* time bearers of such food had the right of safe conduct if there was a war on: *siboan indahan tinabean na so djadi mago* = the bearer of consecrated food must not be harmed, was one of the rules of war which even protected those who were involved in it. A meal which has been consecrated is also called *indahan na marlapatan* = rice which has a meaning, or, *sipanganon na marhadohoan* = a meal which has a purpose.

If, however, the people for whom a consecrated meal is destined are to regard it as such, then the meat must be chopped up and prepared according to fixed rules, otherwise it will be regarded as 'ordinary meat', *djuhut rambingan*. Ceremonial meat must be cooked in its own blood, *na marsaudara*, or *na margota*, — so that the skin of a man who eats it will shine — and be cut up into the *na margoar* = the parts that have a name. This is most important and must be done with great care.

THE NA MARGOAR

If these separate pieces of the meat are to be eaten immediately at a small meal, they are called *niadopan* = that which is placed before someone. At a great ceremony, however, they become the *djambar* = portions of the feast-animal, which are allocated according to the *parsolhot* = family relationship, and the *tohonan* = social position. Anyone who makes a mistake and sets a portion of meat before one of his guests or allocates to him a part to which he is not entitled according to his kinship rank, affinity relation or social status, suffers his displeasure, irrespective of whether the person is *na sumangap* = a distinguished person, or an ordinary man. Everybody sets great store on the constant and proper acknowledgement of his position in the social structure and it is precisely at meals to which a number of guests have been invited and at public feasts, that the social relationships can be so distinctly observed in the distribution of the *djambar*, to which everyone present has his own special right. For instance, everyone will watch carefully that the *adat paramaon* = the acknowledgement that one belongs to the older layer of the genealogy, and the *adat parsihahaon* = the acknowledgement that one belongs to an older branch, is not disregarded, since this entitles one to a portion of the meat and to the right to subdivide it again on behalf of one's lineage, or, one has the right to an upper part of the thigh, *soit na godang*, in contrast to the *anggi* who only receive the lower part, *tulan*. These are trifles in the eyes of spectators like ourselves from a different world, but among those directly concerned they carry as much weight as the status symbols of other societies. A wife will pay as much attention as her husband as to whether the part of the animal which he has brought home, be it from her own relatives or from his, is the part to which he is entitled.

At a great feast for which a buffalo is slaughtered, the *djambar*, piece by piece, uncooked and still with the hide on, are thrown onto a mat, *sosor*, from a platform, *pansa*, the name of the piece and that of the rightful claimant being called out at the same time. (see Appendix I). And woe betide the leader of the feast or his assistants if they make a bad mistake. There will then be protests from all sides and possibly a general quarrel or scuffle will follow as an expression of already long slumbering dissension regarding genealogical priorities.

It is not practicable here to give the *djambar* allocations in great detail, or the relevant usages: the local variations are numberless, but in order to give some idea of its general distribution I will give one or two examples which I noted.

In Silindung affines and chiefs from far and near had been invited to a three-day feast to celebrate the bestowal of the name of a great ancestor on the son of one of his most distinguished descendants. The division of the *djambar* of the slaughtered buffalo was as follows:

the rump, *ihur*, went to the father-in-law of the man who gave the feast, the *suhut*;

the head, *ulu*, to his mother's *hula-hula*;

the ribs, *somba-somba,* to the *bona ni ari* (the *hula-hula* of his grandmother and great-grandmother etc.) ;

the neck, *rungkung,* to the *ianakhon,* the *boru* group;

the thigh pieces, *soit,* to the chiefs of the territory and the *boru na godjong,* its oldest in-dwelling *marga;*

the rest of the meat, minus the bones, *sibuk ni djuhut,* was a counter-present for the edible contributions received, *ulak ni ampang =* returning the baskets; a fourth part of it being for the inhabitants of the village, *isi ni huta;*

the entrails, *raoan,* were cooked for the guests to eat with the other food provided at the meal;

the midriff, *ungkapan,* and the breastbone, *pangaransangan,* were for the village chief;

the lower part of the neck, *panamboli,* was for the members of the lineage, *dongan-sabutuha na saompu,* who had helped with the slaughtering;

the backbone, *hau tanggurung,* was the reward for the male servants, *upa parhobas;*

the haunch, *gonting,* was for the drummers, *pargonsi;* the throat, *aru-aru,* was for the oboists, *parsarune;* the femur, *botohon,* for the men who played on the small gongs, *pandoali;* the feet, *pat,* were for the *pangkesehi,* the metre-beaters on the *hesek;* and there was some meat for those who attended to the three large gongs;

the upper parts of the breastbone, *tuktuk,* were for the *datu* who had determined the day by divination, *sidjudjur ari;*

the shoulder blade, *sasap,* was for the descendants of the founder of the village, the *sipungka huta.*

In Humbáng the division of the pig which was slaughtered at a smaller feast for a *marupa-upa dakdanak =* the wishing of good fortune at the birth of a son, was as follows:

the fat and the blood in which the meat had been stewed were for the co-inhabitants of the house, the *dongan sadjabu;*

the jaw bones were for the elder branch, *sihahaan,* of the father's lineage;

the upper jaw was for the man who had spoken the address;

the shoulder blade, *sasap,* went to the descendants of the founder of the village, the *sipungka huta;*

the thigh pieces, *soit,* were for the rest of the chiefs present;

the neck, *rungkung,* for the *boru;*

the back of the head, *parsanggulan,* for the *boru na godjong*;

the ribs for the *datu*;

the entrails for the slaughterer;

the backbone for the men who cooked the animal.

FOOD AND THE AFFINITY RELATIONSHIP

We have already seen that a man may not set all foods before his various affines. If someone from the *hula-hula* is to be the guest, then the meat, *djuhut,* of a pig, a cow or a buffalo must be given as an accompaniment, *lompan,* to the rice, irrespective of whether he is from his host's family-in-law with whom the latter constantly maintains the affinal relationship, or only a man who belongs to the *marga* which the host regards as his *radja hula-hula.*

If, however, someone from the *boru* is to be the guest, then fish, *dengke,* must accompany the rice and for preference the *ihan,* the fish rich in oil which is found in Lake Toba. But, since it is difficult to get fish in areas which are poor in streams, and since visitors sometimes come quite unexpectedly, it is admissible to substitute a chicken: *balitang do balatuk, molo soada ihan ba manuk* = the cross bar is the rung of the ladder; if one has no fish then one can make do with (the indeterminate) chicken.

Here again, fish is symbolic. *Dengke na porngis* = fat fish, is the symbol of abundance and the fruit of enjoying it is a long and fortunate life. The fish, cooked and prepared with lemon juice, *aek pangir,* and curcuma, *hunik,* is eaten by participants at many a ritual and is called *dengke saur.* Thus it is fish that the sower, for example, must eat when he has sown his fields; herdsmen when they move their cattle to new grazing grounds; and it is fish that is offered when the rice is first in grain. The *boru* is given fish by its *hula-hula* since blessings and prosperity are expected from it. The future son-in-law is given *dengke* when he goes on his first visit to the parents of his chosen bride; *dengke* is the accompaniment to the rice that is given to the bridegroom's father when he and his relations visit the bride's father for the official transfer of the payment that finalises the marriage settlement; *dengke* is placed on the top of the rice which the bridal pair have to eat together. And the parents of a pregnant woman will bring fish with them when they visit her to perform the *mangupa,* etc., etc. On important occasions like these fresh fish, *dengke rata,* from ponds, rivers or from Lake Toba will be provided, because the salted and dried sea fish, which can be obtained in great quantities from Sibolga, has no meaning at all for ceremonies such as these.

There are thus a variety of occasions when the partaking of a meal is regarded as efficacious.

AIMS AND EFFICACY OF MEALS

The object of holding a feast and of offering the invited guests a meal is to obtain their *pasu-pasu* = blessing, for the undertaking for which it has been arranged. The proffered meal, whether it consists of the *na margoar* which are set before the guests and eaten there and then, or the *djambar* which the guests take home, is an expression of reverence towards the guests who, by virtue of their position of honour, which they either had or have acquired by being invited to the meal, pronounce the desired benediction after they have spoken the obligatory words that link the meal they have just eaten with their benedictory words to come.

A man will set a meal before private guests to honour them and to bring their *tondi* into a pleasant frame of mind, so that they will enjoy being in his house; the host on his part will receive blessings for his hospitality.

People who have collectively resolved to undertake something important will assemble at a meal, and if some event of importance has just taken place they do so too. In this way a favourable atmosphere is created, the desired harmony is established and people strengthen each other for the future and congratulate each other when they have been successful in achieving their aims.

Important contracts like marriage, betrothal, the transfer of land, business transactions and similar matters are concluded with a meal, either from established custom or because it is felt to be necessary. The meal acts as a seal of agreement, *hot situtú do nasa na pinadanhon diatas ni djuhut dohot indahan* = what has been agreed over meat and rice is absolutely settled.

If a man wants to ask his parents, his family-in-law, his village chief or a higher chief, his creditor or anyone else for something important, he will go to the house of the person in question carrying on his head a dish piled high with food, *mamboan (manghunti) sipanganon*. He sets this before them so that they will be agreeably disposed towards his request.

When notables and chiefs are summoned to settle a dispute a meal will be set before them before they sit. By this means they are brought to the tranquil frame of mind necessary if they are to carry out their important task of hearing accusation and defence and considering the case in a dignified way. And, when a settlement which satisfies both parties concerned is finally reached at the end of a serious controversy, they will often assemble at a meal to confirm the agreement that has been arrived at. If, however, the arbitrators who have been summoned in a dispute cannot at first succeed in inducing the parties concerned to be mutually lenient and thereby effect the settlement of the quarrel, they will perhaps resort to the beneficial activity that can result from taking a meal together: meat and rice will bring the matter to a satisfactory conclusion, *djuhut dohot indahan pasaehonsa*.

If two parties have been abusing each other or if there has been a fight, and if both are equally at fault, then the judge or the arbitrator can order them to take a meal together. Both contestants have to supply the ingredients. During the meal, with the appropriate words, they will have to acknowledge their guilt, forgive each other and show their mutual goodwill. Such a meal is called *mangan indahan sinaor* = eating 'mixed' rice, and in many cases this is punishment enough.

If a man offends another, by word or deed, then he must go and confess his guilt, *manopoti salana*, by, among other things, offering a meal in the preparation of which his family has assisted. If someone damages other people's property, if, for example, he destroys crops by thoughtlessly burning the forest, or floods fields downstream by careless manipulation of a dyke, then he must set before the community affected a meal of meat and rice, *mandjuhuti mangindahani*, as payment for his negligence. In partaking of it the community accept his acknowledgement of his guilt.

Many more examples of these ceremonial meals, which are *dibagasan adat* = according to usages and customs, will be given in the course of this work. For the moment, this brief mention will suffice since their purpose and efficacy has been made sufficiently clear. Their aim is always to demonstrate esteem and honour; to appeal to calmness and the restoration of peace of mind and to promote tolerance and harmony. One can here recall the offering-community, the *sapanganan*, of which the members share a meal together when the ancestor common to them is to be worshipped.

Besides these meals, there is a peculiar form of serving food which is not done when guests are being entertained at a general meal or when people eat together on terms of equality, but when the server, in any way or for any reason, stands in a special relationship to the one who has to partake of the food. In such cases, the server will show particular respect to his guest, will request particular benediction from him, or desires particularly to be strengthened by him.

Generally speaking, the ceremonial meal takes place with due observance of some established forms which indicate its magical character.
If it is served in a house, it is in the centre of the dwelling, *di tonga ni
djabu,* on a clean mat, *di lage na tiar,* out of a clear sounding dish,
pinggan sitio suara, (this dish is also called *pinggan pasu* = the dish
of benediction) on which the rice is placed in a dome-shaped pile,
didimpu, etc., etc. It is also necessary to pay attention to those things
that are *subang* and which can produce a magically dangerous situation.

MANULANGI

Among the practices relating to meals, there is the giving of food from
the hand, *manulangi,* (see photo IIa). It belongs to the ritual of all acts
of homage which are specifically made to those to whom it is appropriate
to offer a meal: affines, kinsmen, superiors and other persons.

For instance: at a wedding the party of the bridegroom, thus the
boru group, performs the *manulangi* ritual towards the bride's father
and mother. One of the next of kin of the bridegroom's father girds
himself with an *ulos,* and, carrying the *ampang* in which the cut up
meat has been placed, approaches first the bride's mother. He takes
some of the meat in his right hand, puts it into her mouth and says
to her: "I feed you with rejoicing, Aunt, may your *tondi* always give
benediction; your *sahala* fortune, and may your daughter quickly have
her first child". He then repeats this ritual with the bride's father. A
daughter resorts to the *manulangi* ritual when she is in need of special
benediction. If she has no children, when she becomes pregnant and
wishes to receive an *ulos ni tondi,* if all her children die in succession,
in short, whenever it is necessary for her to be the object of benediction,
diupa, she turns to her parents, or other *hula-hula* and expresses her
particular respect towards their *sahala* by the *manulangi* ritual, thereby
asking for their blessing.

The parents can also be the object of this ritual, *disulangi,* without
there being a specific motive, for example, in order that sickness and
calamity will be kept at a distance, and so that their children will enjoy
the blessings which can radiate from the greater *sahala* of their parents.
It can also be done on the order of a *datu.* And in the same way a pupil
feeds his teacher or a subordinate his superior if either desires that
some of the *sahala* of the other be transmitted to him. The *manulangi*
of a father on his deathbed is of importance since he can thereby be
activated into expressing the last pronouncement of his blessing on his
children. When this form of *manulangi* is to take place, all the children

together prepare the meal, *sulang-sulang,* that is to be served to their father. Each child offers some food to him three times and addresses him in affectionate terms. The commands he then gives, the *tona* = instructions for his descendants, are binding on all concerned.

It is worthy of note that the *manulangi* is also done to inanimate objects, such things, for instance, as the wooden images of the *Debatá Idup* which are carried about by a childless couple who hope in this way to ameliorate their piteous condition, or the *porsili,* the small image that is made as a substitute for a sick person whose *tondi* is held in the grip of a *begu.* It is also done when the antidotes, *pagar,* against sickness made by the *datu,* are used or if they have lost their efficacy because they have not been used for a long time. And when the bones of an ancestor are dug up and removed to another resting place, the skull is *disulangi,* etc.

THE BATU NI SULANG-SULANG

A sum of money which is called the *batu ni sulang-sulang* = the 'stone' of the meal, frequently accompanies the offering of a meal. This is done, for example, when the purpose of the meal is to make a request in order to acquire something of value; it is done when, in reaching an amicable settlement, it has been agreed that the one party will satisfy the other with a meal and an additional money gift. It is also given when a money gift is one of the elements of the reconciliation that follows an admission of guilt. The efficacy and purport of the *batu ni sulang-sulang* is as many-sided as is the efficacy and support of the *manulangi.*

THE EFFICACY OF SPEECH

The Batak attaches good and bad 'effects' to words. A word can bring benediction or calamity. Words can summon powers that bring ruin or good fortune. Bad words, invective, insulting words, or words which contain a malediction all stir up evil. And for almost no offence are there so many terms as for the verbal insult. The lips which have expressed such words must be squeezed together, *gatip bibir* or *gansip bibir,* the terms for a customary punishment in such a case. The person who has been affronted by a verbal insult must be offered a meal consisting of meat as a 'medicine' to avert the grievous consequences: *sineat ni bibir djuhut daonna* = when one has been struck with words from the lips, meat is the medicine. The curse, *sapata,* pronounced by people whose *sahala* should be respected, such as parents and chiefs, brings about childlessness or prolonged sickness among the living or in the next generation. The *pangulubalang* (to be discussed later) and other supernatural means of destroying an enemy are not effective if the requisite incantation, *mangmang*, is not uttered. The *pagar* = amulets, used to ward off the calamities that angry spirits can cause, derive their power from, among other things, similar formulae spoken by the *datu* who prepares them. When the *datu* consults his oracle it only gives its pronouncement after being summoned to do so by an adjuration. Hence one of the names of a *datu* is *pormangmang* = the one who adjures with words. And, as we have already seen, a dream can be summoned by words, *marmangmang nipi.*

Good words can promote good by the magical power emanating from them. The *hata na uli* or *hata na lehet* or *hata na denggan,* the 'beautiful words' used when people address each other on all kinds of occasions, derive their value not only from their aesthetic beauty but especially from the power of benediction that is expressed by them. Words of solace, *hata apul-apul,* comfort those in low spirits not because they refer to and emphasise the good aspects of a difficult situation, but because they have of themselves strengthening power. At the exchange of words between host and guest which make the meal effective, *parsaut ni sipanganon,* the host apologises for the scantiness of the meal and the guest expresses his complete satisfaction with it. Each of them uses well-chosen words wishing the other prosperity, *marsiduma-dumaan* (from *duma* = prosperity) as the result of offering and partaking of the meal.

It is even possible for a man to invoke benediction, *tua,* for himself by saying the appropriate words at the beginning of a meal, *mortuahon mangan.*

If a *datu* has given his services at a ceremonial toothfiling or at the first hair-cutting of a young child, etc., he will be requested after the ceremony to proclaim the success of the operation, *paboa horas-horas,* since the mere utterance of the words is conducive to it.

When contracts transferring land or cattle permanently are concluded, the finalised negotiations are closed to the accompaniment of the *hata sigabe-gabe* = the words of 'good fortune' which, by their utterance will give the blessing, *gabe,* that should be associated with a newly acquired property and should promote the prosperity of the new owner.

Thus, whenever it is necessary that one person gives benediction to another there must be an address suitable to the occasion. For example, the *hula-hula* must speak the *hata pasu-pasu* = benediction-bringing words, to its *boru* for without them the *mangupa* ceremony would not be complete. And words of a similar purport are spoken by the village chief or the higher chief of the territory when he addresses a newly-married couple, or a man who is departing elsewhere to try his luck.

All such addresses are strongly interlarded with a great number of standard expressions, *umpama,* in which the play of homonymous words increases their efficacy. It was by means of these old and well-proved sounds and terms that the ancestors experienced their blessings. One finds the same rhetorical expressions in addresses in Toba as one does in Angkola which was populated some centuries ago and where, in the ensuing period, people maintained little or no contact with Toba, their country of origin. The 'born orator', and as such the Batak is well-known, is he who knows the right moment to use the appropriate *umpama* in his feast oration.

The following has been taken from a description in a Batak newspaper, and refers to the consecration of a newly built house, *mangompoi djabu.* After the meal one of the guests first pronounced the *parsaut ni sipanganon* and then asked about the *haroan* = aim of the feast. The host gave his reply and then the guest spoke again as follows: (the standard expressions are in italics)

Gonghon paimaon, djou-djou sialusan.

Ba nunga bosur hita mangallang *indahan na tabó,* djala mahap hita marlompan; *pamurnas* ma i *tu daging, saudara tu bohi,* ba, *haroan ni i* dipaboa suhutta.

One must wait for an invitation and one must answer a summons.

We have been satisfied by partaking of the *delicious rice* and content with the other foods we have been given. Such a meal gives *strength to the body* and *lustre to the countenance.* Let the host now communicate to us *the purpose of it.*

Alus ni suhut.

Anggo *haroan* i, alé amáng, *sai ro ma haroan marharoan tu djoloan on. Djagar hata* dibahen hamú songon *na marlompan hunik,* djala dipatama hamú hata i songon *na martondi eme.* Sai *tubu ma na djagar* idaonta tu djoloan on, tumpahan ni Debatá dohot tumpahan ni tondi ni amanta radja, na liat marlolo on.

The giver of the feast replied:

With regard to its *purpose,* Dear Friend, *may there always be opportunities for festive gatherings.* You have *spoken fine words* like one who *garnishes his meal with curcuma,* you have chosen your words well as is done when *the rice in the fields is imbued with its soul.* May there always *be much that is beautiful to be seen* and may it receive the

7

blessing of God as well as that of the *tondi* of you respected people who are gathered here.

Na hupungka hami do bale-balenami on, ba, i do na pinabotohon tu angka dongan, tondong ro di angka amanta radja *mangido pasu-pasu, panggabean, parhorasan.*

We have built this humble dwelling and we now make it known to all our kinsmen and affines as well as to the other respected gentlemen present and we *ask for your blessings, for prosperity and the good that comes from stability.*

Ro alus musé.

Ba, molo i ma hapé, *sai horás ma tondi madingin, pir tondi matogu.* Sai hot ma di batuna togu di pangarahutna bagas ni inanta, sibaganding tua on.

The reply to this:

So be it. *May your soul be firm and cool, stable and strong your soul,* so that the dwelling of the housewife rests firmly on its foundations, so that the lashings of this dwelling, which is built on such broad ribs, are strong.

Lili ma di gindjang, hodong ma di toru, *riris ma djolma di gindjang, gok pinahan di toru.*

The rib of the aren above, the stalk of the aren below; *may a long line of human beings be in the house and a byre full of cattle below it.*

Sai tubu anak na maló martahi dohot boru na maló marhuhuasi.

May many sons be born who know how to deliberate and many daughters who know how to provide.

Alus ni suhut:

Tutú, ninna anduhur, tió ma ninna lote; nasa na uli na nidók ni radja ba, i ma didjangkon tondi, *unang muba, unang mose.*

To which the giver of the feast replied:

It is true (tutú) says the turtle dove, it is clear (tió) says the quail: may all the good words which you respected gentlemen have spoken be accepted by the soul *without change, without fail.*

Olop-olop, ninna angka na asing.

We agree, the guests replied.

Some other ways of giving and taking the *tondi*-power which have their own characteristics are worth mentioning.

DONDON TUA

The term *dondon tua* can best be translated by "weighted with good fortune" (*dondon* = to press on). This term is applied to objects which are given to a person so that a special measure of fortune will thereby be transferred to him or her. Such objects can be heavily weighted with good fortune by subjecting them to the special effect of important ceremonies which are key points of supernatural activity, such as, the *hordja turun* = reburial of the bones of a great ancestor; when the *gondang* is played and when the spirit of the deceased ancestor is near, and all the various ceremonies have as their object the bringing of benedictions to the living. The small rice cakes that are offered on these occasions are imbued with strong power and are treasured for a long time in case there should be childlessness in the family. When a man uses the opportunity that such a ceremony offers to present an item of value, such as a rice-field, for example, to one of his beloved and child-less relatives during the dancing, then a favourable effect is hoped for with regard to the fruitfulness of the woman. The particular gifts which grandfathers sometimes give to their grandchildren can be termed *dondon tua*. These gifts usually consist of land, and are given especially to the eldest sons of eldest sons in order that as much as possible of the *sahala* of the grandparents' old age and their prosperity will be trans-ferred to the principal descendants of their lineage who will worship their spirits in the hereafter.

SAMPE TUA

Although this term has a similar meaning to *dondon tua*, it is as a rule connected with a definite ceremonial and the gifts associated with it. It is a term that is particularly common in the more southerly parts of the country when a new dwelling is consecrated. The presents that are then offered to the giver of the feast by kinsmen, affines, friends and members of his village have the separate name of *sampe tua* — in addition to the general terms *ulos* and *piso* when the affines are involved — and, like the address just given, aim at bringing good fortune to the host during his sojourn in the new dwelling. And when people make their first visit to the house some time after the consecration, they must leave a small trifle as the *sampe tua* before departing. Such people as widows, women who have had no children and a married couple whose children have all died, are for the time being excluded from a newly consecrated house: they do not carry fortune, *tua,* with them but misfortune, *sial.*

THE HOMITAN NI TONDI

The *homitan ni tondi* = that which is under the protection of the *tondi,* also called *gomgoman ni tondi* = that which is ruled by the *tondi,* is a means by which people endeavour to increase and perpetuate good fortune and avert the threat of misfortune. A *homitan* is some object or an animal. A person binds it to his personality by a small ritual of words and acts from which he expects the favourable effect that is thereby attributable to it. A man is then said to be seeking blessings by means of objects which have been subjected to the power of the *tondi, didjalahi pasu-pasu marhite sian ugasan homitan.*

One form of *homitan* of which the sole aim is the welfare of the individual is the *hadjimat ni tondi* (Malay: *djimat* = amulet). This is sometimes an extraordinary product of nature such as a distorted bambu stalk, a peculiar piece of quartz and similar things which a person can carry round with him. If attention is to be drawn more to the prosperity of the family, then a person will bind himself to an object such as a cloth, a beautiful dish, a domestic animal, and so forth. For, by these means the fortune of the hearth, the cooking pot and the house are thought to be preserved. Sometimes an object or an animal is chosen for this purpose if a period of good fortune began when it was acquired and it has thus come to be regarded as fortune-bearing. Such an object or an animal is sometimes obtained after the *datu* has consulted his oracle.

However, it is the *ulos ni tondi,* given to a woman during her pregnancy by her parents, that is the talisman especially considered as the one which will maintain the fortune of the family and avert calamities. It is then not a cloth that she can appropriate solely for her own use but one which will also serve all the members of the family who find themselves in distressing situations. It derives this quality from the fact that the affines, from whom a special strengthening influence can be expected, have bound their benedictory powers to it.

The larger genealogical communities have their own *homitan* in the *ruma parsantian* with its *raga-raga,* in the *tunggal panaluan* = magic staff, and in former times, in the *pangulubalang,* the remains of a youth who was ceremonially killed by having boiling lead poured into his mouth. These remains were kept in a pot. His *begu* was thought to be a willing tool in the hands of its owners for doing harm to their enemies.

There is also the *hoda miahan* or *hoda Debatá,* the consecrated horse of the gods. As a rule it is bought by a lineage of about the size of a *sapanganan lombu* after it has experienced many reverses of fortune, and after a *datu* has recommended through his oracle that such a horse should be kept. A contribution towards the cost is required from every member of the lineage, the amount being the same for everyone. The animal is consecrated, *dimiahi*, by being sprinkled with water, *pangurasion*, mixed with lemon juice, *aek ni pangir*, and the *gondang* is played to invoke the ancestors to bestow their benediction on the consecration. Neighbouring lineages of the *marga* are invited to the ceremony so that they will be acquainted with the special destiny of the horse. It is let loose to wander in the fields as it will and can eat what it likes without being driven off. It can only be driven out of the fields, and then with caution, by neighbours who are not associated with it, or they can take it back to the chief of the lineage to which it belongs. When the horse is old it will be offered to the three uppermost gods and then all the lineage members will partake of the meat. It is then replaced with another young horse and as far as possible one that resembles the animal which was the companion of the *ompu parsadaan* in his prosperity. Such horses still wander about in Humbáng.

MAGICAL PURIFICATION = PANGURASON

In a world in which a magico-religious way of thinking is an important feature, it is repeatedly necessary for men, animals or a region to be cleansed and freed as far as possible from the impurities with which they have become befouled, *rotak*. The consecrated horse of the gods which is expected to bring prosperity to the lineage, is brought to a state of purity by certain ritual acts; barren women, to whom there obviously clings a stain, are sprinkled with lemon juice during the *mamampe raga-raga*. Purifications relating particularly to the hair of the head will be mentioned in the course of this work. The aim of this purification is to make clean, *ias*, to make pure, *uras*; the ceremony is therefore called *pangiason* or *pangurason*, and is effected by *mamangir* = sprinkling or washing the object with lemon juice, *aek ni pangir*. To ascribe a symbolic purifying activity to such an act is quite logical and consistent in this range of ideas. The purification is also called *parpangiron*. Besides lemon juice other requisites are frequently prescribed, such as *sanggul* = leaves for decorating the hair, *hunik* = curcuma, *baoang* = onions, and *miak* = oil or albumen. The *manguras* is frequently associated with sexual offences.

The *mamangir* forms (or perhaps formerly formed) an integral part of the ceremonial attendant on certain legal transactions and consequently the term is used to denote them. For instance, in the more southerly parts of the country a marriage, among other things, can be

defined by the term *mamangir,* and it is the technical term for the sum
of money which in olden times the *parboru* (who gives the woman in
marriage) had to pay to the husband as compensation when he agreed
to take back his wife after she had committed adultery. Indeed in many
cases the performance of the purification ritual itself, has been reduced
to giving and receiving a sum of money.

THE INFLUENCE OF CHRISTIANITY

I will conclude this chapter with a brief comment on the influence
of Christianity on these religious concepts.

It is not easy to state with any precision in how far the Batak who
has become a Christian has abandoned his traditional religious concepts.
The observations I made in the introduction are applicable here: the
old ideas have never been replaced in a balanced concept-for-concept
manner. The spiritual luggage of a newly baptised Batak from Samosir
contains more pagan elements than that of the youngest generation in
Silindung who, as fourth generation Christians, are at the present time
regularly subjected to the influence of school, church, confirmation,
needlework clubs and choral societies, and so forth, and who associate
little, if at all, with the unbaptised. Naturally, individuals differ considerably. A man who has experienced much misfortune recalls the
sources from which men formerly sought prosperity, and his belief in
the efficacy of those sources will be greater than that of a man who
has been successful: the latter will have no difficulty in keeping his faith
in God. The moulding of the moral personality of those who have
just emerged from a world of thought in which many things are judged
to be the automatic result of supernatural activity, will take different
courses.

There is also the difference in the character of the existing pagan
concepts and usages. The Mission has always been quick to diagnose
that which is demonstrably coloured with animism and directly connected with the veneration of the spirits of the ancestors — elements
easily recognised by the older Christian congregation as being non-
Christian — and has immediately opposed them. In the first decennia
of missionary work, they prohibited the holding or the witnessing of
gondang ceremonies for invoking the spirits or for their veneration. To
enforce this rule, they had to have the help of the Dutch Government,
because the chiefs were in the main still pagans and even where they
had become Christians, they were not strongly opposed to these ceremonies. At the present time the prohibition is supported in regions where

Christianity has found general acceptance, such as Silindung, Balige and Humbáng, by the authority of the parish itself which often exercises stronger disciplinary control than the Church leaders deem necessary. And right from the commencement of their work, the missionaries have opposed the many expressions of the *tondi*-cult. But, because they had for so long approached all the phenomena they encountered as expressions of animism, much that was equally pagan in character and origin, dynamism, for instance, was not initially always clearly understood and was more or less tolerated. Even the Christian Batak himself does not understand the essentially non-Christian character of these concepts, because he sees them either as simply customs of which the real meaning has been forgotten, or as petrified usages, e.g. the many *subang*-regulations. Sometimes he ascribes them to a universal human sphere (such as the interactive spiritual influence of kinsmen and affines), or he draws parallels between them and the Old Testament (the offering of meals and the benedictions of Genesis 27), or he is unaware of their nature because they have acquired a superficial Christian veneer which has ostensibly obscured their pagan origin. Consequently, that which stems from the world of magic merges more easily into the thoughts and life of a young Christian Batak than that which is of a more animistic origin. Yet, in a society such as the Batak, which is strongly orientated genealogically, many remnants of the old animistic concepts will live on for a long time.

It is thus understandable that in the present transitional stage, a variety of intermingled ideas, requirements and usages which are evidence of the concepts of earlier periods, will exist in individuals and groups, alongside their new religious beliefs. The following examples are typical of these interwoven ideas. A man took his wife who was barren and always ailing to the house of his brother, a teacher in a Mission school, with the request that he should perform the *mangupa* ceremony for her. Her brother refused to do so because he realised the pagan purport of the ritual, but, before he sent the couple homewards, he nevertheless gave his sister an *ulos pamontari*, a garment of the kind that is often given by the *hula-hula* as an *ulos ni tondi*. A pagan had a judicial judgement passed upon him whereby he was ordered to 'mangari-ari' the *tondi* of a Christian by having the *gondang* played and by offering a meal. This was thought necessary because the *tondi* had been frightened when inaccurate reports of the Christian's death had been circulated: Christians objected to this judgement. A Batak newspaper carried a brief report of a shortened form of *pangupaon* which had taken place in the office of the Batak District Officer, himself a third generation Christian, after there had been a great fire in the market place: he had offered some rice and money as an *upa tondi* to the "frightened" merchants who were for the most good Christians too; the offering was made with the appropriate words in the old-fashioned style. A Batak pastor was once insulted by one of the congregation during the service. The following week a meal was held: a cow was slaughtered and the cooking pot, *hudon,* the sitting mat, *rere,* and the ladle, *sonduk,* had to bow, *morsomba,* and after the ceremonial meal, the offender, his wife, his father and his mother had to admit to his guilt and beg the pastor's forgiveness before all the members of the parish who had participated. The original intention had been that the gathering would take place in the middle of the chapel, *mordomu di tonga ni djabu,* since the glory of the Christian Church, the *sahala ni huria,* had also been insulted.

A small spring, *homban,* in a field was the object of long and fierce litigation between the elders of two wholly Christian lineages on the Toba plateau — even an elder of the parish was involved. Each party claimed that its own ancestor had been the first to use the spring as an offering place. The only purpose this spring served was as a reminder of the revered *ompu parsadaan.*

Christians are sometimes placed under the ecclesiastical ban (i.e. they cannot be baptised, take part in the Lord's Supper or have their marriages blessed, though they are allowed to attend the service regularly and often do so) and the most usual reason for it is that they have committed bigamy either because they have had no children by the first wife or the children are all daughters. A Batak would rather break his external link with the Church than die without male issue.

CHAPTER III

THE CORPORATE COMMUNITIES (*Haradjaon*)

It is comparatively simple to describe the main features of the smallest of the Batak corporate groups, the village; and the highest, the tribal group. Below the village there is only the hamlet; above the tribal group there is only the Batak people as such. It is what lies between these two extremes that presents the difficulty.

THE VILLAGE

The village-area is a small square with a fine, hard and bare courtyard in the centre of it. On one side of this square there is a small group of houses, usually set in a row; each house has its own kitchen garden at the back. Opposite the row of houses there is a row of rice granaries. There is usually a mud-wallow or two. The whole is enclosed by a wall on which there are tall bamboos: sometimes a village will have a ditch round it. One will find pigs rooting under the houses, dogs nosing about, chickens scratching the ground and a cat sleeping in the sun. A woman will be sitting at her loom in front of one of the houses while a young girl stamps rice in a large *losung* and some children play in the shade beneath a small clump of fruit trees. Baulks of timber and planks lie on a vacant piece of ground and have obviously been there for years. One's eyes and one's mind tell one that this village is a small closed world, a living unit consisting of a small group of people who belong to each other and who have lived together for a long time in this place where their children were born and where they themselves hope to die.

When a number of such villages, *huta*, lie in a cluster, then each one is contained within its own walls. But sometimes one finds what appears to be a continuous village compound divided in half by a wall and then one is told the story of the quarrel between Ompu A. and Si B. This dispute between them ran so high that they separated, each occupying his own half of the village and transporting the houses of the men of his faction, but which lay in the territory of the other, to his own side of the new wall. In regions where there are no longer actual walls in the complex the boundary will then be a hedge, a row of trees, a disused patch of land with ferns growing on it, a footpath, or something else that more or less serves to make a clear separation between the groups of houses. These forms of demarcation are often found where the village groups have been under Dutch rule for a long time. The inhabitants of a village will point to one *huta* as being *huta Lumban* so-and-so, to another as that of Ompu someone-or-other, to a third as belonging to the *marga* this-or-that, being the in-dwelling *boru* of our lineage from olden times, *ai boru-hatopannami nasida.*

THE TRIBAL GROUP

It is somewhat more difficult to present such a clear picture of the tribal group for it can cover whole valleys, large tracts of lowland and plateau, extensive mountain regions, or, half the island of Samosir in Lake Toba. The difficulty is, however, lessened a little because the boundaries between the tribal areas were clearly defined and permanently established when the contending tribal groups made peace after a war. Thus it is possible to show the individual tribal areas on a map. Such boundaries were not so necessary among the *marga, marga* branches and lineages, or for the groupings into which they so often united to form a more or less well-defined community. Therefore boundaries within the tribal group's area were frequently not defined, for though fighting was indeed frequent within a tribal group itself, when one faction might capture the *huta* of another, or some people might be driven from the place in which they lived, the contestants nevertheless belonged to one larger group and if a neighbouring group threatened to invade their territory they had to combine. Such internal boundaries were thought necessary, however, in an area such as the *sidjamapolang* region, the area of benzoin cultivation, where the forests are in fact the actual benzoin fields and where the area under cultivation is extensive.

The boundaries between the tribal groups are sharp. On Samosir the boundary is a straight east-west line. On the Humbáng Plateau clearly demarcated lines go over hill tops and conspicuous stones, over trees and ravines, and elsewhere over a stream, a watershed or some other natural feature. Here and there controversy will arise among the Batak on some perhaps uncertain individual point — but where does one ever find a situation among these people in which everybody is in agreement? But such arguments are never of so much account as to make the drawing of lines of demarcation on a map unjustified.

THE CORPORATE CHARACTERISTICS OF THE TRIBAL GROUP

The tribal group has only one characteristic of a corporate group: its own territory.

With regard to centralised authority, the Toba Batak preferred in the *Pidari* time to live in small convenient units consisting of some hundreds of people, at most a thousand, whose interests were confined to their own affairs. They had not developed the art of ruling to the stage where a large area could be brought under a stable administration. There was no one person or persons in whom central authority was vested. There was no common administration of justice either for disputes and misdemeanours which affected more than a smaller territory or as a court of appeal against the justice administered within such a territory. Disputes between corporate communities were settled peaceably or they resorted to war. And if the internal affairs in a territory became completely disordered, then the *radja* = chiefs, of the affinity groups were often more effective as mediators than the *radja* of the cognate groups.

As far as security was concerned, it was sometimes thought necessary to have a village as a frontier post in places where an invasion from a neighbouring tribal group could be expected. In such cases, after deliberation between members of adjacent territories, a village was founded, populated and maintained as a substantial contribution to keeping the enemy at bay.

Trade and social intercourse were maintained between members of tribal groups and between members of territories hostile to each other, or even formally at war, by the 'peace of the market'. This was an established institution facilitating intercourse between warring or quarrelling factions by enabling them to meet in any of the central *onan* = market places. The 'peace of the market' was observed by all.

The tribal group can be considered in a sense as a unit: its members have a feeling of belonging together; they are of the same blood; and they have sprung from one ancestral village where a common guardian spirit is often honoured at ceremonies to which come members of the group living elsewhere. In the past its members sometimes arranged large communal offering-feasts. They feel that their security and welfare are best promoted by living together in one tribal area and by remaining together within its confines.   .

There is, however, no clear basic pattern, for, since nothing is simple and uniform here, development has not followed a model. The number of tribal areas which, irrespective of the *boru* in-dwelling in the territory of its *hula-hula,* contain an unmixed tribal group in its entirety is very small. I believe there is only one, the Sipaettua area round Laguboti. The other tribal areas, with the exception of South Samosir, generally accommodate fragments of another tribal group in one or more places within their area, and this breaks their unity. Or, two different areas such as South Samosir and Muara, will each contain a part of one tribal group. And there are tribal groups, like the Silahisabungan and Borbor, which only have a small land of origin but no well-defined tribal area because they have spread for the greater part over the whole of the country. On the other hand, there are large mixed areas like Pahae and Upper Barus and small areas like Bakkara, where several parts of different tribal groups live together, each in its own corner, within the territory as a whole. All these phenomena have led to local links, usually of a confederative kind, which are often strengthened by affinity relationships between the allied *marga* and their principal chiefs.

This does not, however, alter the viewpoint from which the spread of the Batak people should be approached, nor does it alter the fact that the tribal group's character is not only genealogical and territorial; it also has juridical significance.

THE VILLAGE AS A CORPORATE COMMUNITY

The *huta* has a much more pronounced corporate character than the tribal group. The area of the village is small and clearly defined. Specifically, it is the piece of land on which the village, with its wall and ditch, was founded. If its founder built it on land that he owned, or on unoccupied land, then the *parhutaan* = the area of the village, is part of the property of the founder and of his descendants and will continue to be so even if the village itself is later moved elsewhere and the *parhutaan* becomes *lobu* = deserted. If the village was founded on unoccupied land, then in most regions, customary law, *adat,* adds an area round it of about 30 feet or more which in some places serves as reserve land for the possible growth of the village: the area is then called the *tamba-tamba ni huta* or the *pangeahan ni huta.* In some regions it forms an inalienable complex of rice-fields which is intended exclusively for the use of the inhabitants of the village and must periodically be redivided among them. It is then called the *upa parik* = appendage to the wall. Elsewhere, it is a means of demarcating the point to which neighbouring villages are permitted to come with their walls and cultivated fields and it is then called the *nilinggom ni bulu* = that which is in the shadow of the bambu, or the *parhaisan ni manuk* = the place where the chickens are allowed to scratch. This area is measured differently everywhere but it can be defined for any village and is always reckoned as being part of it. It serves the interests of the village, and non-inhabitants have no rights there and are excluded from it. The area beyond it cannot be regarded as being part of the village-area proper: it is not a special sphere of interest of the village, nor does it exist for the special benefit of the villagers, and it does not come under the jurisdiction of the village's management. Villagers can acquire the right of use, or a preferential right to unoccupied land beyond the narrow village area only when it has been regularly used as cattle pasture or has previously been used as rice fields, gardens for sweet potatoes, and so on. This is the only way in which such land can be linked with a village.

Land which is cultivated by members of a village can be regarded as belonging to the village. This is especially the case where the village plays a prominent role in the control over the area over which the *marga* disposes. The nature of this link varies because it is determined by the local laws in respect of the relation between village and land rights, and by the mutual relationships of the *marga* and lineages. As a consequence, it is difficult to separate village land from land that is the personal property of the founder and his descendants (who are the village chiefs): the one is often indistinguishable from the other.

The second feature of a village that gives it the character of a corporate community is that it manages its own very diverse activities. Only a few people may be concerned, usually a *huta* contains about 6, 8, 10 or a dozen houses some of which house a couple of families (villages of more than 20 houses are rare), but the internal affairs of the village are, nevertheless, multitudinous. The wall has to be maintained as do the bamboos planted on it, the ditch and the village council house, the *sopo,* though nowadays there are only a few of these left. The drainage has to be looked after as well as the entrance and exit to the village. Among the villagers themselves there will be trifling arguments over their children, their dogs and their pigs. One of the inhabitants will want to build a rice granary, another to fell a tree on the wall for timber, while a third wants to use a vacant plot as a small garden. A child will be born and all the relatives of the parents on both sides will come to give their good wishes: a son of a member of the in-dwelling *marga* plans to marry and must have a plot of cultivated land for his daily sustenance. In another family there will be a daughter who will marry and leave the village, or perhaps she will remain there with her husband who, as the son-in-law of her father, will become an inhabitant. One villager will sell his cattle, another will present a wet rice-field as an *ulos* to his *boru*. A house will be dismantled and sold to someone, or a villager will move far afield or will leave but live nearby and matters relating to his property and land must be put in order. A wife has perhaps fled to the village chief because her husband has driven her out of the house; a *datu* will be consulted because there are many cases of sickness; one of the villagers has died . . . All these events are village affairs and constitute the aspects of the life of a community living in a small group which is secluded from the outer world. Everyone knows everyone else's business: people help each other in disaster and grief, take an interest in each other's welfare and in every change in the composition of a family. There are the changes consequent on a villager departing or a new inhabitant arriving. The villagers are wary of accepting a stranger, but a new arrival who is accepted is given rice, if he needs it, until the land which he will be cultivating yields him a harvest. A builder of a new house finds that everybody is prepared to help in the work. And when a man is leaving the village to seek his fortune elsewhere, he summons everyone to a last meal at which many *hata na denggan* = wishes for his welfare, are expressed, and presents are given to him. Should he fare badly the village is happy to have him back again.

Such is village life, the life of men among their fellow men: it is public life in a nutshell. Anything outside the sphere of actual family affairs is a village affair and comes within the village's control. Private interests and public affairs flow into each other and the smaller the village the quicker it happens.

In the following chapters it is in the main private law that will be discussed, nevertheless, it must be understood that, though the village community may not be mentioned, its administration, its customs and its law are interdependent and the village itself is always in the background.

One should not assume that all the people who form such small village communities are equal to each other in the body corporate of the village. Such is not the case. There is a separation and no matter where the village is situated, it is one that applies everywhere and which is only overruled in exceptional circumstances. One does not find the social classes in the Toba Country such as exist in South Tapanuli, nor does one encounter in Toba the wards within villages as one does in South Tapanuli and the Karo Batak Country. In Toba the internal differences between the villagers result from and are dependent upon the foundation of the village. Once a man has founded a village, *mamungka huta,* whether he did it alone or (seldom) with the co-operation of others, he creates for himself and for his sons a community of its own and in doing so he and his male descendants acquire the right to be masters there and freely to dispose over the admittance of others. This is a right that operates strongly everywhere and which governs village life completely. It derives its authority from the fact that in the territory of which the village forms a part, there are other villages of the same larger kin-group — the descendants of the first occupiers — that have the same rights. It is an idea that is accepted and which will continue to be accepted because it flows naturally from a system of social relationships that is based on a genealogical structure.

The manner in which a village is founded contributes to the firmness of the link between it and its founder. The offering, *bunti,* that is offered to the Supreme God, *Muladjadinabolon,* and the Earth Spirit, *Boraspati ni tano,* with the object of obtaining their blessings and averting the danger of their anger and of summoning a good guardian spirit for the village, *bauta ni huta,* creates a spiritual link and a legal relationship between the person making the offering and the village. This will later be strengthened by the many children he will be fortunate enough to have and by the prosperity they will share. This first village will always be held in great honour, the more so if it has flourished and, becoming too small, has been the starting point for the founding of other villages to accommodate the founder's descendants. In later centuries it will become a place of pilgrimage for them. The 'right' to the village is thus the factor of differentiation between the *isi ni huta* = inhabitants of the village. It is the right of the founder, the *sipungka huta;* of the bearer of the offering, *sihatahon bunti;* the instigator of the founding, the *suhut,* or whatever name he is called, and is held in perpetuity by his descendants so long as they continue to dwell in the village. It ceases to be operative only if the village is deliberately abandoned, *huta na niulang, lobu.* This right also entitles the holders to govern the internal affairs of the village and gives them independence regarding its affairs in respect of interference from outside. But it only operates within the village. This right of internal control in village matters is vested in the entire male line of the descendants of the founder right up to the present-day head of the village, the *radja huta,* who is the one to whom the village belongs, *nampunasa.*

The right to rule in the village, *haradjaon,* is the common right, *hatopan,* of every one of the founder's direct patrilineal descendants and, though according to the rule of law it is vested in one person and possibly limited to his branch, nevertheless, the other descendants of the founder benefit from it. They cannot be banished from the village, *pabalihon*, and they have an unassailable right of entry and residence therein if they so desire. Thus the *haradjaon* is the exclusive prerogative of the lineage of the *radja*, but not of the greater lineage or of the *marga* of which it forms a part. Fellow members of a *marga* can go to live in each other's villages, though they do not often do so if they live in the same territory, and they may then acquire some advantages over members of another *marga* living there, but they have no part in the *haradjaon* of the village. Neither have the so-called in-dwelling *marga* any entitlement in this respect. They are mostly connected with the *marga radja* by affinal ties and for this reason alone are not inclined to usurp the rights and position of their *hula-hula* or *boru*. And, in the light of the relationships in the village, it would not be possible. Were a ruling *marga* in a village to be supplanted by the in-dwelling *marga* it would threaten the legal position of other villages in the territory and probably other territories as well. Such an action would activate them against what they would regard as an assault on the legal order and on the general interest. It has never happened in the Toba Country to my knowledge.

The members of the in-dwelling *marga,* often called *parripe,* or *anak ripe,* or *na hinomit,* the ones who are ruled over, have very little to do with village affairs if they have but recently come into the village. They are simply the dependents of the family from which they took their wives. And if they are not an affine of a member of the ruling *marga,* they are taken into account even less. But as the generations succeed one another and the in-dwelling *marga* becomes a *marga boru* of the second and later generations (in matters such as these too, people easily reckon in *sundut*), its position becomes more important and its influence in the affairs of the village greater. However, the descendants of the *boru* which, in many regions, has assisted its *hula-hula* in founding a village by sharing the cost of its construction always have the most influential position. It is thus from the outset the special *boru* of the village, the *boru ni huta,* which in former times could play an important role in the administration of justice in the village and which is still entitled to privileges.

The difference in the legal position in the village between the ruling *marga* and the in-dwelling *marga* is further established in the law of land tenure.

This difference is particularly clear where the village is one from which land rights are exercised. It is least clear in, for instance, the *bius* of North Samosir where the land is divided into large blocks (either once or repeatedly) between the *marga* comprising the *bius*. There the village as a land-controlling unit has been pushed into the background and the block, the *talian,* has come to the fore.

A man of the ruling *marga* of a territory is a *pargolat* or *partano*, in his village, i.e. if he clears a piece of land it becomes his own, it becomes his *golat*, his share in the *golat* of his *marga* in which are vested the rights of the land in the area it occupies. It is land he can freely give to his children, sons as well as daughters, and he can leave it to his sons when he dies. It is land that belongs to him no matter how far away he goes to live. It is land that he can exchange, loan out, give as a pledge if he is in need of money, and he can give it in payment if his debts are weighing him down and no one will help him. It is land which, within the limits of the local customary law, which usually awards the *uaris* the right of preferential purchase at a reduced price, he can permanently alienate against money. For a man who is of the ruling *marga* the right to his *golat* is his most valuable possession, as it is for his male descendants to whom the land, divided or undivided, is passed after his death. It is the original right of land control of his lineage, *marga* or tribal group which is vested in him personally. His *marga* name establishes his right in this respect: he will say: "I am of the *marga* Malau, the land I cultivate is part of the *golat* of the *marga* Malau, hence this is my land". Such is his reasoning and that is sufficient. Similarly, in Silindung and Humbáng the member of the lineage of the village chief whose *marga* is the ruling *marga* of the territory can say: "I live in the village of Ompu Gulasa and am of his lineage, hence the land that I cultivate in this place is my *golat*". Thus, from olden times there is a natural association between authority over a region and land rights, and still today the right of the ruling *marga* to dispose over land is an integral part of the right of the larger corporate communities and of their villages.

Thus, if a person does not belong to the ruling *marga,* any right he may acquire to land for cultivation is a derived right and not one to which he is automatically entitled. For instance, a man who belongs to the in-dwelling *marga*, to the *na hinomit* = the ruled one, only acquires the right of usufruct, often called the *parripean*-right, of the *golat* of the ruling *marga* with which he is an in-dweller. The precise nature of this right as it operates in different regions will not be examined at

8

present. It is sufficient to say that in one place it is linked with the in-dwelling of the user or his descendants in the village from which the first cultivation of the land was done. If he moves elsewhere then the land must be surrendered, *tinggal* or *tading,* to the village chief unless the relations between this chief and both the user and the chief of the village to which he is going are such good ones that he will be permitted to continue to have the use of the land, *mamboan* = to take the land with him. In another place the right is tied up with the in-dwelling in the cluster of villages to which the village, from which the cultivation was started, belongs. And there are other restrictions on the right to this land by an in-dweller: normally he cannot pledge a piece of land that he himself cleared for the first time or pledge garden plots with their trees without the consent of the village chief; it cannot be used as a redeemable pledge, *sindor,* for the marriage payment for a son, *pangoli ni anak*; it cannot be given as a gift to a daughter, *pangias ni boru,* when she marries unless the user is of the *boru na godjong,* the first in-dwelling *marga* of olden times. A chief cannot, however, take land away from the user, except in great need, so long as he and his descendants continue to live in the village. In short, the right of a man who does not belong to the ruling *marga* is much weaker than that of one who does, the *pargolat,* but it is stronger than a mere right of usufruct resting on a terminable contract. And this right of use becomes stronger as the period of time during which an in-dwelling *marga* stays with another *marga* increases, because, as a rule, many-sided relationships result from the marriages which take place between a ruling *marga* and an in-dwelling *marga.*

In respect of the law of land tenure, members of the village chief's *marga* who live in the village but who are of another branch or lineage, are often treated on an equal footing with the *parripe.* (In the Silindung area they are called *parripe dongan.*) For example, members of the Huta Galung *marga* who live in a village of the Harean branch but who are themselves of the Inaina branch, are there regarded as in-dwelling, though it is a small Huta Galung territory situated in the middle of the Silindung valley where both branches live together. These kinds of relationships too have considerable local variations.

It will already be obvious from the foregoing that the village possesses the third characteristic that stamps it as a corporate community, i.e., its own authority. Some writers on the Batak have gone so far as to say that the *huta* is a small independent republic whose *radja* need brook no outside interference in its affairs. This is not admissible. The *huta* is always a part of a higher community from which, in the *Pidari* time, it could not disassociate itself other than at the cost of great danger to its own existence. It is a cell of a political organism which was formed by the *marga* and tribal groups, but a cell with a corporate life. Everything that happens between the members of the village and within the village's walls, and only there, is, from olden times, a matter which only concerns the village. Formerly, the only exception were those major crimes which disrupted the peace of the whole territory. Minor offences were settled in the village as were also cases between the villagers themselves relating to land and debt, and everything that was of interest solely to the village and its inhabitants was dealt with by the village authority. In such cases the village chief parried any interference from the chiefs of surrounding areas. Nowadays, the sphere of life of villagers has extended considerably through wider intercourse, so that many of their interests, for some of them most of their interests, lie outside the strict sphere of the village. Nevertheless, the village chief is still always on his guard to see that the *adat parhutaan* is properly maintained; that village affairs are handled by the village authority and that there is no interference from outside in these matters.

It is, however, possible for a firm bond to exist between a village and its mother village = village of origin, and then some interference by the latter in, say, a marriage or the slaughter of an animal for a feast, is tolerated.

The authority in the village is usually the village head who is known by various titles: *radja huta* being the most usual one. On Samosir he is called *tunggane ni huta* = village elder; elsewhere he is also sometimes called *siboan bunti* = the bearer of the offering. It is he who is charged with the management of the village and the maintenance of law and custom, order and discipline. He is the patrilineal descendant of the founder of the village who was the first *radja huta*. This office, if possible, is passed from father to son, or to an *uaris*. Formerly a village chief was required to have more qualities than at present now that peace prevails. The village head's administration is as diverse as are the aspects of village life. He is responsible for the maintenance of the village square and the walls; he regulates the alignment of the houses and controls the lands of the village. He can decide whether a small garden must be given up in order to make room for a house or whether it can remain; he guides the legal conduct of his dependents and stands by them if they have to make a claim against anyone, or in the event of their creditors making too many difficulties for them. He conducts their betrothal deliberations when their children marry. He represents the interests of his village and of his lineage where there is involvement with the outside world. And, though he has been pushed into the background in recent years, he is still the authority in the village who executes the orders of the higher authority. Formerly he was responsible for the administration of justice also. The inhabitants of the village must accept his leadership and be guided by him and as proof of this they must honour him in such transactions as marriages, the sale of cattle, alienation of land, etc., with their gifts of homage, *upa radja.* He, on his side, usually consults his elder subordinates, *na tua-tua* or *pangintuai,* from the foremost of whom, the *namora boru,* the most important man of the in-dwelling *marga,* he receives regular support. This is especially the case when the matter relates to a dispute between him and members of his own lineage. Nevertheless, he has the last word. And if he has to assert his chiefly authority by force in order to ensure that his orders are observed, he does so. He is the government and police in one, and in olden times he sometimes had a block standing near his house so that he could place under restraint an inhabitant who would not submit with good grace to his orders. Naturally only a powerful figure who was head and shoulders above the villagers and whose words would not be taken lightly could make a successful village head whose authority would be felt.

Though the position of a village head is thus an important one, in practice, he sometimes has little opportunity of exercising it. If his village is small and consists of only half a dozen simple farming families who are poor, then it may be a long time before anything of note happens, such as a betrothal, the slaughter of a buffalo, a departure elsewhere, or an alienation of land.

In areas where the village is not the focal point for the control over land, legal cases are rare, and it may sometimes be months before the necessity arises to replace a *radja huta* who has died. There are also *huta* which are gradually being depopulated and eventually there may be only one or two families left in them. This may be the result of sickness, a desire to emigrate or, if the *huta* is in a mountainous area, there may not be much possibility of cultivation of rice on wet fields. In such small villages with their lack of vitality, the value of village life declines considerably and the actual meaning of the right of the village's founder or of the village head loses its significance and is sometimes reduced to almost nothing. Miniature villages like these are numerous, a fact that has led the Government to abandon using the village as the smallest cell in its administrative system.

Nevertheless, the general principle of the independence of the village, its area, its internal management and its government, remains what it was and the Batak accord equal honour to these smallest villages and to the large handsome villages of the prominent and prosperous lineages.

THE TERRITORIES BETWEEN HUTA AND TRIBAL GROUP

Links are everywhere to be found between the tribal group and the *huta* grouping the inhabitants of the tribal areas in territories of various graduations. These connections are not clearly discernible everywhere, nor are they always sharply defined by the same characteristics. It is not easy, therefore, to describe them in a few pages and it can only be done by omitting a number of peculiarities which would give an indication of the perpetually deviating local aspects.

When the population occupied their present-day tribal area, or the mixed area roughly corresponding to it in extent and significance, and settled in villages, and when they united in different communities, three connected and interchanging motifs played their part: the genealogical, the religious and the territorial. The foremost of these is the genealogical aspect. Sometimes it governs all layers and sometimes it only concerns one or a couple of them, but it is never completely absent. Second in significance was the religious motif which united villages or groups of villages into sacrificial communities that became corporate groups. In some areas, however, the religious motif has not been significant from a political point of view since it did not produce corporate groups. In these areas the offering community synchronises with the tribal group or lower corporate bodies built up genealogically. Of the three motifs, the territorial has been the least operative as an independent linking factor. It has had little effect in breaking the genealogical line in regions which are strongly marked ancestral areas. The only exceptions of which I know are some parts of Uluan and a couple of stray instances elsewhere. It has, however, been more effective in the older and younger areas of emigration where odd villages united in a more or less firm combination in mixed territories or territories formed by different but kindred *marga*.

Among the territories created between village and tribal group by the action of one or more of these factors, there is in most ancestral areas at least one that bears the clearest character of a corporate community. It does not then, however, always possess completely all the distinctive characteristics of it: its own area, administration and authority. The units above it, as well as the elements which form its structure may, in their turn, display some characteristics of a corporate community that it may possibly not possess itself. Here I will deal with the most important elements that have played a role in this respect but I will not stress one as being more important than another. The *bius* will not be discussed since I have already dealt with it.

ONE LAND-CONTROLLING GROUP

Although the internal boundaries between the territorial communities within the tribal areas are not usually sharply defined, the village groups both large and small are, nevertheless, as a rule so situated in relation to each other and are so distinct from each other, that each kinship group lives in its own corner of the tribal area within which there are no other villages other than, possibly, a *huta* of the *boru hatopan*, the common *boru*. This area is cultivated by members of the relevant group, i.e., the lineage that has sprung from the ancestor who first utilised the land there, *manombang*. But it cannot always be said of every complex that it has the character of a well-defined independent territory which cannot be used by people living outside it — even near kinsmen — to found new villages, to construct irrigation works or to open up new land for cultivation without the consent of the chiefs of the villages concerned. This does not apply as a general rule to the lowest of them, the smallest grouping consisting of a small number of villages. In areas where the genealogical principle has predominated in the spread of villages in ever-widening kinship circles until it takes in the tribal group, one cannot say with any certainty which of the 'links' the greater lineage, *marga* branch or *marga*, groups which have the right to and control of the land, have acquired their sharpest definition. The lower is always within a higher and there is always some irregularity in the location of the villages. Consequently, the villages in these areas are well in the foreground in respect of land rights and the maintenance of community rights. The higher links are only clearly defined in areas where non-related *marga* meet each other. On the other hand, in regions where the religious factor is interwoven with the genealogical motif, a clearly recognisable land-controlling group can be detected because the distinguishing feature of the *marga* is its unity. Samosir is an example. Most of the *bius* there are built up of fragments of *marga* branches each having its own *golat* (*talian*): Uluan and Upper Barus are other examples where the *bius* as a whole is not a land-controlling community either. Everywhere that some fragments of *marga*, which are, as a rule, related, live together, we can delineate more or less sharply a tendency to a separation regarding land rights. This applies, at least for the area that is considered as cultivable and which has in fact, already been cultivated. In the few large forest areas, such as the mountain barrier that separates Uluan from the East Coast, in the Huta Galung forest southward of Mt. Pusuk Buhit and the Dolok Saut complex, the right to them is in the hands of the entire tribal groups.

A somewhat different form is displayed in densely populated Toba Holbung where the rather large *hordja* is a genealogically pure unit as well as being a sacrificial community and a corporate community. It is true that related *hordja* lie beside it but not always in such a way that the nearest kinsmen are also the closest neighbours. In Toba Holbung the large fragments of the *marga* of the Pohan tribal group have become *hordja* and have spread like spots over the entire ancestral area without uniting into a *bius*. The result is that they form the most distinct communities and the most distinctly defined land-controlling groups.

The question of land rights must be considered in the context of the many local divergencies, usages, and special arrangements that give the Toba country its rich variety of land laws which are slightly confusing to the outsider. But, nevertheless, the Batak is always able to say that the land belongs to the *marga, marga do nampuna tano*, a principle he rightly accepts as a basic one in his customary land law.

THE GROUP ACCEPTING RESPONSIBILITY FOR CRIME AND FOR THE ADMINISTRATION OF JUSTICE

Before the advent of Dutch administration among the Batak, these two attributes were important factors in their judicial life.

The motive of self-preservation was a powerful one and the safety of members of a group was ensured through the power of the chief in the event of a crime being committed. And if any member of the group, or his property, was attacked by members of another community, the group acted in concert on his behalf. If one of its members committed an offence outside the group, the entire group was answerable for it and the culprit either had to be handed over to the injured community, or he was punished in collaboration with it.

It was usually the highest kind of corporate community living in the territory of the tribal group that was responsible for keeping law and order in this way. This method of administering justice acted as a kind of bond in that there was no other independent authority above it for dealing with offences and lawsuits. Nevertheless, as we shall see in Chapter X, everything could go by the board in matters affecting more than one village. Here, however, it is sufficient to state that almost nowhere in the Toba Batak country there is any question of a distinctive graduation of authority from the lowest unit, the village, to the largest, such as that to be found in the Karo Batak Country.

The efficacy of the organisation in dealing with crime should not be overestimated. Many a crime committed by a well-known person, either one within the group or someone outside it, could go unpunished for years on end. The result was frequent wars of revenge and a consequent endangering of security. This fact is clearly evident from old missionary literature.

ONE ONAN

The danger to the security of the country due to the defective organisation for keeping law and order and for administering justice, was to some extent compensated for by instituting markets, *onan*, and their so-called "peace of the market". This at least meant that during the actual market-day and during the time when people were going thereto and departing therefrom, a recurring period of security was ensured within the sphere of influence of the market. This usually covered the night before market-day to the day after it. Fighting and killing were forbidden; it was not permitted to fetter a man for debt, or to rob a person on his way to the market, etc. Each territory that was of some consequence and had the vitality to do so founded its own regulated market, the *onan na marpatik,* as the centre of trade and intercourse for the whole of the surrounding area. This *onan na marpatik* was distinct from the *onan manogot-nogot,* the very small morning markets, also called *onan sampang,* the sole purpose of which was to serve the daily household needs of the nearby villages. A territory that founded an *onan na marpatik* was ensured of the co-operation of the territories in its vicinity and consequently the desired 'peace of the market' could be permanently guaranteed. Frequently one of these *onan* rose in importance above the others and became the central *onan* of the area of a tribal group, or a principal part of it.

Of the institutions which the old Batak society produced, the instituted market is the one which has most served the purpose for which it was designed. In some *onan* one can still find the old trees planted when they were founded by the chiefs of the co-operating territories. Under these trees the chiefs sat, each in his own corner of the market, *parampangan,* to receive petitions or complaints and to discuss the affairs of the land.

ONE HOMBAN (spring); ONE PANGULUBALANG (centre of supernatural power); ONE RUMA PARSANTIAN (house for the ancestral spirit)

These three features, which can exist together or separately, are all connected with religious concepts. There is a relationship between them and the genealogical groups and thus there is a connection with the communities within the whole of the tribal group. As with everything else in this cadre, the extent of the group having one or more of these attributes can be small as well as very great.

ONE MOTHER-VILLAGE (*huta parserahan*)

The communal mother-village where the ancestor of the larger and largest genealogical units lived is primarily a place of veneration. For the smaller units the relationship of a village to the village from which it has sprung, has a more practical significance. Each territory has almost always grown from only one village, or sometimes from a pair of separate but related villages, from which there were offshoots, *marserak,* at one time or another. These in their turn were later the village of origin of a number of other villages, and, except in the younger areas of emigration, the founder-village of any village is always known. This is attributable to the fact that when a would-be-founder of a new village leaves the village in which he has lived, he is usually given a formal send off, *dipaborhat,* by the village chief and those who will be staying behind and the chiefs of the surrounding villages, who are on friendly terms with his village of origin. This naturally creates a permanent relationship, which is further strengthened by what is, as a rule, the prime motive in founding a new village: expansion of living space for a lineage. This is termed *pabidang panggagatan* = unfolding the wings. In olden times there was the additional aim of strengthening the lineage's power against enemies around it. But there are and were other reasons that play a role: lack of space in a *huta* when its families begin to increase; a desire to split off from the lineage of the founder when it has become too extensive; dissension between brothers of the same father; the desire of an influential father to set up some of his sons in their own *haradjaon,* and so on. The founding of a new village springs from the inclination of the Batak to provide living room in more than one village for a genealogical group that is growing in numbers and prestige. This leads to a community being formed particularly along genealogical lines, because since early times the instinct of self-preservation among groups who belonged to each other has necessitated their living together in a restricted territorial area. This is still a national inclination. It is not and never has been the custom, except where a new area is occupied (or in former times conquered) which is at a great distance from the mother-village, for a newly founded village to associate with a group of villages of another lineage or *marga*. In the formation of communities, being of one lineage, *partubu*, has always been of more importance than the *parhundul* = the territorial location.

The principal joints above the village are thus usually the complexes of a mother-village with its offshoots which formed small and larger territories inhabited by parts of a lineage or a *marga* branch. Throughout the whole of Ypes' work there are brief remarks concerning the relationships of mother-villages and daughter-villages or relating to the divisions according to lineage and the extended family. These are to be found between the descriptions of the *bius*, the *hordja* and the *sĕmbarur* or *ladang*. They are clearly casually observed details rather than the result of a definite investigation into the internal organisation and structure of the larger units he describes. Nevertheless, they do give some indication of it. My own investigation showed me that the structure of these territories in a number of areas is not to be regarded as a simple formation with the village as the sole unit in its composition, but rather as a complicated one which usually originated because of the repeated creation of mother-villages and their offshoots (conf. App. V).

ONE COMMON IN-DWELLING MARGA BORU

The *boru* group which counts as the in-dwelling *marga* of a territory from olden times, has certainly been linked to the ruling *marga* for a number of generations, and it is therefore usually a territory of some extent and of some age that accommodates such a *marga boru*. There is a relationship with the genealogical character of a territory or of a part of it. Where a territory contains more than one *marga* (the *bius* in the north and west) or more branches of a *marga* (more in the south), one or more of these *marga* or *marga* branches generally has its own *marga boru*. But it can also happen, as in Uluan, that small groups of the *marga boru* common to the whole tribal group (in Uluan from the Silahisabungan tribal group) have contributed almost everywhere in the region to the composition of the different *bius*. It is also possible for this old *marga boru* — also called the *boru gomgoman* = the *boru* that is ruled, in contrast to the *marga boru* with which affinity relationships are maintained but which lives elsewhere — to have provided the newly founded villages with their *boru*, the *boru ni huta*. This can, however, also have been done by other *marga boru*, younger ones, more closely associated with the village's founders.

In many territories the ancient *boru* obtained, at its request, permission to found one or more of its own villages in the midst of the villages of its *hula-hula* or on a *talian* allotted to it. This *talian* then becomes land over which it has control so long as it continues to reside in the territory. In these villages and on this land the *boru* can act as though it were the master. The rights it then has for example, to accommodate people from other *marga*, can vary according to region and local opinion.

A large piece of land was sometimes given as the *pauseang* = marriage gift from the *hula-hula* to the *boru* group. This transfer was then meant to be permanent and it included the right of control over it and this could lead to the formation of an independent territory.

Where the ancient *boru* had not acquired the right to found its own villages — a right that appeared to me to be most coveted — it could have all kinds of other specific rights: it could use some of the land it cultivated as payment (by pledging it) of the marriage payment for a son, or, it collected the contributions, *guguan*, for the offering ceremonies of the territory. This was usually the prerogative of a man from the oldest branch of the *boru* group. Sometimes it had the right to stab the feast-buffalo and to receive a specific *djambar*; to lead the speeches at the gatherings of the territories' chiefs; to arrange the taking of the oath when a political agreement had to be confirmed, and so on. This *boru* can also play an important role in the administration of justice in a territory, as will be seen in Chapter X.

ONE GROUP FOR GIVING ITS DAUGHTERS IN MARRIAGE

The territory has to be viewed as a genealogical unit in this respect also. When the giving of a daughter in marriage is not only a matter affecting one family but also the lineage to which that family belongs, and perhaps even the whole *marga* or the tribal group are affected, (where the rules of exogamy are involved) then, in principle, the actual interest and interference in concluding the marriage is unlimited. In normal everyday life, however, the geographical position defines the natural boundaries and as a consequence, as far as marriages are concerned, a lineage living in an area separate from that of the other lineages of a *marga*, easily regards itself as a unit apart and in the territories which contain fragments of several *marga*, each of them stands on its own in this respect. As far as it concerns the giving of daughters in marriage, the influence exercised by solidarity on the partitioning of the tribal group is as varied as the internal development of the lineages and *marga* and their distribution over the ancestral areas.

ONE GROUP GOVERNED BY CHIEFS (*panggomgomion*)

For a group to follow a *de facto* leader who is a powerful personality is rather different from following a *de jure* figure who has been deliberately invested with his official position by the group itself. In olden times both occurred, with, as always, their attendant phenomena. The first happened mainly where there was no durable formation of alliances with the agreements and growing usages springing therefrom. Thus in those areas where the genealogical arrangement was the prime factor in the formation of territories. Here it can be noted in regard to Silindung, where the *bius* was solely a sacrificial-community and not a corporate group, that Ypes, describing the Silindung Valley as a typical example of an arrangement that is almost exclusively genealogical, deals with the "temporal chiefs of the highest order" without, as elsewhere, referring to corporate communities within the territory of the tribal group. In Silindung the large lineage or the *marga* branches were grouped round a powerful *radja djungdjungan*, a chief who had succeeded in being highly respected in the larger genealogical group to which he belonged. He was primarily concerned with matters of security and with warfare as well as with the internal affairs of the territory. He was assisted in his deliberations by the *radja partahi* = counsellors, who were usually the chiefs of the component offshoots. But if a man who had been a powerful figure lost his influence in the territory's affairs, or if the branch to which he belonged increased less than others in the larger groups, then the mutual rivalries of persons and of the smaller lineages very soon became apparent and a territory that had been a powerful unit could become divided into a number of quarrelling factions of a *marga* in a short space of time. Here historical and personal events played an important role though their effects could be somewhat tempered by a more or less strong feeling of preference for an oldest *marga* branch, *haha ni partubu,* also called *haha ni haradjaon.* This was not only the case in Silindung but also in Central and East Humbáng, or in Muara and — probably — in the Sipaettua area around Laguboti where the situation was not very different. In these areas there can be little if any question of a permanent central chieftainship, or of some measure of fixed division of offices between the component parts of the larger territories.

Where a territory is a separate unit distinct from neighbouring lineages of the same or other *marga*, even though it is also formed internally either exclusively, or mainly, genealogically, as is the case with the *hordja* in Toba Holbung, the chief has become a more established figure for this corporate community which has had to maintain rigidly its existence as a unit. In such a case it would usually be more correct to say that the chief carries his own branch of the waringin tree as a token of his chiefly authority, *mandjudjung baringinna,* and that he stands on his own feet, *djongdjong di hadohoanna.* The only point in respect of the chieftainship upon which there could be dispute was the question of assigning the chieftaincy to the rightful claimant.

Where the alliance aspect of a territory has become its predominant feature, the *haradjaon* = chieftainship, and its administration, *panggom-gomion,* (from *manggomgom* = to rule) have been organised in a sharper and more established form. But not to the same degree or in the same manner everywhere. In Uluan, for instance, where there was not always a communal *bius* chief for the promotion of secular affairs concerning the whole *bius,* it was least apparent. There, the principal element was the chief of the foremost division of the *bius,* namely the *hordja.* In so far as such a *hordja* was of mixed composition genealogically, it had in its turn the character of an alliance and the decision as to who should occupy the position of *hordja* chief was usually subject to the rule of local agreement, otherwise its character was as that in Toba Holbung.

On Samosir the *radja doli* was recognised more clearly as the foremost chief of the *bius* than he was in Uluan. On Samosir the *bius* nearly always consisted of a number of fragments of different *marga.* The chief was recruited from the *marga* or *marga* branch to which the office belonged by virtue of primogeniture, earlier settlement or a-greement of old. Each of the components of the *marga* provided him with one chief as his assistant, *radja partahi.* However, here also striving after the crown was, as elsewhere, always a possibility. The best organised territories appear to have been in West Humbáng and Upper Barus where the administration of the *bius* was conducted by a council of which the composition was fixed. At its head there was an *ompu* (or *bona*) *ni saksi* = chief (or beginning) of the law, from the *marga* or *marga* branch which — as on Samosir — had precedence in this respect, and often there were as many chiefs belonging to it as there were *marga* or *marga* branches participating in the alliance. Most of the titles of these chiefs were derived from the division of the offering-buffalo: *parisang-isang* = the recipient of the jaw; *parihur-ihur* = the recipient of the tail, etc. Indeed, in general the mutual relations of the component *marga* of the *bius* were usually permanently determined by such a fixed division of the animal slaughtered at the ceremonies. It is understandable, however, that the actual position underwent continual change with the modification of the internal power-relationships.

One rarely finds that two or more easily distinguishable joints between *huta* and tribal group have resulted from a concurrence of the phenomena so far described as being active in the formation of a corporate community. The greatest coincidence occurs in the areas where the religious motif has effected the formation of alliances. There, at least in principle, the two layers, the *bius* and the component *marga* are clearly distinguishable. There may have been a further sub-division within the *marga* according to lineages due to rivalry between the chiefs, or because of the splitting off of villages. Stap, the first Controleur = District Officer of Samosir, who had the task of organising the legal communities on the island, mentions in his report that it did not often happen that only one chief, among the many was pointed out to him by everyone as being the acknowledged chief of the *bius,* and that they nearly all laid claim to the few chieftaincies which the Dutch Government had instituted. From this one might well deduce that the practice of the *Pidari* time frequently led to more internal strife and confusion than to a tranquil community life and effective rule over *marga* and *bius.* Where the jointly held *bius* feast contributed little or nothing to the formation of corporate groups as, for example, in Toba Holbung, only the *hordja* acquired a distinct form. Elsewhere it was only the powerful personality who was able to bring larger units under his all-embracing authority; an authority which diminished as his forcefulness waned. The extent of these territories shrank according to the communal objective in view, about which there could often be contention.

DJANDJI

I will only comment briefly on the *djandji* = friendship alliance of magico-religious purport. Such an alliance was frequently concluded in olden times by a *marga,* tribal group or *bius* with another similar group living at some distance. In normal life members of the *djandji* maintained no direct political relation with each other but they visited each other, *borhat djandji*, when it was deemed necessary to ask for supernatural strengthening, for example, after a bad harvest or any other kind of calamity. The *borhat djandji* was led by the principal chiefs or the *parbaringin*. One of the effects of the *djandji*-association was that it gave its members freedom of movement within each other's areas. In some regions a feature of the *djandji*-alliance was mutual support in war.

GOVERNMENT INTERFERENCE WITH THE SOCIAL AND
POLITICAL STRUCTURE

It will be realised from the foregoing that the Government was faced with a singular task when it tried to find starting points in the existing social-political structure for its administration. It encountered great diversity of forms, both in the southerly part of the Toba Country in 1883 and in the northerly parts in 1908. There were, however, a few main lines discernible which provided some indication for a general direction of policy. These have been followed though there have been misconceptions, lack of understanding, and experiments. Briefly, until a few years ago the position was as follows: recognition as a corporate authority was not accorded to the tribal group, or a large part of it; at least no attention was devoted to its further development as a higher authority with its own political character. Administrative districts and sub-districts were organised, each containing one or a few tribal groups or parts of them. The boundaries of these districts seldom fully corresponded with those of the tribal groups and sometimes cut right across them.

With few exceptions and then only temporarily, the *huta* was not officially recognised as the lowest corporate community because of the enormous number of these miniature villages.

Minor chiefs were appointed as early as 1883 with the Malay title of *kepala kampung* = village head. These chiefs were the headmen of one large *huta* or of some smaller ones. When groups of *huta* were formed into *kampung* very little specific attention was paid to such particular features of Batak society as close kinship relationships, common origin from a mothervillage, the natural link between *boru*-village and *hula-hula*-villages and other similar factors that are such important elements in Batak socio-political structure. Instead, it was the *parhundul*, the geographical proximity, number of people, etc., that played the chief role since it provided surveyability from the point of official administration.

The *kepala kampung* had below them the *kepala rodi*, one for every 10 male statute labourers, who were sometimes *huta* chiefs, but not always.

The result of this arrangement was, that in many a sub-district, the lowest step of the social structure, which had always been organic in character, was completely, or anyway for the greater part, eliminated, with the consequent development of a number of grievances.

Where the highest joint below the tribal group was the *bius*, it could in many an instance be acknowledged without reserve as a *hundulan* (later a *negeri*) under a *djaihutan* (later a *kepala negeri*). But, since the Government used the number of inhabitants as a basis for the system, the result was that, where of old the genealogical relations had predominated, there was an arbitrary splitting up or joining together of parts which originally did not belong together. The use of population figures as a basis in areas where formerly the genealogical motif had predominated in the formation of a territory, meant that sometimes whole *marga* or, in some cases, branches of *marga* were declared *hundulan*. It also happened that, by virtue of their geographical position, the natural bonds between villages were severed by incorporation of one of them into an adjacent territory, so that sometimes even Sumba villages came under Lontung *radja*.

In Toba Holbung the *hordja* were in most cases originally made into separate *hundulan* but later, when the *negeri* were formed, combinations were often resorted to by the Government. A factor that very often bore upon all this was the presence or absence of influential chiefs. It was a long time before the position was stabilised with the formation of the *negeri* about 1918. During this period there were confused appointments and discharges; there was organisation and reorganisation; a decrease in the number of chiefs, etc.

The first joint to be formed below the *hundulan* was the so-called *radja paidua*-ship. This institution of 'chief of the second grade' has at no time and nowhere operated regularly in such a way that all the main sub-divisions of the *hundulan*, each of which should have been able to continue its own corporate life, had by right a secondary chieftainship irrespective of its population. This chieftainship, in fact, became a means of mollifying the many chiefs who had been passed over for the *djaihutan*-ship, at least this was certainly the case in the early years of the Dutch administration. If the *hundulan* were clearly such as to call for subordinate chieftainships, these were, in fact, only conceded to the largest of them, the *radja paidua* of which then frequently came to rule over groups alongside which they had lived but which had never been under them. In the course of years the number of *radja paidua* were gradually reduced — as they died or were dismissed — without much fuss. The institution was finally abolished, so that at the time of writing (1932) there are only a few old *radja paidua* left. Their position was never integrated into the framework of the *hundulan* and therefore to revive it, as has been suggested, is hardly sensible after so many years. It can be regarded as having fallen a victim to the *kepala kampung* institution when it will be reorganised. This latter can assume adequately the position of a link between *huta* and tribal group, for which, in general, there is a need. More important, however, than the question of precisely where the level of this link should lie, is the demand that the *marga*, their branches, the lineages and complexes of villages, from all of which elements a *hundulan* is constructed, are all represented in its administration, be it by one or two chiefs for the smaller units and by more for the larger ones.

Not much authority has remained to the chiefs. They had always been responsible for caring for the law, for prosperity and security, and though judged by present-day standards they did not do it particularly well — as will become apparent soon enough — they did bring a certain order and prosperity to this substantial population which could not have existed if there had been no such authority. Initially, under the new Government, they thought themselves firmly in the saddle, for the foremost of them received official recognition. They had the right to impose certain levies to meet their needs and were allowed to play an important part in the administration of justice. But in the course of the last few decades there has been a tremendous amount of Government activity in the Toba Batak Country and a corps of Batak civil servants have been introduced between the European administration and the chiefs. The latter became aware that they were being relieved of many of their former responsibilities. They accepted the fact that in all these new forms of Government care: education, vaccination, control of cattle disease, road building, maintenance of penal regulations, the only co-operation they could provide — co-administration would not be appropriate in this context — would be in giving their services. This they accepted, at least in the beginning, despite the fact that they were deprived of an outlet for their previous activities which had consisted of the defence of persons, village, territory and everything connected therewith. In the long run the interference of the Government also in the internal life of the corporate communities, was such

9

that the chiefs were, in fact, divested of all their authority, of their power to make their own decisions. They became no more than the mouthpieces of Government officials and this, understandably, was a source of grievance. For the population it was an inducement to transfer their respect from the chiefs to the much more influential Batak officials of the Government.

A factor contributing to this change is the singular outlook which the Batak have on life. As I have explained earlier, the Batak have an aspect in their dynamic-religious way of thinking that to a great extent coincides with what the Westerner calls 'success'. A person who has become someone in the world and continues to be someone, enjoys particular respect among the Batak: the person who fails, either wholly or in part, forfeits that respect in corresponding measure. This particularly affects the chieftainship.

THE NATURE OF THE CHIEF'S AUTHORITY

On this issue the Batak's attitude proceeds along lines of reasoning that are different from the Western approach. This cannot be better demonstrated than by quoting an episode from the collection of tales called *Torsa-torsa ni halak Batak* (Tales of the Batak People). Therein is told the story of a mighty *radja* who had lost his wealth and power through his own fault. He had even been struck with the misfortune that his daughter had been abducted by a tiger who had taken her to a desolate forest to become his wife. The daughter knew the circumstances of her father's life, so, when he had tracked her down — with much difficulty — she received him sympathetically and offered him a meal, resolving at the same time to investigate the condition of her father's *sahala* by divination, *martondung*. Her object was to find out whether the *sahala haradjaon* = the particular quality of chieftainship, which a man can have, no longer dwelt within him, *so mian be di ibana*. She therefore divided the small animal she had slaughtered for the meal into three parts. The parts "which have a name" the *na margoar,* she put into one pot; the meat cut up in the ordinary way, *tanggo-tanggona,* she put into another one; the intestines, which are the parts destined for the servants, *naposo,* she put into a third pot. Now, she thought to herself, if the *sahala haradjaon* has already departed from my father he will undoubtedly take the third pot first. If, however, he should choose the one with the ordinary meat in it, then he is still clearly a *radja panonga* = a medium sort of chief. But, if he takes hold of the pot with the *na margoar* in it then that will prove that, although afflictions may have overtaken him, honour and respect will again be his due in the future.

The rise and decline of rulers and their lineages, of their prosperity, their power, their prestige, their influence (outside their own *huta*) is regarded as an indication of the presence or absence of the special potency which the *tondi* of a chief can possess and which is called the *sahala*: in this instance, the *sahala haradjaon* = the quality of power, the natural result of which is the *sahala hasangapon* = the quality of being respected. They are the qualities which dwell in a chief and which, thanks to their existence, entitle him to respect, veneration, and, as the bearer of authority, to docility and obedience. The dependents of such a chief can, as a result, become prosperous. They acknowledge that their relationship to a man who has 'luck' can reflect good on them.

To quote the saying:

baris-baris ni gadja di rura Pangaloan,
molo marsuru radja ingkon oloan,
molo so nioloan tubu hamagoan,
ia nioloan dapot pangomoan;
Rows of elephants in the Pangaloan Valley,
When the *radja* commands people must obey him,
Those who do not comply will suffer,
But obedience brings its reward.

A man who is *tois* = impudent, refractory, toward his chief, is so to his own detriment.

Formerly the outward signs that the *sahala haradjaon* and the *sahala hasangapon* had disappeared, were the decrease of the numerical strength of the chief's lineage (due to a low birth rate or a high death rate), the chief's sickness, his ruin through gambling, bad harvests in the territory, losses due to war, etc. The present-day equivalents are unexpected dismissal and lack of success of a son or a nephew in the subsequent election for a new chief. The signs that a person has the *sahala ni radja* are to be found in some external favourable circumstances; in special traits of a person's character, or in remarkable qualities of which the most important are the following, though not necessarily in this order:

habolonan = largeness, which refers to the large number of members in the lineage of the chief concerned, resulting from the existence therein of men with large families stemming from grandparents and great-grandparents who were richly blessed with sons. Such an extensive lineage is the source of the greatness which formerly could possibly lead to a chief being accepted as paramount chief not only by his own group, but also by other smaller segments of the *marga* branch;

hamoraan = wealth, is also an important source of authority. It reveals a successful life in which the luck of the game, success in arms, prosperity in trade and good fortune in the cultivation of rice and in the rearing of cattle have co-operated in providing great material benefits. It gives a person power within his environment: formerly one could engage in a war of long duration on the strength of it and, then as now, it provided the power to pay a higher marriage payment for a young daughter and thereby obtain influential affines. It also gave one the power to hold a debtor in one's hands, etc.

The main manifestation of *hamoraan*, however, is *panggalangon* or *partamueon* = hospitality, of which the liberality is an expression of the degree to which a chief has the genuine chiefly qualities. Such hospitality is no demonstration of benevolence towards the poor, *na pogos*, or the wretched, *na dangol*, but a public demonstration of one's wealth, a fulfilment of the obligations by one who has acquired honour and respect. It is 'liberality' with which is associated a blessing for host and guest alike: stinginess is not commendable; liberality is praiseworthy.

habisuhon = sagacity, or *parpollungon* = the art of disputation. A person in whom these qualities are natural is likewise thought to possess the true nature of a chief. He will be a *partahi-tahi* = a diplomat, a person who has many-sided relationships with the outside world, or a *parhata-hata* = one who shows himself to be a sagacious speaker in matters of law, a person to whom people will readily submit their affairs under dispute. Formerly such a shrewd chief made alliances for offence and defence;

habeguon = courage in war and firmness towards subordinates, qualities which naturally strengthened one's personal authority;

hadatuon = skill in the science of the *datu*, which could sometimes be found in a *radja*.

Formerly, if a person possessed these qualities, it signified that he had the qualifications to govern. Such prominent chiefs were among those the first Government administrators and the missionaries came to know. The *sahala ni radja* dwelling in them was the source of their success, and this in its turn was the manifestation of it. It was 'power' in the person who possessed it and its expression was in his behaviour and the results of his advice. If it was attached to one's 'house' it could pass to one's descendants. It provided the authority indispensable for the maintenance of order and peace, for the observance of judicial decisions, for obtaining the assistance and co-operation of dependents against the outside world. It contributed to increasing the prosperity of the people as much by words as deeds. An area with a powerful chief prospered. Theoretically the development of a strong personal authority over large groups belonging together could have come about had it not been for the vigorous, ambitious and obstinate character of the people and the crowding together of people who were blood kinsmen: they are like trees that are too close together, they rub against each other, as the saying goes.

And indeed, almost every region has known periods in which powerful and still renowned *radja* have exercised a wide-ranging authority. But in this play of power and counterpower only the mightiest and most capable personalities could assert themselves and maintain their position for a long time.

The status of this type of chieftainship in the old society is well delineated in the exordium of a description of law compiled by Panggading, the well known *radja paidua* of Sisoding (Simamora), a chief in a region where a well-grounded *haradjaon* existed. It is a rather pathetic exordium abounding in set terms. In general it demonstrates how authority is a source of prosperity and law; indicates the all-embracing nature of the chieftainship and can be applied equally to an influential and authoritative village head and to the higher chiefs of a territory.

Ditompa Debatá djolma mangaradjai uhum,
God created men to control the administration of justice;

ditompa Debatá do uhum mangaradjai adat,
God created the administration of justice to control the law (*adat*);

ditompa Debatá do radja, mangaradjai luat,
God created the *radja* to have dominion over the country;

asa radja i ma nampuna adat dohot uhum,
the *radja* is, therefore, the controller of the law (*adat*) and of the administration of justice;

mangaradjai angka na metmet dohot na magodang lahi-lahi dohot boru-boru,
in order that he may rule over the small and the great, men and women.

Asa radja i ma parmahan so tumiop batahi, pamuro so tumiop sior,
The *radja* is thus the herdsman who carries no whip, the watchman in
the fields who has no need of a bow to drive away the birds,

mangaramothon saluhut na di gomgomanna,
the one who cares for everything in the sphere of his administration;

sigarar utang situnggu singir di na balga dohot di na metmet,
the one who pays debts, and who receives the claims of great and small;

manguhumi siuhumon,
the one who passes judgement on what has to be judged;

*Radja i ma sipungka solup, sitiop batuan na so ra teleng, hatian so
bonaron, mula ni hata na sintong,*
It is the *radja* who establishes the rice-measure, who holds the scales
that do not tilt, the balance which does not need to be tested, the
beginning of righteousness;

*na manogihon halak tu panggagatan na lomak, na manarihon hangoluan
ni angka ginomgoman,*
he leads his people to fertile pastures, he cares for the well-being of his
dependents;

Marsoban parsoban pe, parsoban ni radja,
When the woodcutter seeks firewood he is the woodcutter of the *radja*
(were there not one he would not be successful);

mandurung pandurung, pandurung ni radja,
when the fisherman catches fish, he is the fisherman of the *radja*;

mallandja pallandja, pallandja ni radja,
when the carrier bears his load, he is the carrier of the *radja*;

maronan paronan, paronan ni radja,
when the marketeer goes to market, he is the marketeer of the *radja*;

paruma pe, paruma ni radja,
the tiller of the soil is the cultivator of the *radja*;

mangula pangula, pangula ni radja,
when the craftsman uses his tools, he is the craftsman of the *radja*;

saluhutna i pandapotan tu radja,
all these things are dependent upon the *radja*;

*Asa ndang tinanda hau so ingkon sian parbuena, ndang tinanda radja
na maló, so ingkon sian pambahenna,*

Were it not for the fruit one would not recognise the tree; were it not for his acts one would not recognise a *radja*;

Timbó buluna, balgá hutana,
His bamboos are high, his *huta* is large;

gabe parripena maduma dohót ibana,
if his subordinates prosper, he too will prosper;

sinur pinahanna, gabe niulana,
his cattle will multiply, his labour will be fruitful;

Borngin dohot arian ndang nok matana manarihon uhum dohot adat di angka ginomgomna, pasari-sari panganonna asa adóng hangoluanna, he does not close his eyes night or day because he looks after the laws and customs of his dependents and their welfare.

If one compares this past attitude to a chief and the present day situation it is hardly surprising that the chiefs complain of the whittling away of their status and of their lost greatness, and that even in the highest rank they scarcely feel themselves to be more than *radja panonga* = a *radja* of the medium sort. Today appointment and dismissal are arbitrarily effected, a new, apparently all-powerful, *sahala* has come into existence, that of the Native Administration, an Administration which, despite its instructions to see that the chiefs' authority is upheld, strives itself after the much desired *hasangapon*.

Much that was done to undermine the chiefs' authority was unavoidable, but much was also done that could have been done differently. It is true that the Batak, both the people and the chiefs, with their mutual jealousies, their eternal quarrelling and their selfishness, are also guilty of the decay of the chiefs' position. But the officials, although they showed real zeal to develop the country economically, should have shown a greater appreciation of the social system in which the now so badly crippled chieftainship is rooted, and for customary law, *adat*, from which the life of the community mainly draws its sustenance.

Customary law has been subjected to disruptive tendencies and to the various pressures of modern times, so that it is less than ever in a position to be deprived of the regular care and attention which it needs. In olden times this responsibility devolved on the chiefs: they were the supporters of customary law, they were the upholders of the law, *siramoti adat do radja, siramoti ugari.* Each of them, from the *huta* chief upward, had a specific task in this respect within his own group in which customary law was "the customary law of our grandfathers, the glory of our fathers, *adat ni ompunta, sahala ni amanta*." Such a group, however limited, is always a corporate group in which the law obtains its life and form. It is these communities, therefore, which have to absorb the tensions to which the law is exposed by modern life. They have to effect the co-ordination between the new demands of modern life and the forms which have grown during a long period of time.

In these communities this law is withering through neglect and through the breaking down of the chiefs' authority instead of developing, and it is becoming disassociated from the life of the people which, as a result, is exposed to the dangers of disintegration.

Customary law can only continue to be what it should be, a firm base for preserving the unity of society, by a well-guided administration of the law by the chiefs.

CHAPTER IV

SOME GENERAL OBSERVATIONS

Before dealing in detail with the principal parts of civil- and penal law, brief consideration will be given to some general principles and phenomena that are significant in a wide field and thus can throw some initial light on subsequent chapters.

LEGAL MAXIMS, UMPAMA

Umpama are set expressions noteworthy for the frequency with which they are used and for their rather striking form. When they embody a legal concept they can be regarded as a kind of legal maxim.

Though they do not have the normative character of sections of a code, many of them, nevertheless, have become an established legal form since a definite concept of law has been crystallised in them. These *umpama* are known and used everywhere as far as the south of Tapanuli: people apply them in the same circumstances and with the same meaning. They can be considered to be more or less fixed points in an otherwise very mobile whole.

Many *umpama* express what is more or less popular wisdom, but the juridical purport of many of them is greater that one would suppose at first sight. One cannot, therefore, simply divide *umpama* into those which are juridical in content and those which are not, for they are couched in such a form that it scarcely if at all allows one immediately to perceive their legal purport and it is only when they are used on the appropriate occasion that they are judicially efficacious. To give an example:

molo metmet binanga, na metmet do dengke,
molo godang binanga, godang dengke;
If the stream is small, then the fish will be small.
If the stream is big, then the fish will be big.

This maxim expounds the principle that the reward of those who have actively concerned themselves in a legal affair must be proportionate to the importance of the matter at issue. As far as I know, the application of this maxim is confined to the sphere of customary law.

Sometimes *umpama* are moulded in the form of a comparison, but this is not particularly conducive to their intelligibility or to the stability of the interpretation. There are also maxims in circulation which say so little that the most diverse interpretations are given. I quote an example of such an *umpama* to draw attention to the fact that there is much chaff among the grain:

> *martuktuk tao, marbanggua dolok*;

of which the literal translation is, promontories jut out into the lake, *banggua* grass grows on the mountains. This maxim is often used and in a variety of contexts in judgements given by the native courts. I found that it means: a right of refuge (for example in a church or in a field where many women are working); that one may not encroach on the rights of a man who is regarded as the general representative and leader, *suhut,* of a group; a prohibition against embarrassing a respected man in public and, with the addition of, *ndang djadi margabus* = one must not lie, a threat against swearing a false oath. The meaning of this *umpama* is simply that things and people can be out of the ordinary and that this must be taken into consideration. It is, therefore, a maxim that is so vague as to have scarcely any practical value.

It is possible that its meaning has become uncertain because it is the remembered first half of a longer maxim now forgotten but which was originally couched in the usual twinrule verse form. In this form the contents of the first rule are meaningless or have little meaning, only the second rule contains the kernel, cp. the *umpama* quoted in Chapters I and II. The function of the first rule is to provide a euphonious introduction which ends with a word that rhymes with the last word of the second rule. If such a maxim is one that makes an impact on the ear, then it is often sufficient to quote only the first rule in order to evoke the meaning of the whole. This usage can result in the first rule acquiring eventually a life of its own as an independent form, or it may become the introduction to more than one aphorism. In fact, many maxims are used with minor variations either in the rule containing the rhyme or in the rule containing the kernel, or in both. In most cases, however, this does not alter the purport and the deviations should be regarded as slight local variants, or admissible licence.

The examples given throughout this work should not necessarily be regarded as being the only ones used in a given circumstance, or those most commonly used. Variants will only be given in the course of this work if there is a particular reason for doing so.

The use of maxims is undoubtedly connected with the need to give

impressiveness and authority by the spoken word to principles which
have been handed down and that are generally acknowledged and by
which the life of the community must be guided if that life is to be
good. As solemn addresses are readily interlarded with set expressions to
enhance their impact, so legal concepts also gain a normative efficacy
when they are couched in the established and well-sounding form which
gives them the desired solemnity. If a well-known maxim is used at the
right time when a complaint is made, when advice is given, or when a
judgement is pronounced, it emphasises the gravity and importance of
the affair in question. If, for example, an appeal is being made to some
old and acknowledged rule or institution, then, in place of the simple
words, *i do adat* = this is *adat*, use will be made instead of the ceremonial words, *tona ni ompunta do i, tona ni amanta* = it is the command of our grandfathers; it is the command of our fathers.

If it is necessary to draw attention to an existing prohibition that may
on no account be infringed then, instead of the everyday language, the
following maxim will be used:

gandjang abor ndang djadi suruhon,
djempek abor ndang djadi langkaan;
Although the sign saying "forbidden" is high, one may not crawl
beneath it.
Although it is low, one may not step over it.

This maxim has the same support as "no admittance" in Western communities.

If an alliance or a contract is concluded and it is intended to be
permanent and binding, then an *umpama* with an appropriate comparison will be used:

taluktuk na so ra mumpat, pago na so ra morot;
[The terms of the contract are] poles which cannot be pulled up,
boundary posts which cannot be removed.

This stresses the importance of the contract and imprints it firmly on
the mind.

When a case has been settled and if one of the contestants still feels
so aggrieved that he endeavours to rake it up, then the judge may
address him as follows:

ndang tarungkap batang batu,
ndang tarharhar pudun mate;
A stone chest cannot be unlocked.
A knot that has been tied cannot be undone.

The force of this maxim is not only in the graphic use of metaphor but also in its melodious cadence, a fact that even anyone who is ignorant of the Batak language cannot fail to notice. In the *umpama,* the euphony, which is of itself a bearer of great good, is so important that the lack of it can quickly stamp a spoken maxim as a creation of the person uttering it, or as a degeneration of a genuine one. The defective *umpama* of more recent times can be attributed to the decline of the knowledge of the legal rules to which the *umpama* apply as well as to lack of conversancy with the original legal maxims themselves.

In Chapter II I discussed the magical power of words, but the conclusion should not be drawn from this that the use of the appropriate *umpama* in a lawsuit will of itself produce a decisive result. The Batak do not attribute such a force to it. The right legal maxim can sometimes bring disputants together if they have not quarrelled too violently and if they are susceptible to good advice, but if each stands on his rights, or if one has provoked the other with evasions, false pretences, or sophistry, *sidalian,* then an *umpama* of itself will not repair the breach.

Both the law and the maxims used to express it have reached a relatively advanced stage of development, a fact that must be ascribed to the frequency with which the Batak quarrel among themselves, as well as to their obstinacy. Their society produces a great many cunning rhetoricians, sagacious advocates and astute perverters of justice whose one desire in a lawsuit is to catch out an opponent who may not know the rules of the law and the relevant *umpama* sufficiently well. The maxim applicable in such a case states this with relentless candour:

> *idjuk di para-para, hotang di parlabean,*
> *na bisuk nampuna hata, na oto tu pargadisan;*
> The *idjuk* on the grid above the fire, the rattan hanging from the high place;
> The cunning one wins the lawsuit, the stupid one (the loser) goes to the place where the slaves are sold.

These *pangansi* = cheats and *panggunturi* = provokers of quarrels do not, however, get off scot-free according to Batak ideas. A hell has been created for them where they importune each other day and night by pressing for payment of their debts. This is their punishment for the trouble they have caused their fellow men in the mortal world.

THE IMMUTABILITY OF TRADITIONAL LAW

One of the basic principles of traditional law is that it is immutable. The law is conceived as being "the customs of the ancestors who were first born into the world, the *sahala* of the ancestors, *adat ni ompunta na djumolo tubu, sahala ni amanta.*" A concept that extols the intelligence of the forefathers who formulated the law and which supports its authority. It postulates that the law derives a certain sanctity from the fact that it originated at the time when the ancestors lived and this enhances its binding character.

This unchangeability of customary law is expressed in the following *umpama*:

martagan sipiltihon, maransimun so bolaon,

adat ni ama dohot ompu tongka pauba-ubaon;

A thing that is small like a gherkin must be dispersed.

A thing that is like a cucumber cannot be split.

The customary law of the fathers and forefathers should not be altered.

This principle is no longer operative, but in olden times people adhered to it, though they were conscious that its application was relative. That it applied in a somewhat small circle was brought home to them when they visited the great markets where people from all points of the compass gathered, or in intercourse with distant affines for, although their origin was the same, it was apparent that the law had pursued an individual and distinct course in the different areas. This divergence was particularly noticeable in respect of matrimonial and land laws, though it was also evident in matters such as slavery, loot, etc. The following *umpama* makes allowances for these variations:

muba tano muba duhut-duhutna,

muba luat muba uhumna;

A different soil, a different grass.

A different region, a different law.

Local deviations in the law have even led to a rule of intercommunal law:

disi tano niinganhon, disi solup pinarsuhathon,

A man receives rice according to the measure common to the area in which he lives, i.e. a man is subject to the law of the area in which he lives.

INTER-COMMUNAL LAW

Although there is only this rule of intercommunal law, as far as I know, it cannot be interpreted in an absolute sense: land remains under the jurisdiction of the law of the area in which it lies irrespective of where the rightful owners live. For example if a man from Samosir marries a girl from Toba and receives from his father-in-law as a *pauseang*-gift a wet rice-field which is in Toba, the law of land tenure of Samosir does not apply to it; if a man who lives in Silindung goes to the Dairi Country to lay out coffee gardens and leaves his wet fields and dry land in the charge of his *uaris* in Silindung, then his relation to this land is governed by the law obtaining in Silindung. The rule of inter-communal law does also not apply strictly in other fields, because a man who leaves his village or the place of his birth wants to continue the association with the area of his origin. A man who belongs to the lineage of the founder of a village in which he himself was born, wants to be kept informed of the important affairs concerning the village, even though he may be absent from the village for a long or a short time due to his office, calling or for other reasons, since he expects to return in due course. If a Batak departmental clerk and a Batak trained nurse go to the register office in Batavia [now Djakarta] to get married, then both their families living in the area where the couple were born will assemble with their kin at the *marundjuk* at which the ceremonial transfer of the marriage payment takes place. This makes the marriage definite for them. And so on. The rule is, therefore, not operative much beyond the relationships of everyday intercourse. It is one of the tasks of a judge to determine how far the rule is applicable in the cases which come before him and if possible to define the recognised deviations.

THE LAW AND CONTRACTS

The principle of the immutability of the law is also modified by agreements since it is possible to depart from it:

togú urat ni bulu, toguán urat ni padang,

togú pe na nidók ni uhum, toguán na nidók ni padan;

The roots of the bamboo are strong but the roots of grass are stronger.

The precepts of the law are powerful but the contents of an agreement have more force.

The rule in this maxim seems to provide an unlimited right to deviate from the relevant law when entering a contract. This principle is, however, limited by the inviolability of the rights of third parties and by the strict prohibition quoted on p. 139. To give just one example: a marriage which is considered to be incestuous will be unlawful and must be dissolved.

The purpose of the rule is not to promote uncertainty but, nevertheless, the tendency to depart from the rules can be pursued to the point where it endangers the general stability of the law. Repeatedly one encounters relations in a rather limited circle which are singular to it and that have come into being by mutual agreement, *sian dos ni roha,* by the magnanimity of one of the parties concerned, *sian denggan ni roha,* or as a result of former wars etc. Such particular relationships are often created when new affinity links are started or old ones renewed, since these frequently result from or lead to firm alliances or friendship between persons or groups which then search for a particular form to express the strength of their relationship. The regular living together of kinsmen and affines also leads often to relations that deviate from the common pattern.

In Silindung, for example, it is a general rule that the right of usufruct that a *parripe* (someone from an in-dwelling *marga*) has to land given to him by the village in which he is an in-dweller, is lost to him as soon as he leaves the village. One does, however, often find that a *parripe* who has moved to a neighbouring village is allowed the continued use of this land because the village chiefs are mutual friends or are of the same lineage, or because the reason for his departure is dictated by ill fortune, *sori ni arina,* and it is not his own wish, or because he only intends to be absent for a short time. And there can be, of course, many other reasons.

The most noteworthy example that I know of the desire to deviate from the existing law is the following: shortly after the establishment of Dutch authority in Silindung and parts of Humbáng and Toba a decree was promulgated that legal claims could no longer be made in respect of contracts concluded before the sensational battle of Tangga Batu in 1883. The salutary purport of this "limitation" rule was recognised by all and such claims as date from the *Pidari* time are always rejected by a judge. However, some of the groups of the Tampubolon and Pandjaitan *marga* (from the Pohan tribal group) living in the neighbourhood of Pangaribuan agreed mutually that this decree should be ignored.

DIFFICULTIES OF INVESTIGATING THE LAW

This freedom to establish particular legal relationships in a wider or a narrower context does hinder considerably any investigation into the contents of the operative law. The investigator who tries to learn and to observe how the law operates and according to what rules the judges are guided in their decisions, often comes across deviations which are actually practised.

One sometimes cannot escape the impression that, according to popular feeling on the matter, there is little need for a precise legal system. And it is almost impossible to get a clear and understandable reply to many a concrete question. One thinks one has been given the correct answer only to find that, in fact, it can also be otherwise. One tries to find the common element in all these variations and encounters either a particularly cordial relationship, or a special custom in a small group, or a very old basis of living together, or a recent arrangement. One traces the relations of people who are strangers to each other with the object of determining a basic rule and finds that certain relationships do not occur between them or, if they do exist, one finds that the formula one has worked out from what one has discovered cannot be applied generally, or that its principles have been modified in so many ways. Then one can only indicate an outer framework, a sphere within which life is enacted in different manners. Here one can so easily be led on the wrong track by a stray question, a sole observation, a chance sample taken at random. One consequence of this is that the terminology I use will sometimes be found to be vague as well as variable, and that it will appear that I have sometimes deliberately blurred a definition which I have previously formulated.

APPARENT STABILITY OF THE LAW

From the manner in which the Batak talks about his customary law and from the delight and readiness with which he always appeals to it when he thinks he is a wronged man, one would not imagine that it is in any way vague. That the Batak regards his customary law as being stable and having coercive force is shown by the term he uses to define it: it is *patik* = the fixed rule, to which term he readily adds the word *hot* = firm, unchangeable; *patik na hot* therefore means the fixed unchangeable rule. Usually the law is regarded as that established by one's own chiefs, *na pinatikhon ni radja,* but this does not alter its significance: as the law that must be observed, rather the contrary. The Batak also applies the word *uhum*, administration of justice, legal usage, the law enforced by a judge, and thereby emphasises its obligatory nature and its maintenance by sanctions. The word *saksi,* popular in Hurlang and West Humbáng, has the same meaning. Van der Tuuk, who obtained his material mainly from this area, renders *saksi* as "regulations, ordinances which must be adhered to". Here one must also bear in mind specific declarations: there are *saksi ni onan* = the rules for the peace of the market, which are promulgated when a new market is inaugurated; *saksi ni djudji* = the rules to be applied at an organised gambling party. But the *ompu ni saksi* = the chief of the central territory and the *ama ni saksi* = the chief of a lineage or *marga* branch, are also the upholders of the law in its entirety.

SLACKNESS IN LEGAL PROCEEDINGS

Despite the concept of the law as something that is immutable and binding and as something which must be observed, and the sanctity with which the institutions of the ancestors are clothed, the Batak has not failed to obscure its concrete form by his many everyday legal transactions. And, in addition, the position is further aggravated by an unpardonable slovenliness in the execution of a great number of legal matters which are a common feature of Batak life. The legal forms are many and they are sound, but their observance often leaves everything to be desired. As a consequence much that cannot really be dispensed with is steadily worn away. For instance, if a rice-field is to be pledged then the pledger should set foot on the land, *mandegehon*, with the pledgee and the boundaries should be defined in the presence of the owners or users of adjoining land, and the village chief should be informed. In practice, however, it happens that the pledgee has not seen the land, and has given it out on a sharecropping basis or he has re-pledged it though he is ignorant of the boundaries or does not know who cultivates the surrounding fields, and no village chief has been notified of the transaction or consulted about it. Another example: an entire group will sometimes have prolonged deliberations over a matter and will finally come to a decision, whereafter one among them who is competent to do so draws up a document and then everyone neatly signs with a pen or with the top of his thumb. Later, however, if a quarrel arises concerning the transaction it becomes apparent that the document has been drawn up in a slovenly manner and that no one knows precisely what had been agreed. In Toba there are many lawsuits as to whether a transfer of land is permanent, *sipate-pate*, or only temporary, despite the fact that the permanent transfer of land is termed *manggabehon* and that the good fortune-bringing wish, *gabe*, is only expressed at the permanent transfer of land. This is rather surprising against the endless stream of cases that come before the judges. But an explanation for this situation can be found in the character of the people. If the relationship between the parties is a good one, then they are prone to be trusting and to think that no point of contention will arise. But, as so often happens, sentiments later change and friendliness turns to hatred and the former negligence

10

then takes its toll. The weapons of mutual quarrelling are forged by carelessly executed transactions, as the following *umpama* explains:

> *mangkuling taguk-taguk diatas ni arirang,*
> *hungkús nambura saut, bauan nambura sirang;*
> The *taguk-taguk* bird sings on the flower clusters of the palm tree.
> What has just been done has a pleasant smell.
> What has just been broken off stinks badly.

It would seem that people never learn from experience. A contributory factor may also be the old manner of conducting a lawsuit when not much weight was attached to furnishing reliable evidence. The matter was often settled by ordeal and the oath.

When a legal act is executed in which all the relevant forms have been duly observed, so that there is no doubt as to its character, completeness and validity, it is said to be *toráng* = clear, or *tangkás* = clear cut. Thus, when a widow has been returned to her *hula-hula* by her late husband's kinsmen, and when they have accepted the *patilaho* = small sum of money, which indicates that she is free to marry again and which will be deducted in the event of the payment for her dissolved marriage having to be refunded, it is said that she has been returned with due observance of all forms, *tangkás mulak*. If a case which has already been settled according to the requisite forms is brought up again, it can be said of it that it has been dealt with already in the prescribed form, *toráng ditimbang*. A transaction effected at a *sipanganon* = ceremonial meal, is said to have been *toráng dipangan* = clearly eaten, i.e., the parties knew what they were doing, if a dispute later arises.

The term *toráng* is not, however, quite a safeguard. It can be used incorrectly. There is an example in a *hundulan* judgement of a piece of land being transferred from one party to another according to all forms, *toráng dilehon,* when, in fact, the one party had pledging the land in mind whereas the other intended to surrender it with the right of usufruct. Both these forms of land transfer are different and each has its own appropriate term.

The following case which came before a *hundulan* court on Samosir deserves mention: a piece of land has passed from one party to another apparently *toráng dilehon,* but, in fact, the man who transferred it was not familiar with it. Thus no proper alignment of the boundaries had been made and the neighbouring owners had not been summoned. This did not worry the recipient until he saw the plot of land which he had thought had become his being worked by another man. Without more ado, he proceeded to sow it himself despite the warning of the cultivator.

He was duly fined for resorting to force instead of to the law, *padjolo gogo papudi uhum*. What, however, is noteworthy in this case, is that the man who transferred the land did not escape a measure of discipline. He was the one who had provoked the *gulut* = dispute, and the *guntur* = disturbance, because of his carelessness when he effected the transaction. He, too, was fined. And had the judge felt it necessary to quote an *umpama* he would have had recourse to the following:

> *talaktak siugari,*
> *ibana mambahen, ibana manggurgari (gunturi);*
> The small *talaktak* bird, the small *siugari* bird.
> He did it, he was the creator of the disturbance;

which maxim is used to put the blame fairly and squarely on the culprit in various cases of this kind. The Batak tendency to be careless, neglectful, obstinate and rough does, indeed, demand of a Batak judge a firm hand. This he is well known to have and he can be trusted to use it where necessary.

The stability and coercive force of the law will be assisted more by stringent judicial control over the proper observance of the existing and known legal forms, which no regulated society can dispense with, than by the introduction of new measures.

But here again there are limits. Two aspects of Batak society, the closed kinship groups on the one hand and the extensive affinity relationships on the other, always stand in the way of regular and stringent maintenance of the rules of law by a rigid system, since each makes peculiar demands when disputes have to be dealt with. In this respect, the affines have been discussed in Chapter I. The following remarks, therefore, relate to the special features of the law which play their part within the kinship groups.

THE LAW WITHIN THE KINSHIP GROUP

There is naturally no place for a "Kampf ums Recht" within the small group of the immediate family, *saripe*, or of brothers' families. The rule that obtains there first and foremost, is that one expressed by a *hundulan* court: "May everyone prosper". This is the *adat parsaripeon* = the rule that must be observed between members of a family. It is a rule that prevents a sharp delineation of the law obtaining within this group. When quarrels break out between brothers and are vigorously pursued — no unusual circumstance, especially in Toba where manners are uncouth — the judge, as well as the mediating affines, seek

in the first instance a solution which will heal the breach and restore
the disturbed harmony, and only if neither of the parties will budge an
inch will a decision be made according to the strict rules of law. These
integrating factors also play a role in the wider kinship circle around
the families, but to a lesser degree.

Disputes are the order of the day where people daily associate with
each other in a village or in a cluster of villages, the more so where they
are generally of the same social status and belong to one smaller or
larger descent group. Where the question at issue involves the maintenance of the internal relationships in the bosom of the kinship group,
an affronted person always stands his ground in the matter of his rights.
On this point he will tolerate neither negligence in observing them nor
a deliberate failure to do so, since such tolerance on his part is not
consistent with the importance associated with having a fixed place in
a genealogical group: this he must defend and maintain.

I will give one or two actual instances as examples: a man married
off his son to the widow of his nephew even though there was an elder
brother of the deceased to make arrangements for her and a younger
brother who could marry her in levirate, *manghabia*. The uncle was
punished because he had set aside the rights of a kinsman, *mangapus
uhum tu dongan-sabutuha*. Another man made it known in a village
adjoining his own, by beating the gongs, that on the following day
the ceremony of receiving the marriage payment for his daughter,
mangan djuhut tuhor ni boru, would take place. He was punished for
not observing the appropriate law: a couple of close kinsmen lived in
that village and they were entitled to a formal invitation, *gokhon*. A
man went to live outside the district in which he was born leaving his
land in the custody of his *uaris*. However, a more distant kinsman
persuaded the man to transfer the custody of the land to him. The
uaris lodged a complaint to the judge who ruled that the land had to
remain in his custody. Such judgements distinguish the difference in the
relationships and interests within the kinship group.

Whenever acts, legal or otherwise, which have arisen out of general
social intercourse, have led to a dispute between members of one group,
the importance of safeguarding its unity, the clan spirit and the feelings
of affection which bind kinsmen, will, if need be, play a more or less
important role. These factors are nowadays less influential than they
were in the *Pidari* time when a group so often had to maintain itself
against neighbouring groups by force of arms, artifice, eloquence and
persuasion. Then, solidarity took precedence over individual self-interest.

Nevertheless, even today, great importance is attached to good and peaceful understanding within a kinship group, and to avoiding the dissension that arises when matters are forced to a head. Were these factors not operative, living together in a village or cluster of villages would be unbearable and the efficacy of many ceremonial occasions when the genealogical group assemble, would be at a discount because of the prevailing unrest. No matter what happens to create discord there is always a force operating for the restoration of harmony. As the maxim rightly says:

tampulon aek do bada ni na marsaripe;

Quarrels between close kinsmen are as the cleaving of the waters. The judge, knowing this, pronounces a settlement which is a compromise and the parties are quickly mollified because:

pulik dabuon djala, pulik dabuon doran,
pulik do oloan halak, pulik oloan dongan;

One must spread a casting-net on a different way from a drag-net. One settles matters one way with strangers; one settles matters another way among one's own.

Kinship connections can no more be obliterated than the tiger's stripes or the juice be separated from a grain of rice, or, in less picturesque language:

ndang targotap pusuk, ndang tartostos parsabutuhaon;

A palm leaf that has not uncurled cannot be snapped off, kinship ties cannot be severed.

A kinship group is *sisada sinamot* = one in prosperity, and arbitrary withdrawal from it would be disadvantageous. One's lineage members are one's *dongan masiteanan* = those from whom one may inherit, or those who may be one's heirs. They are also one's *dongan masihabiaan* = those from among whom one may marry a widow in levirate, or those who may marry one's own widow. And so often people are each other's partners *marripe-ripe*, in everything that is communally owned and undivided, *ripe-ripe*, within the smaller or larger lineage, such as a *haradjaon* = chieftainship, a complex of dry lands, a previously occupied but abandoned village, *lobu*, a consecrated horse, *hoda Debatá* or *hoda miahan*, an irrigation canal, a venerated tree, a sacred spring = *homban*, etc.,

Naturally, the tendency to leniency is not always present, were it so then most of the quarrels among kinsmen could be nipped in the bud. In fact, there is always a dispute of one kind or another either slumbering or active within the circle of relatives. But when the tensions run high, if a felicitous endeavour at mediation can be made, if a wise man can find just the right phrase, or if people begin to tire of the dispute, then the moment often comes when propositions and arguments lose their force and a solution can be reached and accepted which is more in accord with the special relations involved than with the strict rules of positive law. I recollect more than one case in which a dispute, which had kept a small kinship group split in half for a long time, was settled satisfactorily by the judge. The parties then assembled at a communal meal to smooth out the remaining points of contention, since:

> gala-gala na sabotohon,
> molo tubu bada aha na so boi dohonon;
> A gala-gala branch as thick as an arm.
> Once there is a quarrel so many things are blurted out.

If the inclination to refind concord could not truly be presumed to exist among those concerned — if each party insisted in standing on his rights — then their partaking of a mixed meal, *mangan indahan sinaor*, mentioned in Chapter II, which is often ordered by a judge when there has been a quarrel among a group of agnates, would be a meaningless performance. This desire to re-establish harmony can even cause a territory of more than a thousand people suddenly to throw all its internal disputes of many years standing onto the heap and trample them beneath their dancing feet at an appropriate ceremony. A striking example of this will be found in Appendix II in respect of the restoration of harmony in the *marga* Silitonga.

DEVELOPMENT OF THE LAW

It is clear that no speedy development of the law can be expected in view of much of the foregoing. Any growth of the law that might follow in the wake of modern conditions will be limited either in sharpness of outline or in its sphere of operation by the ambiguity of Batak society. If the law is to operate universally it must be sufficiently broad as to admit of its application in varying circumstances. If it is to be sharply defined, then there must be latitude for deviations. As Batak law stands at present, both the law and its enforcement fluctuates between the two extremes of rather strict enforcement and deviations resulting from feelings of unity, respect, love and mutual confidence. It is a difficult fact that modern relationships have increased rather than decreased the existing contrasts: expanded them rather than limited them. In olden times, when people rarely moved outside the small closed groups of kinsmen, territory, *bius*, etc., and when they periodically gathered only for specific purposes in the great markets where the peace of the market was guaranteed, a certain balance was maintained between and due consideration given to the two spheres, i.e., between those who were mutually related and between those who were strangers. Where satisfaction could not be given, it was probably because the sentence for an offence had to be held in abeyance as a result of a war with the clan of the perpetrator; because the judge who had to settle the dispute could not be impartial in respect of those who were most closely related to him; or because he was corruptible, for reasons, therefore, which were not dependent upon the law itself but on the judges. However, the opening up of the country and the consequent freedom of intercourse guaranteed by the peaceful conditions obtaining everywhere, has been conducive to creating many-sided relationships, to a degree hitherto not possible, between people who are strangers to each other. As a consequence, the balance between what could and what could not happen in a closed circle has been upset and the contrast between the two aspects of the law has been increased. The tendency to individualise would undoubtedly be promoted were large towns built, were the ties which bind a person to his land to be dissolved, or if there were other powerfully operating factors which dictated that people had to live together with people other than their own kinsfolk. But, none of these factors is present. On the contrary, there is still a strong attachment to one's native soil and village. This is so marked that it offers strong resistance to the individualising process and will contribute to a prolonged continuance of the interaction of the two spheres. Like many another situation, it is one that is neither desirable nor intolerable: but it has to be accepted as a fact.

If the administration of justice is localised by being restored to the environment where the conflicts are played out, this will, in my opinion, tend to give the customary law the necessary flexibility and enable the practical answers to the problems facing it at the present time to be found.

THE OLDER HISTORY OF CUSTOMARY LAW

There are only a few written sources to provide us with any information about customary law in the period prior to the ending of the *Pidari* time. The main sources are the *Patik dohot Uhum ni halak Batak,* the *Ruhut Pasaoran di Habatahon* and the *Patik-patik dohot Uhum-uhum ni halak Naipospos,* Dutch translations of which [13] are now

---

[13] *Adatrechtbundel* XXXV.

accessible. Each of these works describes the laws and customs of a particular group at the middle and end of the previous century. There are also some interesting notes on typical legal conduct to be found in the legends and stories about the ancestors of the *marga* and tribal groups related in W. M. Hoeta Galoeng's *Poestaha taringot toe tarombo ni bangso Batak*. However, the times referred to are comparatively recent and therefore the light that is shed on the older law is limited. These stories ascribe the most human acts and words to gods and the sons of gods with the greatest of ease. Such importance as these stories have for a knowledge of the history of the law, is mainly provided by some data referring to the occupation of the areas by the present-day inhabitants and sometimes to the *marga boru* in-dwelling there. It is possible that there may be something of value in the tales of which Dr. P. Voorhoeve has made a survey.[14]

An insight into the general course of the development of Tobanese law can be clarified by a thorough comparison with the laws of Padang Lawas and South Tapanuli as they were in the 19th century (known from the work of Willer and Neumann) [15] and with the law of the Pakpak Country, of which Ypes [16] provides most of the data, and lastly with that of Simelungun, the small Timor kingdoms and the Karo Country which, however, still needs further investigation.

It will become apparent from what follows later that the origin and the explanation of many a present-day legal institution is to be sought in the world of the former magico-religious ideas, about which scholarly investigation has brought so much to light in the course of this century. It is hardly to be doubted that research into this sphere will provide useful material for the study of the older history of Batak customary law. For this purpose the material I present in this work can perhaps serve as a guide, though it must always be remembered that much of it is the result of first observation and still needs to be controlled.

LEGAL TERMINOLOGY

Some idea of the extent of the legal terminology can be gained from the index which, however, is by no means complete.

Here again there is often a lack of sharp definition, due to the

---

[14] Dr. P. Voorhoeve: *Overzicht van de volksverhalen der Bataks,* thesis, Leiden, 1927.
[15] See note 2.
[16] See note 3.

popular inclination to be vague. So often people prefer to use a term which has a wide range of meanings rather than one of which the meaning is precise. There are many legal terms that are rarely used, but which, if used regularly, would ultimately acquire a definite meaning and would thus promote the certainty of the law. To give an example: the terms *ulos* and *piso* denote precisely the gifts and counter-gifts respectively, that go from the *hula-hula* to the *boru* and vice-versa. They do, however, cover a wider field. In the first place they denote all voluntary gifts and counter-gifts given in return for voluntary gifts between affines. Some of these gifts have special names, e.g., *pauseang*, the gift to a married daughter either at the time of her marriage, or shortly afterwards; the *indahan arian,* land given on the birth of a child; the *ragi-ragi,* the counter-present to the bridegroom's father from the bride's father and given when the latter receives the marriage payment for his daughter. These specific terms are not always used on the occasion relevant or when these presents are later discussed, because no need is felt to use them since the reason for giving them is that a close relationship has just been begun or has been renewed and this is generally known. What, however, is bad, is that the terms *ulos* and *piso* are also used in everyday legal intercourse for the transfer of objects of value to far distant relatives, when in fact there are appropriate terms for such transfers which are based on legal transactions of a more general character. For instance, the term *piso ni radja* has become the customary term for all kinds of gifts to which a village chief is entitled. If there is not a demonstrable basis of affinity, these gifts should be defined with their own terms. For example, the gift of homage given to the chief of the bride's village when she marries is called the *upa radja*; the remuneration a chief receives when he has co-operated in settling a dispute or in concluding a contract, is called the *pago-pago*.

The term *piso ni radja* is, in fact, even used when there is no direct affinity relationship between the village chief and the inhabitant who makes the gift, the assumption then being that the man is of the *marga boru* and the chief is, therefore, of his *hula-hula*. And, though these terms like *ulos* and *piso* are technically reserved for gifts between affines, they can also sometimes be used to denote the gifts that are exchanged between agnates. The reason for this incorrect usage seems simply to be that there are no well-defined terms to denote these rarely occurring exchanges.

This lack of precision in the use of words not only applies in kinship relations, which if it so pleases a person can be taken right back to

Si Radja Batak himself; it also applies when legal matters are discussed between persons who are in no way related. For such cases there are precise terms admitting of no alternatives. Indeed, the Batak feel little need to choose exact terms in the numerous circumstances in which the determination of the juridical meaning is necessary. This is surprising, because they are so frequently involved in litigation and, moreover, their language, of which an elaborate vocabulary is at the command of every ordinary man and woman, at least that was my impression, is so rich in words and forms.

The natural consequence of this haphazard use of words has resulted in almost no one term being used to define a fixed and single idea and no one idea being defined by a fixed and single term. In fact, within a more or less limited cadre, many terms and concepts are interchangeable. Due allowance must also be made for genuine misuse of terms because of ignorance or carelessness, such as using *sindor* = pledge placed in the hands of a moneylender, when *singkoram* = security remaining in the hands of the debtor, is meant. This imprecision in the use of terms calls for prudence on the part of the investigator into the laws and customs of the Toba Batak, as does the diversity in local law.

The legal language is, however, by no means lacking in imagination and colour as the following arbitrary handful of examples shows:

parhaisan ni manuk = the point beyond which the chickens may not scratch, i.e., the land surrounding a village and belonging to the village;

hundulan ni boru = the 'seat' for the daughter, i.e., the land surrendered to the bridegroom's father when he betrothes his son to a young girl;

pardjabu talak = she who keeps her house open, i.e., a recently widowed childless woman who wants to have a son as quickly as possible after her husband's death so that she can pass him off as his;

ulos na so ra buruk = the cloth that never wears out, i.e., the land given as a present between affines.

These examples are enough to show that an idea can be picturesquely and clearly expressed in the Batak language and in a form which is of much value to customary law if the link between it and the people is to be kept alive and if the law itself is to have the flexibility necessary for its continued development. The language has such a measure of adaptability that the Batak can accept without hesitation that, in their adaptation of new ways of life to the old and tried legal life, they can use it and give adequate expression to modern legal conceptions. Its root words are a sound foundation upon which to build this modern legal language. With a little imagination they can be turned to account to create descriptive and definitive legal terms that will be preferable to adopting foreign terms that so quickly become garbled in meaning and sound. *Tahan* or *singkoram,* security, are better than the borrowed, and garbled, *borot,* from Dutch "borg" = guarantee, or *ongkos* = hire of goods or loan of money, from the Dutch, "onkosten".

CHAPTER V

MATRIMONIAL LAW

(Adat pardongan-saripeon)

GENERAL CHARACTERISTICS

It is hardly necessary to state here that marriage among the Batak is exogamous. A man does not take his wife from his own agnate group but from another one, and the woman leaves her group and goes over to that of her husband. She continues to bear her *marga* name — a woman from the *marga* Siregar is thus a *boru Regar* even after her marriage, but, as does her husband, she calls her own kinsmen henceforth her *hula-hula* and they similarly regard her as an affine.

Marriage is exclusively patrilineal in purport. Its object is to perpetuate the lineage of the man in the male line. According to the rules of family law, the man continues to belong to his kinship group. Land rights, property, names, offices can only be inherited in the male line. There are no exceptions to this rule among the Toba Batak.

Marriage is a "bride-price" marriage. The woman is released from her group — not just from the small circle of agnates within which she was born — on payment of an agreed amount of money, or the handing over of objects of value. By this means she is withdrawn from the authority of her closest male kinsman who is responsible for arranging her marriage, i.e., her father, or if he is dead, her elder brother, or if he is too young or if she has no brothers, her father's brother, and so on. In this context this kinsman is called the *parboru* = the one who "owns" the daughter. He does not, however, disappear from the scene when the marriage is settled since he takes the woman's affairs in hand again if the marriage does not run smoothly and a judicial decision is required, and possibly also if she is widowed. In respect of her personal position, a woman cannot act with complete independence.

The *parboru*'s opposite is called the *paranak* = the one who arranges the marriage for the young man. Once the marriage has been concluded he disappears into the background.

It will be obvious from the discussion on the affinity relations, that the woman's disengagement from her own kin group on her marriage is not final. She is not dissociated from it either socially or judicially. In fact, she becomes the link which binds the groups of affines permanently to each other. After her marriage the woman, her husband and their children always maintain the particular relationship with the agnatic circle from which she sprang and this is continued with its descendants. And though this mutual relationship is later effected by the men of both groups, the woman, as the ancestress who is the binding link, is honoured by both groups.

THE VARIOUS FORMS OF MARRIAGE

The most usual marriage form is that in which the marriage is preceded by a betrothal. This is entered into either because of parental desire or by the free choice of the young people. The betrothal is followed by discussions concerning the amount of the marriage payment. This is transferred in due course and the marriage is then concluded. In addition, there are, however, the following forms, each of which is of less frequent occurrence:

marriage by abduction — the young man, assisted by some of his comrades, abducts by force a girl whom he desires but who will either not have him, or who is not given to him as quickly as he wishes. He takes her to his dwelling or some other suitable place and satisfies his desires. This act of violence gives the *parboru* the right to demand an increase in the marriage payment as a penalty, and in recent times there has also been a tendency for the Government to mete out punishment.

Besides marriage by abduction, there is marriage consequent upon rape. This is sometimes resorted to in order to force the desired girl to consent to marriage. Rape is mostly, however, committed in the heat of passion. In both cases it can lead to marriage.

marriage by elopement — the young woman departs secretly from the parental home with the young man of her choice. Running away together is usually a reaction to too strong a pressure from the parents for a marriage with a man whom the girl does not desire, or the breakdown of the discussions on the marriage payment because the *parboru* is asking too much;

marriage by 'seduction' — the girl forces herself on the man she wants and surrenders to him with the object of compelling him to marry her or, to force her parents to consent to the marriage;

'living-in' marriage — the young man goes to live in the house of his father-in-law either because his kinsmen are too poor to pay the full

marriage payment required, or because the girl is an only child and her parents do not want to be separated from her. This 'marriage by service to the parents-in-law' is also of a purely patrilineal character;

levirate and widow-remarriage — in this form the widow does not return to her own kinsmen but either marries a near kinsman of her deceased husband, a distant kinsman or a stranger. In the first case no marriage payment is due, in both the latter it is and the *parboru* comes into the picture again;

sister-remarriage — a widower marries his deceased wife's sister: this often happens when the first wife died childless;

bigamy and polygamy — both are resorted to for various reasons, the most usual one being the childlessness of the first wife.

All these marriage forms are dealt with separately later on.

NO ADOPTIVE MARRIAGE

An adoptive marriage, non-patrilineal in its effects, in which a daughter gives birth to issue on behalf of the continuance of her father's lineage, is not known among the Toba Batak, and the word *sumondo,* which in the South of Tapanuli indicates such a marriage, is not indigenous to the Toba Batak Country. The Tobanese term for a kind of adoptive marriage which the Toba Batak practise, i.e., living-in marriage, is *morsonduk hela* = (literally) to ladle out food for a son-in-law, and the son-in-law calls himself *hela sonduhan* = son-in-law for whom food is provided by his parents-in-law. As a matter of fact, a wife in a normal marriage often refers to her husband as *na husonduk* = the one for whom I ladle out food. The details of the *morsonduk hela* form will be dealt with later. Here it should be made clear that the husband continues to belong to his *marga* and maintains normal relations with his kinsmen. His children belong to his kinship group and inherit therein. There is no continuation of the lineage of the parents-in-law in this marriage form.

THE LAWS OF EXOGAMY

There is no uniformity in the application of the rules of exogamy. In the whole northern part of Samosir the *marga* which belong to the Nai Ambaton group are not allowed to intermarry. In 1924 a resolution to abolish the prohibition among the Tambatua *marga* round about Ambarita on North Samosir, was passed at a great gathering of Tambatua chiefs held under the guidance of a Batak district officer. But, although the 'fiat' of the Government had been requested, and had been given, and although nothing stood in the way of its abolition, the position has remained the same. The drawback in this area, which is bathed on three sides by the waters of the lake, is that, apart from the few small Silahisabungan territories, there are not many *boru*-villages, nor are there a sufficient number of persons from the in-dwelling *marga boru*. As a consequence the young girls must stay unmarried for a long time because there are not enough young men to go round. The young men cannot find enough girls in their own area and must seek wives outside it. The result of this situation is a financially unfavourable one since the marriage payment is dependent partly on supply and demand.

A natural restraint on actually breaking the ban of exogamy, *manompas bongbong,* is the fear of arousing the wrath of the ancestral spirits, a fear which was revived by a couple of recent cases of wilful transgression of the prohibition against incest, *marsumbang,* which ended badly for the culprits.

The prevalence of this attitude on northern Samosir is rather surprising when in the adjoining Lontung area in South Samosir, the marriage ban between the four 'head' *marga* of the Lontung group living there has been abolished and they can intermarry, *masiolian* (also called *masibuatan*), which means literally: to take from each other. This process, though initially going in only one direction, sooner or later goes in the reverse direction also and once a start has been made in reversing the kin relationships, *manungsang partuturan,* it then goes both ways. What had been *dongan* becomes *tondong* with the lifting of the ban and what had been *hula-hula* henceforth can also become *boru,* though in the latter case with due observance of a number of forbidden categories which differ locally.

Intermarriage is not only possible between the four 'head' *marga* of the Lontung in South Samosir, but here and there some of the component *marga* can now intermarry, though there is no fixed pattern. For example, in the Hatoguan territory I noted that of the 'head' *marga* Situmorang, which is there represented in its entirety, only the *marga* Lumban Nahór and Siringoringo intermarry, the others do not. Of the 'head' *marga* Sinaga, which is represented by three divisions, only Bonor and Uruk intermarry. The reason for this restriction is not known. Elsewhere the position is different again. In so far as this area is concerned, one cannot say without further clarification that exogamy consists of the prohibition on intermarriage within the (head) *marga.*

In the northern part of Uluan, in the neighbourhood of Sibisa, the

first point of their dispersal, the four *marga* of the Nai Rasaon group
have still not broken the ban, *mardjumbar,* as it is called there, whereas
in the south inter-marriage is permitted everywhere. In the Pohan area
round about Balige, the ban has been abolished in one way; in the
Pohan area in Humbáng in another.

That such different courses have been adopted in this matter can be
attributed to the fact that not every tribal group has felt it necessary
that, in its entirety, it should break the ban. Divisions living separately
from each other have gone their own way. On the other hand, when
a case of a forbidden marriage within the *marga* was under discussion
in 1929 among the members of the *marga* Lumban Tobing, representatives of this *marga* from the Pagarbatu territory in the Sipoholon area
which adjoins the Sihombing area, participated in the deliberations. It
is thus clear that the internal relations within the tribal groups have
developed differently in respect of this question. There is certainly a
basic concept which is generally accepted, but there is no uniformity in
the manner of its operation. It is thus not possible to describe briefly
the rules applicable to the *manompas bongbong,* the method according
to which the decision is reached, and the forms that are observed.

In the Lumban Tobing case just mentioned the emphasis was rather
generally laid on the fact that the lifting of the ban should first be
effected at the top of the genealogical tree: the descendants of Siradja-
djudjur would have to be permitted to marry those of Sariburadja (see
Appendix I) before there was any question of inter-marriage between
the descendants of Sariburadja themselves, which idea took into account
that the genealogical tree is *"mardjodjor martordingan songon tangga
ni balatuk"* (see *umpama* p. 40) and that this regular sequence should
not be broken. It would only seem possible for such a demand to be
made by those *marga* which have continued to live together in a neatly
branched genealogy, not by those *marga* that have been more or less
dispersed. In Silindung this requirement is also related to the fact that
a new *marga* comes into existence with the *manompas bongbong.*
Elsewhere there are other ideas regarding the creation of a new *marga.*

The lifting of the ban can, naturally, be determined at a gathering
of the chiefs without there being a special reason for it. This happened
in Ambarita. In this case, however, it was easy to discern that the
initiative lay with the Batak district officer, since in affairs like this
the people themselves do not, as a rule, instigate such a move if there
is no urgent reason for doing so. The decision was never put into effect
as the official concerned was shortly afterwards transferred. The more

usual practice is that a couple contract a prohibited alliance which provokes action in the matter: they must either be punished and the marriage must be declared null and void, or the marriage must be legalised and a declaration made that henceforth *"marsumbang"* is acceptable. This happened some years ago in the *marga* Panggabean when the *marga* Simorangkir separated from it.

One has, however, to admit regretfully that no particular attention is given to the sporadic instances of unlawful transgression of the ban other than to wait and see what happens. And this is so even though the least punishment that can be imposed on a *na tarboan-boan rohana* = the one who has been carried away by his passions, the one who has committed incest with an *iboto* = sister, member of his own *marga*, the one who has broken the *adat*, is that he will be outlawed, *dipaduru diruar ni patik*, until he has paid the penalty imposed on him. Negligence in this matter must in part be attributed to the fact that the authority of the traditional chiefs and the traditional communities over matters coming within the scope of customary law has been diminished, largely by excessive interference by the European and Native Administration on the one hand, and by the continued lack of interest by those same officials in the proper maintenance of the rules of customary law on the other. A noteworthy case can be put on record in this matter. In the cases just cited of the Tambatua (1924) and the Lumban Tobing (1929), the chiefs concerned thought themselves to be without any kind of authority if the local and provincial administrator had not given his approval. It can be otherwise however, for in 1922, the assembly of chiefs of the *luhak* (*luat*) of Angkola and Sipirok in South Tapanuli had on their own authority punished a *kuria* chief, together with all the *radja adat* of his *kuria*, who had wrongfully approved a transgression of the ban of exogamy prevailing there.

On this point as on many other, regular and conscientious support is needed for the development of the law rather than incidental interference.

With regard to the formalities where a marriage is proposed that conflicts with the existing rules of exogamy, the chiefs and elders of the *marga* or the *marga* divisions concerned must be summoned by the youth's and the girl's kinsmen to a meal for which certainly nothing less than a buffalo must be slaughtered since it is an affair of great importance. After the meal there must be discussions as to whether the marriage can be permitted since it will be the first in the series of breaking the ban. If a prohibited co-habitation regularly occurs, then

11

the chiefs and elders must assemble in order to determine the penalty, *parpauli ni sala*. Here also there is ceremonial and one or more buffaloes must be slaughtered. The chiefs have to decide whether the alliance will be considered lawful or not, and whether it will count as the first in the lifting of the ban, *diolopi radja adat diatas djuhut dohot indahan* = approved by the *adat* chiefs to the accompaniment of a meal. If necessary, the decision will be made as to whether the separated group will be henceforth a separate *marga* and if so under what name. In matters such as these local relationships and opinions will determine which groups have the right to take part in the discussions; whether it will be only the *marga* or *marga* branches concerned or the other *marga* of the tribal group living nearby or elsewhere as well.

If the ban has been lifted, the first thing that the closest relatives of the bride will do is to acknowledge the new relationship: their daughter's husband's small kinship group, which had been *dongan*, has become *tondong* (in this case *boru*). The token, *tanda*, of acceptance of the new connection will be an *ulos* cloth which will be presented by the bride's kinsmen to the bridegroom and his kinsmen from whom they in return will receive the first *piso* gift to be exchanged between them.

There are some instances of exogamy which deserve mention because they have their origin in particular relationships such as, for example, continuous living together in one territory of different *marga* when the rule of exogamy was decided upon as a lasting proof of a brotherly alliance. A case in point is the *marga* Sihite (group Radja Oloan) and the *marga* Simamora (group Toga Sumba-Simamora). In the *bona ni pasogit* = ancestral area, of each of these *marga* there is no objection to inter-marriage though it is forbidden between the parts of these two *marga* which live in the Si Ualu Ompu territory in Silindung. Something similar occurs in a couple of Pohan territories in East Humbáng among fragments of the *marga* Silalahi (group Silahisabungan) which live there. Sometimes the reason is a fortuitous historical event such as that given in W. M. Hoeta Galoeng's *Poestaha* p. 216 where the killing of a wild swine which has a chain round its body, *aili na marrante*, purporting to make the beast invulnerable, plays a role in respect of the *marga* Sitompul and Tampubolon: such a story is also known regarding Huta Barat and Silaban Sitio.

OTHER FORMS OF MARSUMBANG

In addition to the prohibitions relating to groups in their entirety, there are also interdicts applicable to individuals who stand in a special relationship to each other. One very strict ban has already been mentioned: marriage between a man's son and his sister's daughter both of whom regard themselves as brother and sister, *iboto*, as do their parents. It is the reverse of the desired *boru ni tulang* marriage. This latter does not apply exclusively to the daughter of mother's actual brother, since the young girls of the same generation in the larger agnatic circle round the *tulang* are also the *pariban* of his *ibebere*. The just mentioned prohibition in the same way extends to a larger group. As I observed earlier, *marsungsang* is only permitted if for some generations the marriage which was once closed between two groups has not been repeated. It is therefore obvious that a man is prohibited from taking as wife the daughter of his sister, *mambuat ibeberena*, a ban which similarly applies to further classifications in the same category.

Marriage between two brothers and two sisters is also *sumbang*. It is one of the circumstances to which the term *dua pungga sada ihotan =* two whetstones bound by one thong, is applied. This is sometimes related to the address-prohibition which applies to certain relations, for instance, the wife of a younger brother, the *anggi boru,* is not allowed to speak with his elder brother, the *haha doli,* and vice versa. However, a man is always on speaking terms with his wife's sister, his *pariban*. Should his younger brother marry his wife's sister there would be a change in the relationship terminology, *imbar ni partuturan*, which is always to be avoided since it confuses the *partuturan =* addressee-addressor relationship. Not all marriage prohibitions can be explained by these prohibitions on address and their presumed motives since the coincidence of these two factors is not constant. Levirate marriage between a man and the widow of his younger brother is only accepted with reluctance: marriage between a younger brother and the widow of his elder brother is quite normal. This, in all probability, is connected with these prohibitions on address.

Marriage is strictly forbidden between a man and his widowed *bao* — the mutual spouse of brothers and sisters are each other's *bao* between whom there is also an address ban. This does not, however, apply throughout the Toba region. This prohibition is extended to cover a man and his *tulang*'s spouse and a man and the spouse of his *tulang*'s son.

A man is not allowed to marry his widowed mother-in-law even if she is his wife's stepmother, *ina panoroni*.

A father-in-law is allowed to marry his widowed daughter-in-law in levirate, but a stepfather may not marry his stepdaughter, though some say this is permissible.

A man is allowed to have two *pariban* (*boru ni tulang*) as his wives if he married one of them in levirate. This does not constitute *dua pungga sada ihotan*, but it would if a man were to marry two sisters or two women who are closely related members of one *marga*. Here and there it is even absolutely forbidden for a man to have as wives two women who are of the same *marga*.

There is, however, one form of bigamy — which will be dealt with in more detail in due course — which is favoured in which precisely the reverse operates: it is recommended that if a man's first wife is barren he should take as his second wife a close kinswoman of the first. This second wife is called *tungkot*. Any children born to the *tungkot* will be reckoned as belonging also to the first wife. It is doubtful if all these instances, applicable to individuals, apply everywhere to the same degree, as it is equally doubtful that every instance has been mentioned.

When transgressions of these prohibitions occur public opinion and public authority are called in. The drums resound and the tiger roars, *gondang mangkuling, babiat tumale*, as they say on Samosir, and people gather to seize and punish the perpetrator of the act:

> *manuan bulu di lapang-lapang ni babi,*
> *mamungka na so uhum, mambahen na so djadi;*
> Planting bamboos on the path the pigs take.
> To begin what is unlawful, to do what is forbidden.

This is a maxim that is used for all kinds of immoral acts. In olden times one could have seized the village of such a transgressor, *martaban*, or put him in the block, *mamasung*. The marriage constituting the transgression is declared null and void. The man and the *parboru* must make atonement, *manopoti, pauli uhum,* or be outlawed, *dipaduru diruar ni patik* = placed outside social life as governed by *adat*. To atone, they will probably have to offer a meal of meat and rice, *mandjuhuti mangindahani* for which a buffalo or a cow must be slaughtered, to the chiefs and elders of the territories affected by their action. This meal also serves as a purification, *pangurasion,* of the land and its inhabitants.

A noteworthy prohibition, which does not really come into the category of *marsumbang*, is that forbidding a woman who has been divorced by her husband from marrying the man with whom she is suspected of having been cohabiting. This is a ban which a judge can and often does impose.

GENERAL STIPULATIONS FOR MARRIAGE

The principal aim of marriage is to obtain legal male descendants and therefore the first requirement is that both the young man and the young girl must be physically mature, *tang pamatang* = full grown in body, *nunga balga* = grown up. That many child betrothals are entered into with more or less serious intentions and that even unborn children are promised, does not alter the fact that a marriage cannot be consumated until the young couple have reached physical maturity. A marriage that has been arranged between a young girl and an elder man, which does sometimes happen, cannot take place until the girl has menstruated for some time. Formerly the sign that a young man was ready to marry was when he had his teeth filed, *manghihir*. If either party to the marriage has any physical defects that will prevent normal sexual intercourse and if these are found out before the marriage, then the marriage can be called off.

With regard to the age at which Christian Batak youths whose date of birth is known from the parish registers, are permitted to marry, there is still no specific age obtaining generally.

Brothels are not tolerated. The country is still virtually free of venereal diseases and their introduction can be combated. Nevertheless, girls and their parents are fully aware that venereal diseases can diminish the chances of producing healthy and robust children. As a consequence they respond readily to the pressure of the missions to get their would-be husbands to have a medical examination before they marry them if they left their district when they were bachelors.

It is customary for an elder brother to marry before a younger brother and for an elder sister to marry before a younger sister. The reverse, which is not definitely forbidden, can only happen if the elder brother or sister give their consent.

SOCIAL INTERCOURSE BETWEEN YOUNG PEOPLE

In the Toba Batak Country, particularly in the south, young people are expected to act decorously in their social relations with each other. The girls do not lead a secluded life but they keep their daily intercourse with the young men within bounds.

The girls' clothing is rather sober: they wear a long hanging gown made of a rather thick material; it has long sleeves and is closed at the neck. A young unmarried girl is called *na marbadju* = she who wears a gown closed at the neck. Only when a woman has had her first child, termed the *buha badju* = the opener of the gown, can she wear a bodice as her upper garment. However, some changes are gradually being brought about in women's clothing by young school girls.

The outward conduct of the young girls is as sedate as their clothing. They are very jealous of their good names and should people talk about a girl, she will not hesitate to be examined by a doctor and, armed with a declaration of her virginity, will turn to authority complaining of slander.

The young girls of the village usually spend their nights in the house of a widow who lives alone and who has to supervise them. The young men spend their nights among their own group in the village council house, or elsewhere. Visiting time is the evening when the youths go to see the girls in the neighbouring villages, joke with them in the village square or in the house of the widow and make their choice. This *martandang* is informal and usually ends at a suitable hour. It is impolite for the young girls to shut the door in the faces of young men who have called in a group to see them. This once happened to a visiting group of youths who became so angry that they stuck their knives through the cracks in the raised floor of the house in order to cut the mats that lay on it. A complaint was lodged against them and they had to atone, *manopoti salana tu na marbadju i*, for their bad behaviour towards the young girls. The girls, for their part, had a similar obligation laid on them towards the youths since they had locked them out when there was no indication that they had evil intentions.

Free association with the young men is forbidden as soon as a girl is betrothed, *nioro*. This also holds good in a child betrothal which for the parents is regarded as a serious matter and not merely as a financial transaction. Betrothed children are encouraged to associate with each other so that what the parents desire will also become the desire of the children. The *na marpariban* = sister's son/brother's daughter, and extensions of this relationship, enjoy greater freedom of social intercourse. On Samosir, perhaps by virtue of contact with Sumatra's East Coast where other customs prevail, sexual relations are freer than in the remainder of the Batak Country.

Before dealing with those particular points relating to marriage and betrothals which merit further attention, I will first give a general survey of the course of affairs in a betrothal and in a marriage which follow on the usual type of courtship.

THE YOUNG MAN BEGINS HIS QUEST: MANGARIRIT

I have already described one method by which young people become acquainted with one another, the *martandang*, but they can also get to know each other at the market, during the harvest, at the choral society, and when they go to church, etc. A young man will often seek his bride among the girls known to him, but he may also have heard of a girl who is unknown to him but whose acquaintance he would like to make. A young man's parents will also direct his attention to a particular girl whose attributes they find agreeable, or because they want to have her parents as their *tondong*. The idea of young people getting to know each other really well before they take the great step of marrying, is not considered to be of particular importance, though at present the desire to do so is becoming more prevalent amoung young people. There are also other factors which play an important part: the wealth of the parents, the possession of diplomas, a good job and other attractions.

The Batak desire of marriage offspring first and foremost and to this end the *tondi* of the couple should be in harmony, *rongkap ni tondi:* there should be between them the harmony of prosperity, *rongkap gabe*, whereby they will be blessed with children. If this harmony is lacking, if their *tondi* are not able to harmonise, *so olo marrongkap tondina*, it will come to light later and may result in a divorce. On the other hand, once children are born, the bond between the couple is strengthened and mutual love may arise.

If a young man has a *pariban* who is already being considered as a wife who will be suitable, *na ampit*, for him or who might soon be so considered but whom he does not desire then, if he wishes to go courting elsewhere, *mangaririt*, it is good manners for him to inform the girl or her parents and thus avoid their displeasure. In any case it is both proper and desirable that a young man tells his *tulang* what his intentions are in this respect and that he gets his blessing. The young man and his mother visit the latter's brother, who is his *tulang*, taking with them food, *mamboan sipanganon*; sometimes this is supplemented with a *piso* gift of money. In this way they express the respect due to the *tulang*. During this visit — which was formerly of more frequent occurrence than now — they tell the *tulang* of the young man's intention to propose to a certain girl, *manopot boru*, and make the request that the uncle's *sahala* will give its blessing to the project, *asa ditumpak sahala ni tulangna i*. The *tulang* then gives his *bere* his *hata sidenggan-denggan* = good words of blessing, and promises that the chosen girl will be as a daughter to him.

The young man, having received similar good wishes and benedictions from his parents for his plans, departs to make his proposal, *mandok hatana* = "to say the words", to the girl he desires. If she is only known to him by sight, he will previously have inquired of the group or *marga* to which she belongs (see *umpama* on p. 21, *tiniptip sanggar,* etc.) in order to ascertain that there is no marriage prohibition. He must also know whether the girl is already betrothed because:

> *sabur bintang sabur maropot-opot,*
>
> *ia naung oroan di saena pe tinopot;*
>
> The stars are sown in multitudes.
>
> A betrothed girl cannot be asked for in marriage with propriety unless she be free, *sae,* again.

All this information he will obtain by asking the older members of the village where the girl lives, through his comrades, or by using the services of an intermediary called a *domu-domu* or *pande-pande.*

THE DOMU-DOMU

The young man does not always make the actual proposal himself. It can be done for him by his own *domu-domu* who contacts a person whom he considers fit to act as *domu-domu* for the girl. Both these *domu-domu* also frequently act as intermediaries between the parents to enable them to reach agreement, *padomuhon,* on the amount of the marriage payment. They also assist in its transfer, etc. The reward for their efforts is called the *upa domu-domu* = payment for effecting agreement. This they receive when the marriage is settled and the marriage payment has been made. Naturally the duties of such inter-mediaries can sometimes be of a rather delicate nature and it is under-standable that they have to act prudently and conscientiously. Ill-judged mediation can easily lead to a misunderstanding and to quarrels, *guntur,* and in certain circumstances an intermediary will find himself before the judge. A more modern way of proposing is by letter: sometimes a photograph is enclosed. Occasionally one even sees a marriage advertise-ment. This imitating of Western modes is done by young people who want to "play the intellectual".

If a young girl makes it clear that the young man's initial advances are agreeable to her, he will then make inquiries as to whether the course of their life together will be favoured with fortune before he takes the weighty decision and proposes. To do this he invokes a dream vision, *marmangmang nipi,* by which means he determines whether or not to proceed with his marriage plans. If, in his dream, he sees the girl doing things that are beneficial, like scooping water from a spring, he will regard it as a favourable sign. If, however, he sees her doing laborious work like lifting heavy loads he will regard it as fortelling misfortune. It is also quite possible that his choice of a particular girl is the result of a dream vision or that her behaviour at their first meeting was such that it presaged future prosperity. If the girl does not already know the young man she will try to get some information regarding him from her trustworthy friends before finally deciding.

BETROTHAL PLEDGES

When all these matters have been investigated to the satisfaction of both parties concerned and the proposal has been made and accepted then, shortly afterwards there follows the exchange of the betrothal pledges, *tanda hata* = tokens of the verbal pledge, also called *tanda burdju* = tokens of the earnestness of the intentions. This exchange often takes place in the presence of friends or older people. The young man usually gives some object such as a tobacco box, a ring, or a coin, or a small sum of money as his *tanda hata*. The young girl, as a rule, gives an *ulos* which is of less value than the gift she receives from the young man. The purport of this exchange of *tanda* is that both the young people have, *maniop*, tangible proof of the vow they have made and of the faithfulness with which it will be observed. If a young man lets down his betrothed without justification, *magigi di oroanna,* then a severe reproof is merited from the intermediaries, *godang hata taononna,* as well as general disapproval. The pledges that have been given as well as any other presents will then be forfeit, the gifts received must be returned. If a betrothal does not go through because the parents cannot agree about the amount of the marriage payment, then a demand can be made that presents that have been given should be returned. If the young man has given a present of substantial value, or a large sum of money as his *tanda* (for example 25 guilders) then, when the marriage is concluded, it will be regarded as part of the marriage payment: a valuable counter present from the girl will similarly be regarded as being part of the opposite *ragi-ragi.* Objects of little worth are not taken into account should the betrothal be broken off or if the couple are later divorced. These small trifles are regarded as "small seeds" that have been scattered and which cannot be claimed back, *inggir-inggir na mapipil, na so siluluan,* an aphorism applied to all the attendant minor items relating to a transaction of which the return cannot be demanded later in legal proceedings.

INADMISSIBLE RELATIONSHIPS

When a couple have agreed to act in secret as though they were husband and wife, *marpadan-padan* = to have an assignation, also called *marmainan* = whoring, and *marlangka pilit* = taking the wrong path, marriage must take place as soon as possible after it is discovered. The young couple can also be ordered to confess their guilt, *manopoti*, before the chiefs and the parents of both parties. The manner of their doing so will be determined by the circumstances and the relationships. If a young man deserts the young woman with whom he has had such a relationship, or if the parents do not wish a marriage to take place, then the penalty is heavier. The young man then has to defray the cost of the *pangurasion* = purification, and has to satisfy the *parboru* with a *piso* gift.

Open, unlawful living together as husband and wife, *marbagas roha-roha*, is not known to me among young people and it is not consistent with the relationship in which a girl stands to her *parboru*. It does, however, exist — in regions where the discipline of law and custom is weak — among older people who have already been married. This is an offence against good custom, *sala tu adat,* and merits persecution and punishment by authority. In Padang Lawas I heard such conduct called by the general term of *manaporkon ogung ni radja* = breaking the chief's gong, i.e., infringing the laws of the community. It is punishable with an *adat* penalty, which qualification shows that the offence is regarded as an offence against the public order.

INFORMING THE PARENTS

As a rule, the young people inform their respective parents immediately they have agreed to marry, or the intermediaries do so; the betrothal, *mangoro*, is not official until the parents of both parties have agreed upon the amount of the marriage payment. If a *domu-domu* is acting for the young man, he arranges the young man's introduction to the *parboru*, and if the latter's response is satisfactory the first meeting of the young man and his future parents-in-law takes place. (At least, that is what happens in Silindung. In Toba it usually happens when the provisional discussions about the marriage payment have been concluded.) The young man is regaled with a meal, *indahan husip*, or *indahan pangaririton*, which usually consists of rice and fish. As a sign that the girl's father approves of his prospective son-in-law and that he accepts him as such, he gives him a beautiful garment, the *ulos ni hela*, as a *tanda hela* either then or later on the actual marriage. When this introduction has been made the young man can visit his betrothed openly and more frequently and, indeed, is eager to do so because of the tasty morsels which are then prepared for him. During this period the terms of address used in mutual conversation are those obtaining between *hula-hula* and *boru*. Particular attention will be given that the terms used between the parents-in-law and the son-in-law are *dibagasan partuturan*. And from time to time the young man will take meat to his parents-in-law and will also meet the next of kin.

DETERMINING THE MARRIAGE PAYMENT

The next stage is the discussion of the financial aspects, *marhata sinamot*, of which the object is to determine the amount of the marriage payment, *mamuhul sinamot*. The word *sinamot* or *pansamotan* = that which has been obtained, the goods, property, used in respect of a marriage, means marriage payment, and indicates that a certain outlay is necessary to acquire a wife, and, since this duty falls on the *paranak*, he is called the *parsinamot*.

The *paranak* refers to the marriage payment as the *pangoli* = the outlay necessary to get one's son married. *Mangoli* is the term used on the man's side for marriage, hence the bridegroom is also called the *pangoli*; his wife is his *nioli*, and to marry off a son is called *mangolihon*. The more complete term, *pangoli ni anak*, also means what has to be paid as the marriage payment for a son.

From the girl's side the terms used are *boli ni boru* and *tuhor ni boru*. The word *boli* is used exclusively in connection with marriage. The *boli ni boru* is the term for what the girl's kinship group receives for her: perhaps it would be better to say it is that which is placed against the *boru*. The word *boli* by itself signifies marriage payment; when used in the expression *boli ni sinamot*, it defines the *ragi-ragi*, the counter presents which the girl's kinship group gives to the young man's kinship group. I will deal with this later. The term means "that which is the opposite of the marriage payment, the *sinamot*."

The word *tuhor*, in my opinion, should be understood in a similar sense. The term *tuhor ni boru* immediately brings to mind the idea of purchase-money for the bride, because at the present time *manuhor* has acquired the meaning of "buying for money" as distinct from "exchange against goods", *marsambar*. So a man will sometimes refer to his wife as *na hutuhor* = the one I have "bought" and a *parboru* will say that he has "sold", *digadis*, his *boru*. Bride-price marriage is, however, no doubt older than acquaintance with money and therefore the term *tuhor ni boru* must originally have meant "what has to be given and what has to be received" when a girl leaves her kinship group to marry. That this use of the words *tuhor* and *gadis* should not be understood to mean buying and selling in the usual sense, is further clear from the fact that the *parboru*, who is the one who hands over his *boru*, only receives a relatively small part of the *tuhor*, the remainder goes elsewhere, as we will see later on.

The term *pabolihon* = giving a girl in marriage, is formed from the word *boli*. The term most used when a girl marries is *muli*, or, in full, *muli tu hutana* = going to her destined village, i.e., her husband's. To give a daughter in marriage is therefore also called *pamulihon*, and a wife can call her husband, among other things, her *hamulian*.

The terms *boli* and *tuhor* are also current in South Tapanuli as well as the terms *mas* and *sere,* gold. The separate parts of the marriage payment are called *rudji-rudji*, after the small accounting sticks which are used for calculating them. These terms are also used in Upper Barus, while *mas* also occurs in Uluan (from Asahan). Other terms for the marriage payment, such as *niundjuk* and *pamoru*, will be met with in their particular context.

The discussion on the financial details of a marriage is usually initiated by the *domu-domu*, or *pande-pande*. This is their main task. If, for instance, the demands made by the one side appear to be too considerable in comparison with the offers made by the other, then the two *domu-domu* strike a happy medium which both parties will gladly accept, at least for the time being, if they really want the marriage to take place. Sometimes it is the bridegroom-to-be who informs both sides of the provisional amounts which the one wants to give and the other to receive.

Once it is known that the determining of the marriage payment is likely to be successful then, (in Silindung and Humbáng), the *paranak* and his closest kinsmen, affines, and the chief of his village proceed, on a day announced previously, to the *parboru*'s village. They go to his house where he will be surrounded by his relatives. His village chief must be also present at the *marhata sinamot* which is the object of the visit. The matters which have to be discussed and about which there must be agreement, are the *djambar* or *pordjambaran* = the main constituents of the marriage payment, namely, the *djambar na gok* (an abbreviation for *na gok di puluna* = that which consists of round tens) which together constitute the *sinamot* proper and are those portions accruing to the *suhut* (the *parboru*) and his *pangalambungi*, his nearest related kinsmen and affines.

THE ALLOCATION OF THE MARRIAGE PAYMENT: THE DJAMBAR NA GOK

The *djambar* are discussed within the domestic circle, *sihataon di djabu*, in contrast to the rest of the marriage payment which is discussed in public on the mat, *sihataon di lapik*, during the formal transfer of the bride-price.

The *djambar na gok* are:

(a) the portion for the *suhut* = principal person concerned, the *parboru* of the girl. This part is always the largest and forms the core of the marriage payment: it is the yardstick for the other portions;

(b) the portion for the *sidjalo bara*, who is one of the brothers of the *suhut* or, if he has no brothers, one of his nearest kinsmen. When it is the eldest daughter who is being married this portion is received by the oldest brother of the *parboru*. When it is the second daughter who is being married then the second brother receives it, and so on. The other brothers also receive a *pordjambaran*, but this has no individual name and is reckoned under the *todoan* (see under subsection c). Another name for the *sidjalo bara* is *pamarai* which means someone who stables an animal. Neither word is in common daily use. These terms appear to indicate the functions which one of the brothers of the *suhut* takes on himself when he arranges the marriage of the *suhut*'s daughter: he stables the animals which are part of the marriage payment. The *sidjalo bara* receives a portion called the *upa bara* or *upa pamarai*. This is less than that of the *suhut* but more than the other *djambar*;

(c) the part for the *sidjalo todoan* = the recipients of the *todoan*, i.e., the portions for the brothers of the bride and of the bride's father who do not receive an *upa bara*. The portion for one of the bride's brothers is called the *upa simandokhon*, since it is he who will arrange the bride's departure from her parents' house and will order, *mandok*, her to leave it. The portions for the uncles bear the collective name, *upa paramaan* = gift for the father's group. The use of the word *todoan* in this connection is not quite clear to me: possibly it relates to those members of the family who are born in succession, see pp. 38 - 39 (*manodo* = to assign something to oneself, to destine for oneself);

(d) the portion for the *tulang* is called the *upa tulang*. The *tulang* receives it for the care he has given and will still continue to give to his sister's child who is as a daughter to him. It is the custom when the eldest daughter marries for the mother's eldest brother to receive the *upa tulang*, and so on. The other *tulang* are not forgotten, but they only receive a trifle which does not have its own name;

(e) the portion for the *pariban* is called the *upa pariban* and is allocated to the elder sister. At the marriage of an eldest daughter it goes to the father's sister: at the marriage of the other daughters it goes to the next older daughter. The determination of the size of this portion is often left to the sisters and their husbands because of the affection that so often exists between sisters and the friendly relations between their husbands. Sometimes, therefore, the *upa pariban* is not a previously determined part of the *djambar na gok*. It should be noted that everywhere the emphasis is not the same on all these main parts. The *upa suhut, upa tulang* and the *upa pariban* are to be found practically everywhere. In the closest kinship group, however, the brothers and uncles sometimes receive their portions separately, for example, the *amang uda* and the *amang tua* each receives a separate *djambar,* and the *todoan* is then allocated to the closest related kinship group and is then divided among the members. There are also other variations. In Toba, in fact, the portions for the *porlambung* = the nearest relatives, are not all defined individually in the discussions between the *parboru* and the *paranak*. There these discussions take place in a smaller group. The total of the *sinamot* is agreed upon and after that it is left to the *parboru* to determine the *pordjambaran* individually and to divide them. The terms used vary according to the area.

THE RAGI-RAGI

The *ragi-ragi* = the things that are to be divided, the counter presents, are decided upon at the *marhata sinamot* at the same time as the *djambar na gok* are determined. These presents can also be denoted by the word *ulos* or by the word *paruloson*, since the *boru*-relationship is then at its first stage. The total of the *ragi-ragi* is therefore also called the *ulos ni sinamot* = the *ulos* which is the counterpart of the marriage payment: its other name is *boli ni sinamot*. The *paranak* receives the main constituent of the *ragi-ragi*, the *ulos pansamot*, from the *parboru*. The *sidjalo bara* gives a present to the brother or brothers of the *paranak*, while the *tulang* is responsible for the present to the nearest related *boru*, the *boru na sumolhot* of the bridegroom who, as will be seen presently, has to fulfil an important function in the marriage ceremonial. All these will vary according to local custom. In areas where it is customary for a daughter to receive a *pauseang*-present the *parboru* will announce what she is to receive.

CONFIRMATION OF THE BETROTHAL

The alliance between two young people is definitely settled at these discussions and for the first time they can be regarded as being properly affianced. The girl has then become the *nioro* = betrothed, of the young man. The word *nioro* is an abbreviation of *nioro ni hepeng* = destined for the one who pays a sum of money. She is also called *oroan* (*boru oroan*), the girl who is in the situation of having been allocated to someone. The young man is called the *pangoro* or *paroroan* = the one who has a betrothed destined for him.

If a betrothal is broken off, the girl is not really free, *sae*, and eligible for another man until the financial arrangements with the previous *paranak* have been completely settled.

Because of their definitive character, the betrothal deliberations are called *pudun-saut* = tying the knot. Participation in the meal which the *parboru* offers to the *paranak* and his kinsmen on this occasion, is called *mangan pudun* = eating the knot. Not only have the young people become bound to each other, but the mutual kinsmen have also come to regard each other as affines, *tondong*.

If any of the near kinsmen of the *paranak* are not able to accompany the *paranak*'s party when it goes to the *parboru*'s village, the *paranak* sends to their homes the *na margoar*, the vital parts of the slaughtered beast to which they are entitled, so that they will know that the betrothal has been settled.

As a rule the payment of a *patudjolo* = precursor, is made during the *mangan pudun*: it is called the *bohi ni sinamot* = the face of the marriage payment, i.e., a first sight of it. This payment in advance makes the arrangements that have been made even still more binding. It does not, however, guarantee absolutely to either of the young people that the marriage will take place. Among the Batak many things can happen, large and small, which can do much to turn the feeling of willingness, so that the betrothal eventually hangs by a thread. However, if the young people are very set on each other, then they will do everything on their part to clear away any obstacles that have arisen.

It cannot be said that everything is defined precisely and determined with exactitude. Naturally, such important discussions as these should be conducted in the correct manner, so that everybody present knows exactly what has been agreed upon. One learns in the event of a dispute arising later and coming before the courts, however, how carelessly the parties often act, how imprecise are the terms they have used and what little trouble they have taken to stipulate precisely the points of the agreement.

COLLECTING THE PARTS OF THE MARRIAGE PAYMENT

As a rule the *marhata sinamot* is followed by the collecting of the stipulated parts of the *djambar, mangalap sinamot*. The *paranak* will have informed his kinsmen and affines, and some of his friends as well, that his son will be getting married and that he will, therefore, expect their support. His closest related kinsmen will make a substantial contribution, *tumpak*. Those further removed will make a smaller one, and everyone will take into account the fact that they have either previously enjoyed such support from the *paranak* or that they may shortly be in need of it.

The marriage payment frequently consists of money and cattle. Animals should be examined by the *parboru* before he drives them away. As a rule payment in full of the agreed *djambar* is not made on this occasion: a small part remains unpaid and this is handed over by the *paranak* at the great assembly, the *parundjuhan*, which forms the focal point of the marriage ceremonies. This follows shortly when the bride is 'fetched', *mangalap boru*.

THE MARUNDJUK OR MANGAN DJUHUT

The official transfer of the marriage payment takes place at the *parundjuhan*. The *paranak* refers to it as the *marundjuk,* he himself is called the *parundjuk*. The *hula-hula* to which the marriage payment is transferred is called the *parundjuhan*, the marriage payment itself being then called the *niundjuk*.

One of the key points in the *parundjuhan* is the offering of prepared meat and rice to the *parboru* by the *paranak*. This meat is cut in pieces, *tanggo djuhut* and the *paranak* therefore calls the ceremony *tanggo djuhut*. The *parboru* and his relations call it *mangan djuhut*, since they eat the prepared meat. He also calls it *mangan tuhor ni boru* = partaking of the marriage payment for his daughter, an expression which probably stems from the time when cattle, which constituted part of the marriage payment, were so few in number that they were eaten at the ceremony.

The participants in the ceremony from the *paranak*'s side are his own brothers, his married sons, his father's brothers (in photo 1b they sit beside him in a row) and his more distant *dongan-sabutuha* with whom he daily associates. There will also be his *parboruan*, i.e., his brothers-in-law (sisters' husbands), sons-in-law and probably still more of his closely related *boru* group. It is one of these last, to whom the bridegroom is the closest affine, who will perform the important function

Plate I

pp. 59, 176, 179, 180

MARUNDJUK
the transferring of the marriage payment

a. The *marhata lapik,* the discussions held on the compound of the village
of the *parboru.*

b. An *ulos* is about to be placed round the shoulders of the *paranak.*

of carrying the covered *ampang* = basket, *manghunti ampang*, in which the prepared meat has been placed. He is called the *sihunti ampang*. The *paranak*'s village chief will also take part in the ceremony since he represents the public authority from the *paranak*'s side and if the *paranak* is an important person, some chiefs of the neighbouring villages and the highest territorial chief will in all probability be present. In addition, the members of his village will be there entering into the spirit of the event which is so important for them, promising as it does, to bring a new female member into their community, and last of all there will be some friends.

The rank and worthiness of all these guests, who are either related to the *paranak* or are his daily associates, is recognised and established by the place where each one sits during the meal, by the division of the meat, the distribution of the *ragi-ragi* and the *upa radja*, etc. The *paranak* also takes care to have a well-filled purse to hand, since there will be a great number of people from the *parboru*'s side whose status has to be acknowledged by a gift of a small sum of money.

The guests from the *parboru*'s side will be the *suhut*, the rightful claimants of the *djambar na gok*, as well as the homologous family members and a wide circle of *dongan-sabutuha* and *tondong*. There will be present the entire *sapanganan tuhor ni boru*, the circle of agnates which considers itself as a separate unit in respect of the giving of its female members in marriage. Not all will be there because not all of them live in the neighbourhood and many will be prevented from attending because of their work. But, if possible, all the divisions of the lineage or the *marga* branch should be represented at the marriage of "our daughter", *borunami*, as they call her. Both rich and poor relations are entitled to attend and the affines, even including the *bona ni ari*, will, if possible, give as much evidence as they can of their interest. The *parboru*'s village chief will be present and the members of his village as well will be there to give assistance in receiving the many guests. If the wedding is that of a distinguished young couple, then the chiefs of the surrounding areas will also go to it. Many of the guests, particularly the recipients of the *djambar na gok*, will bring with them a *siuk* = contribution of rice, having in mind the large meal that is being given: for them the *parboru* will eventually claim a separate gift, the *upa parsiuk*.

In Silindung and its environs the course of affairs is roughly as follows: the *paranak* slaughters his piglet at home and puts it with the cooked rice into an *ampang* = basket. This meal is the *sibuha-buhai* = that which will open the ceremonies. It is carried to the *parboru*'s vil-

12

lage by the *boru sihunti ampang* = the bearer of the meal that is to be served, (also called *siboan sulang-sulang*) who, because he performs this distinctive operation, will later receive a separate *ulos* or a sum of money, the *tutup ni ampang* = the 'coverer' of the basket. Earlier, however, he will have made a *tumpak* = contribution, to the marriage payment that is larger than usual.

When the *paranak*'s party arrives at the *parboru*'s village the first thing to be done is to offer the meal he has brought to the *parboru* and his wife. The offering of the *sibuha-buhai* and its acceptance is a sign to all present that the discussions held prior to the *marundjuk* have led to agreement and that now the formalities can proceed. It is also the official profession of homage by the *paranak,* thus the *parboruon,* towards the affines on the occasion of their surrendering their daughter in marriage. This means that the *paranak* will enter into a *boru*-relationship with the new *hula-hula* or, where it is a case of *manunduti,* will strengthen the existing affinity link.

This homage is expressed by the act of *manulangi* (see p. 94). This is first done to the *parboru*'s spouse, and then to the *parboru* himself, by one of the members of the *paranak*'s lineage, the *paisulang,* who is assigned this duty by the *paranak.* The *paisulang* eventually receives a separate gift from the *parboru.* The *manulangi* is done to the accompaniment of an invocation to the *tondi* and *sahala* for their blessing. In pagan times the *manulangi* was preceded by offering, *tibal-tibal,* the food that was to be served. Following the *manulangi* the bride's parents partake of a little of the food and then they divide the remainder among the rightful claimants according to the *na margoar,* thus taking into account the *partording ni partubu* = degree of kinship, and the *tohonan* = precedence of office. Such a procedure is usual in distributing portions of the meat, but on this occasion particular attention must be given to it.

In larger marriage feasts of wealthy and prominent persons, the *paranak,* as the *pandjuhuti* = the one who regales with meat, contributes a buffalo to the communal meal. This contribution to the festivities is called the *taragu* and consequently the *parboru*-group calls the ceremony *mangan djuhut taragu.* The cow which the *parboru* allocates for the *paranak*'s meal and that of his kinsmen is called the *sila.* Despite the fact that this is not fish, it is nevertheless called by the general name of *dengke* = fish and the buffalo which the *paranak* gives to the *parboru*-group is also called *sulang,* even when no *manulangi* takes place of all the participants. When the meat of these animals is placed before the guests, the rightful claimants to a particular portion are considered most precisely. The guests sit in two groups or in two rows opposite each other. Sometimes it is said to be admissible to combine the two *sipanganon* into one meal: it is also said to be forbidden.

The bride's father does not partake of the communal meal since he is the host. He keeps an eye on the way things are going and offers his apologies for the indifferent quality of the food set before his guests. The *paranak* in his turn replies that the meal is so good it could not be better. The bridegroom does not eat with the guests either; he is entertained separately with a few friends in a house in the village by the bride and her female friends.

After the meal the customary *parsaut ni sipanganon* = declaration of the conclusion of the meal, is made and then questions are asked as to its purpose, *haroan*, and the answer is given. This is the signal for the *marhata lapik* = the discussion on the mat, i.e., in public (see photo Ia), the *marundjuk* proper to begin. The person who asks what the purpose of the meal is, and thereby invites the *hata na denggan* = the good words, about the meal and its object, is called the *panungkunan* = the questioner. He is a distant kinsman of the *parboru* and receives a special gift from the *paranak*, the *upa manungkun* = payment for asking the question. (In Toba it is called *upa manise*.) After the mutual addresses, interlarded with numerous *umpama*, many of which relate exclusively to the concluding of a marriage, the *panungkunan* asks about the different payments that the *paranak* has already promised to make and which he has partly fulfilled, and about those that must then be decided and honoured forthwith. The sequence of these additional payments is not always the same. Many are of an adventitious character and are different everywhere, or have more or less fallen into desuetude. An indication of the principal ones will suffice.

The *djambar na gok* are announced publicly and mention is made of what has been completed and what remains to be paid: this remainder will then, if possible, be paid on the spot. The *parboru* points out the *parsiuk* who have to have a separate payment because of their contributions to the meal. He also indicates to the *paranak* which of his kinsmen have no claim to the *djambar na gok*, but who can expect a more or less substantial gift according to the nearness of kinship: the same applies to the affines. Each of these relations tries to wheedle as much as possible out of the *paranak* while others oppose their too high claims. The *paranak* and his kinsmen endeavour to get off as lightly as possible until eventually, and after much wrangling, all these relatives, including the farthest removed, will have received the small sums which indicate their relationship to the bride's father. These sums can be very small indeed, often pennies or even a penny. Over and above these payments, there are a number that are not consequent upon kinship- or affinity-relations.

They are:

the *upa djudjur ari* = payment for divining a favourable day for the *marundjuk*;

the *sialabane*, the general gifts for the members of the bride's village because the bride is on the point of being withdrawn from their community;

the *upa domu-domu*, for the intermediaries who assisted in determining the marriage payment;

the *upa radja* or *djambar ni radja*, the gifts of homage for the chief of the bride's village sometimes given to the territory's chief as well. If the chief concerned is regarded as *hula-hula*, the gift is then called the *piso ni nadia*; if the chief belongs to the narrower kinship circle of the *parboru*, then the gift is called the *todoan ni radja*;

the *olop-olop*, the gift of small change for the public who attend and cheer;

the *upa namora*, the gift for the village's *boru*;

the *upa pangabis*, the gift for the member of the *parboru*'s *hula-hula* who is the last to express his benedictory wishes and who sees to it that things proceed in an orderly and peaceful manner. He is the last to receive a gift.

All those payments that are not main constituents of the marriage payment are termed *na muhut, na mempar*, or *remeng-remeng*, all of which terms mean 'trifles'. They are reckoned as belonging to the marriage payment, the *niundjuk*, and in the event of a divorce must be paid back by the *parboru*. He also has to repay the whole of the *djambar na gok* in such an event, but he cannot claim restitution from those who have received their portions of it. They, however, receive nothing further if the woman remarries.

Payment of the *ragi-ragi* = counterpresents, follows immediately after the official transfer of the marriage payment. An *ulos herbang* = upper garment, is presented to the father and mother of the bridegroom (see photo Ib) with the appropriate words and gestures of protection: the garment given to the father is called the *ulos pansamot* = the garment for the one who has paid the marriage payment, that presented to the mother is called the *ulos pangidupi* = the garment for the one who gave birth to the son. They receive these gifts in addition to the sum of money agreed upon which in most cases has been deducted already from the *upa suhut*. The *parsiuk*, who have received a *djambar* from the *paranak*, often give a *ragi-ragi* present to those people indicated by the *paranak* as having supported him with a *tumpak*. The *paranak*'s village chief is remembered by the *parboru* with a gift of homage which can be called the *ulos ni radja*. These last *ragi-ragi* gifts consist of money or cloths, or both. During the time when these presents are given the *parboru* will again take the opportunity to make known what his daughter will receive as a dowry, *pauseang*, if such a gift had been previously agreed upon.

The result of all this continual passing to and fro of gifts will be that, sometimes by the end of the *parundjuhan* the *paranak* will have paid out little from his own pocket because of the many *tumpak* he will have received, whereas the *parboru* will have spent nearly as much on entertaining his guests and on the counter-presents, even excluding the dowry for his daughter, as he has received in the *upa suhut*. The often stated idea that marrying off a daughter is a profitable financial transaction is frequently belied by the facts.

A point worth mentioning is that the *parboru* is often a member of a mutual aid society of which one of the rules is that each time a daughter is married off her father must make a contribution to the cash box.

It goes without saying that those present at the ceremonial meal who are regarded as elders, *pangintuai* or *panungganei*, will express their good wishes, *hata sigabe-gabe,* as will the village chief, the chief of the territory and any other *radja* who may be present. All of them will express their *hata pasu-pasu* and will frame them as far as possible in *umpama* form.

THE PARTY GIVEN BY THE BRIDE AND HER FRIENDS

At the conclusion of the *marundjuk* when all the guests have departed, the young girls in the bride's entourage assemble in her village and there prepare a feast for their expected guests, the bridegroom and his friends who will arrive after nightfall. A meal will be set before them and when they have eaten they must give the young girls the *upa naposo* = payment for the young ones. And, just as though it were a *parundjuhan*, each girl will then claim so much as her *djambar* as she feels she is entitled to by virtue of her relationship to the bride. Here too, though in a more gay atmosphere, there is a good deal of bargaining over the

requests that are made. This can go on well into the night. The bridegroom's friends will have given him their *tumpak* which, if they are
somewhat substantial, can build up the total of the *upa naposo* to the
tune of 100 guilders. Naturally these customs among the young people
vary according to locality.

THE MARBAGAS

In Toba and West Humbáng the bride, the *boru na nialap* = the girl
who is 'fetched', goes with her husband immediately after the *marundjuk*.
She walks behind the basket, *mangihut di ampang*, in which the meal
of meat was originally carried and which is then being taken back to
the village of the young husband's parents. In Silindung and East
Humbáng, however, the girl remains for a few days with the bridegroom in her father's village. In these regions there was formerly an
interdict, *robu-robuan*, operative for seven days after the *marundjuk*,
during which the bride spent the nights among her virgin friends. At
the end of the period the bride and groom ate together, *patophon
mangan*. For the purpose of this meal the *paranak* with his closest kinsmen and his village chief paid an evening visit to the *parboru* who had
also invited some kinsmen and his village chief. The young couple were
placed beside each other in the middle of the dwelling before a large
dish on which cooked rice had been piled up in a dome-shaped pile,
nidimpu, on top of which was a fish that had not been gutted. The
girl sat at the side of the *talaga* = the space in the middle of the house
where the housewife performs her household duties — hence one of
her many names is *portalaga*. The young man sat near the *djuluan* =
side wall, like the pater familias does. The bride's mother then threw a
completely new *ulos*, the *ulos lobu-lobu* = the enveloping cloth, round
the couple, while those present sat down in a circle behind them. The
bride and groom then partook of the meal set before them, the *indahan
sampur* = rice of unification — hence the ceremony is called *pasampurhon* = to mix, to unite — and the *dengke saur* = the fish which
promises a fortunate life. After that the bride's father directed a *tonggo*
to the *sumangot* of the ancestors and to the gods. Those present pronounced their *hata sigabe-gabe*, and the *radja* expressed his *pasu-pasu*
to the accompaniment of an elegant address in which he urged them to
live together in harmony.

The marriage was then regarded as being fully concluded and the
couple had become a *ripe* = family. They had become a married couple,
dongan-saripe, a couple whose betrothal had been transformed into a

marriage, *pardongan-saripeon* or *parsaripeon*. They would then live together in an abode of their own, *bagas*, hence *marbagas* = to get married, to live in one's own house; they had become joined in matrimony, *pabagashon*. The woman was no longer the *boru ni parboru* = girl under the authority of her *parboru*, but had become the *nioli* of her husband.

In later times the seven-day *robu* = interdict has come to be disregarded and the marriage ceremonial of the *pasampurhon* has likewise faded into oblivion. At the present day the couple are permitted to sleep in the nuptial bed on the night of the *marundjuk,* or a couple of nights later.

THE CHURCH'S BLESSING

The blessing in church after the civil marriage of a Christian Batak, which is now common, is called *mamasu-masu*. A week or two before the day appointed for the *marundjuk*, the *parboru* and the *paranak* notify the pastor of the parish, *huria*, to which the *parboru* belongs of the intended marriage. The pastor registers the notification and asks both the fathers for a thanksoffering, *hamauliateon*, on behalf of the church's coffers. He proclaims the names of the couple on the two following Sundays and their intention to marry, *martingting*, so that any objections against the blessing of the marriage can be opposed.

The ceremony usually takes place before the *parundjuhan* but not always, and as a rule, little or no time is allowed to pass between the two ceremonies. If the church marriage takes place first, then the pastor asks for proof that the necessary registration by the *negeri*-chief of the marriage payment and the counter-presents has taken place. Since, however, this registration is not the *marundjuk* itself but only a record of the size of the amounts that have been agreed between the parties, the declaration issued does not guarantee that obstacles hindering the 'civil marriage' cannot crop up. It appears, therefore, to be safer if the *parundjuhan* takes place before the church pronounces its blessing, for then the danger that it will hang fire or be hindered will be completely averted.

Though the Church's blessing is not a sacrament according to Lutheran ideas, and though the 'civil marriage' is to be regarded as being wholly legal, nevertheless, it is not considered desirable for a Christian couple to live together as husband and wife so long as their civil marriage has not received the Church's blessing. This has been accordingly decreed in the Church Regulations, *aturan parhuriaon*, introduced by the

Rhenish Mission into the Christian Batak communities. In these communities, where the ceremony of the church blessing has superseded the domestic ceremony of the *pasampurhon*, which permitted a couple to live together as husband and wife, *marbagas*, it can, therefore, in my opinion be accepted as law among the members of these Christian communities that a marriage is regarded as valid if both the *mangan djuhut* and the *pamasu-masuon* have taken place. In contrast to the former situation, there is the gain of ample calling of the banns and registration in the church's registers, a gain that in Toba is considerable since there the *marundjuk* takes place in a less grand style than has been described.

No definite answer has yet been found to the question whether, among Christians, a marriage should be regarded as having been legally concluded when the banns have been called in the church and the *marundjuk* has taken place, but when it has not received the Church's blessing for some reason or other. It still rests on the judge's decision, given for preference after consultation about the feelings of the Church community or of the ecclesiastical advisers, or on a ruling by a council of civic and ecclesiastical dignitaries.

When a pagan marries a Christian and takes a vow that he or she will become a Christian, the Church gives its blessing to the marriage: a sum of money is sometimes claimed as a guarantee.

CONCLUDING A MOHAMMEDAN MARRIAGE

In Pahae, Tarutung and Balige the Mohammedan Toba Batak finds a *malim* who is able to conclude his marriage according to the rules of Islam. The ceremony also takes place on or about the day of the *marundjuk* and, as far as I know, the latter is not subject to modifications.

In 1923 a Mohammedan man and a pagan woman eloped from Uluan and, without permission being given by a kinsman on either side, they were married by a cadi at Pamatang Siantar. The marriage was declared null and void by a native court (consisting of non-Mohammedans) at Porsea on the ground that the preliminary discussion on the marriage payment had not been brought to a successful conclusion, and that nobody from the woman's side had been present.

THE DEPARTURE TO THE HUSBAND'S VILLAGE

In areas where the wife does not accompany her husband to his village immediately after the *marundjuk*, a few days elapse after the *marbagas* before she departs in the proper manner, *mebat* or *marune*, to her husband's village.

She is formally conducted with her husband out of her own village, *dipaborhat*, by her parents who have given her a *sipanganon* which again consists of *dengke*, for her husband's parents. Her parents go no further than the step of their house, or the village gate. For the rest of the journey the young couple are accompanied by a number of female friends of the wife and some older women. They take with them betel, rice, cakes and similar things. Outside the immediate environs of the bride's parents' village the girls give some betel and cakes to all whom they meet on their way and receive words of blessing from the recipients and sometimes a small gift of money. In this way it is brought to the knowledge of the public that a wife is on her way to her husband's village. On arrival there, she finds on the steps on which she must walk in order to enter the house, the small *dingin-dingin* plant, to tread on which will bring her *dingin*, prosperity. The parents and kinsmen of the young husband strew salt and rice made yellow with curcuma over their daughter-in-law, the *parumaen*. This is an expression of their hope that she will prosper and also a demonstration that she is welcome.

A few days later, the wife goes on a return visit to her parents, *paulak une,* and, accompanied by her husband, she is sent off, *dipaborhat*, by his parents. The couple take with them a meal of rice and pork intended for her parents. Arriving in the neighbourhood of her village, she distributes a little of the meal among the people passing by, and when she reaches her parents' house she offers the meal to them and to her kinsmen on behalf of her husband's family. If the meal has been carefully prepared and the *na margoar* have been specially cut up, the kinsmen take home the portions of meat allocated to them or, if they have been prevented from being present, their portions are sent to their homes as evidence that the reception of the *boru* by her family-in-law has gone smoothly and that she has been sent on her return visit in the prescribed form, *tangkás*. Usages in respect of these visits are also rather varied.

A number of special points will now be considered.

THE ROLE OF PARENTS IN A BETROTHAL

Small children are often betrothed to each other by their parents: this can even be the case of children still to be born. There are two different reasons for it, the one is in reality only a financial transaction, while the other is the *masiboruan* = the concluding of a *boru*-relationship by means of a betrothal which stems from the desire of the parents to become each others' *tondong*, affines, *naeng martondong*. If the circumstances are favourable, the second can develop out of the first and there are transitional forms in which each of the motives plays a more or less clear part.

THE BORU SIHUNTI UTANG

The settlement of an existing money debt or of one to be incurred, by making the marriage payment to be received in the future for a *boru* (usually the debtor's or would-be debtor's own daughter) a security bond for the debt, *utang i niampehon tu boru*, is a purely business transaction. This girl is then called the *boru sihunti utang* = the girl who bears a debt on her head: she is also called the *boru sihunti garar*, or *hepeng*; both terms express the same thing. Most times the girl is referred to by her name, but she is also sometimes spoken of as "the one who has just been born" or "the one who has just been 'divorced' ". This usage is not a desirable practice in the event of there later being a dispute centred around her.

If the future marriage payment for a daughter is placed as security against a money loan, then such a loan is practically as good as always one bearing no interest: the amount cannot increase by non-payment. If the marriage payment relates to the settlement of an existing debt, or to the termination of a legal dispute either by mutual deliberation or after judicial intervention, it is also customary that no interest is calculated for the period between the time when the amount is determined and the debt is honoured. This period can often add up to years.

As a rule, it is not the intention that the *boru sihunti utang* will be betrothed to a son of the creditor by virtue of this debt arrangement, and consequently the ceremony for a child betrothal does not take place, nor is there any other formality with regard to the girl. The reason that this subject is discussed here rather than in Chapter VIII, which deals with the laws of debts, is mainly because the creditor acquires by the agreed contract a right to delay the marriage (and the betrothal?) of the 'pledged' girl if he has not been paid beforehand out of the marriage payment that is to be received for her. He then turns to the *parboru*'s chief, or to the competent judge who, if the claim is made to seem reasonable to him, is obliged to stop further progress towards the conclusion of the marriage so long as the matter has not been settled definitely. The girl concerned, who is usually unaware of the burden she is carrying, as is the young man to whom she is betrothed, has defensive remedies against such an obstacle: she and the young man can resort to some of the ways of forcing the marriage that have already been mentioned earlier.

It is not in the nature of this transaction that other debts can be accumulated against this security. If, when a daughter is being married off, other creditors appear, it will usually mean that one of the contracts has not been concluded with due observance of the requirements of the law, *dibagasan adat*, which in this case means, among other things, that the *parboru*'s kinsmen, as well as his chief, should have been informed. Negligence on the creditor's part will weaken his claim, and bad faith on the part of the *parboru* will possibly earn him disciplinary correction.

If the girl dies before a marriage has been arranged for her, it is quite in order that she be replaced.

If a creditor neglects to make known the facts of his claim for any reason other than ignorance regarding the concluding of the marriage, then he loses the agreed security and also greatly weakens the evidence of his claim. When he learns too late that the marriage has been concluded, and then wants to rectify the matter, he can exercise his patience until one of the daughters that may be born to the woman is getting married. In relationships such as this people easily reckon in decades. If a creditor is wise, however, he will make his claim immediately after he discovers the marriage has taken place and, if necessary, he will make a new agreement in order not to run the risk of being like the man who fails to call his dog properly and loses him, *agoan asu na hurang doda*.

PARUMAEN DI LOSUNG

What is much more serious for the young girl is another type of contract whereby, young as she is, she is handed over by her *parboru* (often her father) to his creditor as security for a debt. She is said, in fact, to be betrothed to one of the creditor's sons but her real status, however, is that of a 'peon': *boru mangadop*. And though such a girl is termed *parumaen* = daughter-in-law, the fact that the qualification *di losung* = at the rice-stamping block, is added, shows quite clearly that the creditor intends to have the benefit of her labour, *mambuat gogona*. The girl is also called *parumaen sinonduk* = daughter-in-law for whom food is provided. If there should happen to be a young man who is regarded as suitable, *ampit*, for her, then there may be a plan to marry them at a later date. The young man's parents will then go out of their way to accustom the young people to each other. If it is apparent that they are not attracted to each other, then the plan can easily be abandoned and the girl can be married off to someone else when she is nubile. The division of the marriage payment will be decided between the creditor and the *parboru*. If the girl is an orphan whose distant kinsmen parted with her in payment for their debts, then the creditor himself arranges the whole matter of her marriage.

This handing over of young girls by their parents into this disguised form of service in settlement of their debts, is still done in areas around Lake Toba, though it does not happen so frequently as it did in the *Pidari* time. This form of child betrothal is distinct from the normal one in that the girl lives with her future parents-in-law.

In Toba Holbung, if a betrothal is sincerely desired between a marriageable girl and a youth who is still too young, then it can happen that his father will secretly have sexual intercourse with the girl. If children are born as a result of it, they are regarded as the grand-children of their procreator. Elsewhere, however, this is looked upon as unworthy.

REASONS FOR CHILD BETROTHAL

Besides the simple reason of settling outstanding debts, there are a number of others which result in a more regular form of child betrothal. The object of the parents is to enter into an affinity relation and the circumstances under which such a betrothal takes place are somewhat unusual to Westerners. Since, however, the entire life of a Batak is directed to maintaining kinship- and affinity-relationships, betrothal and marriage are naturally bound up with other elements of the social organisation. To give some examples: in the *Pidari* time, a father married off his already betrothed daughter to another man. The jilted man declared war on the father and defeated him in battle. Peace was restored between them by one of the *parboru*'s young granddaughters becoming betrothed to the grandson of the man to whom the *parboru*'s daughter had originally been betrothed. And it was also agreed that the *parboru* should settle on his erstwhile adversary two cows and half a house as an *ulos topot-topot*, an *ulos* present which is in the nature of a penalty; the *parboru* received nothing at all. In another case a village chief died leaving an outstanding debt to a friend who was at the same time a fairly close affine. The closest kinsmen of the deceased were poor and were only able in part to bear this burden on the estate. The arrangement was made that some of the kinsmen should make a money contribution and that for the remainder, which was considerable, another kinsman should hand over his small daughter to be betrothed to a small son of the creditor's brother. This appears to be a somewhat involved solution, but it is quite usual to the Batak.

A man living in a small village or a small town outside his own *marga*'s area becomes prosperous. He wants to remain there for good and to build a house on his own land. In order to acquire this land for himself, and later for his son, he betrothes the boy while he is still young to a small daughter of someone who belongs to the ruling *marga*. The boy's father gives a considerable sum as the precursor to the marriage payment and obtains the desired plot of land as a precursor to the dowry.

In olden times when a man wanted to remove timber from a forest but was not entitled to do so because his *marga* had no rights in the area in question, he often entered into, or renewed, an affinity relationship, *mamungka* or *mangaratai partondongan*, with someone from the ruling *marga* in order to acquire the right to cut down the trees. This could also be effected by a child betrothal if no marriageable daughters were available. The present given by the person desiring the timber also served as an acknowledgement of his enjoying a personal privilege within an area over which others had the rights of disposal.

Formerly there were typical political betrothals and marriages which were effected by *radja* of distinction among each other in order to extend a friendship with powerful and influential chiefs as a counterbalance to the growing power of and the danger that threatened them from their enemies. It is known, for example, that the last but one *radja* of Pulo Sibandang — an island in Lake Toba — who ruled the entire south westerly area of the lake, married his seven daughters to chiefs in all parts of the Batak Country, including Silindung, who were as powerful as he was himself.

The old and the new are sometimes intermingled. When a *kampung* chief has to be elected for some heterogeneous *huta*, a candidate from one *huta* will sometimes promise his small son to the daughter of someone from another *huta* for a large sum of money in order to gain the latter's vote and that of his small group of kinsmen.

BETROTHAL FORMALITIES: PRESENTS AND COUNTER-PRESENTS

The formal betrothal of children takes place in the house of the *parboru* after the financial conditions have been discussed. The *paranak*, his small son, his nearest kinsmen and his village chief, go to the *parboru*'s house taking with them a meal which can also be called *tanggo djuhut* = to cut up meat. The *parboru*'s village chief, the *parboru*'s kinsmen and some of the members of his village are also present. When the meal has been eaten the girl's name is spoken by her father, *paboa goar*, upon which the boy's father strews some grains of rice on her head, *mandjomput parbue*, so that she will be prosperous and, expressing his good wishes for her *tondi*, acknowledges her as his prospective daughter-in-law. The *parboru* does the same thing to the boy and gives him an *ulos* as a *tanda hela* = the token that he accepts him as prospective son-in-law. Sometimes the girl has beads hung on her and so this ceremony is also called *manangkothon simata*.

When these ceremonies have been performed the payments are made and there is an exchange of presents and counter-presents. The *paranak* pays the *patudjolo* = precursor of the marriage payment, (also called *bohi ni sinamot* or *niundjuk*) consisting of money and cattle to the girl's father and possibly distributes the portions for the *pangalambungi* = nearest relations. In return he receives the *ragi-ragi*. In Toba particularly, the latter is usually a piece of land which is then regarded as the precursor of the dowry, the *pauseang*, that the daughter will later receive when the marriage takes place. In Toba this piece of land is called *parhaen* = the covering (for the girl: *haen* is a little used synonym for *ulos*). In Silindung, where land is less frequently given as a dowry, it is called the *hundulan ni boru* = the 'seat' for the *boru*. At the same time as these substantial presents are given, small presents can also be exchanged that are connected with the transactions that have been effected and which confirm and indicate satisfaction with them. The formalities in these matters naturally differ from place to place. Such presents are: the *ulos sidjomput parbue* = overgarment for the *paranak* who strewed the rice over the *boru*, and the *sipaboa goar*, a *piso* gift for the *parboru* who spoke the girl's name, etc. The people present receive an *upa domu-domu* or an *upa manggabei* for having given their good wishes, *gabe*.

The formalities of betrothing an unborn girl, a *boru tapang*, to a youth (sometimes, though rarely, to an unborn male child, *anak tapang*) only differ from the usual child betrothal in so far that the ceremonial just described takes place when the girl has been born and when the father of the youth comes to "*marupa-upa*" her.

BREAKING OFF A CHILD BETROTHAL

The death of one of the two children does not mean that the parents must give up the idea of a betrothal completely. If the girl dies, she can be replaced, *singkat*, which will happen the sooner if the *parboru* has a little daughter and no money with which to make a return for the *patudjolo ni sinamot* he has already received. If financial difficulties make it necessary, or if the continuance of the *partondongan* that has already been begun is highly desirable, then close kinsmen will come to the *parboru*'s aid and provide a substitute for the deceased child. However, a kinship relationship five *sundut* distant can be reckoned to be too far back to assume that a kinsman will be willing to do so, as I learned when I was present at the hearing of a case dealing with the point in question. The situation can be different again where people live together in less compact kinship groups. If the boy dies he can also be replaced.

Breaking off a child betrothal either because later on the grown up children or their parents have other plans, will be dealt with for preference in the discussion on divorce since the technical terms used in this connection can also be employed in terminating a betrothal.

THE YOUNG PEOPLE'S FREEDOM

If the betrothal of two young people when they were children was only, or in the main, a financial transaction, or if, during the course of the ensuing years the desire of the parents to contract an affinity relationship should have cooled, the tie so contracted is only formally binding on the young people. It is true that when the small girl has reached an age at which she can be courted, she is regarded as a *boru oroan,* i.e., she can only be asked for when she is again free, but her parents will not make any objections to releasing her from her bond. This holds good even for the *parumaen di losung* who is not strictly obliged to marry the man chosen for her if she does not wish to do so. It is a different situation, however, when the parents still want the marriage to take place, if the financial dependence of the girl's father has increased, or if the circumstances, which can be manifold, have become more pressing. Then the parents will endeavour to influence their children to conform to their wishes by persuasion, gentle pressure or by contriving that the betrothed couple have sexual intercourse in order to ensure that the marriage takes place. They will not even shrink from using strong moral compulsion if there is any opposition, and the girl runs the risk of physical force being used against her. (In the *Pidari* time it was not even against the law to put a recalcitrant daughter in the block, *mambeanghon.*) Parents can also adopt these attitudes when the children have grown up and the parents then set their hearts on a marriage which suits their plans or which, as far as it concerns the girl, promises a large marriage payment. The young man, who is always accorded more independence by his father than a father gives to his daughter, always has somewhat more freedom of action in his search for a bride. And, although he will have to withstand powerful opposition and pressure if he is determined to have his own way, it will not be too difficult for him. The girl, however, by virtue of the relationship between the sexes, always plays a more passive role. She does not continue the lineage of her father but forges other links by her marriage and is the means by which a desired relationship can be effected between the men's groups. She is brought up to accept the superior position of her brothers and her own submissiveness to the wishes of her kinsmen. If her ideas run counter to those of her parents, then she will have to possess great fortitude to triumph over them. If her parents are dead, if her brothers are too young or are dead, and if her uncles, who would then act as her *parboru*, are heartless and selfish men who live in an environment where customs are rough — the area round Lake Toba in particular — it is not out of the question that her kinsmen will use physical force to make her submit to sexual intercourse with the man, often much older than she, to whom she has been promised in marriage. Her kinsmen will excuse such callous behaviour by saying that they have a right to decide the girl's fate, and anyway they do not see such conduct as offensive. They believe that affection between the young people before marriage is not necessary, because in their opinion genuine love will grow after the birth of children, particularly after the birth of a son. It must be remembered that the principal aim of marriage is to beget children. A wife who has given her husband a son is considered to have fulfilled her destiny, and at the same time, his dearest wish. He is grateful to her and honours her the more for the son she has given him. Such a wife is then called the *boru naung gabe* = the woman who has been blessed, and she is assured in the future of her husband's respect and appreciation and she knows that her life is then secure, even if he dies before she does. It is therefore assumed that a marriage for which neither the one nor the other had much desire and which was brought about by pressure, will take a turn for the better as soon as the couple become "*marrongkap gabe*" because this can lead to a prosperous life together and to a large family of healthy sons and daughters.

I found this belief confirmed during the period when I practised as a leader of the judicial administration when many lives were laid bare. Many women who had been persuaded into marrying with an *upa mangunung* = an inducement, such as a rice-field for example, had had a happy married life after giving birth to a number of children.

However, the love between young people who are not allowed to marry each other, or their opposition to a forced marriage, is often stronger than the power of the parents against which they do have some means of defence such as the forms of marriages mentioned earlier of which the manner and the consequences will be discussed later.

DEFENCE AGAINST PARENTAL COMPULSION

The most serious thing that can happen as a result of parental pressure is for the girl to commit suicide. Each year there are one or more cases of suicide that can be attributed to this cause. A girl can run away from her husband after the unwanted marriage — and this does happen — but she knows the fate that awaits the *boru mahilolong* = the wife who has broken up her marriage. It is the form of divorce in which the affronted husband can make the greatest possible demand on the *parboru* who, as a consequence, will frequently take the husband's side against his own daughter. Knowing this, the wife will sometimes resort to cunning. She seeks out a knowledgeable old woman and following her advice, acts with a passive indifference in the first nights of her marriage so that her inexperienced husband appears to be impotent. This she soon spreads abroad as a motive for her deserting him and for a divorce.

A young man who meets opposition from his parents will frequently go out into the world in an endeavour to make himself financially independent. And, as I found out, if he fears that the girl of his choice might be forced into marriage with another man, he will drive the cattle from his father's pastures to the *parboru*'s village and give them to the girl's father as payment for his daughter, thus forcing his own father into the *marhata sinamot* = discussions on the marriage payment, which he had previously refused to consider.

It is obvious that the young girl of today who has been to school is opposed to the use of force or of too strong a moral compulsion by the *parboru* (and by his wife also for the older women are often in complete agreement with their husbands). The present generation of young men are also becoming more and more averse to what can no longer be regarded as conduct worthy of a man. If, therefore, the Government should take measures against this form of compulsion it will have a growing opinion on its side.

THE PARBORU AND THE PARANAK

The *parboru* is normally the girl's father. If he is dead the girl's

13

mother cannot, as a rule, take over his role. In Toba Holbung, however, where both a wife and a widow have more independence of action, a widowed mother can give her daughter in marriage without acquainting her deceased husband's kinsmen if they are distant relatives and if she has a small son for whom she is considered to be acting. Elsewhere, however, when a son has not reached manhood and also where there is no son, the girl's father's brothers or more distant kinsmen will stand on their rights. When the kinship relationship between her *parboru* and her deceased father is a distant one her fate, as we have already seen, can be very unfavourable and the more distant the relationship is the worse the situation can be. If a widow has a son who is married, then he becomes the *parboru* and will arrange the marriage of his sisters in consultation with his mother. An unmarried son is also entitled to act as a *parboru* provided that he has reached manhood. Such an unmarried adult son of a widow is called the *dagang ina* and, as will appear later in the discussion on attaining majority, will come forward on behalf of his deceased father, if possible, in collaboration with his father's brothers, but if necessary, without them.

It is unthinkable for a girl to be without a *parboru*. It did happen in the *Pidari* time when there were occasions when a man, whose ties with his kinsmen had all been severed, died and left only a daughter. If he had been a slave or if he was held in pledge for a debt, then his creditor had rights over the girl.

There is one occasion when the normal *parboru* is dispensed with and replaced by another person and that is when a wife is divorced on the understanding that if she remarries, the marriage payment made by her ex-husband will be returned to him out of the marriage payment acquired on her second marriage. The reason that the *parboru* does not handle the financial arrangements of such a second marriage is that he might be prejudiced against the first husband. The financial settlement is arranged by the chief who acts as an intermediary, *pangulu*, in such circumstances. The wife is then called the *boru ni radja* or the *boru ni pangulu*. This feature has almost as good as disappeared from customary law: it will be discussed later.

The *paranak* is the young man's father. If he is dead, then his eldest son or one of his brothers takes his place, and should there be neither then, at the outside, a cousin will act for him. After that the young man usually handles the business himself. A widow is allowed more independence of action in marrying off her son than in marrying off her daughter. If by chance father and son are in conflict, and the latter takes his fate in his own hands and abducts the girl, or elopes with her, then, should the *paranak* refuse to co-operate in the arrangements for the marriage, the father's brothers will come to the young man's aid and the affines will use their influence to restore peace.

The young man attains his majority on his marriage but this does not mean that his father forthwith allows him independence as far as property rights are concerned, *mandjae*. Should the marriage miscarry before the young husband attains his full rights, then the *paranak* will act for him in the dealings with the *parboru*.

THE PARBORU AFTER THE MARRIAGE

It must be remembered that the links between a woman and the group from which she came are not severed once and for all when she marries. The relationship is regularly maintained so long as the marriage goes smoothly, and the *parboru* will intervene if there is a rift. The woman can then be returned to him with the request that he "teach her a lesson" if her husband feels that he has reason to be displeased with her behaviour and conduct towards him. If she has in fact mis- behaved, the *parboru* will take her to task and will then either send her back to her husband on her own or he will accompany her himself in order to heal the breach. The *parboru* also becomes involved again if there is a marital dispute and his daughter goes to him with just cause for complaint. If, for instance, she has been ill treated. He will then take his daughter's part because he feels that he too has been insulted. The husband must then make reparation for his misdemeanour, *pauli uhum*, which is also an expression of his regret and of his willing- ness to ask the *parboru* for his forgiveness.

If a wife runs off with another man or if her husband suspects she is unfaithful and as a consequence there is a dispute about her then, so long as the matter is pending, she can be given into the custody of her father, *pinarhundul tu amana*: she is then a woman in dispute, *boru panggulutan*. If a wife has been brutally raped, the *parboru* will also seek satisfaction, *marlulu*, and both he and the husband have a right to legal redress, *rap mandjalo uhuman i*.

When a woman is widowed and puts on widow's weeds, *tudjung*, her *parboru* and his kinsmen come after some time has passed to put an end to her mourning, *pasae tudjung*. If the widow later marries in levirate her late husband's *uaris*, or somebody else, the *parboru* receives a sum of money, which is large or small according to the circumstances, from the new son-in-law as an acknowledgement of his status as *parboru*.

These are just a few of the instances which demonstrate that the wife, contrary to the idea accepted by some writers, does not become the exclusive property of her husband; that he does not have complete control over her and that the severance from her kinship group is not final.

THE UPA TULANG

The continuance of the woman's relationship with her kinship group after her marriage is clear from the fact that at the marriage of her daughter her own closest *marga* kinsman, her brother who is the bride's *tulang,* has a right to a portion of the marriage payment. This portion is even one of the main constituents of the marriage payment, with that of the bride's father. But, in contrast to that of the agnatic circle which is defined by the terms *tu suhut, tu sidjalo bara, tu todoan,* etc., for the *suhut,* etc., this portion is always termed *upa (upa tulang),* and means a gift of homage. It is not in the nature of "compensation" but it has probably superseded a former *mangupa.* The allocation of this portion to the *tulang* is an acknowledgement of the important function the *tulang,* the mother's brother, who also acts for a father after his death, fulfils in respect of the beneficial activity which the *hula-hula* can transfer to its *boru.* The *tulang* is constantly by his sister's side and assists in the upbringing of her children of whom the eldest son will possibly be his future son-in-law. He treats his sister's daughters as his own and they will be as sisters to his sons.

CONSTITUENTS OF THE MARRIAGE PAYMENT

In view of the facts already given regarding the marriage payment, it will be no surprise that, unlike what is often the case elsewhere, it does not contain objects having a magico-religious significance. The idea that objects imbued with strong supernatural power go from the weak *boru* to the strong *hula-hula* is not consistent with the relationship which comes into being with a Batak marriage. No instance is known to me of such a thing. In the addresses which are given in Silindung at the *marundjuk,* the set phrase, *horbo na poso, mas na lobangon* = young buffaloes and old milled-edged gold pieces, is often used to describe the whole *sinamot.* I doubt that this indicates a supernatural purport attaching to golden objects which, with cattle, must formerly have frequently constituted the marriage payment. At the present day one finds all kinds of movable property serving as the constituents of the marriage payment, but in the main it is usually paid in money or cattle.

Formerly, among wealthy persons, it was also paid in male and female slaves.

If cattle are given in payment, then their transfer is permanent as a rule: they are not redeemable, *sindor*. At present the amount of the marriage payment is assessed in terms of money, the cattle being valued at so much per head, *asam*, but this was not the practice in olden times. If the cattle are not actually delivered, then their transfer is effected by handing over a small whip or a halter for each animal. Very often payment consists of a quarter, *hae*, of a buffalo, a horse or a cow and when the remaining quarters belong to another person or persons these should be informed that there is a new joint owner. More often than not, however, this is neglected. When the cattle are *niasam*, restitution can be made at the value fixed, or another beast or beasts provided in the event of there being a divorce.

If land is included in the marriage payment, it is always as a pledge, *sindor* for a money debt, *sindor ni hepeng*. The size of this sum must therefore be clearly established (this is also called *niasam*). This land can be redeemed by closely related kinsmen of the man who pledged it. In some areas the in-dwelling *marga boru* living of old with its *hula-hula* has the right to use the land it cultivates as *pangoli ni anak* = payment for the marriage of a son: younger in-dwelling *marga* are not entitled to this right.

Gold and other things, such as houses, for example, can also be handed over as *sindor* but they can also be transferred permanently. Many a time kinsmen make their property available as *sindor* which is then their *tumpak*. *Ulos* cloths can never form part of the marriage payment because these cloths come from the *hula-hula*.

In the *Pidari* time the total amount of the marriage payment was small. Nowadays it can vary from between some tens of guilders among the poor to some hundreds among the wealthy. It rarely exceeds 1,000 guilders and sometimes it contains spare items called *gadja ni mas* which are added for the sake of honour and to dazzle the public. The introduction of money into the country has gradually increased the amount of the marriage payment, though not excessively.

Formerly there seem to have been many endeavours by the Government to fix a maximum (I heard amounts of 30 and 150 Spanish dollars mentioned) but they were unsuccessful and, furthermore, they appear to be unnecessary since, unlike South Sumatra and Nias, there is no question of excessive amounts being demanded. It is probably the fact that the bride's father can be called upon to refund the full amount in the event of a divorce that has acted as a brake. Usually the marriage payment is completely settled at the *marundjuk*. If a part of it remains unpaid and no pledge is given for it, this fact must be clearly announced. Whether it is settled in full or only in part has no influence whatsoever on the relations between the married couple, nor does it affect the relationship between the wife and her own kinsmen, nor that of the husband towards his parents-in-law: settlement of the part outstanding has as little consequences. On the amount still owing, *na so sahat* = what the opposite party has not yet received, also called *utang di pudi* = the debt outstanding, no interest is ever claimed.

EVIDENCE REGARDING THE MARRIAGE PAYMENT

Because a number of people attend the discussions, many of which are held in public, and because a meal is eaten, the assumption would be justified that the arrangements relating to the marriage payment are always properly recorded. On the contrary. There is hardly any subject in Batak customary law that presents so much dissension as does the composition and amount of the *sinamot, ragi-ragi* and *pauseang* in the event of the marriage failing and there being a divorce. This applies as much to the arranging of the betrothal as it does to concluding a marriage. In these relationships especially, excessive cordiality and good-will are likely to result in carelessness. Moreover, the Toba Batak, as distinct from the Batak of South Tapanuli, lack the feeling for the dignified and the dramatic that makes the purpose of a series of cere-monies clearly perceptible to everyone and, in fact, serenity is often con-spicuous by its absence at the *marundjuk*. Often there is more tumult than peace. Also, not everyone pays the attention that should be given to all the details of what takes place. If everything were conducted in the right way then the *domu-domu* or *pande-pande* who co-operated in both parties reaching agreement would be fully cognisant of the whole course of the negotiations, so that in the event of a dispute rising later they could give the fullest and most factual testimony. They have after all received the *upa domu-domu* as a reward for their mediation. In practice, however, they are not infrequently in disagreement with each other or are but half in possession of the facts and are therefore some-times not even brought before the judge by the parties concerned. As for the other witnesses, the chiefs, kinsmen, affines and the casual spectators, they alas, are often not much better informed.

As a rule, the best guarantee of a regular and clearcut progress lies in the co-operation of the chiefs, primarily the village chiefs, the *radja ni huta* — though they are sometimes unsatisfactory witnesses — and, if required, the higher chiefs as well. Their efforts are almost indispensible. Whether the negotiations concern a *marboru tapang*, a normal child betrothal or the first *marhata sinamot* after a young couple's courtship, it is always correct for the *paranak* to be accompanied by his village chief when he goes to the *huta* of the *parboru*, and he must insist that the *parboru*'s village chief is also present at the latter's house. Whosoever comes must be accompanied by a *radja* and must be received by a *radja, marradja ma na ro, marradja na nidapotna*. If both chiefs are absent then, though the agreement reached is not void, it is regarded as being less conclusive, *hurang denggan*. Their presence is obligatory at the *marundjuk* proper otherwise the marriage can be declared illegal. If later there is a dispute, the judge has in these chiefs a pair of witnesses, *sibege hata*, who should be able to state the facts of the matter to him clearly and without any doubt, *andár*. They do not witness the negotiations as casual observers but represent authority in their village. They must know what important contracts are concluded by their people, commit the details to memory, and give their blessing to the agreement. They are also obliged to support their subordinates with their reasoned discourse and, if the parties cannot meet on common ground, the chiefs, knowing the position with regard to the disputants' property and their circumstances, will make such proposals as may lead to agreement. For this and their further co-operation, they receive the *upa radja*, a gift of homage consistent with their status and also an acknowledgement of their fitness to bear witness. Whosoever neglects to acquaint his village chief about matters relating to betrothals and marriages, merits disciplinary action being taken against him. Similarly, the chief who is negligent and careless in providing his legal co-operation deserves the same treatment. Both parties, in neglecting their duties have endangered legal security and legal order within the community concerned.

The evils which can result from failure to give due attention to the evidence, are for the greater part counteracted by the regular application of the swearing of the oath which is always regarded as decisive in a dispute concerning the size of the *sinamot* and the *ragi-ragi*. It is the principle (discussed in more detail particularly in Chapter X) that is embodied in the *umpama*: *unang pabalga hae-hae ni horbóm* = no one is permitted to increase his own quarter of the buffalo, i.e., no one is allowed to use the oath as a means of increasing his claim. Thus, when there is a divorce, the *parboru* states on oath the size of the *sinamot* he has received and which he has then to pay back. The *paranak* does likewise in respect of the *ragi-ragi*. This is the established rule from which no one departs other than in exceptional and unusual circumstances.

The written record provides an additional certainty of correct evidence. The value of such a record was understood immediately after the first missionary schools were established in the Batak Country. It was to the village teacher, who could provide the desired record by virtue of his qualifications, that people turned in the first instance. The chiefs also appreciated the value of this procedure, as appears from the signatures on many a "certificate". But it fell by the wayside in most districts when a so-called marriage register was introduced by the district administration. This register gave people the opportunity to put on record the property that was part of the marriage settlement. Ostensibly the registration was optional but from many a criminal sentence by the lower courts it is clear that it became gradually to be regarded as obligatory. Nevertheless, numerous marriages were not registered. In later years this registration has been delegated more and more to the *negeri* chiefs who usually follow the prescribed model. According to this the names of the persons concerned, the principal *djambar*, one or more of the smaller payments — sometimes all under their collective name of *suda di lapik* — and the *ragi-ragi* should be listed. The value of all the items must be expressed in terms of money. In addition, what the bride has received as *pauseang* must be stated as well as what has been paid and what remains unpaid.

As appears from the numerous lawsuits, special agreements which are frequently made, are seldom stated, neither is what has been given as *sindor*. This is a deficiency arising directly from the restrictions which the model form imposes. Worse, however, is the disadvantage that the desire of the parties concerned to be complete in the details of the agreement is thus not furthered: in the case of the *sinamot, ragi-ragi* and *pauseang*, these can often be very complicated. As a result, those concerned do not fully realise the importance of the registration and consequently time and time again it is apparent that the formal statements deviate from the reality. It adds up to this: where the registration takes place in the sub-district offices, verification of the statements made at the *marundjuk* is virtually impossible, and no other control is feasible. With the prevailing idea that no marriage can be regarded as being concluded until the registration has taken place, the consequence is that it is always rather deficient and doubtful. Where the *negeri* chiefs keep the registers there is better opportunity of supervision, of seeing that the record accords with the actual facts. The *negeri*-clerks, however, with their usual incompetence, need more freedom to write their records in their own way. Then, if a dispute later arises, the judge may have placed before him documents from which he can learn albeit with difficulty what in fact has been agreed upon by the parties concerned.

It has always surprised me that in these circumstances the supervising officials have always been inclined to persuade the judge to accept as factual what is stated in the register so long as no reliable counter evidence is furnished. Bearing the facts in mind, it can hardly be considered satisfactory to bind litigants to a written statement of this kind. In doing so greater importance is attached to a written record as evidence than is usual in customary law. The conclusive force which the record then acquires clashes with the swearing of the oath, of the reasonableness of which those concerned are still convinced.

THE ASSISTANCE OF THE HIGHER CHIEFS

From what was said in Chapter III it will be clear that it is not generally applicable throughout the Batak Country that the higher chiefs appointed by the Dutch administration had, by the rules of customary law, to be acquainted with the settlement of all marriages. Marriage has always been primarily a matter for the village and the somewhat larger lineage. The principal chiefs of an entire *marga* or *marga* branch did not attend every marriage, neither did they always claim a gift of homage. Even in those regions where the *bius* was politically coloured, such as Samosir, where the *radja doli* could be a powerful figure, or in West Humbáng with its distinctive figure of the *ompu ni saksi*, the highest chief only concerned himself with marriages which took place in ruling *marga* other than his own if he wished to give proof of his interest out of friendship or because of affinity relationships. Generally marriage was not the concern of the *bius*; it was a matter only concerning the component genealogical units.

Consequently, when the Government made the regulation that a fixed *upa radja* had to be paid to the "acknowledged" chiefs, the *kampung* chief, *radja paidua*, *negeri* chief, etc., it was regarded as an innovation and met with little response in a community when its own *huta* chiefs were not among the "acknowledged" ones. Moreover, the incorporation of non-related *huta* under one *kampung* chief, or the incorporation of small territories which either did not belong together or whose relationship was inadequate, into one *negeri*, also awakened in those who were the victims of these arrangements a disinclination to pay the *upa radja*. They looked upon it as an order, a *printah*. The formation of the *negeri* was not attended with a definite mandate to the *negeri* chiefs to give systematic care to customary law in the communities they ruled, either on their own authority or in conjunction with the lower chiefs. In fact, the formation of the *negeri* tended to coincide with a concentration of more and more power and authority in the hands of the Batak district- and sub-district officers and in the lower courts which came under their jurisdiction. All of them undermined the authority of the chiefs who were left with little more than an interest in the levies.

That there is, however, a need for a powerful chiefly authority that extends above the narrow village milieu, is nowhere more obvious than in matrimonial law. The state of affairs in marriage and divorce — especially in Toba, but elsewhere also — is such that it can hardly be left as it is. And that the population is aware of this need may be concluded from the fact that some of the few native municipalities which (up to 1930) had been established, have concerned themselves with the position of illegitimate children, the transfer of the *pauseang*, the regulation of levies at marriage, and so on. In general these efforts have been fruitless, because the Government, and as a consequence the "supervised" administration of justice, have withheld the support without which no act can be an operative force. All too often irregular marriages and divorces take place at which only a couple of more or less near kinsmen and one or two of the lower chiefs — sometimes not even those of the parties concerned — have been present and which have been effected in such a manner that one is justified in saying that there has been a certain degree of degeneration. It is therefore desirable that, instead of curtailing the authority of the chiefs in respect of divorce and marriage to such scanty proportions, which is the result of the excessive concentration of authority in the district administration, the Government and the judiciary should give a stimulus to the chiefs and show them that they have a real interest in the proper maintenance of law and custom on these important matters. The opposition that the *upa radja* levy now encounters among the people would then lose much of the justification which it does, in a certain sense, have.

THE DOWRY, PAUSEANG

The bride's dowry, the *pauseang*, is the gift given by the *parboru* to his *boru* and her husband when the *parboru* gives her in marriage. It is given at the time of the marriage or shortly afterwards. It usually consists of land, particularly a wet rice-field. The transfer of land by means of an affinity relationship is, in general, one of the principal ways in which land, unredeemable, passes from one *marga* to another and the *pauseang*-gift is one of the most important forms by which this is achieved. It is not, however, a frequent occurrence in every part of the Batak Country. In Silindung and its environs it only occurs to a limited extent since there is the fear that it would result in too great a loss of *golat*-land for the *marga* and tribal group. There, preference is given to a conferment of land rights upon the in-dwelling affines in the form of the right of *parripean*, a kind of usufruct for the duration of their sojourn in the village or region. In Pahae the practice of giving land as *pauseang* does not occur. In Toba, on the other hand, the *pauseang*-gift is often given and nearly every daughter who marries profits by it. It gives rise to an ever-increasing alienation of land to *marga* other than the ruling *marga*, especially in recent years now that marriages can be concluded outside the neighbouring groups of territories. It also leads to a further splitting up of land that has already been parcelled out and, since the place where the *parboru* lives and the fields which he allocates to his *boru* are often far from the dwelling place of his son-in-law to which the *boru* will go, it gives rise to a number of kinds of contracts such as usufruct, sharecropping, land pledging and exchange. Because of this and because in Toba marriages so often end in divorce, this alienation of land is often the origin of many lawsuits of various kinds.

It is thus important that a subject which lies in the domain of both matrimonial law and land law should be dealt with in some detail. It must, however, be said at the outset that on this point, as on many others, Toba is not exactly a region where the nature of a legal institution is always strictly observed by everyone. It should also be noted that in the abundance of forms and terms which exist in respect of the alienation of land by the *hula-hula* to the *boru*, it is easy for one form to merge into another, while many a term is elastic as to its meaning and sometimes varies according to area. First we will deal with the precursor to the *pauseang*. This is given at a child betrothal to the *paranak* as a counterpresent of the *bohi ni sinamot* which he has paid. This precursor which, for the time being at least, will only be of benefit to the father of the youth, is as indefinite in its purport as the betrothal itself. By its designations, however, *parhaen* and *hundulan ni boru*, it does show that its purpose is to serve the donor's daughter later on. The conditional nature of the gift will naturally restrain the donee from actions which would bring about permanent alienation or cause difficulties in the event of its having to be returned to the donor. I once saw a contract that stipulated that the *hundulan ni boru*, which was land, was to become the permanent property, *sipate-pate*, of the *paranak* should the betrothal come to naught, declared void by the judge because it was regarded as a disguised and unlawful alienation of *golat*-land to a member of an in-dwelling *marga*.

The terms *hundulan ni boru* and *parhaen* are not used if the counter-present of the precursor of the marriage payment is not a piece of land: in such a case the more general terms *ragi-ragi* and *ulos-ulos* are used.

The *pauseang* has also a precursor, the gift of affection, the *bangunan*, consisting of a rice-field which, especially in Toba but elsewhere also, is often given by a father to his still unmarried daughter. A wealthy father will give such a present to his daughter out of pure affection or, if she is deformed, to enhance her chance of marriage. A further dowry can follow when the girl does marry. This present is a *silean-lean* = permanent gift, which cannot be reclaimed by the donor, *ndang siunsatan naung nilehon*. The girl cultivates the land herself and harvests the rice from it which she stores or sells. When she marries she brings both the land and its produce with her. The *hauma bangunan* occupies a separate place in the matrimonial property and is distinct from the other plots of the family's land, each of which has its own legal origin. The woman's children will later regard it as their mother's contribution to their prosperity. Her husband is not at liberty to make any decision regarding it without first consulting her and possibly he will leave all matters concerned with it to her. Should the land be the subject of a lawsuit, she can appear herself before the judge with or without her husband. If she returns to her *hula-hula* because she is widowed and has not remarried in levirate, or if she is divorced, this piece of land is the first thing that she retains. From all these features, which are apparent in one region more than in another, it can be seen that there is a close and permanent connection between a woman and such a piece of land transferred to her personally. The *bangunan* has also some features in common with the *pauseang*.

The principle feature of the *pauseang* is that land so bestowed is intended for the descendants of the daughter: an objective not so clearly discernible with other property. It is not a transfer of land between the men over the head of the wife, it is a gift given to her as a dowry, *asa sangap boru i*, so that she will be held in esteem by her husband. It has the additional object that the land will remain in the possession of her descendants, *siihut-ihuton ni pomparanna*. It is the donor's first contribution to the welfare of the *boru*-group that comes into being for him when he gives his daughter in marriage. This feature is observed during the first generations at least. It is upheld least scrupulously where there is a continual passing to and fro of the *pauseang*-gift as a result of marriage, divorce or remarriage.

A number of phenomena which do not everywhere appear together in the same context, are connected with this feature. In many regions when the marriage is concluded and the *sinamot* and *ragi-ragi* have been discussed and settled either fully or in part in the usual way, the *parboru* gives a verbal promise, *holan hata dope*, of a *pauseang*, but its actual transfer, *pasahathon*, only takes place upon the birth of a child. And it is then immaterial whether it is a boy or a girl. The birth of a child has proved that the couple are fruitful, so that their union can be reckoned by the woman's father as durable. His object in withholding the *pauseang* was intended as a safety measure in case the son-in-law should attach the land unlawfully in the meantime. If the father-in-law is still cultivating the land himself than, as a rule, he surrenders its harvest to the married couple, but if he is rather dubious of the durability of the marriage, he stores the harvest in his own rice granary and only at his daughter's request does he let her have sufficient for her sustenance and that of her husband. This sort of things is typical of Toba Holbung. It does not exactly promote stability in the marriage bond, because this public token of lack of confidence sometimes induces the son-in-law to divorce his wife. It is this situation that compelled the council of the native municipality of Parmaksian in 1924 to fix the *pauseang* at 20 per cent of the marriage payment on condition that, apart from the *ulos ni mas*, it could be deducted direct at the settlement of the marriage payment. And, since money is not a usual *pauseang*-gift, it will be seen from this how the chiefs are sometimes led to simplify customary law because they are weary of the great number of cases (Mal. *perkara*) they have to deal with in this field. It is also typical of Toba that a wife's father once pledged the promised *pauseang* to a third party out of sheer refractoriness over the remaining unpaid portion of the marriage payment. Such an act will be declared illegal by a judge since the *parboru*'s promised gift to the young couple is not to be mixed up with his claim on the *paranak*: a man must claim his debts from those who owe them and must pay his debts to those who claim them, *masitunggu singirna be masigarar utangna be,* as the old saying goes.

It is contrary to the purpose of the *pauseang*-gift (and consequently held unlawful in Silindung) for a person who has been given one to use it for purposes other than those for which it was intended, i.e., the *pandjaean* for a son born of the marriage when he sets up his own house, or as a *pauseang* for a daughter on her marriage. It cannot be used, for example, as a *pauseang*-gift on behalf of the husband's own kinswomen. On Samosir, I was told that its use for such a purpose is only possible when the *hula-hula* agrees and, as proof of his acknowledgement and acquiescence he must then be given a small *piso*-gift.

Other restrictions on the husband's right of disposal over the land which he has received as *pauseang* are also connected with the purpose for which it was originally given. I was told that in Toba the giving of a *pauseang*-field is called *mandanggurhon batu na marihur-ihur* = throwing a stone which has a tail (by which it can be retrieved). This should not be construed to mean that the *parboru* can withdraw the gift: once it has been promised and given it cannot be withdrawn, *niunsat.* What it means is that the *hula-hula* has a right of recovery, *mangeahi,* a preferential right in case the land is to be disposed of in any way. It also refers to the *hula-hula*'s right to oppose, *mangambati,* a transfer which has already been concluded to another. All this results from the affection which the *hula-hula* expresses towards his *boru* in presenting the *pauseang.* This imposes an obligation on the young couple when they are in need to turn in the first instance to the *hula-hula* for support. The exercise of this right also tends to prevent an item of property as highly valued as land, and which was surrendered with a specific object, from falling permanently into the hands of strangers through carelessness or maladministration on the part of the son-in-law.

The frequent complaints by the *hula-hula* to a judge of *pate,* permanent, alienation to strangers of land which the *boru*-group had acquired as *pauseang,* must be seen against this background. Such complaints relate not only to alienation by the husband-recipient, but also when his sons and even grandsons have not acknowledged the *hula-hula*'s right of *mangeahi.* Complaints of this kind are not only made in respect of alienation against money, because of house-moving, payment of debts, and so on, but, also in the case of a permanent exchange against another piece of land, *marlibe pate.* The underlying idea is that such a piece of *pauseang*-land was perhaps first cultivated by the *boru*'s own father, *na pinungka ni damang,* or was possibly brought as a *pauseang* by her mother, *boan-boan ni dainang*, and then given again as a dowry to a daughter and it is not desirable that it be replaced with another piece of land chosen arbitrarily. In this context the magico-religious value ascribed to land must be taken into consideration.

A similar care must be exercised towards the origin of a *pauseang*-field when it is used as security, *tahan*, for a money debt. The danger of permanent loss which this implies should restrain the holder of a *pauseang* from entering into such a transaction without the *hula-hula*'s consent, while the creditor should place great value on the *hula-hula*'s clear acceptance of the transaction. Whosoever is neglectful in this respect and thus provides a motive for wrangling is a trouble-maker, a *panggunturi*, and merits a reproof from the judge before whom the dispute is brought. Even pledging is not permitted over the *hula-hula*'s head. Several times in Toba I came across cases where one of the closely related affines of the pledger, for example, a brother-in-law, had originally forbidden the land to be pledged but had afterwards given his consent after he had asked for a recognition of his right, *mangido adat* and had received a *piso*-gift. I am doubtful, however, whether the right to withhold consent to the alienation of land is everywhere as strong as it is in Toba. So long as the recipient has no male issue, he cannot arbitrarily pledge this land, but once he has a son he can do so though he must acquaint his family-in-law of his intention and offer them the land in the first instance: this is a matter of good form, *patut*.

I never encountered a case where the *hula-hula* appealed against the alienation of *pauseang*-land as a result of judicial decision.

Since it is lawful for a *pauseang*-field to be used again as such when a daughter marries, there is, I presume in general no objection to its being used as *sindor* = pledge for part of the marriage payment for a son, *pangoli ni anak*.

As a rule, if there is an objection to an arbitrarily concluded contract, the judge will pronounce the unlawful transaction void. There are, however, conceivable circumstances, friendship, kinship, etc., which may weaken such opposition and necessitate the *hula-hula*'s being content with a small *piso*-gift as an acknowledgement that a right of *mangeahi* did exist. The right is, naturally, surrendered by the acceptance of such a gift.

It is not possible to say for how many generations the right of *mangeahi* can be exercised. It does not have the same force everywhere and the production of evidence as to the origin of a wet rice-field becomes more difficult with the passage of time. In my opinion, it would not be possible to establish a right deriving further back than a grandfather or at most to a great-grandfather.

In respect of the management and disposal over the *pauseang*-field, the husband's authority is also restricted by the rights which a wife who has born him children has in regard to it, though this restriction does not apply to the same degree as it does to the *bangunan*. In a sound marriage the wife is an agent for the well-being of the family and whenever her own *boan-boan* = property which formed her dowry, is affected, in the interests of her children she will, if she is not too weak a character, stand in her rights, even against the outer world. But neither her influence nor her rights are such as to make her co-operation in a transaction indispensable. It is her male kinsmen who are indispensable.

In view of all this one would expect to find a firm rule by which the *pauseang* would be returned to the donor in the event of childlessness, on the death of the wife or her widowhood and her returning to her *hula-hula*. But such is not the general rule. In many regions it is even the contrary. If a son, with or without sisters makes no difference, is born to the woman then the case is simple: the land, irrespective of what happens to the mother, remains with the son and his father: the gift has achieved its purpose. If only girls are born and then the mother is divorced, the girls and their mother's *pauseang* stay with the father. The same applies if the mother dies. Should the father die, then the *uaris,* brothers, uncles, etc., assume their rights and both daughters and land go to them, even if the mother returns to her *hula-hula*. However, whereas their father would have given them the whole of their mother's *pauseang*, and perhaps even more when they married, his *uaris* might not always be so generous and might sometimes scarcely provide an adequate *pauseang* for the girls. In such a case the judge will have to decide what in fairness is their due.

If a marriage is childless, then there is difference in concept and practice.

If a divorce takes place shortly after a marriage, there is a tendency in one region to return the marriage payment as well as the *pauseang* to its source; elsewhere each person retains what he or she has received. I think it can be said that this tendency is the stronger in a region where there are many divorces and lawsuits. When an old wife who is childless is repudiated, *mangambolong padang tua* = parting with an old pasture,

I frequently noted that the judge allowed her for her sustenance all the *pauseang* which she had brought to her marriage.

If a childless wife is widowed and lives with her late husband's *uaris* without remarrying, she will then be allowed as much as is necessary for her sustenance, and here first consideration will be given to the *pauseang*-fields which she brought with her, but in this matter, too, much depends on the circumstances. If she does not stay with the *uaris* but returns to her *hula-hula* then, as in the case of divorce, the matter is settled in various ways: in one region there is an inclination to leave things as they were; in another the *pauseang* and the marriage payment are exchanged. Between these two extremes there are a variety of inter-mediate solutions to the matter.

If a woman dies childless, then the predominating idea is that the *pauseang* which she brought with her on her marriage belongs to the husband, irrespective of whether she is replaced by a sister or not. This applies the more so if she had children who have all died.

If her husband and children die after her, then the *pauseang* also remains with the husband's family group. In a few areas, however, I learned about another point of view and also saw a judgement which carried it out. I only mention this fact but I will not give details regarding it. Anyone who has to deal with this aspect in legal practice should find out what the local concept is and in doing so he will frequently find vacillation and contradiction.

Even if the *pauseang* remains with the husband and his kinsmen when a childless marriage is ended by death or a divorce, the right of *mangeahi* and of *mangambati* remain unimpaired, as far as I know, at least where these rights are strongly acknowledged.

The foregoing, which makes it clear how much diversity and uncer-tainty there can be in respect of one of the branches of the law which are of great importance in daily life, relates almost exclusively to land. There are areas where uncultivated land cannot form any part of the dowry. If land is given at all it will be rice fields or gardens on dry land. Apart from land anything may be used for the dowry: gold, cattle, rice, money, benzoin, a house, a *sopo*, a number of trees. These items, which are of a more or less non-durable nature, are of less consequence than land when they are given as *pauseang*. A wet rice-field which has been taken as pledge can serve as a dowry but should the pledger desire to redeem his land, then the pledgee who has given the field as a *pauseang* must give the recipient the money recovered if he has no other land to offer him as a substitute.

14

Here and there the custom of a fixed ratio between the marriage payment and the dowry exists, perhaps three to one, but here again there is the greatest diversity.

At the present time it is becoming more and more the fashion to give a daughter a trousseau consisting of furniture, kitchen utensils, clothes, etc. According to old custom a married son is settled in his own house, *mandjae,* by his parents sometime after the marriage. The family-in-law contribute little other than the clothing and ornaments of their daughter, and a pair of mats or carpets. In olden times the young couple also had the dish from which they had eaten as bride and groom. However, as a result of young people earning wages, the bride can contribute to furnishing the home. If I am not mistaken the general idea now is that the goods the bride brings with her on her marriage are her personal property in so far that, if a divorce should follow shortly after the marriage, she can claim these items.

PRESENTS DURING MARRIAGE

I mentioned in Chapter II that there are many occasions during a marriage on which presents can be made to the couple from the affines. Any present given to the wife at a *mangupa* ceremony held when she is ill, etc., is, in general, subject to the law concerning the *pauseang* and any present given at the *marupa-upa* ceremony held for a firstborn child is, as a rule intended, as the *indahan arian,* for the child and is also subject to the laws of the *pauseang,* whether the child lives or dies.

There is another category of presents known as *ulos-ulos* which are not directly connected with the concluding of the marriage or the birth of a child. For example, a married couple whose needs are obvious when compared with the wife's more prosperous brothers and sisters, can ask for special help from the wife's parents. Husband and wife offer a ceremonial meal to the wife's parents, and the other married children, and then they submit their request. If it is directed to the wife's brother or her father's brother both of whom are childless, the idea behind it is that such a man will give some of his property during his lifetime to those asking his help in their need so that, when the brother or uncle dies, they will not be too dependent upon the *uaris'* willingness to hand anything over. It should, however, be noted that this kind of *ulos* present cannot be given without the knowledge of the closest kinsmen, the *sisolhot,* of the donor, because they already have a right to his property in prospect by virtue of his childlessness and it should not be sprung on them later that a part of it has been transferred in private as an *ulos-ulos* to the affines. At the same time, the *sisolhot* are not able to withhold such a gift if it is made to the *boru hapundjungan* (own sister or niece of the donor). Where the *sisolhot* have been duly notified, the *boru* acquires complete freedom over the disposition of the property, though he will only use this right if a good relationship with the affines is no longer valued. Such presents are not intended to be returned, *ndang simulak-mulak*; they are given for good, *sipate-pate*. If a present consists of land, then it is for preference called *ulos na so ra buruk* = a garment that never wears out.

When a pledged wet rice-field has been given as a present, the customary rule obtains that it may not be redeemed within a minimum period of two years.

Gifts to the *boru* accruing from the estate of a deceased parent will be discussed in the following Chapter.

Before discussing the relations in and during marriage, some further attention will be given to other forms of concluding a marriage than described so far.

MARRIAGE FOLLOWING ABDUCTION = MANGABING BORU

I have already mentioned the marriage resulting from abduction as one in which the young man, aided by some companions, abducts by force a girl whom he desires but who will either not have him or is not given to him quickly enough in his opinion. After abducting her he takes her to his house or to some other convenient place and satisfies his desires. Such a proceeding deprives the *parboru* of the free disposition over his *boru*, but if suitable atonement is made for this transgression, the abductor can keep the girl as his wife. Her wishes are not considered, or hardly so. Her fate depends on whether her *parboru* will let the abductor keep her or not, and whether the latter can pay the penalty demanded. If the girl does not want to marry the young man, she may try to flee before the marriage is a *fait accompli*, thus cancelling out the abduction and embarrassing the abductor. She may hope that her *parboru* will be on her side, but if she is doubtful she can go to a man with whom she has an agreement to marry, if there is such a one. Abduction must not be viewed as a barbarous act towards the girl in all cases. The young man does not necessarily abduct a girl simply to gratify his passion: it can be a forceful expression of his wish to honour, *mangaradjahon*, the girl of his fancy because he wants to elevate her to the status of being his spouse, the mistress of his house. And, indeed, what woman was ever wholly insensible to such a demonstration of affection and strength of character? Sometimes a girl will refuse to co-operate in such a wayward method of bringing about a marriage, even though she is not averse to marrying the young man, but simply because she does not want to force her *parboru*'s hand by such a step or because she will not depart from the usual course and thus miss the Church's blessing. If a young man abducts his mother's brother's daughter, *mangabing pariban*, or a girl to whom he is already affianced, there are strong mitigating factors, since in each case he is only forcing the issue in respect of a girl who is either actually betrothed to him or promised to him, but about whom the deliberations concerning the marriage payment are not making much headway. Not infrequently in such cases the girl's friends are in the plot, and, in fact, these cases are often indistinguishable from marriage following an elopement, *mangalua*, when the girl acts in concert with the young man and forsakes the parental home.

The treatment of abduction cases will not, therefore, always follow the course as described in *Patik dohot uhum* and neither will this have been the case in the *Pidari* time. Indeed, the many penalties mentioned in *Patik dohot uhum* relate to a time when the *parboru*, in conjunction with his village chief, had to look after his own interests.

Marriage after abduction was a recognised marriage form and the penalties claimed were compensation for forcibly abducting the girl. Formerly it was especially the son of a *namora* = a rich man, who resorted to abducting a girl — his father could afford the heavy penalties — as a means of demonstrating his courage, *patuduhon habeguonna*, in this exceptional way. He also established his name and renown as the son of a wealthy and influential man, *paungkap goarna paboa barita, tanda ni anak paradongan*. It was thus somewhat unlikely that the *parboru* would have been unwilling to leave his daughter with her abductor. The high penalties were tempting, she had by then almost certainly been deflowered, she was probably not at that time betrothed and, moreover, would possibly not want to return to him. If, however, the *parboru* did not desire the affinity relationship, he claimed so high a penalty that the abductor could not pay it. He would then proceed to demand that the settlement must be a *dangdang* = penalty, and that his daughter had to be offered a *panguras* = cleanser, a *pangias* = purifier, he could demand that this satisfaction had to be given in public by the abductor's father, mother, brothers and sisters at a meal of atonement so that the dish and the water cask would bow down, *marsomba sanihe marsomba ramboan*. This attitude the *parboru* could only adopt if he thought his own power and influence greater than those of the overbold young man.

At the present time arms are not resorted to and neither are the many penalties listed in the *Patik dohot uhum* demanded. Now, the *parboru* whose *boru* is abducted joins with his village chief in laying a complaint before the higher chief, and, if the girl has been taken out of the area of jurisdiction of the latter, they forthwith lay a complaint before the Governmental police. The first duty of these authorities is to ascertain whether in fact the girl was abducted against her will, for naturally the *parboru* is inclined to represent the affair in the worst possible light and, whether it is still against her will that her abductor keeps her. They have to determine whether or not it is a case of *manga-bing*, abduction by force and against the wish of the girl. It is this feature which gives the *parboru* the right to demand a higher marriage payment than he could do in normal circumstances. This is an idea still considered reasonable. The modern approach to this subject, however, also regards it as reasonable that the girl herself shall have the right to decide whether she will marry her abductor or not. This is the more reasonable when one considers that it may be a question of the girl's being protected against her *parboru*.

However, even though there has been this shift of emphasis, there is still a place for atonement to be made to the girl, *pangias ni boru*, who has probably been deflowered, if no marriage results. But whether such an *adat* penalty should be imposed to satisfy both the *parboru* and the sense of justice of the public, or whether the sentence should be imprisonment for a misdemeanour which is regarded more and more as in the first place an offence against public order, is a matter for a judge to decide conscientiously in each individual case.

Formerly the amount of the marriage payment for a girl who remained with her abductor was left to the *parboru* to decide. Now, however, the girl also has a say in her affairs and she will not accept her *parboru*'s asking too high an amount, if she wants to marry her abductor. The latter's financial position has to be taken into account and the chiefs of both the *parboru* and the abductor must try to come to agreement. Naturally, in the first instance the abductor's father is responsible for the sum that has to be paid. He may perhaps not be sympathetic towards his son's behaviour, or he pretends not to be, and does not want to pay anything at all. In such a case his kinsmen, the *sisolhot*, and the young man's *tulang* and brothers-in-law will endeavour to induce him not to leave his son in the lurch. They will remonstrate with him, with the help of the appropriate *umpama, anak sipanunda ndang digadis* = one does not sell a son because he has inflicted great damage on one, and, if necessary, will take the arrangement of the matter into their own hands.

MARRIAGE AFTER ELOPEMENT = MANGALUA BORU

The girl's acquiescence from the outset is a characteristic of this form of marriage. The enamoured couple revolt against parental authority. The girl who anticipates stubborn opposition to her marriage to the young man of her choice, or who feels that she is the victim of delay in or the breakdown of the discussions on the marriage payment because her parents are asking too much, will go her own way, *manuntun lomo ni rohana*, and will secretly forsake the parental home with her beloved. And, since putting the girl in the block, *mambeanghon*, to compel her to accept an unwanted marriage is no longer permitted, marriage following elopement is becoming more and more frequent, particularly on Samosir. And despite the fact that it is the girl's action that is decisive, in this patrilineal society it is the young man who is held responsible. He is as a rule the one who has endeavoured to bring her under his psychical power by means of a *dorma* = charm. He is therefore regarded as the abductor, she as the abducted, *na niluahon*. By taking her as his wife he has shown his courage and his disregard for the rights of her *parboru*. He must eventually pay the penalty.

The course of events is roughly as follows, though there is naturally diversity both in respect of conventions and individuals: the couple make an arrangement for the actual time of their flight, the place of meeting and their destination. The girl takes one or more of her girl friends into her confidence and asks them to accompany her for her honour's sake. She may leave behind in her sleeping place some recognisable object as her *tanda*, the sign that she has forsaken the house deliberately. This is an old custom that still survives in South Tapanuli, but it is frequently forgotten in the Toba Country. At the appointed hour in the evening the flight takes place. The couple go to the house of a kinsman of the young man's father or, if the pair are Christians, to the house of a church elder, *sintua*, so that this church dignitary can be a further guarantee of the girl's honour. It would be quite unacceptable for the couple to start to live together immediately. It would be *marbagas roha-roha* = unlicensed marriage, and as such punishable: the young man must even avoid being temporarily alone with the girl.

The following morning the *parboru* is apprised of the facts and then the discussions on the marriage payment can commence.

If the girl has already reached marriageable age, the *parboru*, who has been unable to forestall her flight, or to hinder it, cannot use force to get her to return to him (formerly when a girl eloped it was sometimes the signal for war). He must resign himself to his *boru*'s wish which is implicit in her action, *guru ni boru do i*. He may, however, endeavour to dissuade her by argument, sending envoys to her or by using charms, but he must bear in mind that if he succeeds he does not have the right to claim a *pangias* for her since it is he himself who has virtually sullied (made impure = *rotak*) her name. If he allows his *boru* to remain with her abductor, he is then entitled to an increased marriage payment in the fixing of which the chiefs of both parties will then co-operate. Where marriage payment discussions concern a marriage consequent upon an elopement where honour and decency have been observed, then the *adat sigararon* = the increase of the marriage payment as an *adat* penalty, will naturally be much less than where it concerns a marriage by abduction proper. The chiefs have now also to take into account the young man's financial position. Sometimes a young man will take upon himself a large debt, *utang di pudi*, in order to please his father-in-law in the hope that in the course of time the amount will be reduced. Sometimes the *parboru* who has had to bow to circumstances, shows his resentment by withholding his *boru*'s ornaments and *pauseang*.

MARRIAGE AFTER SEDUCTION BY THE GIRL = MAHITURUN or MAHUEMPE

In this form of marriage the girl goes on her own initiative to the young man of her choice. The decision is entirely her own though she is sometimes egged on by her father if he desires the marriage and the resulting affinity relationship. As a rule, however, she acts alone and in the knowledge that her father or brother is anything but sympathetic to the step she is taking either because he does not want the young man as prospective son-in-law or because he will bring too small a marriage payment, or for other reasons. The *boru sipahuempe* herself, for that matter, brings her *parboru* less marriage payment than is usual since the young man to whom she has surrendered herself is the stronger party in the negotiations which will then be conducted in his village. A girl who throws herself at a man is not usually regarded with favour. It seldom happens.

MARRIAGE AFTER RAPE

There is little difference between rape, *manggogoi*, following abduction and the rape of a long-desired girl. The object is either to break the girl's will or the opposition of her parents. The legal position is about the same as that applicable to abduction.

If the rape of a young girl is a result of the sudden upsurge of passion, it can also lead to marriage. For example, if the rapist is some-one from her own village or region and if the girl is still a *boru ni parboru* = daughter under the authority of her *parboru*, i.e., she is neither betrothed nor married, and if other circumstances argue in its favour. In such a case no punishment will be demanded, such as im-prisonment for instance. It will be regarded as sufficient if the offender confesses his guilt, *manopoti*, to the injured party in a form which will be determined by the relationship between the parties concerned. If no marriage results, then at the present time imprisonment, with which can be associated a *panguras*, is the punishment that is preferred.

LIVING-IN MARRIAGE = MARSONDUK HELA

In this form of marriage the son-in-law goes to live in the house of his parents-in-law. He is then provided with his board, he is *disonduk* = being provided with food, literally, food is ladled out for him. This form occurs comparatively rarely. The cause may be the poverty of the young man's father who does not have adequate means to make a normal marriage payment. The son's labour makes good this deficiency. It is then at the same time a marriage of service. This is the most frequently occurring form. Such a son-in-law, naturally, is only desirable where the family needs an extra hand when, for example, there are many small children who are too young to contribute their labour. Often, therefore, the young man will have moved into his parents-in-law's house some considerable time before the marriage, having regard to the girl's age, can be concluded. When the young people have grown up and if the circumstances permit the termination of the arrangement, the girl frequently insists on her father's allowing her and her husband to live independently since she is well aware of the humiliating situation.

In this form of marriage too, a small part of the marriage payment is paid immediately. The marriage payment is called *hudali* = mattock, because the greater part of it will be met by the young man's labour. As far as the remainder is concerned, diverse agreements can be made: it can be deducted on an annual basis; the service can be terminated on full payment, etc.

It is quite understandable that the *parboru* often allows the young couple to live independently before the whole debt is paid. It is then he and not the young man's own father who sets him up in his own household, *mandjae*. The *pauseang* which the *parboru* will give to his daughter (also called *bangunan* in this context) also serves as a *pandjaean* and is usually of a size equivalent to that which he would give to a son of his own. The kinsmen and affines, *na mordjambarhon boru i*, who in the normal marriage are entitled to a specific portion of the marriage payment but who in this instance get nothing, testify to their agreement to the *mandjae* by, for example, making a contribution to the meal which is eaten to celebrate the separation. So long as the living-in continues the son-in-law does not conduct his own household, he does not work for himself but for his father-in-law and he does not cultivate the land on his own behalf. If the father-in-law allows his son-in-law, *hela*, to keep what he earns in his spare time, *duru-duru ni ulaon* = the perquisites of his labour, it is an act of benevolence.

The motive for such a living-in relationship is not always the poverty of the one nor the need for labour of the other. It may be that a father is very attached to his only daughter and does not want to be separated from her, in which case the young man is generally lured by the promise of a good dowry. His "living-in" is, then, however, usually of short duration since he will always be rather looked down on. Sometimes the married couple will then stay in the wife's father's village but this is not always the case.

In neither of these forms of living-in marriage is there any question of some kind of matrilineal modification of the normal patrilineal matrimonial law. The rules of the law of inheritance in particular remain in force and the father who dies without male issue, *na mate punu*, has not acquired in his son-in-law a substitute for his son. The son-in-law does not continue his father-in-law's lineage nor does he revere his spirit when he dies.

SETTING UP ONE'S OWN HOUSEHOLD = MANDJAE

In a normal marriage the young couple do not set their own family, *ripe*, immediately after they are married. They continue to belong for some time to the husband's parents' family with whom they reside and take their meals, *sinonduk*, and who instruct them how to behave towards each other. So long as this living together continues the young couple are not a separate household with their own finances, *dabu-dabuan*. The young husband has not become a fully fledged member of society and the young wife does not do household duties for herself and her husband but helps her mother-in-law run the home. The young couple only become independent when they are formally set up in their own household, *mandjae*. It is not possible to say precisely when this will happen. If the mother-in-law, *simatua boru*, and the daughter-in-law, *parumaen*, get on well together, then the arrangement can go on for a considerable time, otherwise the *mandjae* takes place after only a few months. In any case the young couple have their own household before the birth of their first child.

The *mandjae* is always accompanied by a meal, *diatas ni indahan dohot djuhut*, which is offered by the young couple. This is sometimes attended by *manulangi* = feeding from the hand. If the house where the young couple have been living accommodates more families, *dongan sadjabu*, then they will be present since they will be the first to be affected by the separation of the families, particularly if the young couple will, like them, occupy their own corner of the communal dwelling. In addition, the father's closest kinsmen and possibly his closest affines will also be present if they live in the neigbourhood as will his village chief, though his presence is not absolutely essential, and some members of the village.

The son asks his parents for his own property, *pandjaean*, when he expresses the appropriate *hata na uli* at the end of the meal, and his request will be granted amidst suitable expressions of benediction, *pasu-pasu*. The young wife then receives from her mother-in-law a bag of hulled rice and some kitchen utensils or things of this kind, with which she can start her duties as a housewife on her own. The husband receives a *hauma pandjaean* = ricefield, from his father and perhaps a plot of garden land, *pargadongan*, as well.

The young couple then constitute an independent family: they cook their own food, *tumutung hudonna*; they have become financially independent; they incur their own debts and make their claims independently of their parents. With the gift of a *hudon* = cooking pot, as a *pandjaean*, the *talaga* = space in the middle of the house, separates the families, *marhudon pandjaean martalaga olat-olat*, to quote the maxim. This same maxim is also used to indicate the separateness of the households of two women in a bigamous marriage.

Though the act of *mandjae* is primarily domestic in character, even the presence of the village chief is not strictly necessary, one consequence of it is that henceforth third parties cannot make claims against the father for debts his son incurs. In the old-style rural way of life the question of claims by third parties was not a complication since a young couple could not undertake important monetary transactions without the assistance of close kinsmen and their village chief. Moreover, village gossip would quickly make the fact public. In the course of time, however, a class of enterprising young traders has gradually emerged, who conduct their businesses primarily outside the village in which they live. There is also an increase in the cultivation of cash crops, and types of trade are more varied. All these increase the possibilities for young married couples to enter into more or less important financial transactions outside their villages. Their partners do not always know precisely the position in respect of responsibility for debts, whether or not they can make a claim against the debtor's father. Thus a situation has gradually come about where there is the need for a clearer public demonstration of the *mandjae* thereby precluding chicanery. This I encountered a few times. The least that should be required is that the village chief should attend the ceremony or be notified of it. The administration of justice may gradually steer in the right direction.

A definite *mandjae* is not always held for an eldest son who has succeeded to the rights of his father on the latter's death and this too may give rise to uncertainties.

The youngest son, the *siampudan*, who continues to live in the parental home after his marriage, is often not given a *pandjaean* in the real sense of the word. He is the *sitean panutuan* = the inheritor of the pepper-grinding stone, a term which implies that he will care for his parents in their old age. I will return to this subject in the next chapter in the discussion on the relationship between the *pandjaean* gifts received by the various sons and the property to be inherited after their father's demise.

The *pandjaean* naturally comes from the father in the first instance. If he is dead, it comes from the eldest son. It can, however, happen that an uncle or grandfather's brother with no sons of their own will present a *pandjaean* to one of their nephews. For such a present there must be a counter-present which, among kinsmen, can also be called an *ulos*. An orphaned young man may sometimes be given a *pandjaean* by his uncle if he has not inherited any property from his father. In areas where the *parripean*-law, which usually gives the in-dwelling *marga* of a village only a temporary 'right of the inhabitant' to the land, is strongly developed, a young couple's village chief should have a *parripean* rice field at his disposal to give them an opportunity of cultivating a piece of land if they cannot receive a plot of their own from the young man's father. In areas where there are land reserves for the cluster of villages, *punsu tali*, a part is given to the *anak mandjae*. It is worth noting that in the neighbourhood of Porsea (and perhaps else-where also?) the trousseau which a father gives to his daughter is also called a *pandjaean*.

THE MARRIED COUPLE'S MUTUAL RELATIONS

The husband is indisputably the head of the family, *pardongan-saripeon*. He rules the home, has control over the children and his wife, and the property. He entertains and is entertained according to his pleasure. He conducts lawsuits; (formerly he declared war on any who offended him, took part in the fighting, concluded the peace and could dispose over the fate of his daughters and lead the family into bondage). He performs the heavy work of cultivation, the digging and the felling of trees but hands over to his wife the time-devouring and disagreeable task of weeding. He can refer to his wife as *djolmanghu* = my creature, or *na hutuhor* = the one I have bought. He is the *porhalangulu* = the one entitled to the top of the sleeping-place, the place of honour; his wife is the *portalaga* = the one who does the household chores on the *talaga*.

Things like this as well as the superior position of the male sex — inheritance law applies only in the male line — are the natural conse-quence of the patrilineal system with its bride-price marriage. One would therefore assume that the position of the married woman can only be an inferior one. In reality it is not quite so. The wife is also called the revered mistress of the house, *inanta soripada*, the more so if she has children. She is the centre of the house and its good spirit. She is part and parcel of the building up of her husband's 'house': she gives him his sons and daughters, manages the household, prepares the meals for his guests in such a way that he gains credit by his hospitality, and plays her part in accumulating wealth. The wife is the *pardihuta* = the one who has the interests of village, house and compound at heart; her husband is the *pardibalian* = the one who promotes the family's affairs outside the domestic sphere. According to the description in the *Patik dohot uhum*, if a new house is to be built it is the wife who must give a send-off to the people who will go to the forest to cut the wood and she must provide them with offering cakes; she must also accept the wood personally when they bring it back. It is the wife who picks the first fruits of the harvest of the fields and these she solemnly carries home. If there is a feast at her house, she starts the dancing. She is the first person to whom the cut up meat is offered by hand, *manulangi*, when the bridegroom's father comes to pay the marriage payment for her daughter and, although she is in the background during the actual discussion, she can have considerable influence when it comes to the matter of furthering or delaying her daughter's marriage. If she and her husband have a serious quarrel, she has the right to remain in the house; he must go and sleep with the young men in the village council house, *martarisopo*.

All this applies particularly to the wife who has become a mother. At the beginning of the marriage the young couple display no obvious affection for each other, but once the wife becomes pregnant the husband makes a fuss of her with small unexpected attentions. When her confinement approaches he cuts the firewood for the small fire which must be placed behind her back. Thus he acts as *sitaha saganon* and the husband performs this task with the greatest of pleasure hoping that when the neighbours ask: "What is it?", *songon dia,* he will be able to reply, *"Taho ma i"* = it is well, i.e., it is a boy. The husband also provides the *bangun-bangun,* a dish of chicken mixed with lemon juice and Spanish pepper which is thought to promote the return of the uterus of a woman in childbed. From then on he will look upon his wife with respect and she is assured of his faithfulness and affection. And, if she has the good fortune to give him a large family of sons and daughters, then the jealous glances of those not so blessed will increase her pride, and his love and gratitude. Despite this, however, I found more than one married couple who had no sons, and even those who were childless, who were deeply attached to each other and who accepted with resignation what is regarded as the greatest affliction a married couple can suffer.

It goes without saying that the relationship between husband and wife can often not be a good one. Quarrels between them are then frequent. A husband can be brutal to his wife, he can kick her and beat her and abuse her if he is dissatisfied with something she has done. And to a certain degree such treatment is accepted, for example, according to the judgement of a native court, a man who struck his wife in a field with a shovel had not acted beyond the bounds of what is regarded as lawful in marriage. A wife will sometimes have to flee from her husband and will seek refuge with neighbours where he cannot seize her. Often she runs away and seeks sanctuary with her *hula-hula.* When this happens, he has really gone too far and the village chief, the inhabitants of the village and the wife's kinsmen get together and take the matter in hand in an endeavour to repair the marriage. If they succeed and the husband is ready to take his wife back again, then the wife, who has expressed her willingness to return by preparing a meal of rice or by taking with her a garment, is led to her husband's house by her *parboru*. There she must be received by her husband with respect and he must welcome her home by setting before her a small piglet to eat and he must ask her forgiveness in the appropriate words while at the same time offering her and her *parboru* a *batu ni sulang* = a sum of money which is in addition to the meal, or a *pandjoraan*, as an earnest of his good intentions in the future. In doing all this he has made up for his neglect and has restored what was broken, *na tinggal diulahi, na sega dipauli*.

Conversely, a wife can also give her husband such good cause for complaint that he takes her back to her *parboru* to be taught a lesson, *paadjarhonsa*. If the justice of the husband's reproaches is not particularly evident, then much will depend on the sentiments of the father-in-law towards his son-in-law and his ability to return the marriage payment, as to whether he will earnestly persuade his *boru* to go back to her husband and to behave as an obedient wife should or whether he will give her his protection and heed her counter-charges. If, however, the husband's complaints are well founded, then the wife, accompanied by her *parboru*, must return in a chastened mood taking with her a meal and probably an *ulos* present. All of this will be in accordance with the proposals of kinsmen and affines, or as determined by a judge. If the woman refuses to return, then a lengthy period of separation, *padao-dao*, can result which usually leads to divorce. The *parboru* can reclaim any expenses incurred for his daughter's board and lodging during the time he has had to keep her if her complaints against his son-in-law have proved to be just.

THE LEGAL COMPETENCE OF THE MARRIED WOMAN

In view of the legal position of the *pater familias*, one would not expect to find that a woman has any authority to execute legal transactions. In fact, she not only handles the daily expenditure for the household, but she also sells the things she makes herself at the market, the pots, mats, clothing, etc.; she sells the fruit from the garden and the rice from the field; she disposes of the small domestic animals and she can also be a trader in different goods, a buyer for a wholesale trader or a keeper of a small shop. She can enter into loans of rice for the family with the proviso of payment after the coming harvest, she can borrow money against interest, she can buy standing coffee trees without consulting her husband and can lend money against a wet rice-field as security. She can even appear in a lawsuit with her husband as the plaintiff about items belonging to the marriage property and can legally oppose a contract entered into by her husband. This is over and above her special rights in respect of the *pauseang-* and *bangunan*-fields which she brought to her marriage. (In many families the husband has to hand over to the wife all the money he receives for working at odd jobs.)

This marked independence of married women is particularly noticeable in Toba. Elsewhere the wife is more restricted to the sphere of domestic economy. Even in Toba, however, not all women make use of their accepted independence. Naturally, it also depends on the character of the husband. I never saw a married woman engage in transactions such as alienating fields, taking or giving rice-fields in pledge, cattle deals, buying houses, betrothing children or marrying them off, handling disputes, acting as witnesses at agreements, participating in village discussions, etc.: these are the husbands' spheres of activity. Where, however, marriage property is involved, many a husband will allow his wife to act as a co-consultant and to be a signatory to the contract. It is thus difficult to say with any certainty that the property of a married couple is not under joint ownership. The 'theory' is that the property belongs to the man and is inherited from him, that in this respect he has the reins in his hands. He owns his wife, she is 'his', a being who has no rights of her own: she looks after his children, his house, the pigs and the fields and is at most his assistant in incidental domestic matters. But in practice one learns the extent of the wife's influence how far she is tacitly thought to be competent to handle legal matters and how far her co-managership can extend. In the 'theory', however, lie opportunities for an ill-disposed husband to act badly. Should the marriage miscarry, he can always appeal to the strict rules if it suits his purpose and more often than not he will find other men, and the judges, on his side. Nevertheless, there is a starting point for the gradual consolidation of the present position of the married woman into an authorised legal status which will give her and her property protection against the malevolence of a husband with whom she can no longer live in harmony. It cannot be predicted how this will develop in the future. It must be made quite clear however, that there is no question of the Batak woman's being entirely without rights, either now or formerly, and therefore, in granting her legal rights on the above basis she would not be emerging from complete darkness into an unfamiliar light. The possibility of strengthening the legal position of the married

Batak woman will, in fact, find support in the real situation in Batak society.

I will deal with further relevant points in the sections on widowhood, divorce and inheritance.

RELATIONSHIP TO MEMBERS OF THE FAMILY; SUBANG, PANTANG

Social intercourse between the married couple and their mutual kin is not without its restrictions. There are a number of *subang* or *pantang* prohibitions which must be observed. Certain relations result in a ban which prevent certain members addressing each other, touching each other, or nursing each other in sickness. Only if there is danger to life can people who stand in the *hasubangan*-relationship to each other act as they do towards other people. If speech is necessary between them, then there must be an intermediary, for which purpose even an object can serve. There are other relationships in which the proper name must not be spoken. The nature of these relations vary as do the prohibitions and regulations applicable to them. The main ones are as follows:

the foremost is the address-prohibition between a father-in-law, *simatua,* and a daughter-in-law, *parumaen.* It is not permissible for them to be alone together, and even when they meet on the road they must step aside a little. This prohibition of association can be easily explained. Apart from the *sahala parsimatuaon* = the particular respect which is imposed in relationship to the parents-in-law, this bears on the "Incest-Scheu". A daughter-in-law who lives in the house of her husband's parents can arouse erotic desires in her husband's father which are thus restrained by this prohibition. That this restraint is not always effective, is proved by the fact that it is sometimes necessary for the young couple, after complaint by the wife, to be permitted to live separately.

A similar speech-prohibition obtains between a mother-in-law, *simatua boru,* and her son-in-law, *hela.* It also obtains between the *haha doli* and the *anggi boru* (elder brother and younger brother's wife). This can be traced back to the fact that the eldest son of the house will in due time assume the rights of his deceased father.

The strict address-prohibition between persons who are each other's *bao,* i.e., husband of sister and wife of her brother and the extensions thereto, a man and the wife of his *tulang*'s son, is less easy to explain. This prohibition does not apply universally. It is with difficulty that one attributes it solely to the respect that a man should always feel towards his *tunggane* = his wife's brother.

What is somewhat strange in these usages is that they arose in a sphere in which a marriage that binds closer the already existing affinity relationship is the preferred one and that even if the wife is chosen from a circle with which no affinity relation exists — a feature that is becoming more and more common — the terms which relate to a preferred marriage are all the same often in use: an engaged couple will call each other *boru ni datulang, ibebere ni damang, pariban,* and the prospective mother-in-law calls her prospective daughter-in-law *maen,* a shortened form of *parumaen,* daughter-in-law. When actual *pariban* marry each other the speech prohibition is not so rigidly observed, at least not between the parents-in-law and the children-in-law.

A married couple are prohibited from calling each other by their proper names, *goar*: a woman will speak of her husband as 'the father of this boy'. Of one's relations one is not allowed to use the proper name of the following: elder brother's wife, wife's brother, wife's elder sister, husband of wife's elder sister.

The use of proper names in the following relationships, although not directly connected with one's own marriage, is also forbidden: one's own father, mother, grandfather, grandmother, *tulang, tulang's* wife, father's sister, thus generally those persons who are of the preceding generation to one's own, the *digindjang ni tutur,* the persons whose *sahala* should be treated with respect and more ordinary reverence by not using the name which is an embodiment of their personalities. And even in kinship and affinity relations in the broader sense, it is not usual to use the proper name: for preference one says of a man, "this [is] my *tulang*", etc.

THE CHILDREN OF THE MARRIAGE

The husband is the father of a child born during the marriage. If he is present at the birth he makes this clear by cutting the firewood, *manaha saganon* (or *soban*) and by serving the *bangun-bangun.* If he is absent then, immediately upon receipt of the news of the birth, he should return home or send a token of his satisfaction. If the child is born after the husband's death, then the absence of a *sitaha saganon* is proof that no other man than the deceased was the procreator of what is then called the *sagak ni panabian* = the fruit of reaping a field of stubble. In Toba and Humbáng the death of a husband without male issue sometimes gives his widow an opportunity of having a child and passing it off as his. With the agreement of the deceased's *uaris,* she makes herself available to any man, *parsangge talak* = having an open

15

pouch, also called *pardjabu talak* = having an open door, and should she become pregnant the child is regarded as being that of the deceased. I heard of a similar custom, but never encountered an instance of it, where a widow who has had no son marries in levirate a kinsman of the deceased husband and any children of the marriage count as children of the deceased.

If a child is born during the marriage of which the husband knows, by virtue of his length of absence from home, he is not the begetter, he nevertheless still regards himself as its legal father: it has sprung up in his garden, *na tubu di porlakna do i,* as the saying goes.

The *sihahaan,* the eldest son, who is destined later to assume the mantle of his father where his brothers and sisters are concerned, possesses the *sahala sihahaanon* = the *sahala* of the eldest son. This is a weak reflection of that of his parents and finds its expression in, among other things, the *hasurungan* = the privileges he enjoys in respect of the property (Chapter VI).

GIFTS TO THE CHILDREN: THE INDAHAN ARIAN

I have already mentioned the interest of kinsmen and affines in a kinswoman's pregnancy and the birth of her child and that gifts are often given to the infant during the *marupa-upa.* If the gift is a wet rice-field it is called the *indahan arian* = the daily rice, or the *togu-arian* = daily midday meal. Sometimes there is in addition a small sum of money, *pasingkau* = small change to buy vegetables, or a head of cattle, *andor ni ansimun* = like a cucumber tendril, i.e., increasing of itself. The terms *indahan arian* and *pauseang* are, however, interchangeable in the case where the actual handing over of a promised *pauseang*, is often done after the birth of the first child. I have already commented upon this loose use of legal terms.

Custom with regard to these gifts differs regionally. There are areas where the *indahan arian* is only given by the father's father to the first born of his eldest son as his extra portion, *hasurungan*, which is his due as the first born of all the grandsons. Elsewhere all first born sons of sons receive it, or even second and third sons. The *indahan arian* is sometimes also given to sons of daughters (thus an *ulos* gift) or the eldest daughter of a son since she is the 'jacket opener', the *buha-badju*, and it is even given at the birth of the first born daughter of a daughter, but it then approaches the nature of a *pauseang*. One cannot, therefore, say with certainty whether the gift must always be regarded in all regions as being a particular and permanent portion allocated to the infant and which he receives over and above his ordinary share, or whether it can be regarded as a constituent of the marriage property. In respect of the law relating to the *indahan arian*, it is sufficient to say that, in general, when the gift is given by the *hula-hula* it resembles the rules applicable to the *pauseang*.

DISCIPLINE, REPUDIATION

The disciplining of the young is influenced by the fear that punishments that are too severe would injure their *tondi* and cause them to forsake the children's bodies so that the children would become ill. Conversely, children stand in awe of their parent's *sahala*. From this it follows that their upbringing is tolerant and gentle. Yet in the *Pidari* time they could be put in the block or, what was worse, they could be absolutely repudiated, though this last measure was not resorted to lightly. To quote the appropriate *umpama*:

anak sipanunda ndang digadis,
boru sipahilolong ndang diaup;

One does not sell a son even though he has brought great damage upon one.

A daughter who is averse to her husband is not cast to the waters. I have not heard of recent cases of repudiation, *ambolonghon*, or *pabalihon*, but when they did occur they were coupled with the pronouncement of a curse, *sapata*, which was intended to strike the *tondi* of the recalcitrant one with a strong, harmful, supernatural force which was thought to result in childlessness especially. Sometimes a father even put a price on the life of his child, if his *anak siambolong-bolong* had done something really infamous. A curse could only be removed by magical means, and when a child had been repudiated and cursed the other children would sometimes endeavour to induce their father when he was on his deathbed to retract it. If they failed, then the outcast continued to be disinherited.

RESPONSIBILITY FOR OFFENCES COMMITTED BY ONE'S CHILDREN

A father is responsible for the harmful consequences arising out of offences committed by his still unadult children. He must pay the debts his sons incur, *manggarar utang ni anakna*, which includes any penalties imposed upon them. This is also the case in respect of damage caused by his children's negligence or imprudence. The degree to which the responsibility for the acts and the behaviour of an adult extends to the wider circle of kinsmen will be discussed in the chapter on the law of misdemeanours and offences.

COMING OF AGE

Usually a son is not reckoned to have reached his majority until he is married and has been set up in his own household. Before his marriage an adult male, *naung balga* or *tang pamatang,* is called *doli-doli.* This unmarried youth has not as yet his own family, *ripe,* or dwelling: he sleeps in the *sopo* = village council house, does not contribute to the communal expenses — nor in former times, to the contributions, *guguan,* to the communal offering-feasts — he is not financially independent and his debts are still a charge on his father. Formerly his teeth would not have been filed. He has no part in the deliberations in the village, in short he is still a minor. In the *Pidari* time he did have to take his place beside the adults in defending the village from attack from outside and his being able to bear a gun, *tang marbodil,* was a token of acceptance in the groups of youths. Until then a youth was only good enough to herd cattle, *tang marmahan.* An intermediate category is called *marsiadjar doli-doli* = learning to grow up.

This situation changes with his marriage and the subsequent *mandjae.* From then on he is accepted in the *adat ripe.* As the head of a family he is a full member of the community; he has his own finances and takes an independent part in all the pleasures and obligations that accrue to all the families living in village-, territory- and kinship communities. At the same time he acquires citizenship and he stands on his own in respect of the rules relating to family, debt and land tenure. The *anak mandjae* is considered fit to be a member of the societies, *parsaoran,* of which the aim is mutual support as and when required. He can be invested with authority. And, since it is extremely rare for a Batak male to remain unmarried — it is regarded as proof of a sexual abnormality — each youth thus reaches his majority in this way.

A married man's legal power is, however, limited in the *hela sonduhan* relationship (see p. 216).

In addition to the *anak mandjae,* the adult sons of a widow, the *dagang ina* or *dagang marina,* men who have only a mother, are regarded as having reached their majority before they marry. In every fatherless family, since the eldest son as soon as he becomes *doli-doli,* will not long delay marrying, there is usually only one *dagang ina.* After his marriage he acts as a father to his younger brothers and sisters. Thus the fatherless family, which on the death of the husband and father had no one to represent it in the obligations and pleasures of an independent family, again acquire a representative when the eldest son attains adulthood, and it again takes a normal part in the *adat ripe*.

The *mandjae* proper as it takes place among the sedentary rural population, cannot at the present day always be carried out. Many young people have found their work outside the village of their birth and remain in it after they marry. Many a time a father will, in fact, allocate a field as the *pandjaean* to which they are entitled and if this is done the young men are regarded as being *anak mandjae*, but the actual proceedings of a *mandjae* do not always take place. The result is that the marriage becomes the token by which they reach their majority — in Java marriages between Batak are concluded without the parents being present. These young men have, in fact, already acquired some legal independence in providing either wholly or in part for their own support with their earnings: among the country population a great number of youths are now often employed before their marriage as road workers, casual labourers in Deli, chauffeurs, and so on. But this independence only applies in respect of their daily outlay for food, clothing and accommodation. Debts contracted by an unmarried son are still the father's responsibility.

In former times participation by the sons of the principal chiefs in the organised gambling parties was a regular pastime which many a time cost their parents dear. If the sons got into debt and were not in a position to offer personal or real security, they could be bound until their fathers came to redeem them.

As far as the girls are concerned, where they have a job and are earning money — a modern phenomenon — what applies to the young men applies to them also. With regard to girls who are not earning, one cannot say that they have any legal independence although they sometimes own their own land, frequently keep a brood of hens, weave cloths and take part in selling all the products of the house and the fields in the market. There is no question of their providing for their maintenance. Girls on their marriage, unlike the young men, do not reach their emancipation.

ADOPTION OF CHILDREN

It is not unknown for childless married couples to adopt children, but it is rare. To the pagan way of thinking for a man to have no male issue, *ndang morrindang* = being unlike a creeper which spreads out, means that his lot in the hereafter will be a wretched one. And even

Christians still think it is a very unfortunate thing to happen to them. Apart from the means to avert childlessness that I have already mentioned, there is bigamy, and adoption. The latter only has meaning if it is possible to adopt a son since only a son will continue the lineage of his adoptive father.

It is not easy to find a boy who can be adopted for no man readily parts with a son, if he has many or few, since they are the promise of an extensive posterity. If a man does so it is because he wants to help a kinsman. In olden times, when there were many uprooted people and slaves, adoption was easier than at present.

The procedure of adopting a son, *mangain* or *paranakhon*, is as follows: the family groups concerned with their chiefs are summoned to a gathering; a buffalo is slaughtered and the announcement made that henceforth the adopted son, the *anak niain*, will be regarded as the son of the man who has adopted him, particularly in respect to succession and inheritance.

That a woman could adopt a father to acquire a *hula-hula* for herself and her family, justifies the assumption that in the *Pidari* time it was possible for a man who had no known kinsmen to adopt a father also.

NAMEGIVING

Part of a man's *tondi* dwells in his name, his *goar*, which is tied to him and can influence his fate. A man attributes his prosperity to his name, among other things, and if misfortune and sorrow strike him he will cast off his ill-omened name and take another in the hope that the result of the new alliance of name and personality will be more favourable.

No man readily uses his own name or that of others. A man is often referred to and addressed by his *marga* name and a woman is also known by the name of the *marga* from which she came — usually with the omission of the syllable 'Si'; for example *boru Tumorang*. A Batak seldom uses the names of his kinswomen. And, as I mentioned earlier, some close kinship- and affinity relationships involve a definite prohibition on the use of each other's names.

A newly born child is forthwith referred to by the general name of *sibursok* for boys, and *sibetet* and *sitatap* for girls. These are in the nature of pet names and are often used even when the children have their proper names.

A child receives a Batak proper name, *goar Batak,* not long after its birth. It is chosen by the parents, formerly with the aid of a *datu*, and from then onwards, where it is a first born, boy or girl, is the name by which the parents will be referred to. If the eldest child, *panggoaran*, is given the name of Si Hudi, for example, then the father will be called Ama ni Hudi, the father of Hudi and the mother, Nai Hudi, the mother of Hudi. ('Ama ni' and 'Nai' are contracted to 'aman' and 'nan' before some consonants.) The parents have then become each other's *dongan sagoar* = namesakes. And when an eldest son becomes Ama ni Hudi, his father may call himself Ompu ni Hudi, grandfather of Hudi.

In addition to this name there is the baptismal name, the *goar tardidi*, which is given to Christians and by which a Batak Christian is also known in daily life. This Christian name is usually taken from the Old or New Testament, or it is a German name (the influence of the Rhenish Mission), or a name taken from the early Christian era: a Dutch name is seldom given. The fact that the baptismal name has come into such general use, is probably due to the religious beneficial activity which was and still is attributed to such names and to many objects of the Christian cult. However, a father of a small son whose Batak name is Hudi but who was baptised Fridolin will never call himself Ama ni Fridolin.

On Samosir and its environs, which were formerly distinguished by the prevalence of slavery, many aged people still call themselves Ompu Radja N. which distinction indicated that he was freeborn (*radja* as opposed to *hatoban* = slave). There, as elsewhere, older people of some wealth and position like to assume an elegant and powerful sounding name, such as Ompu Sodjuangon, The Irresistible One; Ompu Sosuhaton, The Immense One; Ompu Sabungan Bosi, The Iron Cockerel, etc., in order to have the desired congruence between name and position.

If a man intends to assume the name by which one of the great ancestors of his lineage has become famed, *mambuat goar ni ompu*, or *mamampe goar*, or if he wants to give such a name to one of his adult sons, then it is proper that the whole of the lineage concerned should be consulted about it. Such a name-giving is often done at a great festival to which kinsmen, affines, chiefs and prominent people are invited with the object of honouring the forefather in question and, at the same time, to emphasise the *hasangapon* = position of prominence of his descendants, particularly that of the giver of the feast and his narrow kinship group. Much less ritual attends the giving or assuming of a name of a less renowned ancestor.

The Batak does not have from of old titles other than those connected with kinship or his being a freeman. The prefixes *Sutan* and *Baginda* have been borrowed from Malay and are an attempt in recent times to give expression to acquired prominence. And at the present day, the addition of titles such as *sintua* = elder, *pandita* = evangelist, *guru* = teacher, *kepala kampung* (abbreviated to *kampung*), etc., are never neglected before the names of people who hold or once held office, however minor. The desire for distinction even places a high value on the word "candidate" which indicates that its bearer had once been a candidate in an election for a chieftaincy. Signboards in front of shops have such names as Sintua Marinus and Guru Javet.

BIGAMY

One of the principal motives for taking a second wife is childlessness, in particular failure to have sons. It is a motive that still brings many Christians, among whom are good Christians, into conflict with the discipline of the Church which, on this issue, is adamant: polygamy places a Christian outside the Church community. In fact, in such predominantly Christian areas as Silindung, bigamy is the foremost reason why members of the Church community, with their second wives, are affected by the ban, *dipabali*. This insistence by the Church is not only because the Mission is committed to the relevant decision of the Edinburgh Missionary Conference of 1910; it is also because the Batak ecclesiastical dignitaries themselves will not risk the danger of relaxing this rule.

Taking a second wife because of childlessness does not mean that there is not a good relationship between the spouses. It is, in fact, often the wife herself, who may already have given her husband daughters, who urges him to take another wife so that he may perhaps have sons. If she is not past the age of child bearing, *saep ladang*, then she still hopes that she may also have sons, since it is a folk belief that the presence of a co-wife, *imbang*, may result in the first wife becoming pregnant, *martuahon parimbangon*.

In pagan regions, an important factor conducive to bigamy is levirate marriage. An investigation carried out over a number of years by the Mission showed that a quarter to a half of the cases of bigamy were the result of taking as a second wife the widow of a close kinsman, the *haha boruna*, the *anggi boruna*, or the *inana*, the last being the widow of father's brother or father's second wife married bigamously.

There are also other motives for bigamy: a cantankerous wife, *ala djungkat tunggane boru,* the desire to spread one's wings economically, *pabidang panggagatan,* by increasing the numerical strength of the family and thus its workers and its welfare, or simply because a man has a carnal disposition, *roha daging.* It is these reasons that frequently activate the well-to-do and the distinguished to commit bigamy.

There are two kinds of bigamy and in both kinds the man is said to be *marsidua-dua* = having two wives. Bigamy itself is called *parsidua-duaon.* The wives can be the *imbang* of each other, they are then *marimbang* and they term bigamy *parimbangon*: they are then about equal in status. The second wife can, however, also be the *tungkot* = assistant, of the first wife, in which case her position is a very humble one. I have already mentioned the important difference between *imbang* and *tungkot*: a man cannot have two wives as each other's *imbang* who are close relatives. Sometimes they cannot even be members of the same *marga.* On the other hand, the *tungkot* for the first wife is for preference her close kinswoman.

A man will only take a *tungkot* if his first wife is childless or especially if there is no male issue. Both spouses have to agree on the step, a decision sometimes reached on the advice of a *datu* whom they have consulted. The wife herself usually chooses as her assistant wife one of her close kinswomen. The *tungkot* does not have her own household, she is entirely subordinate to the first wife in domestic matters and she does not receive from her husband any property as her own or to manage. She serves exclusively to give children to the husband in the name of the first wife, as it were. These children are regarded as children of the principal wife who is then called Nan so and so, and they have the same rights as would her own children. If, for example, a man has a chief wife, another wife who is her *imbang,* and yet another who is the first wife's *tungkot* then, if the first wife is childless, the children the *tungkot* bears are regarded as the children of the principal wife and they will succeed to her portion of the husband's property, while the children of the *imbang* will succeed to such part of the property as accrues to their mother. The *tungkot* mainly occurs on Samosir and on the shores of Lake Toba where one of the terms applied to her is *siambolong-bolong* = the outcast, or *panindi* = the subordinate one. Elsewhere, the position of the second wife acting for a childless first wife is not so inferior and approaches that of the *imbang,* even though the term *tungkot* is still used for her.

The relationship of a wife and her *imbang* is quite different. The rule governing their mutual relations is expressed as follows:

niduda rimbang nilaokhon gala-gala,
indang tihas na marimbang masiula di ibana;
The small *rimbang* fruits are crushed, the small *gala-gala* fruits are mixed.

It is best that each co-wife provides for herself.

This principle is also expressed in the term *martalaga olat-olat* = their households are separated from each other by the *talaga*, the domestic space in the centre of the Batak house. When two households have come into being in this way the property relationships must be kept distinct, both in respect of the two wives and of children born to them. When a man takes a second wife he sets aside for her a small part of his property. The first wife must agree to this arrangement since she has first claim on the matrimonial property existing at the time when the second marriage was contracted. And the husband cannot hand anything over to the second wife or to her children during the marriage without the knowledge and consent of the first wife. Only in the case of wet rice-fields (other than those originating from the *hula-hula* of the first wife) does the husband have more freedom of disposal — at least so it is asserted — but even then not to the extent that it would place the first wife and her children in a less favourable position than the second. The first wife lives in the main dwelling, while the second lives in a subsidiary one.

When a *pangoli* = marriage payment has to be given for a son of the second wife in order to procure a wife for him, it must be drawn from such property as his mother has been able to amass if the first wife does not permit that anything be taken from her part of the property. The *tuhor* for a daughter of a second wife accrues to the latter's property and if this daughter is later divorced the marriage payment that has to be refunded has to come out of it. In the event of the father being dead, the divorced woman's full brother is responsible for providing it, and not any of the woman's half-brothers. And when a father divides the part of his property still in his hands before his death among the children — which frequently happens and is advisable in the case of a bigamous union — he will have to pay close attention to the acquired rights of both of his wives and of their children. And he will have to make these arrangements in such a way as to nip in the bud possible quarrels.

If a child is born to the wife who is the *imbang* before one is born to the first wife, then this child becomes the *panggoaran* for the husband who will thenceforth be called Ama ni so-and-so. Whether the child, if it is a son, will be regarded as the *sihahaan* = the one who has acquired the *sahala sihahaan,* is a question to which the answer differs from area to area.

When bigamy is the result of marrying in levirate the widow of a close kinsman, the property of the deceased is intended in its entirety for his own children and is kept separate for them. Children born to the woman after this marriage have no rights to it, nor to the property of her second husband amassed during his first marriage. In a case such as this, however, the half-brothers seldom object if the father divides some of the property accruing to them among the less endowed group.

Some most involved relationships are brought about as a consequence of bigamy, for example: if a son of the first wife marries in levirate the bigamously married wife of his late father, or if a man marries bigamously in levirate the wife of his father's brother. In these cases the law of levirate, the law of inheritance in respect of daughters, and the law of the *parimbangon* are so interwoven, that, in the event of a dispute, it is hardly possible to make a judgement according to the strict rules, and the wisdom of Solomon and a great measure of persuasion are then necessary in order to reach a settlement that is reasonable and satisfactory to all concerned. And even in the more simple cases, the judge often has to interfere because it is said that disputes between wives in a bigamous marriage and their children are often less easy of solution than disputes over land, and that is saying much. Moreover, the *hula-hula* of the respective wives often come to their assistance also and interfere in the quarrel, thus aggravating the position still further.

Can the first wife with whom the husband lives in a regular marriage make objections to his taking an *imbang*? According to old Batak law the answer should be in the negative. In this respect the husband is free so that the wife who would wish to oppose it by withdrawing from her duties as wife would be regarded as shirking a duty inherent in the marriage contract. She would be regarded as a *sipahilolong* = one guilty of breaking up her marriage, and would be subject to all the disadvantageous financial consequences that might result for her and her kinsmen. This law is still so strong that the idea that it could be otherwise for a Christian woman is by no means generally accepted among Christian Batak. Many a man will no doubt be disposed to take into consideration the loyalty of a wife to her faith, and its moral commands, as mitigating factors in determining the measure of her guilt in breaking up her marriage and what has to be repaid to a forsaken husband. But people are still not always willing to grant the justice of her complaint, particularly when her barrenness is the reason for her husband's taking a second wife. In this context it is worth noting that, as far as I know, while there is a prohibition against divorce in the formula used in the Church blessing, there is none against bigamy. Were such the case, then the man would be bound by sacred oath to his wife and she would be the more powerful party in the event of her husband's wanting to marry a second wife. His position as the *siose padan* = breaker of an accepted obligation, would be weaker than it is at present when church law and traditional law are in conflict over this issue.

In 1928 this question was deliberately brought up for discussion and decision in connection with some legal cases before the highest native court at Tarutung (Silindung). The court was augmented by a number of chiefs (all Christians) of Silindung and Sipoholon (Si Opat Pusoran and Naipospos) and the co-operation of some Batak church officials was also enlisted as advisors. The Rapat decided (though by no means with general accord) that a Christian wife, although childless, who refused to live with her husband in bigamy, can be divorced without there being any question of guilt on her part. As far as the husband is concerned, if the barrenness of his first wife has been the cause of his taking a second wife, he has not infringed customary law which permits bigamy. His wife, if she then sues for divorce, is acting in the proper manner judged by the *patik ni huria* = rules of the Church to which she has remained faithful.

No decision was made on the question of whether, if the first wife does not want a divorce, she has a right to demand that her husband part again with the second wife. Such unwillingness to be divorced is usually due to the fact that the woman has children (among whom there may be sons) with whom she wants to stay. In such a case the accepted motive for bigamy does not exist, i.e., lack of male issue, and therefore taking a second wife does not find favour among Christians. The argument will be in favour of the wife who wants to preserve her monogamous marriage. Whether it would get support in the case of a wife who, though she has had daughters, has failed to have sons, is another matter.

This same customary court also decided that a man could not arbitrarily get rid of an old first wife because of his partiality for a second wife. In the popular language there are terms defining the difference between the privileged one, the *tuan laen*, and the neglected one, the *na so hahua*, and it is understandable that in many cases a preference for one of the wives does develop. It will usually be for the one who has had sons and if this happens to be the second wife, it does not mean that dislike of the first gives the husband a right to repudiate her, *ambolonghon*. It is well that this was once again established definitely, because there were two cases about which there had been complaints and in both of them the second and young wife had borne a son: in the one instance the old wife was already a grandmother, and in the other the woman had been married to her husband for 25 years and had given him eight children of which only a small daughter was still alive. The state of bigamy was permitted to continue in these cases — approved by the Church's advisors — on the condition that the old wife should continue to live in her old house and that so much land and property should be allocated to her as was thought adequate to provide for her in her old age.

It seems to me that the determining of the legal consequences of taking a second wife by a court of justice at which all bodies concerned are represented, is of greater value for the gradual development of the law in a Christian spirit, than the drafting of penal provisions as was the case in the adat regulations for Christian Batak of 1892 (Adatrecht-bundel VII), 1913 and 1914 (Adatrechtbundel XI) in which there was the threat of a penalty sometimes coupled with nullification of the second marriage. It would also be of more value than dismissing chiefs who had contracted a bigamous marriage, which was the Government's practice about 1915 on the insistence of the Protestant Mission. It may result in a withdrawal from the Church community, but it hardly strengthens the people's moral judgement.

As far as the formalities of the second marriage are concerned, a detailed *marundjuk,* such as described earlier, does not take place. The marriage is concluded in the smallest possible circle of kinsmen and members of the village, so much so that one sometimes has to ask one-self if the simple eating of a meal together by related kinsmen can be regarded as establishing such an important alliance which, in fact, a bigamous marriage is.

It is very rare for a man to take more than two wives.

DISSOLUTION OF A MARRIAGE

First we will discuss the consequences of a marriage terminated by the death of one of the spouses, and then the ending of a marriage by agreement or on the decision of a judge.

In all cases a legal tie can continue to exist between those who had become affines by the marriage.

DEATH OF A WIFE; HER REPLACEMENT

When a wife dies childless the fact that according to traditional law and custom the prime object of the marriage payment was to obtain a wife in order to have children, particularly male issue, comes to the forefront. Her surviving husband could then ask her *parboru* for another wife, *singkat* or *ganti*, to replace his deceased childless wife, or he could ask him to refund the marriage payment either in part or completely: on Samosir I heard that it was half the amount. This was the case formerly if the deceased wife had even had only daughters.

I doubt, however, if this claim was rigorously enforced in all cases, seeing that among the numberless legal cases on all kinds of subjects that came before me there were none that related to this rule even in the widest sense. In Silindung and Pahae this may perhaps be attributable to the fact that the Mission, which has been established there since 1864, has made use of the regulation promulgated at its instigation by the Government (established since 1882) whereby it was forbidden, *sumbang*, to insist on a replacement for a wife, or restitution of the marriage payment. Elsewhere, the Government may have later adopted the same view, but personally I am not convinced that there was any need to stamp out what was a supposed evil, bearing in mind the fact that neither "bride-price" marriage nor levirate marriage originally found favour with the Mission. The husband will almost certainly only have demanded a substitute if his wife died shortly after their marriage when the dominant feeling would be that he had sustained damage by her untimely death. In the event of his wife dying after they had been married for a long time, his affection for her and the mutual attachment of the affines would have restrained him from making such a demand. It must also be remembered that, particularly in olden times, marriages were frequently concluded within the same small circle where people were already related to each other in various ways. The wife's father therefore sometimes brought the *ulos tudjung* = mourning cloth, to be worn by the husband immediately after his wife's death, as a sign that he as *parboru*, had a substitute available.

It is therefore not surprising that despite the official prohibitions, one can still find *parboru* who are prepared to replace their deceased daughter by another one upon receipt of an insignificant *piso*-gift or who are prepared to assist their widowed son-in-law financially if he should seek elsewhere for a new wife. Many *parboru* adopt a similar attitude where it is a case of divorce by mutual agreement because of childlessness. Replacing a wife, *singkat rere* = replacing the mat, as it is called, is not yet a thing of the past. There is, of course, never any right to claim a substitute when a deceased wife leaves sons, but if the widower, *na mabalu,* is left with young children, then he will seek a second wife for himself and a mother for his children for preference within the circle of the next of kin of his late spouse. This situation presents a younger marriageable sister of the late wife with a task which she sees as being reserved for her, and one which it is difficult to shirk. If she is willing, her father will not be of a mind to claim a full marriage payment for her but will be satisfied with a *piso*-gift. Should nothing come of this replacement by a sister, then the *parboru* will readily support his son-in-law, who is the father of his grandsons, in getting together a marriage payment for another wife.

The second wife called the *panoroni,* continues in the life of the family where the first wife left off. She is the substitute mother, *ina panoroni,* for the children of the first wife; she has the same rights to the property as the first wife had; and any children born to her will have the same rights in respect of the father's property as have those born to the first wife. Only the *pauseang,* which the first wife brought with her on her marriage, is especially for the benefit of her own children only.

THE DEATH OF THE HUSBAND

The death of the husband creates a situation that can give rise to all kinds of relationships. The authority over the wife is then transferred to his closest kinsmen who act independently if there are no sons and if there is an eldest son who is not adult, they act on his behalf. The widow, *na mabalu,* can either remain under the authority of and within the circle of these kinsmen or she can be returned to her *parboru.* She can be married in levirate by someone from the kinship group of her late husband, or her kinsmen can marry her off to a distant relative, a fellow *marga* member, or someone from another *marga.* All these possibilities have varying consequences in respect of the marriage payment and other things. She may wish to remain in her late husband's kinship group with her children as an unmarried widow, in which case the extent of her control over the property must be determined. It may happen that illegitimate children will be born to her as a result of an irregular sexual union or as a result of a more permanent, though not properly regulated one. In the many cases that come before the courts daily concerning widows, each of these possibilities must be considered indi-

vidually because each presents particular aspects according to whether
there are sons, no sons, or no children at all.

PASAE TUDJUNG

A widow wraps herself in mourning clothes, *tudjung*, as soon as her
husband has breathed his last (see photo III) and begins her lamen-
tations, *mangandung*, in which, in her language of grief, she particularly
makes public whether her husband has died childless or has been blessed
with progeny. So long as the widow wears the *tudjung* she must not
leave the 'house of mourning' nor may she associate in the usual manner
with those with whom she normally has social intercourse. Removal of
the widow's weeds, the *pasae tudjung* = the ending of the wearing of
mourning clothes, takes place a short time after her husband's death.
In Toba she is taken to her *hula-hula* for this to be done. In Silindung
and Humbáng members of the *hula-hula* go to the 'house of mourning'
and purify, *mamangir*, her. In the course of this ceremony they partake
of a meal and address their words of comfort to her and to her deceased
husband's kinsmen. The future of the widow is frequently discussed on
this occasion and she is not entirely without a say in the matter.

If she is pregnant, then the birth of the child must take place before
anything is decided. If she is not pregnant, then it is proper that she
delay marrying again for a year, a period which is only really observed
if the proposed second husband is not a close kinsman of the first.

In considering the widow's position the first thing that is given attention is whether there is a close kinsman of the deceased whom she can
marry in levirate. A younger brother has first right in this respect. An
illustration is provided by the judgement of the Rapat Hundulan of
Parbaba of 10th March, 1913 and 20th November, 1913 [17] in which a
member of the court gave the advice that the defendant should marry
his younger brother to the plaintiff, the widow, the object being to
effect a suitable solution to a dispute over land between both parties.
He worked on the assumption that neither party would refuse. It is
difficult for the widow to offer any objections to marrying such of the
sisolhot = very close kinsmen, as the father or a cousin of the deceased
who is willing to have her. For that matter she frequently does not desire
it otherwise. For many women it is far from agreeable to live in widowhood among people who regard her as a useless being, who neglect her,
and who because of the misfortune that has befallen her, are inclined

---

[17] See the publication mentioned in note 1, appendices V and VIII.

to shun her. In Toba, where, in general, a widow who is not past the age of child-bearing is sought after by men, she can marry again quickly but in Silindung it is less easy for her to do so. Levirate marriage is also less frequent in Silindung than elsewhere since bigamy, which among pagans is often the result of levirate marriage, is forbidden to Christians.

At the present day a wife is free to refuse a levirate marriage. She may have various reasons for doing so: she may prefer to stay with her children on her late husband's property until they are grown up, though only the well-to-do can afford to do so. She may have had children who have died, or she may have had no children at all, in which case she may prefer to return to her *hula-hula*. Perhaps she has her eye on a man who is a complete stranger to her late husband's kinsmen or perhaps she has never felt at home with her husband's kinsmen and wants to get away from them (this can also be called *so marrongkap* = unsuited to each other). Her *parboru* may not view her return to him with any great pleasure because it means that he has to refund the marriage payment with the possibility that there may be no other man who will want to marry her. If, however, he heeds his daughter's wish, then he has to attend to a suitable settlement of the relations between her and her deceased husband's kinsmen.

THE PASAEHON: THE COMPLETE SEPARATION OF THE WIDOW

Before a *parboru* is entitled to give his *boru* again in marriage, a formal and clear separation and disassociation must have taken place between the woman and the kinship group of her late husband. If this has not been done and if the *parboru* permits or encourages his *boru* to live with another man, then the rightful claimants to her have reason to make the charge of *langkup* = adultery. This charge is frequent in Toba and will be discussed in detail later.

The *pasaehon* = termination, separation, which can be arranged quite amicably between the parties concerned, or on the intervention of a judge, consists in the first place of establishing what part of the marriage payment has to be refunded by the *parboru*. The amount will depend on many things: the reasons why and the manner in which the separation has come about; the eagerness of the deceased's *uaris* for money; on the prevailing custom; the chance of remarriage, etc. If the widow has a son then the *pauseang* belongs to him and no further demand for repayment of the marriage payment will be made. If she is still young and without children, the most likely thing is that the whole sum will be paid back, if need be, against the return of the

16

pauseang. I also frequently saw the rule followed that is often applied in an ordinary case of divorce and that is that 2/3 of the marriage payment to be received on remarriage is allocated to the deceased's kinsmen and 1/3 to the *parboru*. This 1/3 is then called the *sibalun amak* = for rolling up the mat. This arrangement, as will be seen in the discussion on divorce, presumes, however, that the wife becomes the *boru ni radja* = the wife placed in the mediatory hands of the chief. Prospective suitors must apply to him, must reach agreement with him as to the size of the new marriage payment and they have to pay it to him.

A decision must also be made with regard to the children. If they are still young and if there is no one else to look after them, then they remain for some time with their mother — a baby naturally always does so — until they are about three years of age when she must surrender them. So long as the children stay with their mother, then it is fitting that she has a piece of land or some money placed at her disposal to defray the cost of food and upkeep.

In Silindung and its environs (and elsewhere?) as soon as the separation discussions are finalised, and irrespective of whether the marriage payment is refunded immediately, whether it is held in abeyance pending the woman's marrying again or whether the children remain with her or not, the *patilaho* must be settled and accepted as proof that the woman is free, that she is a *boru na sae-saean* = a woman free to marry another man. This *patilaho* is a small sum of money paid by the *parboru* and deducted from the marriage payment which he has to refund. Even when restitution of the marriage payment is not demanded, the *parboru* still prefers to pay the *patilaho* because, in accepting it, the other party gives a clear sign that they have surrendered control over the woman. This point is important because it is becoming more and more usual for a widow who has no children to be allowed to return to her *hula-hula* without a demand being made for the marriage payment to be refunded.

It is not inconceivable that it is not the wife who wants to be separated from the circle of her late husband's kinsmen but the *uaris* who wants to get rid of her because, for example, she is misbehaving. If, however, the woman has a son then, according to a decision given by a *Rapat* = court at Sipoholon, she has a right to stay with him, to care for him, and to be maintained from the property destined for him.

LEVIRATE, PAREAKHON; WIDOW-REMARRIAGE

If there is a close kinsman of the deceased available and if the widow is not averse to marrying again, he will be able to marry her in levirate, *pareakhon*. The first person to be considered as a prospective husband is a younger brother of the deceased:

butar-butar mataktak butar-butar maningkii,
molo mate hahana anggina maningkii;

When shingles fall off the roof they are replaced by others.

If the elder brother dies the younger brother takes his place.

So runs the saying. If the widow has children, she will readily accept the younger brother as a second husband since he can be expected to be a good father to them. Kinsmen more distant of the deceased who might possibly desire the woman, should respect the prior claim of the deceased's brother and should refrain from making any agreement with the widow without the whole group of which they and the deceased husband form a part, having consented to their *pareakhon*. Failure to do so provides a motive time and again for minor and major dissensions. To give an example: a cousin of the same great-grandfather as the deceased marries the latter's widow without discussing it with the other nearer kinsmen, among whom there are those who want to marry her. In such cases it is the wish of the woman herself that tips the scales one way or the other, but the precipitate one will have to make good his infringement of another's rights by offering as a penalty a meal with a *batu ni sulang-sulang*.

When a member of the narrower kinship circle marries a woman in levirate, it is also termed *manghampi* or *mang(h)abia,* from which the words are derived for levirate marriage, *panghampion* or *pangabiaon,* as well as the terms denoting the second husband, *panghampi* and *pangabia.* The term *pareakhon* does not lend itself to derivations. In such a marriage no marriage payment or part thereof has to be paid. If the *pangabia* is not the next of kin, then he only pays a small *piso ni begu* = gift to the spirit of the deceased, and the *parboru* receives a small gift that I heard called the *paruba-ubaan* = proof of the change, so that he knows henceforth who his *hela* = son-in-law, is. If the *parboru* feels that the close kinsman whom he thinks suitable does not evince sufficient inclination to 'manghabia' his *boru* he will in all probability give him an *ulos pandasdas* (or *pangapo*) = a cloth or gift to stimulate him.

The formalities of concluding a levirate marriage are quite simple: a meal is arranged in the kinship circle concerned to which the village chief and the *parboru* are invited. During the meal the spirit of the deceased is invoked and his blessing on the remarriage of his widow is requested. The Church blessing does not always (never?) take place among Christians and the marriage property is seldom registered.

If the *pangabia* is not decided upon by communal deliberation, then each of the kinsmen has the right to hang up his girdle in the woman's sleeping place, *manangkothon hohosna*, which means that he is a suitor. This act, without any formalities, particularly in Toba, is sometimes followed immediately by the couple's living together. That this sets up no strong links and that it is often the source of disputes in which more than one man lays claim to the woman and the child that might be born to her, is quite understandable. If the principal chiefs were to exercise greater discipline on this point it would promote both the stability of marriage and legal order.

The right of kinsmen to marry a widow in levirate does not extend much beyond the circle of those stemming from one great-grandfather, but, as always, local variations are possible which are dependent, in the main, on the compactness of the group concerned. Members of the same *marga* cannot be regarded as rightful claimants, only as those who (other than complete strangers) have some claim to a reduction in the marriage payment. The writer of the *Patik dohot Uhum* classifies the *pangabia* (for Silindung and its environs) according to the ever extending lineage and gives different names for the payments each has to make to the nearest *uaris*. Many of these names have fallen into desuetude and so has any practical use of them. The term *panimbangi* = that which has to be weighed out, has remained in use for distant kinsmen as well as for people who are not *marga* members: it indicates that a sum is due to the *uaris*. This is determined with due allowance to the amount of the marriage payment paid originally and its size is proportionate to the distance of the existing kinship. A *panimbangi* for a complete stranger is in the nature of a new marriage payment.

The portion of the amount given to the *parboru* is usually defined by the general term *piso*. I also heard it called *sibalun amak* = rolling up the mat, but this term, which points to a complete change in the relationship, has, in my opinion, particular bearing on divorce.

If there is no close kinsman who can marry a widow, she is not usually subjected to pressure as to whom she should marry, and when she does marry there are usually few formalities. Outside the circle of the *uaris*, whose members receive the *panimbangi*, no one else participates at the meal other than the *parboru* and the village chief. The *uaris*, naturally, keep a watchful eye on their rights. It frequently happens that while the widow is living temporarily with her father or in

Plate II   pp. 94, 245, 357
MANOPOTI SALA NA MAHODJORHÚ

to confess guilt after having committed the offence of marrying a widow in unseemly haste. In this case of levirate marriage, the nearest kinsmen of the deceased husband had not been informed about it in the proper manner.

a. *Manulangi radja*, putting food with the hands into the village chief's mouth.

b. *Manopoti salana*, confessing guilt to the village chief and the elders and asking for their forgiveness.

another dwelling of her own which is outside the direct supervision of her late husband's kinsmen, a more distant kinsman will court her secretly and then the *uaris* are faced with an accomplished fact. This failure to observe the proper formalities is most indecent and rude, *madjordjorhú*, behaviour towards the rightful claimants and merits a reproof. This may take the form of having a duty imposed to '*manulangi*' the *uaris*, the *radja* and the *parboru* and to pay a *batu ni sulang-sulang* and a *piso*-gift over and above what is due as the *panimbangi*. Photos II a and b show a *manopoti* which in this instance was performed because of misbehaviour that, in the relevant judgement, was defined as *pangabiaon na mahodjorhú* = the all too desirous taking of a widow.

If it is a stranger who offends the deceased's *uaris* in this way and if it is clear that he is wilfully arrogating the rights of others, then the offence comes in the category of adultery, *langkup*. This will be dealt with later.

CHILDREN AND PROPERTY IN LEVIRATE AND WIDOW REMARRIAGE

If the deceased leaves a son, then he receives what the *uaris* would otherwise get as the marriage payment or *panimbangi* for his mother. The father's property that the son inherits includes the *utang singir* = claims and debts, as well as the *boli ni boru* to be received for a full sister. Only if the father's actual brother, or at most the father's uncle's son, marries the widow will the new husband be regarded as the second father of the deceased's son which latter will share alike with any sons born of the second marriage. In such a case the law of levirate and the law of inheritance give way to each other.

If, however, a widow, having sons, marries a distant kinsman and if she gives him sons also, then the sons of each of the husbands succeed to the property of their respective fathers, *masiihut-ihut di ugasan na pinungka ni amana be*. To this there can be exceptions: if a son of the first marriage has always helped his stepfather, *ama pangabia*, in the cultivation of his land or has helped him in business, then he has also a right to what has been acquired during his mother's second marriage. Disputes arising from this source are not infrequent between half-brothers and are settled with due observance of the particular circumstances.

If the deceased leaves no children or only girls, then his property reverts to his *uaris*. An immediate kinsman who marries the widow acquires property rights above anyone else, but a more distant kinsman only acquires what the close *uaris* are willing to surrender. Consequently, if the woman brought to her first marriage two *pauseang*-fields, it often happens that one field goes to the *uaris* while the other is left to the woman as her *boan-boan*. This could also happen if she had a son. If the woman has small daughters, then some fields, among which are her *pauseang*-fields, are often allocated to her and her daughters. If this is not done then the *uaris*, who naturally receive the *boli* for the daughters, have to provide their dowry. If the *uaris* have received a considerable *panimbangi* or marriage payment for a childless widow, then they must allow her to keep her *pauseang*.

THE WIDOW WHO REMAINS UNMARRIED

I have already said that a widow who does not remarry can continue to stay in her own household, *marnangkar-nangkar*.

A widow who has some property and has sons has nothing to worry about. She handles her late husband's property and manages it until her eldest son reaches adulthood. This control will be limited to the upkeep and use of the property and to the daily expenditure for the family. And the *uaris* will only interfere if she is blatantly extravagant, if, for instance, she slips gifts to her *hula-hula*, and so on. The *uaris* also have a say in the event of legal proceedings which fall outside the boundaries of usual domestic management, such as pledging or taking in pledge a wet rice-field, selling the dwelling, marrying off the daughters, or if the widow is summoned on a matter other than domestic, which often happens. Many a time, however, the widow is also allowed to go her own way in these matters and she is sometimes also permitted independently to petition a court with a claim.

A widow has the greatest freedom in those areas where the married woman also has the greatest independence. Since, however, the independence of the widow in the more important transactions is always dependent upon the graciousness of the *uaris*, who can take action against an agreement concluded which they do not like, it is always best that the widow be supported in such transactions by one or more of her nearest relations. A widow's adult and married sons will sometimes not act in such matters, though they are entitled to do so, out of respect for their mother and will let her go her own way. On the other hand, a widow who is urged by a judge to enter into some kind of transaction may refuse to do so without the assistance of her eldest son. And in my opinion, it would be a help to legal security to encourage this attitude.

A widow who has only daughters is dependent to a greater extent on the *uaris* of her deceased husband. Such *uaris* are the legal heirs of the deceased and can take as much of the inheritance as they want to either immediately after the husband's death or later and can leave the widow in control of as much or as little of it as they feel disposed. There are, of course, the covetous ones who, either straight after the husband's death or at a later date will leave the family barely enough to live on, so that a judge has to intervene and decide what must be given to the wife. There are also the *halak na burdju* = the honest, right-minded ones, who take nothing for themselves and confine themselves to some supervision of the wife's management of affairs and co-operate in the more important transactions. Men such as these will allocate the greater part of the property of the deceased to the daughters when they marry and will themselves take only a small part of the estate as an acknowledgement of their executorship. The *boru*-group of the deceased, his sister, her husband and sons, his father's sister or her husband and descendants and so on, often play an important role in finding a solution which precludes the men of their *hula-hula* from profiting by too great a self-interest.

The widow who is without children and is no longer young and who does not remarry is virtually without rights. Usually so little of her husband's property is left to her that she cannot live properly and there are miscreants who would even withhold that from her. Outrageous examples of inhuman conduct still occur every now and then. Many a time her *hula-hula*, i.e., her own kinsmen do not stand up for her and, especially if she is old and decrepit, they often leave her wholly dependent on the benevolence of the *uaris*. This is a point to which the younger generation might give attention.

THE WIDOW IS NO PART OF THE ESTATE

In the literature dealing with inheritance and succession, the widow is often indicated as being part of the estate of her husband. This position, however, is not in accordance with the actual situation.

The *uaris* of the deceased do not have a free hand with the widow and neither does her son. Were this the case, then there would be good reason for regarding her as belonging to the estate. What the *uaris* have is a right to claim that the woman, who at her marriage was released from her own group against a sum of money and thereby came under the authority of her husband and after his death under that of his kinship group, does not withdraw and is not withdrawn from this authority without a similar settlement. A widow is without doubt freer to refuse a marriage with an *uaris* and to demand separation from the circle to which her late husband belonged than the married woman is to get a divorce. In the case of a widow there can be no question of the stigma of being a *mahilolóng* as applied to a married woman who desires to leave her husband. The question of *langkup* = adultery can arise but in such a case the *pangalangkup* = the man who takes as a wife a woman who is either under the authority of her husband or her deceased husband's *uaris*, is the active agent and he must atone for his action. Repeatedly one encounters a widow who is defending her rights before a judge against an *uaris* who tries to withhold from her what is hers by right and reason. It cannot be denied that a widow who has sons and who does not marry again has, in fact, authority over her property and her children that approaches that of a widow in Western society. The idea that a widow has no rights at all has clearly been furthered by the gross roughness that men can adopt towards women whose position is weak and who do not have the support of their *hula-hula*, and also by the 'theory' of patrilineal relationships. But on this issue, as on others, theory and practice rather differ.

DIVORCE, PORSIRANGAN

The subject of divorce is one of the most difficult in the whole of Batak matrimonial law. The wishes of both the husband and the wife play a role, the *parboru* has a hand in the matter, the circle of kinsmen of those concerned are affected by the consequences. Not only the personal circumstances are important but also what had previously been given as the marriage payment for the wife and what she had brought with her as her dowry. Here, too, theory and practice often differ. There are areas where there is a great stability in marriage and areas where there is less. The Government has also interfered in many ways, there has been the influence of the Mission, and when cases were no longer dealt with before the courts according to native practice and procedure, the handling of divorce suits began to differ from that formerly operative and has sometimes followed a very unusual course. In addition to these factors, there has also been the development and the influence of Christian law and Christian morals alongside ancient usages. Thus old and new, good and bad, are no longer easily separable and there is therefore a need for detailed description.

CAUSES

The first cause that brings a marriage to an end is the apparent sexual impotence or some other defect preventing regular coition.

I have already said that physical capability to reproduce is one of the conditions for marriage, as I have also noted that a wife upon whom a husband has been forced will sometimes succeed in making her husband think he is impotent, *na so hasea* = one who is useless. Even if it can be established by a medical examination that there is no question of impotency and that the possibility of procreation is normal, nevertheless, if the woman persists in her attitude divorce is the natural result. Neither party is compelled to continue a marriage that does not offer the usual opportunities for having children.

There is also another cause which is physical and that is the presence of leprosy, *huliton*, in either spouse. A person suffering from this feared and incurable disease, which in former times could lead to the afflicted persons's being killed, is now admitted to a leprosarium, which means in effect permanent separation between the spouses. The healthy spouse then has grounds for divorce though it is far from always being used. The same applies to mental sickness that is apparently incurable.

Childlessness is another important cause of divorce. This is usually attributed to lack of harmony of the couple's *tondi* which can prevent children being born. Both husband and wife then have grounds for divorce, to which the *parboru* and the *paranak* will agree, since:

saut na marrongkap, sirang na so marrongkap,

With harmony a marriage endures, without it it has to be broken up.

This absence of harmony is regarded as existing solely between both spouses and not between either of them and other people around them. And many a time a *parboru* whose *boru* has been returned to him will forthwith provide another *boru* as her substitute.

Childlessness may continue for years before the couple take the decision to separate. I mentioned in earlier chapters that the woman's kinsmen endeavour to ameliorate her childlessness by a magical enrichment of her *tondi* of which the weakness is seen as the cause of her unfruitfulness. A divorce may sometimes take place on the advice of a *datu* who, after divination, sees it as the only solution. However, the mere wish of one of the spouses for a divorce is also sufficient.

On a level with childlessness as ground for divorce, is the continual loss of children which is likewise attributed to an absence of harmony if other reasons, such as a wrong dwelling place necessitating removal, cannot account for it. In such a case divorce is also at the wish of one or both spouses and is an amicable arrangement. The explanation of this ground for divorce is again the desire to have healthy offspring and this induces the spouses to part in order to enter a new alliance that may be more satisfactory in this respect. One ground for divorce that is less easy to explain, is the desire of a man to divorce a woman who has only given him daughters but who has not passed the age of child-bearing, *saep ladang*. Yet it is often done and in conservative areas the chiefs and the wife's kinsmen are sympathetic towards the husband's desire for sons to continue his lineage, if that is the only motive for his wanting a divorce.

Where a divorce takes place at the wish of the one party, or by agreement of both, it is frequently the result of a growing disharmony between them. If the couple have children, particularly young children, there is a great measure of possibility of the marriage bond and love between the parents being strengthened thereby. Where there are no children, or where they have all died, there is a serious impediment to the couple growing together during their married life. But there can be other reasons which make both the parties concerned feel that divorce is the most reasonable solution to their difficulties. These factors are sometimes related to parental pressure in respect of the choice of the marriage partner, or it can be that estrangement results because of too short a period of acquaintance before marriage. Prolonged absence from the home by the husband, continual quarrels, the wife's deserting to her kinsmen and similar factors are the symptoms of a situation expressed in the following aphorism:

> *sada rantiti sada soná,*
> *sada magigi sada so rá;*
> a *rantiti* tree, a *sona* tree,
> the one has an aversion, the other no desire;

which means that there is incompatability of temperament and that both husband and wife desire to separate.

The word *magigi* = to have a dislike of, to have an aversion to, is also the technical term for the antipathy of only one spouse towards the other and against the continuation of the marriage. This, too, can lead to divorce. This distaste may arise from the fact that a man wants to get rid of his wife, *baoa na magigi*, because living with her has become intolerable; because he has a feeling for another woman; because he is angry with his father-in-law who did not give his daughter a *pauseang*; or because he is incited to do so by his second wife. It becomes apparent from the circumstances and the husband's behaviour towards his wife: for instance, he will return her to her parents, *paulakhon*, so that they can admonish her, *adjarhon*, without his being able to show good reason

for his action. He then concerns himself with her no longer. He may
drive her peremptorily from the house, leave her unprovided for a long
time, repudiate her, *mambolonghon*, in short, he acts in such a way that
there is nothing else for her to do but to invoke the help of her *hula-hula*
with the object of trying to get a divorce. A divorce arising from these
causes, as also one caused by mutual antagonism, is sometimes preceded
by a long period of separation, *padao-dao*, from each other. Usually,
however, the wife and her kinsmen do not wait too long before making
their request since they are anxious to convince the judge who must
make the decision, that the responsibility for the break up of the
marriage must be laid at the husband's door. This is important in respect
of the size of the portion of the marriage payment that has to be
returned.

If a husband acts arbitrarily towards his wife, and thus towards her
parboru, the latter sometimes takes matters into his own hands and,
instead of laying his complaint before the judge, gives his daughter in
marriage to a third party as though she were a free woman, *boru na sae*.
This happened more frequently in the *Pidari* time than it does nowadays. Should he do this, it usually results in the new couple living
together and for want of the co-operation of the chiefs their position is
not regularised by a formal marriage. The husband from whom the
woman has not been legally separated can then lay a complaint of
mangalangkup = unlawful taking as wife a woman who still belongs to
another man, against the third party and a claim against the *parboru*
of being a *palangkuphon* = promotor of *langkup*. In olden times such
an act on the part of the *parboru* could be the signal for a war. In the
event of such a complaint, however, the third party, the *pangalangkup*,
who acted wholly at the instigation of and in concert with the *parboru*,
will disclaim any responsibility by sheltering behind the *parboru*.
Mangalangkup is one of the worst crimes a Batak can commit and he
will plead the following set expression in his defence:

manuk-manuk hulabu ompan-ompan ni soru,
ndang dohonon pangalangkup ia so dituduhon parboru;
A grey chicken is the bait to catch rats.
A man cannot be called a *pangalangkup* if the *parboru* does not
indicate that he is.

And, indeed, it is the *parboru* who is guilty of an unlawful act. He was
not in a position to dispose freely over his *boru* because no definite,
tangkás, divorce had taken place. His blameworthiness is expressed in
the following saying:

sada lombuna naeng dua hodana,
sada boruna naeng dua helana;
A man has a cow but wants two horses.

A man has one daughter but wants two sons-in-law.
The measure of the *parboru*'s guilt and the subsequent consequences of his action, however, will obviously be determined by the attitude the complaining husband had previously adopted towards his wife.

If the *magigi* = aversion, is on the wife's side, it is called *mahilolóng* = having an aversion for her husband, and the woman is called the *boru sipahilolong.* A man who gets rid of a wife who does not want to leave him, acts arbitrarily towards her and towards her *parboru* who takes her part. For this he must pay a penalty even though he is entitled to sever the tie that binds him to his wife formally, even in so high-handed a fashion.

A married woman, however, according to the old rigid law does not have the power to put an end to her marriage of her own free will by, for instance, such an arbitrary act as running away. She is under the authority of her husband who took her out of her kinship circle and so long as he lives and acknowledges her as his wife she remains under it. Here the patrilineal character of marriage comes to the fore: the wife exists for and belongs to her husband. It is the same attitude often adopted by the *parboru* when he wants to force his *boru* into a particular marriage. And once the *parboru* has taken this stand, he takes it for granted that there will be no question of aversion on her part either initially or later. He imposes his will on his *boru* the more readily because, if the marriage is terminated because of her *mahilolong,* the consequences for him in respect of refunding the marriage payment can be much more disadvantageous than is the case when the *magigi* is on the husband's side. The *boru* who, once she is married, has other ideas than her *parboru,* not only finds herself up against his obstinacy but also his strong legal position and his unwillingness to suffer any damage on her account. The misery to which she could be subjected in olden times for refractoriness is described in the *Patik dohot Uhum*: she could be put in the block or physical force could be used to compel her to submit to the sexual act. A case of this kind described in the *Patik dohot Uhum* evidently concerned a young virgin who was married to an older man against her wish and who immediately afterwards showed a great aversion for him.

As far as a young couple are concerned, there is none of the boldness on the man's part in the first period of the marriage as in the case described in the *Patik dohot Uhum*. The matter then has a milder aspect and it is mainly the parents who will decide whether or not the marriage will continue. The case in the *Patik dohot Uhum* is one of the worst that could happen, because it suggests a great heartlessness on the part of the *parboru*. However, blood being thicker than water, the *parboru* is often moved by his *boru*'s lot, or perhaps he fears she might commit suicide. Even in olden times, there was a limit to which the heartless treatment of a wife could be carried. This is expressed by the following saying:

ndang tarseat boru na so olo adjar;

a daughter who will not be obedient cannot be killed.

This means that a *parboru* will not resort to extreme measures, but it is obvious that this applies rather more to his own daughter than to a niece whose father has died.

At the present day inhuman compulsion is, naturally, absolutely forbidden. Moral pressure can, of course, be exerted and is permitted in accordance with the prevailing attitude about the law and custom that will not acknowledge the right of a wife voluntarily to put an end to her marriage which she no longer desires, and which still endeavours to curtail more vigorously her freedom in comparison with that of her husband. However, a determined wife can at the present time always contrive the dissolution of her marriage.

This being the case, there is apparently no reason now to introduce special measures favouring the wife who wants to leave her husband or whose husband wants to part with her, by making the financial arrangement of a divorce more disadvantageous for the husband than would be the case under the old law or under present-day law. European district-officers sometimes tried such a procedure as well as the missionaries, on the assumption that the bondage of the woman was primarily caused by the financial tie. Nevertheless, the possibility that the woman's freedom will be contracted by men must always be guarded against. At the moment the legal position of the married woman in respect of continuing or dissolving her marriage already so much approximates that of her husband, that the fault of breaking up a marriage, whether it lies with the husband or the wife, can be expressed in the size of the marriage payment that has to be refunded. This is in accordance with Batak law and it promotes the stability of marriage. The Batak usually attaches more value to such a gradual change than he does to imposed innovations which, as a rule, are badly misunderstood and as a consequence work out other than was intended. It must be admitted that it is distasteful to see men squabbling over the marriage payment as though they were discussing the price of a cow when it is the preservation of the marriage and the fate of the wife that are at stake.

A woman cannot be divorced when she is pregnant. If the husband is responsible for her conceiving then *magigi* on his side is regarded as the height of indecency. The birth of the child should take place before any definite decisions are taken bearing on the husband's motives which, as a rule, will not be very noble ones. It can also then be determined that he is the father of the child.

If the *magigi* is on the side of a pregnant wife, then it is more than likely that her pregnancy is the result of intercourse with another man and, in order to place the legal parentage of the child beyond all doubt, no heed is given to the woman's desire for a divorce until the child is born. Another reason for refusing the woman a divorce in those circumstances, is that there is no desire at all to be accommodating to the man who has probably alienated the woman from her husband. This same attitude was adopted by a judge at Simormata [18] when he forbade the wife whose request for a divorce was based on childlessness, to remarry the man who was accused of inciting her to sue for divorce, even though no valid proof was adduced in support of the allegation. It was also the attitude of the chiefs of Silindung who, according to the *Patik dohot Uhum*, pronounced a similar prohibition, *hata siunang*.

Any attempt by another man to induce a married woman to be unfaithful, meets with strong opposition from a Batak judge. If, however, the wife's adultery is confirmed, then her husband can return her to her *parboru* if he wants to get rid of her. Extra-marital intercourse by a man is no ground for his wife to ask for a divorce.

Another reason for not acceding to a husband's request for a divorce, is the fact that his wife may be a *boru na gabe* = a woman who has had children. I only found this motive operative in Silindung. In Toba, on the other hand, there was many a judgement in which it scarcely made any difference. (I am not clear regarding the attitude in other areas.) The idea is that a woman, in marrying a man and bearing his children, has achieved her natural purpose, she has given him all that he could desire of her, she has contributed to the building up of his 'house' and therefore she should not be at the mercy of any inclination of his to get rid of her. It is right that a man should then keep his wife, care for her and maintain her even though there are no further sexual

---

[18] See the publication mentioned in note 1, p. 135.

relations; that she should be held in honour and be respected as his lawful wife who belongs to the main room of the house, *djabu bona*.

It is preferable for a man to take a second wife and live with her in a subsidiary dwelling rather than repudiate his first wife, *paulakhon* or *ambolonghon*, and thus place her in the position of being a divorced woman who may not remarry and who has no individual means of sustenance. A divorce with payment of alimony is not consistent with the principles of Batak matrimonial law which only admits divorce as a complete severance of personal and financial relationships. Therefore, the only way in which such a wife can retain the respect that is her due, is for her to remain her husband's legal spouse. These principles were expressed in the judgement discussed earlier of the highest native court at Tarutung, and furnish further proof of the high position that a wife who has had sons can acquire among the Batak.

A divorce need not necessarily affect the relations between the kinship circles of the spouses concerned. If the couple were each other's affines before the marriage, these relations naturally remain unimpaired after the divorce. If children are born of the marriage, whether sons or daughters, then they continue the existing affinity relationship. If the couple are divorced because of childlessness, the existing affinal link, *partondongan*, may be continued, if desired, by providing another *boru*. Or, this relationship can be renewed by a marriage of another young man with another young woman. In very backward areas, where marriages were repeatedly contracted between the same patrilineages, the marriage of two people and the reasons for maintaining it have been submerged in the relationships of the groups as entities. I once observed a change of persons in the out-of-the-way mountain territory of Sagala (near Pangururan) that can only be called staggering.

A marriage that has ended in divorce can be remade, though it is rare:
   sigarang-garang sibulu tobu;
   boi do naung sirang djumadihon mardomu.
   The *garang-garang* herb, the sugar cane leaf.
   What has been torn asunder can be reunited again.

MODE OF DIVORCE

The great host of kinsmen and affines who showed their interest in the marriage by assembling at the *marundjuk* do not foregather at a divorce. It is more an affair of the closest kinsmen and the village chiefs of both parties concerned. This is because, among other things, the *suhut* (the *parboru*) is the only one responsible for the refund of the marriage payment. None of the other recipients of the main constituents, *djambar*, is required to surrender what he has received as a contribution to the amount that has to be returned. (At the later remarriage of the woman they naturally do not receive a new portion.) And neither have the recipients of the *na muhut* any responsibility.

There are areas, such as Silindung, in which a high value is placed on the stability of marriage and where divorce seldom takes place, where kinsmen and affines, chiefs and friends leave no stone unturned to reconcile a couple who find they cannot go on living together and wish to part. If their efforts are unavailing and if it finally comes to formal discussions on the divorce, *mangholting*, strictly speaking, only those who are concerned financially are affected. Their village chiefs act as their legal assistants and as intermediaries who can bridge over difficulties that may arise. According to traditional law, it is hardly necessary that the higher chiefs of the territory, who had previously given their *pasu-pasu*, are consulted, though if those in the small circle fail to arrive at an agreement, they may well be called upon. Thus it is not to be wondered at that in areas such as Toba, where in general not such a high value is placed on the stability of a marriage, divorces occur in which hardly anybody bothers to interest themselves except a small circle of, say, five or six persons. Nor is it surprising that the Mission, in order to promote stability in marriage, has always advocated that its European and Batak ministers should have the opportunity of exercising their influence, by advice and exhortation, to heal a breach before Christians are finally divorced. It also recommended to the Government that divorce proceedings should be dealt with by the courts of justice under the chairmanship of Europeans and Batak civil servants: the Great and Small *Rapat*. This two-fold aim is commendable, but the raising of the moral standard which can result from the first object will be less consistently supported by the compulsion and pressure that goes with the second, unless the view can be developed among the populace that marriage, its laws and its practice, is not the private affair of the smallest possible group, but a matter of general concern.

As I have already remarked, many a time a divorce is preceded by a lengthy period of separation, *padao-dao*, during which time the spouses do not have sexual intercourse. It may also happen that the husband is continually absent from home. He may go to the East Coast, for example, and his wife will hear nothing from him and he does not inform his kinsmen regarding his intentions in respect of his marriage. It goes without saying, that in the course of time the wife and her kinsmen will insist on a divorce and in such circumstances many a court will speak of *sada rantiti* (see p. 250) rather than *magigi* on the part of the man. In such a case, provided the husband's attitude regarding the non-continuance of his marriage is clear, his absence is no impediment to a divorce. His *paranak,* who must co-operate to this end, will assume all responsibility on behalf of the absentee.

The pronouncement of the divorce is not attended with any symbolic formalities performed by or on behalf of the spouses. A couple of payments confirm the pronouncement and are evidence of agreement by both parties. The chiefs who have co-operated receive the *pago-pago,* sealing money, as they always do when a dispute is settled. This must be paid by each party as proof that they accept the decision. In the case of divorce, *sirang,* this money is called *pago-pago sirang* but it can also be called *pangholting* and *sae-sae.* In Silindung and its environs (and elsewhere?) the *parboru* gives the *paranak* a small sum and in accepting it the latter acknowledges that he has surrendered his authority over the woman: this sum is called the *patilaho* and will be deducted from the marriage payment that is to be refunded. It is said that the *patilaho* is only given if the married couple are childless and if the affinal relationship created by the marriage is completely severed by the divorce, *tos partondongan.* But this is a distinction that is too subtle for the Toba Batak to appreciate. If the affinity relationships continue because there are children, then the proper term would be *parsaean* or *sae-sae* = termination of the marriage. I also learnt, however, that these terms can only be used if the marriage payment has been refunded in its entirety. If the affinal relations continue, then the term *ulos* is used to denote what the *parboru* gives to his divorced son-in-law.

All these payments imply agreement between the parties, not only as regards the divorce but also as regards the financial consequences. The two things are, in fact, inseparable, and to treat each separately would be taking it out of its context. As I have already said, the motives for the divorce determine to a great extent the nature and the size of the *parboru*'s financial commitments. However, if one or both of the parties are shown to be guilty of the marriage miscarrying, or if one of them is absolved of the guilt, reaching agreement is often made more difficult especially in respect of the financial arrangements. In olden times, people frequently pestered each other with protracted negotiations or waged war until they got so tired of it that they were in a mood for amicable discussion, for ending the dispute, which they then handed over to the chiefs to settle. If the chiefs felt themselves powerful enough,

17

they simply imposed their decisions on the parties. War being nowadays excluded as a means of settling disputes, complaints of one or both parties are brought straightaway before a judge who can pronounce a divorce and can settle the consequences without it being necessary for both sides to agree to it. Nevertheless, he should not be deterred from striving to reach mutual agreement if it is possible.

It is not necessary for the *parboru* to pay immediately in cash the sum that he has to refund. An advance can be given provisionally and a definite arrangement made with regard to the remainder. If the woman is still young and can easily remarry, then an arrangement is often made that the payment of the remainder will be made when she becomes married to another man, *di laku ni boru i*. Meanwhile, she is the *sihunti garar* = the one who carries a debt on her head. Formerly in such a case the woman was placed in the hands of the intermediary who had arranged the divorce as the *boru ni radja* or the *boru ni pangulu* and her remarriage was also arranged by the intermediary. A would-be suitor had to turn to the intermediary with his request to marry the woman and it was he who fixed the marriage payment that could be claimed for her, received it and handed it to the rightful claimant. He saw to it that the woman did not remarry until after the debt resting on her had been properly paid. He was expected to attend to the interests of all concerned in like measure. This system made it possible for the amount the *parboru* had to pay back not to be a fixed one: an agreement could be reached whereby the husband would receive whatever amount the negotiations with the new husband would yield. Such an arrangement might be necessary if, for example, the wife was elderly or if the fault for the marriage failing could be laid more on the husband. A part of the amount received, for example, 1/3 was allocated to the *parboru* as the so-called *sibalun amak* = for rolling up the mat, which term indicated the change in the relationship which had been created by the divorce and the subsequent remarriage. This arrangement can still be applied if there is someone in whom both parties place sufficient reliance in respect of arranging a new marriage. Usually, however, the courts of justice that deal with divorce cases will decide upon a fixed sum at the outset and stipulate a period within which it must be paid. The *parboru*, however, then has to take the risk that the woman does not marry again and he will usually raise objections if the *magigi* is found to be on the husband's side and not on that of the wife.

If no amount is laid down and if no agreement is made that the amount will depend on what will be received *di laku ni boru,* it will then be fixed as the whole or a definite part of the first marriage payment received for the woman. For this purpose the whole of the *djambar na gok,* as well as, usually, the *na muhut,* are added up and from the total is subtracted the *ragi-ragi* that the *paranak* received. The cost of meals and such like are not taken into account. Things that are given *in natura,* such as cattle, are generally valued at a certain amount, *asam.* In such a case restitution cannot be claimed *in natura* but the claimant must be content with their value in money. The counterpart of the marriage payment, the *ragi-ragi,* must be repaid by the *paranak.*

The *indahan arian* and the *pauseang*-fields have already been dealt with in this context.

Presents that the *parboru* has given his *boru* during the marriage, usually return with the wife if they have not served the purpose for which they were given. For example, a *tano na niupahon* given to a married daughter who had failed to conceive and was still childless at the time of her divorce. If a child was born but died later, then the land can either be returned with the wife or it can remain with the husband.

THE AMOUNT OF THE MARRIAGE PAYMENT TO BE RETURNED

As already stated, the amount of the marriage payment to be returned is definitely related to the cause of the divorce. Here also, however, there is a difference between theory and practice.

In cases where apparent impotence, sickness or childlessness or mutual estrangement are the motives for the divorce, the principle is generally that the marriage payment is returned completely. However, there can be a number of circumstances by virtue of which the *paranak* will be content with less. In Silindung, for example, where divorce is not frequent and where people are rather ashamed to associate financial claims with it — the favourable influence of Christianity and civilisation — the *paranak* does not usually insist on complete restitution even though there is no demonstrable reason for reducing the amount. And even where a couple are childless or have lost all their children, their personal relationship can be a good one despite the mutual desire to dissolve the marriage. Similarly, a good relationship between husband and wife's kinsmen, or an existing affinity link can continue. In these cases the husband usually lets his former father-in-law keep a considerable part of the marriage payment as a *piso-piso,* perhaps half or a quarter of it.

In cases where there is mutual aversion, the question of guilt is relevant and each of the parties usually has reasons to demand that less guilt on their side should be taken into consideration when the amount of the marriage payment to be refunded is determined.

The announcement that a marriage is to end in a divorce is usually preceded by prolonged disagreement and all kinds of major and minor questions that have arisen as a result are raked over. These are placed before the mediating chief or judge. If the resulting decision is that there is no question of *magigi* on the part of the husband nor *mahilolóng* on the part of the wife, then the husband usually wants the entire marriage payment returned to him. It may also then happen, however, that he will renounce a part of it as a proof that he values the relationship in which he stood, and continues to stand, to his wife's kinsmen.

Children, or absence of them, make a difference as does their being girls or both girls and boys. Local usages, mutual relationships, age, attributes of character and other factors of this kind will further determine the right judgement. People who are acquainted with both parties and know their circumstances are, in this respect, the best mediators or informants for the judge.

If it is clearly established that the husband has repudiated, *dibolonghon*, his wife, has returned her to her parents, *dipaulakhon*, without well-founded reasons, that the wife has done nothing wrong, that the husband has acted out of malice, *djungkat ni roha*, so that it is obvious that the *magigi* is on his side, then either he gets back nothing or only a small part, usually a half or a third, of the marriage payment: he has trampled the remainder under his own feet, *tinundjang ni patna*. In such cases, it is usually decided that the amount to be refunded will be paid from the new marriage payment that will be received for the woman when she remarries. The ex-husband thus runs the risk that she will not remarry or that she may die soon. He may get an entitlement to the whole of the future marriage payment for his divorced wife, but he must then immediately give a considerable sum to his former father-in-law as *piso*. On this point many variations are possible and it often happens, naturally, that a wife is not wholly free of any responsibility for the divorce, so that clemency towards the husband has to be exercised.

If the wife is of an age which makes her marrying again doubtful, so that the *magigi* is a question of getting rid of an old pasture, *mangambolong padang tua*, then it is usually decided that restitution of the marriage payment will be made out of a new marriage payment. If, however, the wife is guilty of *mahilolóng*, then the husband has a right to a refund of an increased marriage payment. The generally known rule runs:

> *sidangka sidangkua tu dangka ni singgolom,*
> *na sada (dua) gabe dua (tolu) na tolu (opat) gabe onom,*
> *i ma utang ni sipahilolong.*
> The branches of the *sidangkua* round the branche of the *singgolom*,
> One (two) becomes two (three) and three (four) becomes six,
> That is the penalty for the wife who deserts her husband.

The words in brackets given the more recent and milder version of this *umpama*. In reality, the doubling of the marriage payment no longer occurs and the increase by half only in cases where the wife has clearly shown an unreasonable aversion for her husband. In general, there is a growing tendency not to express the guilt of the wife in the break up of a marriage in terms of a large sum of money. Here, as with the *magigi* on the part of the husband, there are all kinds of nuances conceivable that either mitigate the guilt of the wife or induce the husband to accept a lesser increase than he would normally be content with. Often he is quite satisfied with restitution of only the marriage payment provided that it is clearly stated verbally that the wife is *mahilolóng*. In practice, therefore, the maxim only means that it is a limit which cannot be exceeded. It is only applied in the most serious cases and not to the intermediate cases which are those most frequently occurring. The judge must always bear in mind, that many a time one party will endeavour to place the other in the most unfavourable light by pretending that their one desire is that the marriage should continue whereas, in reality, both are anxious to part from each other.

If the decision is that the wife is guilty of *mahilolóng* then, as a rule, a small sum of money is claimed from the *parboru* as *panulaan*. This recalls olden times when the *parboru* had to conclude divorce proceedings of this kind with a 'meal of separation'. Such a meal was also demanded when someone had committed an offence and made atonement to the injured party, the chiefs and the village. This shows that a woman's unwillingness and her resistance to the continuance of her marriage was, in olden times, regarded as an offence. The *magigi* on the husband's part was by contrast merely unseemly.

After the divorce the children of the marriage remain with the husband. Only infants stay with their mother until they are old enough to be separated from her, *sirang susu* = to leave the breast, which is when they are about two or three years old. During the time that a child is with its mother, the father has to provide for its maintenance.

BREAKING OFF A BETROTHAL

Though a betrothal is of a provisional nature, the side that breaks it off does not go unpunished. Here also the word *magigi*, in the context *magigi di oroanna*, is in common use to indicate that one of the affianced has no further desire for marriage with the other. (The term *mahilolóng* is not applied here.) If it is the young man who no longer desires the marriage, then the *patudjolo ni sinamot* which then has to be paid back is decreased, and this decrease is then called *piso*. If it is the young girl who does not desire the marriage it is increased and this increase is then termed *ulos*. In the case of a girl, it will in many a case be the father who wants the betrothal, entered into perhaps when his daughter was a child, to be broken and another entered into. If, because of this the *parboru* should engage his *boru* to another man when she is already betrothed, it is called *palangkuphon* = the giving of the wife (in this case the girl who is betrothed) of one man to another, but it is also called *mangose padan* = breaking an agreed contract. The last term is used for preference when the circumstances show that the first betrothal was not regarded seriously and the *parboru*'s action was only an arbitrary departure from the agreed contract without proper consultation with the other party.

If the *magigi* is on the part of the young man, then he will receive back (part of) the *bohi ni sinamot* only after a new marriage payment has been received for the girl. If the guilt is on the girl's side, then the amount is reclaimable immediately. It is not usual to give a *patilaho* if the betrothal is broken off by mutual agreement.

I have already mentioned that a young man must refrain from associating with a girl who is betrothed. If, nevertheless, he desires her and abducts her, he is then guilty of *mangalangkup* in respect of a *boru oroan*, i.e., taking a girl who is betrothed to another man. It is a special form of *mangalangkup*.

LANGKUP

Mangalangkup is a crime committed by one man against another. It is the taking of the wife of another man with the object of permanently possessing her while she is still under his authority, or under that of other persons. Thus a woman who is not free. There are degrees of gravity increasing according to whether the woman is:

the betrothed, the *oroan*, of another man;

a widow, *na mabalu*, who has not remarried within the circle of her deceased husband's kinsmen and who has not been separated from them;

a wife who has already lived for a long time without regular sexual intercourse with her husband, and who is therefore in a state of *padao-dao*: this is called *anggi ni langkup* = approaching *langkup*;

a wife who has regular sexual intercourse with her husband: this is *langkup djongdjong*, and is *langkup* in its strictest sense. Distinction is made between *langkup badju-badju* when the woman is still young and childless and *langkup tataring* when the wife has had children.

In the first three and milder forms of *langkup*, the woman may have lived with her *parboru* who has married her off to another man, *palang-kuphonsa*, before she was a free woman, *boru naung sae*. In that case, as we saw, the man whom she has married will shelter behind the *parboru*. He will have the best chance of doing so in those areas where divorce is effected in the very small circle of those primarily concerned. At present, the man is also considered guilty when he is supposed to be in a position to know whether or not the woman is free.

If the *parboru* stays completely outside the case then, as soon as he learns of the unlawful intercourse of his *boru*, he will, as a rule, tell the rightful claimants what is going on with the object of completely disclaiming any responsibility. He also regards himself as the injured party, *rap marlulu*.

Though *langkup* is primarily regarded as an offence committed against the person to whom the woman belongs, it must nevertheless be regarded as also a disturbance against the public order. As such the authorities can take the necessary measures — this applies especially to the most serious forms of *langkup*. *Langkup* is: *mangapus uhum tu parnioli dohot tu radja* = a violation of the right of the one to whom the woman belongs and to public authority.

The mildest form of *langkup* is the taking of another man's betrothed. If it is coupled with abduction, then the rightful claimant joins the *parboru*, in conjunction with whom he seeks satisfaction, *marlulu*. Abduction is an aggravating circumstance for which an *adat* penalty must be paid, *digarar adat*, to the injured betrothed. This will vary according to whether the young couple also desired the betrothal or whether it was mainly a contract between their parents. In the case of a marriage that followed an elopement, the disappointed one will have to content himself with a single *ulos*-gift over and above the *bohi ni sinamot* which has to be refunded to him. This is also the case when the *parboru*, in conjunction with his *boru*, contracts a marriage other than that originally agreed.

More onerous is the *mangalangkup* of a widow. It is a crime against the *uaris* of the deceased husband from whom the woman had not been separated according to all the prescribed forms. It is obvious that the woman has co-operated in it, but she is not directly concerned in the lawsuit. She is regarded as the one who has been violated, the means by which a violation of the rights of another has been committed, *tangko uhum*. At the present time, as a result of European influence, this offence is often disposed of by ordering the *pangalangkup* simply to restore the marriage payment with, at most, an extra supplement as a penalty. According to the traditional law, however, he had to make good his misdemeanour, *pauli uhum*, by slaughtering an animal, a pig or a buffalo according to the gravity of the case, and to offer it to the *uaris* and the chiefs of the deceased and his kinsmen and, in addition, he had to pay a sum of money, *batu*. He also had to repay the marriage payment as determined by those concerned. It seems to me to be in the interests of legal order and a check on lawlessness and the degeneration of morals, if the violation of other people's rights in these circumstances is not allowed in too sentimental a manner. As soon as a Batak realises that a thing may be done, he is apt to assume that it can be done: that the sanction is neither checked from above nor supported from below, *di gindjang so dokdok, di toru so halang*, and will soon come to think that he can act as he chooses, *di rohana adat parradjaon*. Most chiefs know that their countrymen need discipline if good order is to be maintained in the community. They do not, therefore, readily take to a relaxation of authority for motives which they do not fully appreciate.

This same attitude applies to taking a woman whose marriage has not been formally dissolved. This approaches *langkup*. Her husband may, indeed, have neglected her for a long time, but this does not give her or another man the right to act as though the marriage has been dissolved according to the proper forms. Now, more than formerly, the woman and her *parboru* can go to law and can claim restitution of conjugal rights or demand a divorce. If they do not take this course, then the abductor has to pay the penalty which the judge will impose, having due regard to all the circumstances. There are also occasions where disciplinary action has to be taken against lower chiefs who have given their consent to the couple living together — there can be no question of calling it marriage. As a rule a number of mitigating circumstances can be adduced on behalf of the woman but her responsibility for her conduct is greater than that of a widow because she is still the lawful spouse of another.

The following *umpama* makes this point:

> *ansimun sada holbung dohot pege sangkarimpang,*
> *manimbung rap tu toru mangangkat rap tu gindjang;*
> A tendril of the cucumber, a root of ginger.
> Both go downwards and both go upwards;

i.e., though the man must pay the penalties, *manggarar adat,* imposed, the woman must also accept her part of the responsibility. Formerly, in the worst cases, she could be put in the block, bound to the pole with the *pangalangkup,* have her hair cut off, her ears pierced, and so on. At present, both she and the man may be imprisoned, but milder and even more effective punishments are conceivable.

The most serious form of *mangalangkup* is taking a woman away from a husband with whom she is living a regular married life. It is one of the worst crimes known to the Batak. In olden times it was the crime of a vicious man who was so determined to have the woman he desired that he did not shrink from bringing about the most terrible strife to get her. This usually meant that the entire kinship group and the authorities of the territory of the injured party took up arms, not only against the criminal but also against the lineage that supported him. His village was pillaged, he himself pursued, and no one rested until he had either been killed or put in the block or one of his kinsmen had been captured. The penalty he had to pay was assessed in buffaloes of which the number varied according to different areas. In addition, he had to offer a meal to the inhabitants of the injured party's territory.

At present the culprit is imprisoned in the few cases that occur.

MARITAL INFIDELITY AND OTHER MORAL TRANSGRESSIONS

Committing morally offensive acts is generally summed up in the following *umpama*:

> *manuan bulu dilapang-lapang ni babi,*
> *mamungka na so uhum, mangulahon na so djadi;*
> Planting bamboos on the path the pigs take.
> To begin what is unlawful, to do what is forbidden.

Such acts befoul a region (make it *rotak*) and bring shame upon the persons injured (make them *maila*). For such acts the culprit must pay with a punishment which, besides giving satisfaction to the injured party, must result in a purification, *pangurasion,* of the woman who has been violated and of the region that has been befouled by his act. This is done by means of the *parpangiron* that I have described on p. 101.

The simplest form of moral transgression is to importune a girl or a woman with evil intent, *manggunturi boru* or *mangaroa-roai*. The guilty party must confess his guilt, *manopoti salana*, and must give to the woman or girl an *ulos* = cloth, *diatas ni indahan dohot djuhut* = during the eating of a meal of meat and rice. This meal must be prepared by his wife, mother or sister. During it he must confess his guilt and declare that he will reform, *mandok djora*. The woman must accept this act of penance, *mandjalo uhuman i,* in the presence of her husband, (or betrothed), her father or brothers and the chiefs concerned, all of whom participate in the meal and who receive a small sum as an acknowledgement that their rights also have been violated.

The rape of a young girl, a married woman or a widow has always been regarded as a serious crime. If a man rapes a young nubile girl and is then permitted to marry her, then his punishment is mitigated. If not, as in the case of the rape of a married woman or a widow, a considerable penalty is demanded.

Sexual intercourse between young people, *marmainan* = whoring, can take the particular form of *marpadan-padan* = behaving like husband and wife before marriage, or it can simply be *morlangka pilit* = walking in bad ways. The term *morlangka pilit* also denotes adultery committed with a married woman. When a man is caught with another man's wife in the act of adultery, the applicable term is *targombang* or *tardege di pinggol ni dalan* = caught by the wayside, i.e., in the act. Formerly the injured husband had the right to kill the man caught in the act of adultery as he would kill a pig in a rice-field.

The term *targombang* can also be used when a man approaches a bathing place, *tapian,* and has not indicated his approach in the approved manner by calling out *bo* and has thus caught the woman unawares, or when she has not made her presence apparent in any way. When a man and a woman are caught in the act of exchanging meaning-ful glances, it is called *targombang di panaili.*

If a man is willing to take back his wife when she has committed adultery, the *parboru* must pay him a sum of money as *panguras* in paying which he delivers his *boru* to her husband in a state of purity again.

When a man commits adultery with another man's wife, the penalty is only demanded from the man. This gives satisfaction to the woman's husband but none to his own wife. Formerly an adultress was treated as a *na nilangkup* (p. 265). At the present time the Christian sense of justice also regards the man as guilty of bad conduct towards his own wife.

Imprisonment is at present expedient in those serious cases which approach *langkup*, either with or without a supplementary order. The less serious cases, however, can still be dealt with according to traditional law and custom of which the penalties can restore peace and extinguish the rancour caused by the offence.

Adultery committed by married people is relatively rare, for the Batak value marital fidelity highly. Extra-marital intercourse is more frequent between a man and a widow who has not remarried and who is still under the authority of her late husband's *uaris* and with a married woman who has been left by her husband for a long period, *padao-dao*. When it is found out it is *langkup*, but often it is not committed openly.

ILLEGITIMATE CHILDREN

If a child is born as a result of extra-marital intercourse, the applicable law is the so-called *adat porlak* = the custom of the garden, whereby a child is accredited as being that of the man to whom the woman still belongs. This idea is expressed in the following *umpama:*

> *lata na nidanggurhon tu porlak ni deba, nampuna porlak nampu-nasa;*
>
> The cutting that is planted in another man's garden belongs to the owner of the garden.

Strictly interpreted, this maxim says that, irrespective of the relationship of the woman to her husband, or of the widow to her late husband's *uaris* and, irrespective of her relationship to the begetter of the child, the child must always be regarded as belonging to the husband or to the late husband's *uaris* if it is conceived or born before its mother is formally separated from the man/men who have authority over her. This principle is, however, particularly applicable in respect of married women. To give an example, a man goes off to military service leaving his wife with a couple of fields in the place where he was born. Now and then he sends her an insignificant sum of money and returns for the first time some six years later on short leave. He arrives to find that his wife has a small child born as a result of an intimate relationship with another man. The husband lays a complaint to a court of law and they are divorced. The court forbids the woman to marry the child's begetter and awards the child to the legal husband. I never came across such a rigorous application of the principle in respect of a widow. But, as regards married women who have not formally been divorced, I did also encounter a milder practice and found people who advocated it. It was said that the maxim only applies to people who have been united in a regular marriage and in such a case only the husband can assert his right to the child of which he is probably not the begetter. As far as a widow is concerned, it is argued that she must have lived regularly within the circle of her late husband's *uaris* for the latter to lay claim to the child. If neither the one nor the other has been the case, if the woman has had ample opportunity to have a constant, uncontrolled intimate relationship with another man, the maxim would lose much of its force. Then, after the divorce, she could be married to the man in question and the child could be awarded to her and her new husband.

I regard this approach to the question as an expression of modern concepts which are not supported by the traditional law. It seems desirable that the establishment of a rule applicable to present day conditions should be the aim to strive for. Now there is an absence of stability in the law and the great variation in decisions compromises the administration of justice. In some judgements I noted that a child was awarded to a woman and its begetter although the latter had been punished as a *pangalangkup*.

If a widow has a child of which the begetter is unknown, or if the man indicated as such by the woman denies it, then the child is regarded as being the deceased husband's. If the child is a boy, then the *uaris* have no authority to send the woman away. In the case of a married woman, the legal parentage of the child is never doubted in such a situation: it is the husband's. The procreator can make himself known as such by providing the wood for the fire which is burnt when she is in childbed.

A child born to a woman who has never married (in Silindung called an *anak gampang*) does not have its procreator as its legal father. If such a woman is not a *sibabi djalang* = roving pig, i.e., a woman who lies with any man, her pregnancy will, as a rule, lead to marriage, if necessary a bigamous one. A child born as a result of an unlawful alliance between a woman who has been married and another man, *marbagas roha-roha*, which sometimes does happen, would not be regarded as the child of its begetter, so long as no legal marriage has taken place. If, however, in such a case, no other man comes forward as being the child's father, it is regarded in practice as being the begetter's child. It can never be regarded as belonging to the *parboru*. The best attitude would be that for a man and a woman to live together in a 'wild marriage' is punishable in itself. At the same time the further relationships and the consequences could be determined.

I remarked earlier that the carelessness and the lack of formalities sometimes associated with a levirate marriage can easily lead to a dispute over the status of the child.

CHAPTER VI

INHERITANCE LAW

(Adat taringot tu tading-tadingan)

MAIN PARTS

The Batak term used here for the law of inheritance means literally "the law relating to property left by a deceased". If one seeks one term which will define this law as a whole, then one is confronted with the fact that this part of customary law has many aspects, and that it consists of several separate sub-divisions, each of which has its appropriate term. These terms are sometimes mixed up with each other in the popular language, but native law makes the distinction between each one quite clear.

The three main parts of the law of inheritance that must be distinguished are: succession in direct descent in the male line; the accrual to the collateral male line; the allocation to the daughters.

Succession in the direct male line, which is effected through the birth of sons, is the natural complement of the male descendants' continuance of the lineage of the father. According to pagan ideas, the earthly life of deceased forefathers is continued by their sons. Their descendants honour and care for them while they are in the realm of the *sumangot,* and the ups and downs, the waxing and the waning, the prosperity and the poverty of the living descendants are reflected in the honour and respect which the spirits enjoy. The material goods acquired by the forefathers will be preserved by the sons, if possible, augmented. The renown of a wealthy and mighty ancestor is their renown, and they expect that the blessings which he so patently enjoyed will descend to them. The members of the lineage remain together for their mutual glory and strength. But, charity begins at home, and a man's foremost desire is that his own direct male line remains in possession of the property which he will leave when he dies. Inheritance in the direct male line is, therefore, called *mangihut-ihuthon* = to succeed to, to continue on: the sons must succeed to what their father leaves, *na tinadinghon ni amana, siihuthonon ni anakna.* In Silindung, people also speak of the *ganti* (*gansi*) = substitute, thereby denoting the son who is his father's heir. This word also indicates uninterrupted continuity in the line of descendants.

The estate accrues to the collateral when the deceased has no male issue. The direct lineage of such a man, *na mate punu*, becomes extinct. His *sumangot* is not honoured in the hereafter by surviving descendants: it wanders alone and forgotten and finally disappears. His goods accrue to his nearest lineage members, the *uaris* and the *sisolhot*, a form of acquiring property termed *manean*, the person so obtaining it being called *panean*. The concise term for inheriting by the collateral is *na punu siteanon* = the property of the deceased leaving no male issue must go to the collateral. Then there is the allocation to the daughters. Unlike the sons, daughters have no definite right to inherit the property of their father, but if they respectfully request that some part of it be allocated to them, then the male heirs, sons or collateral, must accede to their request. Their father can also set aside a part of his property for them during his lifetime over and above the dowry they have already received. Either such property is given to them at the time, or they can receive it later on as *pauseang* when they marry. The portion assigned to the daughters after the father's death is called, among other things, the *parmano-manoan* = that which they receive in remembrance of the deceased.

The peculiarities of these three main forms of inheriting will be discussed later. First, we will discuss the composition of the inheritance.

THE INHERITANCE

The inheritance, the *tading-tadingan*, or *tean-teanan*, consists of the land belonging to the deceased and his other property, *sinamot*, i.e., his house, the *sopo* = rice barn, his cattle, trees, moveable goods, his *utang singir* = debts payable by him and debts due to him, and his money. It is sometimes also necessary to reckon as part of the inheritance the marriage payment which can be expected for a still unmarried daughter, for if the debts exceed the assets, then an agreement can be reached by effecting a (quasi-)betrothal contract whereby the amount which a creditor claims will be considered as the *bohi ni sinamot*, precursor of the marriage payment. The girl is then bound to the creditor's son, and, as far as the creditor is concerned, his claim has been met.

Land left by the deceased can either be unpledged, *na so morutang*, or pledged, *morutang* (also termed *tu gadis*). In both cases it is reckoned as part of the estate. If a man inherits a pledged wet rice-field, then it is his responsibility to redeem it. It is still part of the deceased's property and is inherited by his heirs: *haumanami do i* = it is our field, they say: or *hami do nampunasa* = we are its owners, it is ours.

Partnership of the deceased in undivided land (dry, usually not regularly cultivated land) *tano hatopan, tano ripe-ripe* = land belonging to a smaller (or larger) family, is passed to the heirs, but this partnership expires if a man dies without male issue. In that case it augments the portion of the nearest kinsmen who then become the legal heirs.

If the deceased had taken a wet rice-field as a pledge, then this also belongs to the estate, though it is not land that passes from father to son but *sindor ni hepeng* = security against a sum of money. What the pledgee has acquired is a plot of land that is a substitute for a sum of money and which can be replaced with a sum of money. This land he can use so long as it has not been redeemed by payment of the money, and he can repledge it against a sum of money.

The standing harvest on land worked on a sharecropping basis, *bola pinang*, belongs to the estate of the deceased, though the land itself does not belong to him. Similarly, rented land, *niongkos*, (which is rare), or land on loan, *niindjam*, as well as land on temporary exchange, *nilibehon*, does not constitute part of the estate as land; there is only a right of use.

Land used by a member of the in-dwelling *marga* of a village under the *parripean*-law, which only gives the right of usufruct for the duration of his sojourn in the village, whether he cleared it himself or whether he received it from the village chief, does not by right belong to the estate. It can, however, according to proper usage, be left to a son if he continues to live in the village.

Land which is security, *tahan*, for a money debt incurred by the deceased, passes to the recipient on this footing, so that the creditor retains his right of security.

The house and the *sopo* are always parts of the estate and are distinct from the land on which they stand. The deceased can have owned his house outright, *himpal*, or have had it in joint ownership with others, *ripe-ripean*. In the latter case the part owned by the deceased, the *pardjambaran* (*bagian, toktok,* etc.), belongs to the estate. The Batak regards such a part as an individual item that belongs to him personally. The same applies to cattle, trees and moveable goods.

I have already remarked that a widow is not inherited with the estate and that she does not belong to it.

Debts owed to the deceased, *singir*, are part of the assets, and, like fields given as pledges, are enumerated by the dying man on his death-bed when he informs his children what he is leaving them. The person who acquires the *singir* can recover the debt(s), *martunggu*. If possible he does so before the estate is divided up. The *singir* pass to the recipient on the same terms as existed under the deceased, for example, the arrangements regarding land accepted as security, *tahan*, for it, or regarding a daughter of his debtor who had become a *boru sihunti utang*, etc., remain as they were.

Rights which can only be realised in the future and then only under specific circumstances, such as the right of *mangeahi* and *mangambati* in respect of a *pauseang*-field given to the *boru*, also pass to the male next of kin of the deceased, but they are not reckoned as assets of the estate.

The right which the deceased shared with others in the *pusako* (or *pusaha*) = goods of the larger (or smaller) lineage to which he belonged, is treated in the same way as his partnership in *tano hatopan*. His own personal things to which he was particularly attached, the *ugasan na tanda* = the things which played an important part in his life, may be held in honour by his children as *pusako*, as objects with which the welfare of the lineage is bound up. Gifts that the mistress of the house has received and which were beneficial and have brought prosperity to the 'house', and the *homitan ni tondi* may be similarly treated. These *pusako*-objects are inalienable.

The accrual from affairs started by, *na pinungka ni*, the father or the grandfather, i.e. what they acquired and amassed by their own hard work, have a special place in the estate. It is distinct from anything gained by other means. For example, the field the deceased received as pledge for part of the marriage payment for his daughter, the *hauma sindor*, which can be redeemed, cannot be reckoned as something he himself started, *dipungka*. The same applies to the rice-field which the *hula-hula* presented as an *ulos* to his wife when she was sick; to the *sopo* or the cow he inherited when one of his brothers or uncles died without male issue; and to the benzoin gardens opened up by his *parripe* who left them with him when he moved elsewhere; and to the rice-field which he, as the *uaris* of someone who has moved out of the village, redeemed from someone to whom the absentee had pledged it before he left the village. These goods are, in a sense, impersonal as far as the heirs of the estate are concerned. They have no personal value to them. The property in which they all desire to share is the house, the *sopo* which their father built himself, the fields he cleared with his own hands, the progeny of the cow he bought, the coffee garden he laid

18

out or bought with money earned in trading, the hoarded and interest-bearing money, and so on. These are the particular things they wish to inherit so that the blessing, *tua*, which their father had so obviously enjoyed and which after his death may possibly continue to be associated with them, will be passed to them.

THE EXPENSES ON THE ESTATE

The first expense on an estate is the cost of the funeral. This is accounted for by a pall, *saput*, the coffin, *batang*, and the *boan ni na mate* (in Toba called the *ola*), consisting of a chicken, pig or buffalo that is slaughtered and eaten by the next of kin. In pagan regions these animals are regarded as offerings and as provisions for the deceased on his journey to the world of the spirits, and as his introductory gifts to them. It is not always necessary, however, for these costs to be drawn on the estate. If, for example, a daughter is allocated a *parmano-manoan*, she usually takes care of the *boan*. If another man was responsible for the death of the deceased, then he has to bear the cost of the *saput*, the *batang* and the *boan*. If the death was the result of the deceased's being kicked by a horse, then the animal must be surrendered as the *boan*. In Toba, when a man dies without male issue, a great death feast will, as a rule, be held at which the *sigale-gale* puppet, which represents the dead man (see photos III a and b), is made to dance with the object of ameliorating somewhat his miserable life in the hereafter. A small model house, *djoro*, is erected on his grave and the objects which he used daily and those on which he placed special importance are buried with him. Quite often it is seen as an honour to spend the greater part of the deceased's assets in this way.

Debts, *utang*, are an expense on the estate, even if after paying them there is deficit. This has particular relevance to the sons as direct heirs, a relevance expressed by the following *umpama*:

> *singir ni ama, ba, singir ni anak,*
> *djala utang ni ama, utang ni anak;*
> Debts owed to the father are naturally owed to the son;
> Debts incurred by the father are debts the son must honour.

It is not, however, only the deceased's sons who are responsible; the brother, or the brother's son of a man who has died without male issue must reckon it as a family obligation to pay the debts of brother or uncle, if at all possible. In certain circumstances, for example, if the deceased's line is a meagre one, a cousin stemming from a common

PAPURPUR SAPATA

to remove a curse: this is done some months after the death of a childless
man, in order to rid the land of the curse which had been upon him.

The women, wearing on their heads the *tudjung* = cloth of mourning, are
dancing and wailing on the village compound. The *sigale-gale,* a dressed puppet
(wearing a white neckcloth) representing the deceased, is also made to perform
a dancing movement. The woman waving her arms about is lamenting the
fate of the deceased and recounting his qualities, *maronda-onda.*

Plate IIIb

PAPURPUR SAPATA

The *sigale-gale* embraces one of the female relatives of the
deceased and bemoans his fate.

great-grandfather will take the debts on himself. This is not generally applicable to more distant kinsmen. They can wholly disclaim any responsibility for the dead man's debts. As far as they are concerned the debts must be met out of the existing assets, despite the well-known maxim:

niarit tarugi pora-pora,
molo tinean uli, teanon dohot gora.

If one cuts a *tarugi* rib it always stays dry.

Whosoever inherits the good things must also inherit the drawbacks. This aphorism is also pertinent outside the direct sphere of the law of inheritance, though it contains an unmistakeable principle of that law and appears to be even more far-reaching than the maxim quoted just previously. It is not the purpose of this maxim, however, that an obligation to meet all the debts without regard to the assets shall be laid upon the collateral, no matter what their distance is from the deceased. The fact must be taken into account that a debt of any size usually has its own cover in a gold or other pledge, in an encumbered daughter, in land placed as security, etc., though this does not mean that a creditor can only procure payment by way of that cover. As a consequence, not many of a man's sizeable debts are without cover when he dies and there is thus not often a great deficit. Should there be one, however, it can frequently be attributed to speculative loans of a kind arranged for by a candidate at an election; to gambling debts, which are a danger in themselves in that a debtor may default; or to the harsh terms of a rice loan when the harvest was bad. In Toba these latter loans formerly led to peonage and slavery, and even at the present time lead to the complete penury of the borrower, since the last of his possessions must be given in payment. Thus, if the aforementioned maxim is interpreted and applied in a more restricted sense, it does not cover a very extensive field. A fact that should be especially borne in mind, is that payment of large, old and heavy debts is hardly ever demanded to the last farthing, and partial payment, for example, a valuable plot of land, a garden, a house and similar things, is deemed sufficient if no definite unwillingness to pay up is presumed. This becomes particularly clear in the event of the demise of a debtor.

The maxim does have a direct bearing on the obligations that the deceased incurred on the special parts of the inheritance allocated to his heirs and which they must take on their shoulders. For example, if a wet rice-field which had been pledged by the deceased is allocated to one of his heirs, then its redemption is his responsibility. If distant uncles give

a daughter of the deceased in marriage and it then comes out that there
is a quasi-betrothal contract with another man, then they must meet
the obligation that had been incurred. If a *sisolhot* of a man who died
without male issue marries his widow in levirate, he takes upon himself
the obligations which are attached to the inheritance to which he
succeeds. A similar responsibility must be accepted by an *uaris* who
marries off a widow. If a lawsuit was in progress when a man died, then
his heirs who have acquired the estate, must continue the suit, and
they also have to be answerable for any claims that may be brought
later on. To quote a relevant saying: *sidjalo singir, sigarar utang =*
whosoever acquires the right to make claims also gets the debts. Then,
of course, it depends on mutual agreement as to whether all the heirs
will join together to meet the obligation before the estate is divided up,
or whether they will allocate that part of the estate carrying an obligation to one of them. Debts which do not lead to creating deficit in
the estate are those that are all, or as good as all, contracted within the
circle of related kinsmen, co-inhabitants of the village, the affines, friends
in the neighbourhood, village chiefs and the chiefs of the surrounding
villages. More than likely some of these people had a hand in the matter
which created the debt and are thus partly responsible for it. They
know each other's financial position, have been able to restrain thought-
less moves and feel obliged to come to the man's aid in case of need.
They are the circle within which the debtor is wholly at home, where
he is known and people are aware of his obligations.

Special mention must be made of trading debts which, with the
advent of shopping and trading centres, have in recent years been
incurred by traders in the market place. A trader or shopkeeper who sets
up in a market place and deals with people with whom he has no
connection, or who enters into speculative transactions in imports and
exports, or who runs his own big business, is in a position where the
members of his kinship-circle to which he belongs cannot keep track of
him, exercise any control over him, or advise him. Such a man may
accept advances and receive credit from non-Batak firms to an extent
outside his financial competence. Transactions of this kind are a new
experience for him. There are dangers and temptations and mere confidence must provide a great part of the security for the creditor. This
does not necessarily mean that such a man has separated himself completely from his known circle of kinsmen and affines, for in the event
of his defaulting or of his death, the responsibility may fall on them,
and naturally these small farmers in the village of his origin feel more

and more oppressed by the great risks which their kinsman or affine is taking. It is not possible at present to determine where the development of the law will lead in this respect: this point will be discussed in Chapter VIII. Naturally, it depends upon the extent to which a man's circle is held responsible for his debts.

A man can make known his debts to his relatives when he is dying, when he is telling his children the detailed facts regarding his property, and it is then that a creditor will recall, if possible, outstanding debts due to him, in the presence of one or more of the dying man's relatives and will then expect an implicit or definite agreement. It is advisable· that a creditor makes known any other contracts that exist between him and the dying man which may later lead to disputes, such as, for example, a rice-field that he cultivated and which is held in pledge or the part-ownership of an animal he looks after. This is not strictly necessary as proof of the existence of such a contract, anymore than it is necessary for the dying man to tell his children all the details of his property obligations and other legal aspects relating to it. It is obvious that only those persons who live in close proximity to the dying man and who are therefore fully aware of the seriousness of his illness, are in a position to draw attention to their claims on his deathbed.

Creditors have another opportunity to state their claims just before the dead man is buried. The eldest son of the deceased will proclaim in a loud voice to those assembled at the funeral that he accepts all responsibility for his father's debts which will then be made known or of which he will be informed later. If the dead man was a *na mate punu,* then his brother makes the announcement and assumes the responsibility. This is called in Silindung tapping the bier of the dead, *maniktik batang ni na mate.* If a creditor is present and fails to make his claim known, this is likely to be regarded as strong proof against its validity, though he will often defend his omission by saying that he did not want to shame the relatives. And even where no public declaration of responsibility is made at a funeral, any claims should, nevertheless, still be made then. A creditor does not have to make known a claim in this way if he can produce a written document that has been properly witnessed.

If the debts are few, they will be paid immediately out of the estate and the only question will be whether they are to be accepted in whole or in part or on the terms decided by the creditor. It is not always possible to have to hand ready money or other liquid assets with which to pay all debts immediately, and if prompt payment is demanded, then land can be given as a pledge, *sindor.*

If the debts are so large that there is either a certainty or a likelihood that the total assets will be insufficient to meet them, then an endeavour will be made to reach an agreement. The son or brother who makes himself responsible for the debts will summon the creditors to a meeting, for which he will slaughter a piglet and to which the village chief, his close kinsmen and close affines will be invited. After the meal he will put the position clearly to the creditors and, if necessary, he will make his urgent request, *mangelek-elek*, to them and perhaps will even make a respectful plea, *somba-somba*, to them to be lenient and compassionate, *asi ni roha*. His village chief will add his support to the appeal as will his kinsmen and affines. The matter will be talked over, proposals will be made and reprobated and after one or two more meetings, agreement may be reached. Everything depends on the circumstances whether all the creditors will have their claims met to the same extent. Good friends or relatives of the deceased will be more lenient than others. Loans on which the interest has been paid regularly, or which are for the greater part paid off, will be remitted more willingly than debts on which the creditor has always had difficulty in collecting his payments. One cannot say that, in general, creditors are inclined to allow the heirs to keep a considerable part of an encumbered estate or that they will demand nearly all that is due to them. Much depends on the demonstration of willingness to pay, on the inclination of kinsmen and affines to contribute to the settlement, on the circumstances of the close relations of the deceased, for example, whether there is sickness, many small children, and so on. Naturally, in these discussions neither side is allowed to try to trick the other, *marsimaloi*, by adroit, *malo*, talk as is done in debt cases among the living. A discussion on the debts of a deceased person is governed by adat, *dibagasan adat*, and the intention to reach agreement is a sincere one.

Debts must be very large when the only way they can be met is to alienate land permanently, *sipate-pate*, in order to effect complete settlement, *parsaean ni utang*. Usually such debts are met by transferring cattle, a *sopo*, a gold ornament, etc., to which is sometimes coupled the pledging of one or more rice-fields, *manindorhon*. I have already observed that the future marriage payment for small daughters of the deceased, of his son, or possibly of another helpful relation, is negotiable in these circumstances. If necessary, creditors have the right to compel the heirs to agree to such an arrangement. However, in such a case, no interest is reckoned, no matter how young the girl is. If the object is also to enter an affinal relationship, then the natural consequence is a decrease in the claim which is effected by fixing the *bohi ni sinamot*, at a lower amount than that owing.

The threat of failure is always in the background of these consultations with the consequent claim that the debt be paid in full. The judge will then take the matter in hand. Formerly, he not only had control over the assets, but he also had the possibility in his hands of using peonage in one form or another as the final remedy: beyond that a creditor could claim nothing more. At the present day a firm order to pay in instalments over a long period would be the expected judgement, though I never heard of one. In a few cases known to me, all the deceased's possessions were distrained on and sold and the creditors accepted such money as was received from the sale and let it go at that.

My information as to whether all the possessions of the deceased can be distrained upon for the settlement of debts, varies. In the case of an old father or a widow with young children it was said that the judge can decide that a part of the property should be allowed them for their subsistence. I once heard that a quarter of the estate should not be touched, but I also heard it said that only household utensils and farm implements and the rice, and sometimes the house, could be left to the heirs. These varying data originated from one and the same region and I attribute the variation, as also the hesitation in much of the infor-mation, mainly to the fact that more often than not the assets exceeded the liabilities and agreement could easily be reached, and as a conse-quence there was hardly any need for fixed rules. The few cases that occurred could be left to the discretion of the judges. I never saw a judgement of this kind.

With regard to payment of gambling debts that were formerly incurred at the organised gambling parties to which people from all points of the compass gathered, legal usage acknowledged the most rigorous appli-cation of all existing legal remedies, such as attachment, being put in the block, peonage, etc., but land could not be forfeited without the consent of the debtor's wife.

In respect of debts for which the deceased had assigned a rice-field as *tahan* = security, for which he had 'encumbered' a daughter, or for which he had given some other kind of cover, there is in my view no doubt that the heirs had to accept these commitments. Fields which the deceased had pledged to a third party remain pledged to him, but I did come across an agreement according to which a creditor was declared qualified to take over such a pledged field which could then be redeemed from him by the heirs by settling the amount of his claim, plus the sum that he had paid to the original pledgee. As is often the case in such circumstances, the possibilities for unexpected and complicated agreements are considerable.

THE HEIRS

The principal rule of the law of inheritance is that sons inherit the estate of their father. If there are sons, they are the sole heirs. It is possible for some part of the property to be allocated to the affines, but they are not the deceased's heirs and they are not responsible for his debts, though they can make a contribution to the settlement. A widow with or without sons, cannot inherit. It is illegal for a mother and a son to divide the assets between them with the object of splitting up the estate in order to avoid the risk of distraint for debts incurred by the son. There was once such an instance in Silindung but the judge declared the arrangement invalid.

Sons by different mothers of a bigamous marriage form separate groups, as do sons of different fathers and of one mother who has married in levirate. Sons of one father and two mothers, the second of which the father married after the demise of the first, belong to one category except in respect of the property that each of the wives brought to their marriage as *pauseang*.

The eldest son, the *sihahaan*, who replaces the father on his death, and the *siampudan*, or *sianggian*, the youngest son, who looks after his parents in their old age, occupy a special position in inheritance law in relation to the middle sons, the *silitonga*. This will become clear when their portions are discussed later.

If a son who was already independent dies and leaves no sons, then his father becomes his heir. This is called *munsat tu* or *mulak tu* = reverting to the father.

An adopted son inherits from the father who adopted him: repudiated sons are excluded from inheriting.

Sons born to a woman who is not legally married to their procreator do not inherit from him.

If there are neither descendants nor a father nor a grandfather, then the inheritance accrues to the collateral, the *panean*. Principal among these are the brothers by the same father as the deceased and, should there be none, then the uncles and cousins of the same grandfather, and so on, the appropriate claimants going a step further back in the genealogy each time on the same principle.

If the deceased left neither a widow nor daughters, then the *panean* can forthwith take the whole estate. But if there are either, then the *panean* must allow at least a part of the estate to the bereaved family and either then or later must allocate portions for the daughters.

In principle there is no limit to the accrual to the collateral. If a man who has no close relations dies in the area where his lineage, *marga* or *marga* branch is settled, there are always people to be found who are related to him, since their connection with the branch to which the deceased belonged and of which he was the last representative is fully known. If such a man dies in a strange place outside the area of his lineage, then it may be that his fellow villagers do not known where to look for his closest *uaris*. If he had received land as a member of the in-dwelling *marga*, then it accrues to his village chief under the *parripean*-law. Land that he had bought or had obtained otherwise and which was definitely his own, as well as the rest of the estate, can be left to his daughters or, if there are none, can be allocated to a fellow *marga* member who is willing to attend to the funeral arrangements and to pay his debts. If there is no one who is disposed to take on these obligations, then his estate goes to his village chief. This is one of those rarely occurring instances, where the man is usually poor and the settlement then depends mainly on the incidental circumstances.

If there is a known *uaris* but he is absent and his place of residence unknown, then the deceased's village chief administers the estate until the absent *uaris* returns. In Toba and Samosir the village and territory chiefs claim an *upa radja* when an inheritance accrues to the collateral. I did not gather any details about this.

ALLOCATING THE PORTIONS OF THE INHERITANCE

There is no question of dividing the estate as is known in European law. In a general sense each of the heirs is equivalent in status and they are treated in a similar way, but there are one or two definite prerogatives and, in addition, there are a variety of different factors affecting the distribution of the estate. The inheritance is not regarded as an entity that can be split up precisely into a number of parts and, in fact, this would hardly be possible since the parts are never valued in terms of money, neither are they converted into money. For example, the dwellinghouse of the testator, with the *sopo* = rice-barn, and (sometimes) a smaller dwelling than the main one, are always separate parts of the estate and special rules are applicable to them. Whatever a father has obtained by his own efforts, *dipungka*, can never go to only one of the sons, even if he were willing to take on himself the settlement of all his father's debts. It must either be divided among all the sons or remain undivided. There are regions where the rice-fields which have been in the family for generations and generations cannot be allocated to the *boru,* but must be inherited by the direct line and then, if possible, go from eldest son to eldest son. If the number of plots of land originate from different sources and are as large in number as the number of the sons, then it is not necessary that all the plots are so divided up that their distribution will be equal as to size and quality. Approximate equality is aimed at but it is not necessary to balance exactly size and fertility. It is not even necessary to stipulate that all the sons will have a share in the redemption money received later when fields taken in pledge are redeemed, nor is it necessary that a rice-field which has been given in pledge has to be redeemed before the estate is divided. The solutions which will satisfy everybody will be found in mutual consultation between the brothers, supported by the chiefs and the mediatory help of the affines.

Frequently a father will have already simplified matters for his children by dividing his property among them during his lifetime, except for a small part which he sets aside for his own sustenance. The first opportunity the father will have for doing this will be when the youngest son has been married off and the marriage payment has been paid. Daughters can also be favoured by a settlement their father makes during his lifetime. It is rare for a man without male issue to divide his property among the collateral.

Whatever the father in such a case retained for himself during his lifetime, then goes to the one who looked after him while he was still alive, *patuahon ama,* who is, as a rule, the youngest son, the heir to the pepper-grinding stone, *sitean panutuan,* and in such circumstances he regards it as his *pandjaean.* A father has to allocate the *pandjaean* to his sons when they marry and the *pauseang* to his daughters. He must therefore always look ahead and consider the interests of all his children, and also bear in mind that when the last of them has been married he has enough for his own subsistence. If his prosperity has increased over the years because of his diligent application then, in the course of time, he will probably have presented a rice-field as *indahan arian* to one of the children of one of his own children, or will have given land as *niupahon* at the *mangupa* ceremony held for one of his childless daughters, or he may have given a field as an *ulos-ulos* to one of his daughters who had requested one of him. He keeps a general account of all these items when the time comes for his final division, but he does not regard what each has received as a precise portion to be placed to their debit, and if he does not wish to do so he need not endeavour to equalise the portions which each child will ultimately receive. If one of his children has not fared well, if one has had many children, then he may allocate more to them than to the others. If a son has remarried two or three times, then his father may decide to give him correspondingly less because of the marriage payments that will have been made. A father can stipulate payment of certain debts as a prerequisite to receiving a certain part of his property, and so on.

If the estate has not been divided up before the father dies, then the children will often ask him on his deathbed, amidst the respectful serving of food, to make known his instructions in respect of the property, so that no dispute will arise among them later. Such instructions given by a father on his deathbed, either to his children alone or, for preference, in the presence of the village chief and a couple of the inhabitants of the village, his affines or friends, are called *tona ni na mate ndang boi muba* = the immutable instructions of the deceased. They act as a brake on the eldest son who replaces his deceased father in the management of the estate. To give an example: if a father has indicated that a particular field should be given as a *pauseang* to an unmarried daughter on her marriage, then the eldest son, her brother, must observe the command. A man will often recount on his deathbed the legal history of the principal parts of his estate; will enumerate monies outstanding; will tell anew the facts about pledged fields; and will sometimes acquaint his children with the details of a dispute pending between third parties; or he may tell them that at one time he wrongly supported someone in a lawsuit against a common enemy. These and similar communications also constitute the *tona* to which his heirs attach great importance.

Allocations made on a deathbed are final, as are all gifts, and the testator cannot revoke them should he survive his illness.

If a man has not divided up his estate during his lifetime, then it is not necessary that his children do so immediately he dies. It is never done if the sons are still young, and even if some of them are already married it is not done, for such married sons will each have received his *pandjaean* and the remainder of the estate must serve primarily to defray the cost of the marriage payments that will have to be made for the still unmarried sons and to set them up with their *pandjaean* or, if there are promising school-going children among them, to complete their education. Naturally, exceptions can always be made if there is a special reason for them, for example, if one of the sons cannot work or if a son has died leaving behind small children. If all the sons are married then, as a rule, most of the estate will be split between them. Usually an estate does not long remain undivided, though some goods may be left in joint-ownership for a longer or shorter period. *Pusako* objects cannot be portioned out.

When the final division of the estate is made, no precise account is kept of what any child has received as *pandjaean, indahan arian,* or as other gifts. Here, too, the law of inheritance retains its elastic character. The only thing that is taken into consideration is what the sons have received in a general sense, which is how the father would have approached the subject had he made the allocations, and some endeavour is made to see that the apportionment to each is approximate.

A particular exception is the dividing up of a house and *sopo.* The general rule is that the youngest son gets the main dwelling, a fact that bears on his duty to care for his parents in their old age. The eldest son gets the *sopo* or, if there are more sons who must live in the house and the *sopo,* then the youngest gets the main room of the main dwelling, *djabu bona,* and the eldest that of the *sopo.* These are the special privileges of the eldest and youngest sons. The eldest son also has a claim to extra privileges, *hasurungan.* These he may already have received in one form or another, but if he has not, then he can still lay claim to them. It is possible that he received from his grandfather the *uma panggoaran* because, as the eldest son, he had given him the so greatly desired title of Ompu ni N. or the *pangoli* which his grandfather may have paid when he married: this is something he would not do for any of his other grandsons. As the eldest son he may have received at a *turun*-feast the *dondon tua,* a gift intended to transfer to him, as the bearer of the *sahala sihahaanon,* the *sahala* and the *tua* of his forebears. If there was no opportunity for any of these expressions of the eldest son's privileges to be made during the father's lifetime, then he can reserve something for himself, either by keeping a special part, or by taking a larger part than the other sons, at the division of the estate. Here and there it is the custom — I heard of it on Samosir among other places — that if the deceased had several fields lying along an irrigation canal or a rivulet, the eldest son gets the one lying upstream. There are probably more examples of typical local usages.

If the property goes to the collateral, then nobody has any privileges over anyone else. Everything can be divided equally. Property deriving from a predeceased common grandfather or great-grandfather may be subject to a different mode of division than the rest, or it can remain undivided.

When the estate or part of it is not divided up it comes under joint-ownership, *ripe-ripean, hadosan, hatopan,* because of death and by mutual agreement of the heirs. Such a part of the estate often consists of dry land which, remaining undivided, may eventually become property owned by a large lineage, *ugasan ripe-ripe.* The origins of such property may have been various. The land may have been the cultivated fields surrounding the village founded by the ancestor and may have later been abandoned; or it may have formerly been irrigated from an old neglected conduit; it may have been used as a sweet potato garden, *pargadongan,* and then left unworked; or it may have been used for outer defence in a protracted war; it may have been captured from a former enemy; or it may have been left unworked after a flood, etc. There are also other things besides land that can remain the undivided possession of a larger kinship group: a house, a wet rice-field, a grove of fruit trees or trees for timber. The house can be inhabited by the family most in need of it, the rice-field cultivated from year to year on a fixed rotation arrangement or according to who is the first comer, the trees can be utilised as necessary. Since this property is owned by a group, anyone using it must not do so in a way that shows that he is greedy to possess what is in fact communal property, *tung na so boi impul iba di ugasan ni dongan marripe-ripe.* It must always be used with due observance of the general rule of *ripe-ripean*:

  ugasan ripe-ripe ndang tarbahen panghimpalan,
  ugasan panghimpalan ndang tarbahen ripe-ripe.

  What one holds in joint ownership one may not take as one's own.
  What is another man's property must not be made the joint
  property of a group.

This is a rule which a judge is frequently called upon to apply, since it is not always fixed precisely what is communally owned and what is privately owned. The rule also holds good for *pusako* objects which naturally are always *ripe-ripean.*

THE RIGHTS OF DAUGHTERS

In the previous chapters some ways have been given by which daughters can enjoy the property of their father. There is the gift which a father can give his daughters while they are still young; there is the dowry and its precursor given at a daughter's betrothal when she is still a child; there are the presents given to her during her married life, or to her children. All of these gifts show that the father, or on his death his eldest son, is always ready to observe towards his daughters or sisters respectively and their children, the *adat ni boru* = the obligations to be observed by the *hula-hula* towards its *boru*. Among other things, this means seeing that part of the family estate is allocated to them and assisting them when they are in trouble or need.

If one can speak of a daughter having any rights in respect of property left by her deceased father, it is in the sense that she can make a last appeal to her brother to be given a contribution from the property that has thus far supported the family which is then breaking up. If there are no brothers, then the appeal must be made to the uncles or further kinsmen to persuade them to surrender to the daughter of the deceased as much of the property that has accrued to them as will be adequate for her. The death of their father changes nothing for his daughters in so far that, had he effected the division of his goods to his children during his lifetime, the daughters would then have been allocated a portion, and they can therefore request the nearest brother(s) or uncle(s) to give them a corresponding part.

They must, however, request that a portion be given them, as they must also ask their father on his deathbed for it, to the accompaniment of a respectful *manulangi*. It is thus fitting that they treat their *hula-hula*, from which their help must come, with similar respect. They offer their *hula-hula* a meal and after it they submit their request, in the appropriate form, that they should receive something from the estate. If their request is directed to their brothers in the prescribed *adat* forms, *dibagasan adat*, the latter can hardly refuse to grant it. Usually, however, they make a counterclaim that the *boru* must attend to the *boan*. Whatever a daughter receives in this way is usually termed a *parmano-manoan* = keepsake, as is whatever her dying father allocates to her. If it consists of land, it is also called the *daon sihol* = the means of alleviating distress, *parsiholan, pardaon siholan*.

A daughter cannot make such a request if there are still unmarried sons who have not received a *pandjaean*, or young unmarried daughters who have to have a dowry, or if there is a mother who must draw her subsistence from the estate.

The size of the portion surrendered to a daughter depends entirely on the existing circumstances. The eldest son, who decides, must take into account the rights and interests of all his brothers and the allocations to be made to all his sisters. It is not consistant with the *hula-hula* —

boru-relationship that brothers withhold a part of the estate from their sisters, and they hardly ever do so. There is, however, often wrangling over an alleged promise and its non-fulfilment and occasionally a complaint wil be laid before a judge of their stinginess. He is not, however, as a rule, much troubled by such a dispute between the *hula-hula* and the *boru*. The apportioning of a reasonable part to the *boru* is usually accepted as a just solution by the parties concerned who could not agree and who only needed the opinion of a neutral third party. When the daughters make a stand against their father's brother or against their other and distant kinsmen, the matter is not quite so simple. In many cases anger and resentment are not aroused, nor is there a quarrel, for the desire that the administration of the estate should proceed peacefully will induce the *uaris* voluntarily to arrange a meeting with the sisters or other *boru* affines of the deceased, or to submit the request for a proper apportionment to the judge, or a meeting of the elders. The aim of the *uaris* is not that they will thereby benefit themselves but that they will also have determined the portion the daughters ought to receive.

If the mother is still alive and the daughters are unmarried then, as we have already seen, the mother is often allowed to manage the greater part of the property and the *uaris* will earmark this part for the girls' *pauseang* when they marry and will only want a small portion for themselves as an acknowledgement of their rights as the *uaris*. But, nevertheless, many are the bitter complaints of girls, and women who have only daughters, that immediately after the father's or husband's death, the *uaris* insist on their rights of custodianship and management and distrain on everything, show no willingness to allow them more than barely sufficient for their subsistence, and are also unwilling to grant anything to the married daughters over and above what they have already received as *pauseang*. The judge must then intervene and, guided by the affines, must determine independently what in fairness the daughters should receive. In this he has no fixed standard to go by. He can count the father's brothers as the daughters' brothers and then can divide everything in about equal parts among them all; he can take the distant kinsmen collectively as one brother of the father and arrange a division of the property accordingly. Criteria like these are followed in some cases and not in others, for here too, there is conflict between the narrow and strict law of the partrilineal system, according to which girls and property accrue to the *uaris* who can decide at their discretion what part of the girls' father's estate should go to them, or can adopt the more tolerant practice, supported by the demands of the *adat parboruon* = the custom towards the *boru*, which provides that an adequate part of the deceased's estate should go to his daughters. There is, however, no indication as to its size, and the need of more certainty on this point seems undeniable.

SUCCESSION TO OFFICE

On the death of the holder of an *adat* office, the transfer of that office is only subject to fixed rules in those cases where no special demands are made as regards attributes of character, personal capability, social influence and so forth. Thus the *radja ni boru*-ship, which is primarily the representation of a genealogical group, as opposed to the *marga radja* ruling in a territory, can remain in and be continued in the oldest branch, always passing from father to son. The *parbaringin*-ship, which is only of importance in the sphere of religious ceremonies, may likewise continue to be passed on in the oldest line, or it can be transferred in rotation between two or more lineages, or according to other fixed rules which vary from area to area. In a small village, where the inhabitants are either kinsmen or affines; where legal proceedings of any weight rarely occur; where no marriage takes place for perhaps five consecutive years; where people seldom move elsewhere; fields are pledged only once or twice in a season; lawsuits are quickly ended by mutual agreement; and where there is little incentive or opportunity for the village chief to exercise his authority over the inhabitants, the chieftainship can also continue to remain in the lineage that has arisen from the village's founder and can always be transferred from a father to one of his sons.

The chieftainship of the *radja na sumangap*, however, of which the holder is a prominent chief of a territory comprising several villages, and a great lineage or a *marga* branch, and having an important *onan* as its core, a *bius* alliance, an area over which it disposes and its own administration of justice, demanded in ancient times of the bearer strength of character, personal courage, public ascendancy in wealth and a number of other qualities which guaranteed internal and external authority. For this reason it was never certain whether the *hasangapon* acquired by a father would pass to one of his sons or whether the son could continue it. The inhabitants, who were interested in having a powerful central leadership, might well wish to reserve for themselves the choice of a successor to a deceased territory chief. This provided the opportunity for rivals for the office to strive to augment their power acquired by virtue of their increasing wealth, the expansion of their lineage, or gain accruing from a war. In view of these factors, the only law that could develop was a flexible one that gave the notables of a territory the authority to select the most suitable person as their leader from among the circle of the deceased chief, and even to disregard that circle if it had declined in power and prestige. Thus the *sahala haradjaon* did not automatically pass from a man to one of his descendants or to a near kinsman.

CHAPTER VII

THE LAW OF LAND TENURE

(*Adat partanoon*)

It is not necessary for me to deal with land law at length for to do so would merely be to recapitulate the extensive and detailed information on the subject which Ypes has given in his recent work.

In the course of the previous chapters I had occasion to touch on rules of land law when presenting certain of the data I had obtained. The following are the instances in question.

More than once I dealt with the role that land and the giving of land as a present, plays in the affinal relationship regarding the *ulos*-presents from *hula-hula* to *boru* in Chapter I, Section B. p. 69; Chapter II, p. 87, the transfer of *tondi*-power; in Chapter III, pp. 112-3, 123, temporary right of usufruct to the *boru* as the in-dwelling *marga* and even the surrender of the right of disposal over land to it; and in Chapter V, p. 202 *et sqq.*, gifts of land to a daughter before, at and during her marriage.

In Chapter III I dealt with the connection between land tenure and the autonomous community, (village, tribal group, *marga* and territory, p. 118) where I endeavoured to clarify the connection between the right of disposal over land and authority vested in genealogical groupings.

In the following Chapter the position of land transactions in respect of the law of debts will de dealt with as well as share-cropping agreements, the financial aspect of pledging land, land as security for a debt, and here and there reference will be made to the law relating to land contracts.

Ypes deals at length with these aspects and the material I present on them is only an amplification and perhaps also an elucidation.

If I have any comment to make on his work it is this: first, the normative value of many of the judgements of which the content is given, would be more accurately assessed if the milieu in and the circumstances under which the lawsuit was conducted were more

thoroughly known. Some light will be thrown on this point in my
Chapter X in the section entitled 'The judgement and its content'.
Secondly, a number of rules, sometimes given in great detail, are stated
by Ypes as comprising the applicable land laws, but, as I showed in
Chapter IV, it is a fact that the Batak has an indestructible inclination
to allow the working of his customary law to be predominantly influenced by particular relationships or circumstances and to adapt the
rules accordingly.

CHAPTER VIII

THE LAW RELATING TO DEBTS

(*Adat dibagasan pardabu-dabuanon*)

TERMINOLOGY AND NATURE

There is no simple term in the Batak language by which the law of debts is defined. One could perhaps use the compound term *utang-singir* = claims and debts, and invest it with the meaning of the "law relating to claims and debts", but this would be an oversimplification and not sufficiently embracing of the broad and extensive nature of the financial relationships into which a person can enter. The more appropriate term is *pardabu-dabuan* which, though it means current account, statement of account, in its narrowest sense, also refers to the financial obligations in general, the contracting of them and the discharging of them. The term is derived from *mordabu-dabu* = mutual reckoning up, making the final settlement. This was formerly effected with the aid of reckoning sticks, *rudji-rudji,* each of which represented a debt or a part of a debt. These sticks were collected together as the debts were tallied up and as each debt was settled a *rudji* was dropped, *mandabu.* This procedure was formerly also called *mandabu rudji-rudji* or *mordabu-dabu,* this means literally: to be engaged in the operation of 'dropping'. The derived form, *pardabu-dabuanon,* acquires the meaning of 'that which is embraced by the settling up' and in a broader sense indicates the whole sequence of the relationships resulting from entering a contract. Thus the expression *adat dibagasan pardabu-dabuanon* is intended to define the law applicable to these relationships.

This law, of which the following description is rather superficial on some points, has reached a fairly advanced stage of development, to which the delight in litigation which is in the Batak's blood has been a considerable contributory factor, as has been its natural counterpart the desire for mediation and adjudication. These attitudes have also played their part in the law of land tenure and family law. A number of rules and delimitations have been evolved which are directed to the maintenance of good moral order and the preservation of the foundations of public confidence on the one hand, and which look ahead to possible procedures which can result from a claim to honour an agreement on the other. In view of this, it is very important that everyone knows and takes into account the rules of the law of debts which have been embodied in a great number of *umpama*. It is as detrimental to a party to ignore them when entering a contract or after a contract is concluded, as it is for a third party who is involuntarily involved to do so. Negligence in this respect gives a shrewd adversary the opportunity to play a game of questions and answers, which he will continue should the case later be brought before a judge. He will then profit by the advantages which the rules of the law offer him and will place his opponent in an unfavourable position. Consequently, anyone involved in a legal action must be constantly on his guard and must choose his words carefully. Many a time a Batak judge upbraids a hard-pressed victim of his own carelessness and says to him: "*i ma dohononmu* = you should have said it in such and such a way". Mistakes are nearly always fatal to the victim's case, for does not the old saying read:

siala ilió, mago do halak ia so maló,
he who is not sagacious is lost.

This aphorism, in conjunction with the one quoted earlier on p. 140, "The clever one wins the lawsuit, the stupid one goes to the slave-stand in the market", demonstrates quite clearly that a judge respects a man who conducts a transaction in an adroit manner and who is versed in the art of litigation.

Before discussing the general principles of the law of debts and the characteristics of the various transactions, I will deal with those things over which transactions are conducted and the shift of importance that has taken place in recent years.

OBJECTS OF TRANSACTIONS AND CONTRACTS

Formerly land was less frequently than at present the object of transactions, and agreements relating to it had for the greater part a different character. There was an abundance of land and a sparse population, and as a consequence, it was possible for individuals to clear land, and fields that were not so productive or which were difficult to reach could the more easily be allowed to lie fallow for a long time. This naturally led to the development of the legal practice described in the *Patik dohot Uhum* as *mangarimba* = reclaiming and recultivation over a stipulated number of years by someone other than the man who originally cleared the land. And pledged fields were sometimes allowed to remain in the hands of the pledgee so long that both parties forgot the amount received or given at the pledging. Land was not sold permanently. If land was permanently transferred, then it was in payment of a gambling debt or of other sizeable debts, or it was a gift. One of the main forms of a gift of land was the *hula-hula*'s giving land to its *boru*. Under the *saksi ni gade* = the rules of pledging, which were impressed upon the assembled chiefs and players at a gambling party by the leader of the party, the *ulu porang,* as described in the *Naipospos Manuscript* [19], the debtor could be fettered for a gambling debt, objects could be pledged and an affine could give a personal guarantee to settle a debt, but land could not be attached for it.

When a man moved elsewhere, he preferred to leave his land in the hands of his *uaris* who lived in the village, rather than pledge it against a sum of money to help him in cultivating new land as is done at present. He would be helped in the village to which he was going by the inhabitants who would give him rice until a new field yielded its first harvest.

The change in the relationship between supply of land and size of population has taken place in the last 50 years simultaneously with the change in the function of money. Before Dutch administration extended over the Toba Country, intercourse with the outside world was mainly limited to the export of benzoin and the import of salt and tobacco. The amount of money in the country was small and it more or less stayed constant — this money consisted of Spanish dollars and small coins introduced by the (Dutch) East India Company. Among the Batak themselves, money was not the usual medium of exchange for procuring all the goods they needed. There was too little of it for that. In the village and in the market goods were still exchanged in the main on a goods-for-goods basis; rice for pots, fruit for meat, etc. Trading, *martiga-tiga,* was either conducted by professional traders, *partiga-tiga,* or was carried on casually in the *onan* = markets, or was conducted in the villages by itinerant traders. This trade was not on a money-for-goods basis: the trader acquired cattle and gold, linen and rice. A builder of large canoes, *solu,* could dispose of them against a bride for his son. In the main, money had other functions and served other purposes than just as a medium with which to buy goods. (A Croesus sometimes nailed all the *ringgit* = dollars he possessed on the front wall of his house just to let the public see how rich he was.) It could be used to denote a girl who was destined to become the bride of one's son and she would then be termed *nioro ni hepeng* = one who is designated with money, and

---

[19] Translated into Dutch in *Adatrechtbundel* XXXV.

who thereby became unavailable to any other man. Men gambled with money. It secured the protracted use of a plot of land belonging to another man who needed ready cash, and when he claimed the land back he paid back the money he had received. Copper money was exchanged against tobacco, weight-for-weight; money was loaned out at interest to a man who wanted to profit by using it, loans on this basis being termed *manganahi* = having the use of it with the stipulation that it increases, i.e., carries interest (*anak*, literally 'children'), in contrast to *morsali* = loans carrying no obligation other than to pay back the value of the object received. But it was not only money to which interest could accrue: if rice were loaned because of a rice shortage, *morlali eme,* it had to be returned augmented. Money could also be used as a medium of assessment, though there was not much need felt for this because the marriage payment was for preference expressed in the things which constituted it, for example, the total was a quarter of a house, half a buffalo, a golden earring and two horses. The *guguan* = contribution to a joint ceremony, was reckoned in measures of rice. And fines were as often paid in cattle and rice as in money. Money in common with many other things, was a valuable item, but it could not be acquired to the same degree, and neither was it available in such quantities that it could supersede exchange of goods-for-goods and make trade by exchange superfluous.

This situation is gradually changing. Land is acquiring greater value as something on which one can borrow money or which one can sell. Money itself is becoming a more and more general medium of exchange, though the term *manuhor* = to buy, is not yet exclusively applied to the conversion of money into goods required. The process is still going on, but so far it has been rather slow because the supply of money only increases slowly. Even now only a few products are exported from the Toba Country: of old benzoin was exported and later coffee from a few places, but no rubber, timber or cattle. Money does come into the Toba Country each year in the form of the wages earned on Sumatra's East Coast by labourers engaged in temporary work, especially during the dry monsoon, but this amounts to only a few thousand guilders. The salaries of officials and school subsidies bring Government money into the country but taxes take it out again, and a year of excessive purchase of cars for hire work quickly disposes of the money acquired on the East Coast during the monsoon. Only the cheapest goods are imported into the Batak Country.

It goes without saying that alongside the increase in the quantity of money, there has been a steady increase in the quantity of movable goods, in buying them and in the significance of contracts relating to them.

Cattle, gold, boats, household utensils, fishing tackle, kitchen utensils, foodstuffs, clothes, implements, ornaments and so on, are some of these movable goods, among which houses and crops must always be included.

Houses are regarded as being separate from the land on which they stand. In the village, the village ground is an item in itself and the whole area within the village's walls, *parik*, the walls themselves, the ditch, *suha*, around the village and sometimes also a strip of arable land belonging to it, stand as a whole in relationship to the village's founder or his legal successors. Houses in the village have their own owners, and the right whereby the houses stand on village land is subject to the rules which obtain in general in respect of living in a village or to those rules which are fixed or agreed upon by a particular village community. Houses built outside the village are built on the owner's own land, on land owned jointly, or on another man's land, by agreement. The rule applicable to all these forms is: if a dwelling house is built on a piece of land, the owner of the land does not lose his rights to it, *ndang taragohon pardjabuan partanoan*.

Crops must also be regarded as being separate from the land on which they are grown. Trees and plants within the village or on its walls are subject to special village law; one can have fruit trees and trees for timber on one's own or on another man's land, or on land held in joint ownership; coffee trees can be sold separately from the land on which they grow, etc.

Throughout this chapter I will indicate, where necessary, and if possible, where the discussion refers to land or movable goods. In respect of land transactions, the reader is also referred to Ypes' work.

Formerly, legal transactions could be effected over human beings, slaves and peons; at present only over their work, skill and services.

GENERAL REQUIREMENTS OF LEGAL TRANSACTIONS

All legal transactions other than those relating to trifles such as borrowing a knife, buying some fruit, etc., are bound by relevant rules which must not be neglected. They are also subject to some requirements which are prescribed by custom, decency and good order. Important transactions may not be referred to or recalled in casual conversation and without special deliberation, nor so concluded. Such a course is not legal and makes for disorder. For instance, suppose that during the period when men are resting after their work in the fields and are chatting to one another, one man tells another that he wants his money back the following day. This sort of behaviour would not be regarded as being proper: there was no reasonable motive for mentioning the matter; it had no connection with the work which the men were doing or with the people who heard the discussion. It was, therefore, not the correct way to press for payment of a debt, because the people in whose presence the matter was mentioned did not know what it was about, they were not familiar with the circumstances, and neither the time or the place were suitable. If people meeting casually on the wayside, *di pinggol ni dalan,* effect a transaction over a cow or a buffalo when neither a chief, a member of the village nor a middleman is present, then it is open to suspicion in the event of there being anything wrong afterwards. A claim will not then be supported by a judge. It is not regarded as good form to redeem a pledged rice-field when there are only women present, because this is a man's business and should be transacted with men. Contracts made without the knowledge of those who should be informed are valueless. As the *umpama* says:

padan sidua-dua atik behá patolu begu,
padan sitolu-tolu paopat djolma;
Agreements concluded between two people in the absence of anyone else only have the spirits as the third party.
Agreements concluded with three people have human beings as witnesses, *i.e.,* they are public and therefore valid.

A judge will reject an agreement entered into behind another person's back because:

parhudjur mundi-mundi, partotoran hau halak,
parpadan sibuni-buni, sipaguntur-guntur halak.
Someone who uses a javelin as a lance, with a shaft of *halak* wood.
Whosoever enters an agreement in secret creates disorder.

He must be subjected to discipline in some way or other.

A proper place to conduct discussions which are likely to lead to a legal transaction is the *partungkoan* = dry ground under an old tree, which is usually to be found outside the village gate and where people gather for a sociable chat after work and the evening meal. The *lapo* = small eating house, at the nearest intersection of paths is also a suitable place. The most important agreements, however, are made indoors, since they are, as a rule, associated with eating a meal.

CONTRACTING AGREEMENTS

For a contract to be regarded as having been properly made, it must be entered into with due observance of the formalities and requirements pertaining to it. It will then have been discussed and concluded according to *adat, dibagasan adat*.

Part of these formalities in the case of important contracts is, as a rule, the common meal which is eaten by those concerned, such as the meal the *parboru* prepares for the *paranak* when the latter comes to his house to arrange the betrothal of his son to the *parboru*'s daughter; the meal that is given by a debtor when he wants to reach agreement with his creditors; the meal given by a man who is moving and wants to make the necessary arrangements regarding the disposal of his movable and unmovable goods which he is leaving behind; the meal given by a man who has returned to his village and who wants his property back again. In general the meal which is given by those who are taking an important step and who wish to acquaint the circle who should be informed about it, namely, kinsmen, affines, members of the village and friends.

If a man's kinsmen have an interest in what he does as the *suhut* = the main person concerned, then they are entitled to be properly summoned either by the *suhut* himself or by an envoy, to foregather at a meal, *digokhon*. If they are not properly notified they can absent themselves if they wish, and a meeting often founders because they have done so — this is particularly the case in land contracts. But if a proper invitation is extended, then it is correct form that they accept it unless there are pressing reasons to prevent them doing so:

> *gokhon sipaimaon, djou-djou sialusan,*
> One awaits an invitation and one answers a summons.

Which aphorism also applies to feasts and attending them. If a man fails to attend, then he forfeits the right to complain later that something has been done without his knowledge for, if he is present at the discussions and finds that the course the matter is taking is not acceptable to him, he can always express his dissatisfaction verbally or, if necessary, he can withdraw from the discussions and leave the meeting. It is then left to the judge to determine whether an agreement reached in a man's absence is valid or not. What criteria does the judge use in such a case? Here it is difficult to be precise. His judgement will be based principally on the local relationships and the actual circumstances within the group of which the persons concerned constitute a part, thus within the general genealogical and social framework. In these and many other disputes, the factual elements and the juridical elements cannot be separated and differentiated sharply from each other, their boundaries are not well-defined; they blend into each other.

I have already observed that the village chief should be acquainted with all transactions which are of some importance and which directly concern the inhabitants of his village. He must be invited in the correct manner to be present when anything is contemplated in his village. When people are negotiating with an inhabitant of a certain village with which they are not connected, they often prefer to deal with a dignitary above the village chief, since he is the one person who can safeguard them against the undesirable consequences which may result for them from a too close family relationship between the villagers and their village chief. They also bear in mind that if a dispute should later arise, the village chief is in duty bound to be honest in giving the facts regarding the transaction, but he is also in duty bound to support and assist his villagers, even if they are in the wrong.

In some important transactions it is definitely illegal if the village chief is not called to attend them, especially those which bear on the management of the village, such as someone going to live outside the village, the sale of a house in the village, and so forth. This also applies to those transactions of which the purport is the definite transfer of land to a *marga* other than the ruling *marga*, and those which may lead to encumbering land occupied by a *parripe* under the *parripean*-law, etc. Other transactions such as pledging a wet rice-field, burdening an unbetrothed daughter with a debt, selling cattle, etc., are not exactly illegal if the village chief has been by-passed, but it is considered a less proper way of conducting business. Such transactions are *hurang denggan* = less good. They are more easily open to question than those effected entirely according to *adat, dibagasan adat,* and where both kinds of contract are at issue, preference will be given to the latter.

The importance of observing all the *adat* formalities when effecting transactions, lies in the superiority it confers on them. There is no agreed precedence between the different sorts of contracts which can be concluded over a particular object of property other than that of precedence of time, but to neglect the *adat* formalities is to make a contract definitely inferior. Principal among these formalities is the co-operation of the chief. It is his duty to prevent his villagers acting improperly by concluding contracts concerning parts of their property over which they do not have the free and complete disposal, such as selling a buffalo held in joint ownership, giving as security, *tahan,* a field which is already held for another debt, reburdening with a debt a daughter who is already betrothed, etc. He can keep track of all these matters for, though he keeps no record of all his villagers' obligations in this respect, the number of people for whom he is responsible is not very large and the number of transactions are also small and therefore no great demand is made on his memory. If the chief neglects to make known to the opposite party in a transaction that he is entering into a contract concerning something about which a previous contract exists, then he should be corrected, and the possibility is not excluded that he will be held responsible for a part of the damage which has resulted from his concealment of the facts: such concealment can seldom be attributed to accidental neglect.

THE HELP OF THE DOMU-DOMU

We have already discussed the function of the *domu-domu* in respect of the discussions on the marriage payment. It is the *domu-domu* who effect agreement, *pardomuan*, a.o. regarding the size of the marriage payment between the parties concerned, and for their services the *domu-domu* receive the *upa domu-domu* = fee for effecting agreement. Intermediaries also render their services, *mandomu-domui*, when a number of other kinds of contracts are entered into, particularly those which concern the sale of movable goods, cattle and houses, irrespective of whether the agreements are made in the village or in the market. The function of the *domu-domu* is then to bring the parties to an agreement in respect of the price, method of payment and other conditions of sale, which the parties themselves would not reach alone. The obstinate and tenacious Batak evidently cannot dispense with the help of a neutral third party who, when neither of the parties would be prepared to see each other's point of view of their own accord, forms the bridge over which they can reach one another. The activity of this third party is called *manguhum* = to decide like a judge, or *manola* = settling the point at issue. If, for example, a vendor of a buffalo asks 100 guilders, and the buyer offers only 70, then the *domu-domu*, there are usually two or more present at the negotiations, name a price of, say, 80 guilders as being the right one in their opinion, and after some more persuasive talk the sale is forthwith concluded. Such a broker can also act as a go-between when parties are not in the same place. The *domu-domu* do not often take part in contracts which are not of a durable character, such as hiring a house, or those in which no proper valuation occurs, such as pledging a rice-field; neither do they take part in the settlement of debts. They are very frequently used when cattle are to be sold. They hardly ever (never?) appear in land transfers, which seldom have their origin in a simple sale: the chiefs are the intermediaries in these transactions.

The fee the intermediaries receive, the *upa domu-domu*, is a reimbursement for the good services they have rendered. Both parties usually contribute to it, or it is stipulated in the agreed price of the goods, for example, 80 guilders, one of which is to be given to the *domu-domu*. If a concluded contract has to be set aside later, then the amount is reckoned according to the so-called:

> *inggir-inggir na mapipil, lombu-lombu na tartading na so sidohon-dohonon;*
> the scattered seeds of small fruit, shields left behind on the battlefield; no one bothers about them any more.

In respect of the *domu-domu* who co-operate in the discussions on the marriage payment, the complaint was made in Chapter V that they are of such little use when it comes to furnishing evidence in the event of a later dispute. The *domu-domu* who take part in sale agreements are usually more useful as witnesses. They are frequently the only ones, besides the parties concerned, who have taken part in the transaction; they have concentrated on the discussions and the mediation was entirely in their hands, so that they usually also fulfil the function of *sibege hata* = witnesses who heard what was negotiated.

WITNESSES, THEIR FUNCTION AND REMUNERATION

Though the function of witnesses is not to take part in the price-fixing, they seldom, in fact, take part merely as observers at an assembly at which an agreement is deliberated. They are usually co-deliberators, though not always to the same degree, and they help the parties to come to an acceptable solution. It is not expected of a witness, *na umbege hata* = one who listens to the proceedings, that he will simply take cognisance of the expressed wishes of both parties. They should also acquaint themselves with the content of what has been agreed and how agreement was reached. For this service they receive the *singot-singot* (*ingot-ingot*) = reminder money, which is paid to them where the matter deals with trade or debt, or the *pago-pago* = sealing money, which accrues to them in land transactions. The term *pago-pago* means not only that in paying this fee the witnesses will be expected later to remember the facts, if necessary, but it also means that the contract has indeed been concluded: *pago* means a pole that has been driven in and *pago-pago* indicates that a definite agreement has come into being. If the witnesses are in any doubt that agreement has really been reached, then they must not accept the *pago-pago*. Hence, as a rule, it is required that both parties contribute to it, or at least the party who has taken upon himself a certain commitment. When an agreement concerns land, the chiefs of both parties are seldom absent. Where the chiefs are present at other transactions, their fee is usually also called *pago-pago*.

If land is transferred permanently, then the money which the chiefs receive is called in Toba the *upa manggabei* = the fee for the good wishes of prosperity, *gabe*, which are expressed at such a transfer. The term *upa manggabei* can also be used for the sum of money which the parties concerned give to those present as a token that agreement has been reached in other transactions at which similar expressions of good-will are given, such as, when a betrothal contract is made, when a broken marriage is mended, and so on.

I will deal further with the question of evidence in Chapter X. Here I will only mention the gift of notification which is sometimes given to members of the village, even though they were not present at the trans-action. I only came across it in Silindung, in the southerly part of the Toba Country — where it is called *sialabane* — at a marriage and on the permanent transfer of land. I am unable to explain the term: in Upper Barus when contracts of importance are concluded, it is called *uang boto-boto* = so that is known what has taken place; and in Pahae a small amount of cents is set aside for the members of the village, apart from the *upa domu-domu*, when cattle are sold. In Silindung, the same thing is done when a house is sold. The purport of all of them seems to be that such a gift acts as a notification to all the inhabitants of the village that a transaction has taken place whereby something which had been under the control of the village is henceforth beyond its jurisdiction. The *indahan pamonggar* = meal of rice, which is given to the villagers when a house is removed from their village or is sold out of it, has a similar purport.

MUTUAL BINDING OF THE PARTIES

Frequently the one party will require from the other a token, *tanda,* that the contract has been concluded and the resultant obligations accepted, or that the right thereby endorsed is acknowledged. This token is called *tanda saut*, a sign that the matter under discussion has been brought to fruition by the act of agreement (*saut* = to take place, to come about). This token is given, for example, at a betrothal when the young people exchange the *tanda burdju,* followed later by the *ulos ni hela* from the prospective father-in-law. It is given at a divorce and also when a widow is separated from her late husband's kinsmen. On this occasion the *parboru* pays a small sum of money, the *patilaho,* to the spouse or to the *paranak,* who, in accepting it, signifies that the woman is free and can marry again irrespective of whether a claim is outstanding for the balance of the marriage payment, or whether such a claim has already been settled. A *tanda* (which is not given in land transactions) is in these cases a visible token that an obligation has been accepted; that a certain situation has come into being.

The sum of money given as a bond (Mal. *pandjar*) when an agreement of sale is reached, has the same purport. This is especially common in buying and selling cattle, but it is also given at other agreements of sale at which an immediate exchange of the full money value of the goods does not take place. This bond is a part of the total price and is paid immediately after the contract has been concluded and consists of, perhaps, about 1/20 of the full price, and in accepting it the main object is that the seller confirms to the buyer that an arrangement regarding the transfer of the goods he has bought has been made. I heard a buyer of a buffalo say that the bond he had given was a public token that the buffalo was then his, *i ma tanda ni naung saut horbo i di au.* The bond is called the *patudjolo ni gagaron* = the precursor of the payment, and *bohi ni garar* = the 'face' of the payment, i.e. getting a sight of a small part of the full sum actually owed. When poultry is sold, the term *tarintin* is used this being the word indicating the knot, the distinguishing mark which is tied on the bird's foot.

The payment and acceptance of the bond must be considered as separate from delivering the goods. For example, it is paid when a fourth part of a cow which is in the hands of, and is managed by, a third co-owner is sold; the new co-owner can be introduced to the latter some time after the sale. Conversely, it can be paid when the beast is actually handed over to emphasise the fact that the handing over means that the animal has been sold and is not being lent or given into custody to be looked after (to my knowledge cattle are not pledged). A transfer of responsibility for the goods bought is not, in my view, bound to the handing over and acceptance of the bond, at least not in those cases where actual transfer of the goods has to take place. Once the bond has been paid, however, the buyer can demand the actual delivery of the goods he has bought. Furthermore, and this is also characteristic, once the seller has delivered the goods he cannot claim the dissolution of the agreement and the return of the goods on the ground that the buyer has not paid the remainder of the agreed purchase price.

While in general it can be stated that, in negotiations concerning the sale of valuable movable goods, the agreement must be considered to be deficient if neither payment of the whole of the purchase price nor payment of the *patudjolo* has been made, it must always be borne in mind that this statement only applies to transactions concluded between people who are strangers to each other. Kinsmen, affines and good friends place great confidence in each other's word. I did not come across the bond in land transactions, but I did find it paid at the sale of cash crops. I do not know whether the bond is paid in other contracts like hiring, exchange, pledging of gold, etc., in addition to sale agreements: it seems to be doubtful.

EXTRA-CONTRACTUAL RIGHTS AND OBLIGATIONS

There are numerous rights and obligations which do not arise from agreements but from general legal usage. They are a direct consequence of living in small communities. They arise primarily from the principle of reciprocity which is generally expressed in the following *umpama*:

   sisoli-soli do uhum, siadapari gogo,

reciprocity is legal custom; exchange of help in work is strength. *Marsiadapari* means the exchange of manpower, mutual assistance. This is still required when a dry rice-field is laid out; when the harvest is gathered; when houses are built; when a village is laid out; and when the dead are disposed of etc. This custom exists side by side with the new idea which has sprung up of providing services against wages. A distinction is sometimes made, though it is not a sharp one, between *marsiadapari* and *mangarumpa* = to render general assistance, which is the help given by anyone present when, for example, a house is being roofed and the builder asks everyone to lend a hand. *Marsiadapari* proper is rather the agreed exchange of manpower *(adap = alap = to fetch, marsialap = to fetch mutually)* for previously determined recurring aims, such as digging up each other's wet rice-fields. Wages and remuneration are not given, but those for whom the work has been performed provide a meal for those who have given the assistance requested, *na hinara*, and if the work they were asked to do was of a pleasurable nature the meal has something of a festive character. Warneck, in his dictionary [20], defines the word *tondja* as sanctions: to

---

[20] J. Warneck: *Tobabataksch-deutsches Wörterbuch,* 1906.

call on someone who has been unwilling to participate in collective work; his co-villagers then go to him in numbers and he has to give them a meal as an atonement for his disinclination to help. I surmise, however, though I did not check it on the spot, that this is intended as a punishment for someone who was unwilling to co-operate in collective work in which he has the same interest as the others, for example, work on the village wall, after a fire, or on a dyke of an irrigation canal after a flood. Sanctions for unwillingness to participate in mutual assistance lie in the general censure of the village and in a corresponding unwillingness of the other villagers in the future. If it is a village chief from whom the *marhara* = summons, emanates, then reluctance to comply with it is readily interpreted as disrespect towards the chief, *tois tu radja,* which deserves reproof.

Besides mutual help, mention must be made of the gifts that are exchanged mutually such as the *tumpak,* which is given to help a kinsman, an affine or a friend who has to make substantial payments, for example, when a son marries; the *siuk,* the contribution of rice, etc., to a great feast which is given by kinsmen or an affine; the *sampe tua,* the gifts guests give when they attend a feast for the consecration of a house; the *silua,* which, in general, are the gifts given on a number of ceremonial occasions to the persons who organise these ceremonies. If the immediate reason for these gifts is not the replenishment of the kitchen supplies, or the purse, they are, as a rule, presented during the ceremony, for example, during the dancing, and have therefore a ritual and public character. They are all given because general legal usage demands them and to neglect giving them, or to be unwilling to do so, is a discourtesy which arouses the displeasure of the persons concerned as well as public opinion. These and similar kinds of gifts may have been received earlier or they can be anticipated later, and, if need be, can even be claimed before a judge. Here and there the size of the contribution of rice which people in a particular group are accustomed to give each other, is fixed by mutual agreement. At a festival of some size to which a large number of guests will come who stand in all kinds of relationships to the host, the *suhut,* a scribe notes the names of the guests and their gifts which, in total, sometimes exceed the outlay for the occasion.

There are also the portions of the slaughtered feast-animal, the *djambar,* to which people have a right on grounds of kinship and affinity, as well as the portions of the marriage payment, also called *djambar,* which accrue to the *parboru*'s side when a marriage is con-

20

cluded. In coming to the *marundjuk*-ceremony, the members of this group are entitled to a portion. Kinsmen who are not closely related to the *suhut* sometimes receive a gift called the *upa ro* = gift for those attending.

Finally, there are the *ulos* and *piso* gifts which have been frequently mentioned and which are known by many names according to the occasion on which they are exchanged between affines. A voluntary gift from the one side is followed up by a counter-present from the other, and a request for a gift of some consequence can be preceded by an introductory present. There is great dissimilarity in the value of mutually exchanged gifts, as well as great freedom in choice of occasion for a voluntary gift or for a requested one. But there is a general tendency to fulfil the obligations which affinal relationships impose on all kinds of important occasions. In respect of this, it is never necessary to resort to a judicial claim, at least among close affines: mutual obligations are met solely from what might be called moral motives. If, as can happen, there is a dispute between affines which is of a kind that a judge's verdict imposes an obligation on the one party to perform an act which will obtain as an *ulos*, then there must always be a counter-act by the opposite party which will obtain as *piso*.

An act which is not founded on the principle of reciprocity but on emergency, is called *mangasahan gomos* = the arbitrary appropriation of another man's goods, which is not punishable if the motive is of a pressing character and restitution of the value of the goods follows. If, for example, a *datu* commands that a woman in childbed must have a particular sort of fruit, it can be taken from someone else without request; if a child is born and there is no chicken or piglet which must be killed for the meal that has to be given to the visiting women, then a chicken or piglet can be taken from an inhabitant of the village, even though he forbids it. The principle of *mangasahan gomos* also applies to an *ibebere* = nephew who appropriates something from his *tulang* = mother's brother, to pay pressing debts.

FULFILLING CONTRACTS

A later contract cancels out an earlier one, *tading hata pardjolo dibahen hata parpudi,* as does a later promise cancel an earlier one. But, once a person has bound himself, he may not go back on his undertaking:

> *parhudjur mundi-mundi, parsoban hau halak,*
> *parhata simuba-muba, paago-ago halak.*

Someone who uses a javelin as a lance, who seeks *halak* wood as firewood.

A man who continually changes what he has agreed causes great damage to others.

Contracts must be fulfilled:

hori ihot ni doton,

padan siingoton.

Flax is the binding twine of a fishing-net,

Contracts must be fulfilled.

Maxims such as these appear to contain undoubted truths with which all will agree. But, in point of fact, they demonstrate the development of a law of debts because a judge so often has to turn to the medium of these simple axioms when he is confronted with sophistry, quibbling, craftiness, and so on.

Anyone who does not hold himself to an agreement; who acts in a manner other than that to which he has committed himself; who refuses to fulfil the obligation he has contracted, is guilty of *mangose padan* = violating a contract entered into. If such *mangose* is confirmed without doubt and if it is a deliberate act of bad faith, the *pangose* = the perfidious violator of his word, can be disciplined by the judge. The Batak judge, knowing the contrary, irrational, and, above all, obstinate disposition of his fellow countrymen when they have set their minds on something, frequently finds it necessary not to limit himself to ordering that an agreement must be observed; that what has been neglected must be carried out and compensation paid for any damage suffered; but to take disciplinary measures such as imposing a fine, or to ignore counter-claims, and generally to act in accordance with what he deems will best serve the case in question (see Chapter IX).

As a rule, a commitment is automatically discharged only when an act to fulfil an undertaking has to be carried out, when, for example, goods are actually handed over following an earlier promise to do so, or when a promised service is performed. If the agreement concerns a money debt and its discharge, then a claim for settlement will usually have to be made. This is due to the manner in which debts were dealt with and settled of old. Agreements requiring prompt periodic payments such as called for by European contracting parties, banks, shops and car dealers, etc., are alien to traditional law. They are innovations and are still seldom followed even by the richer Batak money lenders. The old style of contract, in which payment is usually coupled with an important event of some kind, such as the marriage of a son, or when a man finds a husband for his daughter, *di laku ni boru,* is still preferred. In more recent times, with the greater use of money, more and more precise data are required for debentures, both for their redemption and for the payment of interest, and sometimes there is the added threat that something given as a pledge will be disposed of immediately if the debtor defaults, though this threat is not always meant seriously. I had to deal with a great number of contracts, written and unwritten, from which it appeared that even before a dispute had arisen, the initial circumstances under which the agreement had been concluded were no longer operative, since in the meantime various things had been discussed, tacitly agreed, or decided upon by the parties concerned. In small communities such as those in which the Batak live, in which the mutual relationships are many and varied, some matters will often acquire a different aspect and this again repeatedly requires delimitation of the varying current obligations. Thus it is a common Batak practice to draw up a statement of account, *mardabu-dabu,* at some time or other.

A debtor usually avoids discussing his debt with his creditor; he is silent about it and waits for the creditor to press for payment, *martunggu.* Hence the reason that pressing for payment, *martunggu singir* = to claim payment of an outstanding debt, is, as a rule, quite an important event for the parties concerned. Pressing for payment may not be done casually or at an unsuitable time, for instance, it is not good form to do it at night. It must be done with due observance of the rules of property. The creditor must carefully consider the way in which he frames his claim, and the debtor must similarly choose his words in reply with equal care, because he may later be confronted with them. Observance of this rule is necessary because the verbal terms agreed upon are often more important than the written word, especially if a long time has elapsed since the contract was made. And, if a person desires to make a claim that an agreement be honoured, it is of the greatest importance that he approaches the same person who has bound himself by the agreement. On this point there is a rule of law which serves as a rule of conduct both for the creditor and the debtor, and which the smallest child has to take into consideration when he is sent out to buy a box of matches:

ansimun na martagan ama ni mandulo,
ia i donganmu marpadan, tusi ma ho uso-uso.
A small kind of gherkin; the father of *mandulo*;
The person with whom one makes an agreement is the person whom one must approach with one's demands.

This rule seems to be simple and self-explanatory, but, nevertheless, it is continually under discussion in legal matters. Time and time again a party has to invoke it or a judge has to be guided by it. This can be the result of a variety of circumstances, for example, an irascible man who thinks that an injustice has been done to him, will often lose sight of how he should act in the matter, and will take what he thinks is due to him wherever he finds it. A frequent cause of mistakes is the close relationship which can exist between brothers and cousins, so that an outsider sometimes has difficulty in disentangling what is individually owned and what is owned jointly. In the case of third parties having an interest in a debt, or in a part of something jointly owned, there is repeatedly carelessness in failing to carry out the obligatory notification of transfer without which the person with whom the original contract was made remains bound, and, consequently, when a dispute arises, the claim is made to the wrong person. The rule just mentioned lays down the proper course that should be followed. To give some examples: a pledger who wants to redeem his pledged field must deal with the pledgee and not with the person to whom the latter repledged it; a debt must be paid to the creditor and not to someone who contends that he is entitled to take payment; borrowed goods must be returned to the lender; pledged goods to the pledger and not to his brother or son. At the same time, there are also cases which prove that this rule, which has an apparent general validity, does not always hold good. Does not a man who has taken a rice-field in pledge from a man who moves elsewhere have to allow the *uaris* to redeem it? Does not the closest affine, usually sister's husband, of a refractory man who does not want to accept a reasonable solution to a dispute, conclude or fulfil a contract on his behalf? And does not a *radja* in conservative areas pay a debt of a subordinate who is pressed for payment when the *radja* knows the relevant circumstances? All these are deviations which, not less than the rule itself, are grounded in law and custom. They are the result of those particular relationships between kinsmen and inhabitants of a village which limit the rigid application of the law.

In this connection, special attention must be given to pledging land which is then repledged and again repledged. When objects (usually gold ornaments) are pledged, the just mentioned rule, *ansimun na martagan*, etc. applies without modification. If A gives something to B in pledge, he must redeem it from B; if B has repledged it to C, B must redeem it from C, and so on. Now, if A wants to redeem and B cannot meet his claim because C makes difficulties, has mislaid the object, for instance, then B must compensate A since C's objections are no concern of his. In such a case, compensation to A can adequately replace the pledge, since objects so pledged are seldom other than things that can be bought in the market and normally pass from hand to hand. If, however, land is pledged, this rule, according to the opinion of many good judges of *adat*, does not always apply. The guarantee that the man who owns the land will again be in possession of it, ranks above the guarantee that the man who holds the land in pledge will get back the money he paid out. To express it in the Batak language: *tano mulak tu partano, parhepeng tunggu singirna* = the land returns to its rightful owner; the money-lender has to claim the payment of the money he loaned. A frequently occurring example is illustrating: A gives a wet rice-field in pledge to B for 40 guilders; B repledges it to C for 60 guilders without informing A (which is improper). When A wants to redeem, B defaults in the payment of the 20 guilders owing to C. When the case goes before the judge he will return A's land to him against payment of the 40 guilders. C will be induced to bring a separate claim against B for the remaining money. It sounds hard on C and appears to be a violation of the law of pledging, but many times I encountered judgements which all demonstrated the same concern that land should be returned to its original owner. This factor predominated when a way out of the difficulties that had arisen had to be sought. It is based on the idea that the ties which bind a man to his land are relatively stronger and are considered to be a more important factor than ties created by the possession of money or movable goods: land is not yet regarded as a commodity in the ordinary sense. It is a means primarily of sustenance for the person who inherited it, cleared it, or who has received it as a present from his *hula-hula*. Therefore a man who invests his money by taking in pledge a plot of land runs some risk: he must ascertain clearly the footing on which the would-be pledger holds the land if he does not want to fall between two stools.

A companion aphorism to that just quoted expresses a similar idea which refers particularly to returning something after using it, or after the dissolution of an agreement, or when an obligation has to be fulfilled:

> *tabo-tabo sitarapullak,*
> *sian i didjalo tusi ma dipaulak.*
> The sap of the *sitarapullak* plant,
> The person from whom one has received something is the person to whom one must return it.

A variation of this idea is contained in the following maxim:

pitu pe batu martindi, sada do sitaon na dokdok,

when seven stones lie one above the other only one bears the full weight;

which means that one person has to be held responsible even though others have used a thing or have profited by it. If, for example, errors are made during the dividing up of the meat of a feast-animal by the kinsmen of the giver of the feast who are in charge of the operation, it is the giver of the feast, the *suhut*, who is held responsible for the errors; if a number of sons of one father contract gambling debts right and left and then abscond, the father has to honour all the debts; when a betrothal is broken off or a marriage ends, the *parboru* is the person responsible for the restoration of what kinsmen and affines have received as *todoan*, etc.

APPEAL FOR CLEMENCY, ASI NI ROHA

The Batak law of debts has some harsh aspects. The rate of interest is high, a consequence of the scarcity of money, and onerous for those who are in debt. In Toba, rice is loaned, and on Samosir the harvest is pledged under such oppressive terms that formerly such transactions often led to peonage for debt. But besides an acute awareness of the power of wealth, there is at the same time a distinct feeling of sympathy for the predicament in which a debtor finds himself (particularly in Silindung and its environs) and to which an appeal can always be made. The fact that a large category of impoverished people does not exist, can be attributed to this factor. A merchant who has provided a man with trading capital and who knows better than anyone else the difficulties facing him, will be lenient if the man fails and is not in a position to repay his debt. If an inhabitant of a village has had to contend with his own and his family's sickness and, on the suggestion of a *datu*, moves elsewhere in order to escape his fate, then his fellow-villagers who have small claims on him do not press for payment; the son who, after his father's death, perceives how large is the burden on the estate, will call the creditors together to a meal in order to talk the matter over; if someone has caused another to suffer considerable damage as a result of his carelessness, and if it is very difficult for him to make reparation, then he will plead absence of intent in the hope of being treated leniently.

But in all such instances, a person must definitely make a plea for clemency. And if the need is indeed great, the request must be made in the form of a supplication and in a manner appropriate to softening the heart. This entreaty because of need is called *mangelek-elek,* which presumes acknowledgement of the debt as well as dependence on leniency. *Na mangelek ahu* = I beseech you earnestly, are the words which should be introduced into the appeal. The appeal can also be called *marsomba,* the emphasis then being on the display of respect, the *somba-somba,* towards the creditor. When a plot of land is offered as payment of the debt, *hauma parsomba,* which is to be transferred permanently to the creditor but of which the value is less than the amount of the debt, it is called *manombahon.* A rich man who is known to be hard-hearted, is not usually asked for a loan because he would not observe the *adat parsingiron* = the right way of conducting oneself towards a claim in respect of one's fellow men. It is not consistent with good legal morals that a hearing should not be given to a reasonable appeal. The chiefs and judges who handle matters of debt sometimes suggest that the debtor makes an appeal, *mangelek-elek,* or support him in his endeavour to soften his creditor's heart. And if the creditor is not agreeable to considering the appeal, though the reasonableness of the request is such that he should, then the suppliant can turn to the judge who will decide accordingly. For, since it is the custom that payment of debts that have accumulated or of debts that it is hardly possible to meet fully, should not be claimed to the last farthing, the judge has, correspondingly, the power to mitigate the force of the applicable law if he deems it just.

It must be noted that in olden times clemency was not customary in respect of those who joined the organised gambling parties, of which a detailed description is given in the *Naipospos Manuscript.* The rigorous laws relating to gambling debts which were enumerated at the gambling party put the full burden of the debt on the loser.

THE ACTUAL TRANSFER

The actual transfer of anything, either by virtue of an agreement or not, from one person to another is called *pasahathon,* to make *sahat* = to arrive at. When goods are handed over from one person to another the responsibility, the risk, *mara,* is also transferred. When the transfer has been made, the responsibility is said to rest with the person to whom the goods have been handed, *nunga sahat mara* = the responsibility has been passed on. The transfer is thus, in general, more important to the person who makes the transfer than to the person to whom the transfer has been made. The emphasis is not on the fact that, when a bond is given as a token of sale, or where there is a symbolic handing over, especially in the case of presents, the actual transfer of the goods must be made later, because a person once so committed neither objects nor neglects to do so. The emphasis is on the fact that the risk which lies with the owner of the goods must be transferred. The transfer is therefore also called *pagomgomhon* = to transfer the control, from *manggomgom* = to rule, to control. When a man returns a rice-field he says: "*gomgom haumám* = henceforth you have control over your field".

Mara can also be understood and interpreted as the threat of interference with the peaceful possession of the goods because of the claims of a third party, against whom the person who transferred the goods has to put up a defence. This responsibility regarding third parties is often mentioned in a clause in the written deeds of all kinds of contracts: *asa mara ni na hugadis i di ahu do* = I am responsible for the thing that I have sold. If this safeguard is found to be false, and if it becomes apparent that the seller has disposed of the goods without having the right to do this, then the judge may deem it advisable to mollify the person who has been duped, by ordering the guilty person to give him an *upa sala-sala* = acknowledgement of guilt.

The particulars of the actual transfer in the different contracts will be discussed later. Here I will only refer to what has already been noted, namely, that the formalities which should be observed are frequently neglected. Again and again it happens that the actual transfer of land, or of part of an animal that is in the hands of another joint owner, or of fruit trees, etc., was not accompanied by any sort of formal act. According to my observation, this has almost become customary when a written contract is drawn up in respect of the transfer of any object which is not handed over forthwith.

ARBITRARY ENFORCEMENT IN RESPECT OF AGREEMENTS

The practice of arbitrarily enforcing the observance of a contract was in olden times, in principle, unlawful. When it was permitted it was only in specific circumstances or with due regard of certain rules. According to the usual course of affairs, a dispute could be settled mutually among those concerned by using intermediaries; by resorting to an ordeal (war, trials of various kinds, the oath, etc.,) or by turning to a judge with the request for a decision. But one could not first use force and then invoke the law, *padjolo gogo papudi uhum*. If a man thought that an agreement had not been observed; that an obligation had not been fulfilled, then it was proper that he turned in the first instance to the person concerned with a request for an explanation:

topot mula ni uhum,

sungkun mula ni hata;

the beginning of proceedings to obtain justice is a visit,

interrogation is the beginning of a lawsuit;

and only after a fruitless endeavour could the aid of the chiefs be invoked as mediators or as judges, or recourse be had to war:

djolo mulak sian topot asa djumadihon parbadaan;

one must first have failed at a visit for the purpose of explanation before one can commence a war.

It was not lawful arbitrarily to fetter, *marnihot,* a refractory debtor, or to put him in the block, *mambeanghon.* Such acts could only be committed with the knowledge of the chiefs; as, for example, in the market place in respect of debts that originated there. However, as mentioned elsewhere, at the organised gambling parties, at which the numerousness of the debts incurred and the fact that the participants lived in widely scattered regions, made summary justice necessary, it was permissible to fetter a man who was not in a position immediately to meet the debt, or who could not give sufficient security, as a means of securing the rights of the creditor. However, escaping from the block immediately released a man from such a debt. But men were frequently fettered unlawfully in other circumstances and had no legal redress, as many an aged man told me.

The Government has now forbidden such high-handed actions to be inflicted on a debtor and it no longer occurs. What does often happen, however, is that a piece of land in dispute is actually seized, *padjolo gogo,* an operation effected by digging up, driving off the cultivators, forbidding access to the land, etc. This usually happens at the end of the dry monsoon when the working of the fields has started again. It is an unlawful act. It is also unlawful to pick the fruits of a tree which is in dispute and managed by another man; to tap benzoin trees cultivated by another; or to carry off cattle about which there is an argument.

When a dispute is pending, the item at issue can be placed out of reach of both parties by the judge. It can either be placed in the hands of a chief, *di tangan ni radja,* or of the judge himself, or a prohibition order, *hata siunang,* can be issued to both parties that the object must be left untouched. Land can be placed in the hands of the last, and disputed, cultivator, a measure which is usually given preference above others by Government officials. It is said that the Government devised this measure, but it seems to me to be founded in customary law. This measure and the rights it affords the last cultivator, is called *hot ni paksa*, a somewhat unusual term which apparently intends to convey the idea that the compulsive nature, *paksa*, of the situation will provide the required stability, *hot*. Such a provisional measure can also refer to the right of continued use, *paksa ni ulaon*, deriving from previous cultivation. I did not hear of arbitrary seizure of valuable objects from someone who had not, or would not, pay his debts. This could not even be done in the case of a gambling debt, even if the loser had been put in the block, according to the *Patik dohot Uhum*.

One can only take back one's own goods when they have been stolen and have been passed to a third party by the thief.

RESPONSIBILITY OF THE GROUP TO WHICH A DEBTOR BELONGS

In olden times, the tie which held together a group of kinsmen, affines and members of a village or of a territory, had to be more powerful than is now necessary, because at that time a group frequently had to maintain itself against the world outside by force of arms. Therefore, what was in the interests of one member of the group was always to a certain extent in the interests of the whole group. Any weakening of the position of one member affected all, and the maintenance of the social position of an individual was thus the task of the whole group. There was hardly a matter which, though initially entered into by one member of the group, could not in particular circumstances come within the sphere of interest and be of importance to the whole group. The aim of fettering a man for his own or someone else's debts, was to get his kinsmen to pay a ransom for him which was often forthcoming immediately, or to reach a settlement. Such an act, could, however, also lead to war. In principle, therefore, the whole group to which a man belonged stood behind him and whenever he made a contract this group would come forward should the observance on his side or on that of the other party leave much to be desired. The motive of self-preservation of the group, which compelled it to place itself behind its members, has at present largely disappeared, now that personal safety is guaranteed everywhere. But it still exists as a communal feeling which makes the individual realise that he will always be weaker alone than when united in a group in which the one can rely on the others and which can provide mutual assistance if necessary. This sense of community manifests itself primarily as a consciousness of belonging to an extended family and lineage according to which descendants of

a revered ancestor are still regarded as a natural unit whose prosperity
is the prosperity of every member of it. Cutting across this awareness is
the feeling of village-solidarity which can activate all the inhabitants
of a village and this is supplemented by the affinal relationships which
create their own obligations. It must be appreciated, however, that at
present the extent of the circle which the person belonging thereto
reckons as his sphere of interest, has dwindled to a small group. But the
solidarity is still evident whenever a member of a group is affected by
adverse circumstances. And it is still so strong that in certain circumstances an absentee feels compelled to give his help. There is, however,
no longer any question of the group being legally responsible in respect
of claims made upon a member by a third party. The solidarity of the
group is voluntary. If I am not in error, direct responsibility for each
other's debts only applies in the direct line in connection with the law
of inheritance, by which the property of the deceased father goes to
the sons and *vice versa:*

> *singir ni ama, ba singir ni anakna do,*
> *djala utang ni anak, utang ni amana do.*
> Debts owed by the father are debts owed by his son.
> Debts of a son are debts of the father.

As has already been indicated, however, the financial position of the
father must be taken into consideration, for example, when a son has
suffered considerable losses in trade.

NO MIXING OF CLAIMS

The Batak is averse to mixing claims. In the small communities in
which he passes a great part of his life, a person is so closely bound to
the other members by all kinds of ties, that it is often necessary to keep
concrete claims separate in order to prevent the complications becoming
too great. Besides that, each claim must always be seen against its own
background; it is characterised by the manner of its origin and by its
own observance and settlement; consequently each claim can create its
particular problems. As a consequence, mixing claims is not a feature
of village life and judges dislike counter-claims:

> *masitunggu singirna be, djala masigarar utangna;*
> let a man claim payment of debts owed to him and let him pay
> his own debts;

so runs the relevant aphorism. It does not only refer to the *utang singir*
which may exist between several people, but also to those which exist

between two people. It expresses a generally well-known and well-observed course of action. Nevertheless, it has to be invoked repeatedly in lawsuits against people who encounter difficulties in getting their claims accepted and who find therein a motive not to perform their own obligations. Once a person has deviated from the course of good conduct, he is seldom averse to mixing his obligations towards the one with his claims against the other. It does not need saying that there are cases in which mutual claims are so closely linked that they can only be settled by dealing with them as one.

We will now turn to the particular forms and will deal first with those which are considered as being the oldest, though naturally, there can be no question of a strict chronological sequence.

GIFT-GIVING

It seems unquestionable that among the Batak the giving of gifts of some substance to someone is particularly to be regarded as being in origin and essence a ritual act with a magico-religious purport. The numerous occasions when gifts are given, which I have mentioned earlier, point to it: there are the *dondon tua* = gifts loaded with good fortune, which are given to childless married couples, or to grandsons by their aged and prosperous grandparents; there are the *ulos*-gifts of various kinds which are given by the *hula-hula* to the *boru*. All these gifts have as their aim the passing on of the prosperity and blessings of those who are regarded as strong to those who have need of prosperity and blessings by means of objects, words or acts which are laden with supernatural strength. These presents are handed over to the soul of the donee, *dipasahat di tondi ni na mandjalo,* so that he will receive strength from them. Of old, and even now, they are the sole means by which certain categories of mutually connected persons, close kinsmen of successive generations, or close affines, can transfer certain things (e.g. their own house) since it is considered outside accepted usage for them to deal with such objects by means of a financial transaction. To most of the reciprocal gifts there is attributed a magico-religious character, like the *sampe tua,* but there are also those where the economic motive predominates, the *siuk* and the *tumpak.*

It is a characteristic of all these gifts that they are *sipate-pate* = permanent: they are not *simulak-mulak* = returnable:

sirungkas di paremean,
ndang siunsaton naung nilean.
The creeper on the rice heap.

What has once been given away cannot be taken back.

This permanency is not definitely expressed in the word meaning 'to present to', *mangalean*, since this verb also means 'to give' in the more generale sense of 'to hand over', 'to part with', but the idea is expressed in the specific technical legal term, *silean-lean*, which indicates not only the gift as such, but also the actual act of handing it over.

It cannot be said that every present is made voluntarily and disinterestedly. In many cases it is a compulsory gift, such as the counter-presents for the presents already received, or when a gift is given in anticipation of a counter-present. We have already seen in the discussion on the *pauseang* how the donee can be limited in his freedom over the disposal of an object presented to him, and we have also seen that gifts given at and during a marriage can revert to the donor if there is a divorce.

It is not always necessary that a gift is actually handed to the intended recipient: it can be given verbally, *holan hata dope*. Cattle that are given as *andor ni ansimun* at the *marupa-upa* of a firstborn are not usually given there and then; the gift of a *pauseang*-field is often effected on the birth of the first child. A provisional symbolic presentation is also possible, such as that which takes place when the guests at feasts offer their *silua* when it is their turn to dance. The person who is offering money holds it clearly visible clasped between the upright fingers of his uplifted hand and hands it over afterwards. A person giving cattle holds a small whip, and anyone giving rice holds a number of ears of rice or a ricesack in his hand. The dance and the show of symbols combined constitute the act of presentation: the actual transfer of the gifts follows later. If I am not mistaken, in the case of such a ritual presentation, the donor does not actually hand over the gifts himself; the donee fetches them or has someone do so on his behalf.

EXCHANGE

The exchange of goods against goods is called *pasambarhon* if the emphasis is on the items exchanged, and *masisambaran* when the persons making the exchange are to be stressed. To exchange is also termed *manumbang*, while the term *maningkati* = to substitute, can also be used. In the exchange of land, the term *marlibe* is mostly used and, since such an exchange usually has as its object the obtaining of land closer to hand in place of distant land, it is also termed *masigembaran* =

to bring (the owner and his land) closer together. In olden times, when money was still scarce, the incidental exchange of movable goods against a medium of exchange, or in regular commercial intercourse in the villages and the markets, the *onan manogot-nogot* = morning markets for the smaller village clusters, as well as in the large markets instituted by the territory and the tribal group, was called *martiga-tiga*. A much used medium of exchange then was *eme* = rice in the husk, a product for which there were official measures in many of the large markets. One could get practically anything for rice. This conversion of rice into goods was also termed *manuhor*, a term now used for the exchange of goods against money. Any kind of merchandise that was bought against rice was termed *situhoran*. The function of rice as a medium for buying goods has for the greater part been taken over by money. That the term *tuhor* was not only used to denote an exchange of goods against rice, is clear from the expression *tuhor ni boru* and the composition of the marriage payment.

The exchange of more important items could, and can, be attended with the paying of a sum of money equivalent to the excess value which the one item has over the other. This is called *manendek*, or *masiten-dehan*, as well as *maniha*, to add money to the exchange. This is done for instance when two people, each of whom owns a half of two buffaloes of different sizes, exchange them, and the man who obtains sole possession, *himpal*, of the largest buffalo, makes up the difference in value in money.

In the exchange of land, a distinction must be made between permanent exchange, *libe pate*, and exchange whereby the land can revert to either party, *libe mulak*. Exchange of the produce of land, *libe gogo*, by which two men harvest each other's fields after each man has planted and cultivated his own field, aims at economising on transport charges for the harvest. Particulars regarding these matters can be found in Ypes' book.

JOINT OWNERSHIP

Joint ownership of goods, which is still frequent among the Batak, is a (gradually disappearing?) form by which men are bound mutually by means of goods of one kind or another. Formerly this must have been more common than at present. Joint ownership may arise from the desire that inherited goods remain undivided, or by deliberately contracting an agreement of joint ownership. In the first case the property has come under the joint ownership of a group of people who are bound to each other by kinship ties. In the second, separate individuals have voluntarily bound themselves and their legal heirs to each other. All goods and land can be held in joint ownership.

Joint ownership is called *ripe-ripean,* when the emphasis is on the profit which the goods can furnish each individual owner, *na morripe-ripe,* by an alternative arrangement of their use by each of them. If, however, all joint owners profit to the same degree at the same time, then the more correct term is *hatopan* or *hadosan* (*top* = together, *dos* = alike to each other); thus the joint ownership of a buffalo or a house is termed *ripe-ripean;* that of a village or an irrigation channel, *hatopan:* the boundary of this word usage is, however, not sharp.

The part held in joint ownership is termed *tohap, toktok, bagian* or *ripean.*

The motive for entering into contracts of joint ownership is frequently a friendly relationship of one kind or another. Joint ownership can be a means whereby one may acquire some part of the prosperity of one's companion, *mambuat tua ni donganna,* and, since people see in joint ownership a means of participating mutually in each other's prosperity, its purport is therefore not only a matter of economics. This applies especially to cattle which, during the period of joint ownership grow and increase, particularly in the hands of someone who seems to be destined to be prosperous. A stranger cannot buy a part of a cow or a buffalo in the market because such a part is not regarded as general merchandise.

Most new joint ownership arises as a result of a marriage being concluded, when parts of cattle are given in settlement of the marriage payment, and from presents between kinsmen, affines and friends. The mutual relationship existing between the joint owners should, therefore, be characterised by friendly feelings and a desire to abstain from doing anything that could endanger it. For example, if there is a point in dispute regarding their joint ownership, they will, for preference, prevent the dispute coming to the point where the oath must be taken. In the case of cattle, the joint owners exchange gifts when young are born.

A rule common to all forms of joint ownership is couched in an aphorism already quoted:

> *ugasan ripe-ripe ndang tarbahen panghimpalan;*
>
> goods held in joint ownership may not be appropriated by one of the joint owners;

which rule owes its practical significance especially to the fact that in a small group of kinsmen, it is not always clearly fixed what belongs to an individual and what is jointly owned. Anyone who knows quite definitely that he is a joint owner of goods, or thinks he is, always takes care that his partner(s) perform no act of management, and still less of disposal, which could later be used to substantiate a claim of sole ownership. Should a co-owner attempt to do so, he would be accused of being a *siago ripe-ripe* = a robber of goods jointly owned, which is a serious allegation since joint ownership still is a main constituent of Batak juridical institutions.

Each joint owner has a right to take over the goods, *manantan,* if one of the other joint owners wants to relinquish his part. This part should first be offered to the other joint owners, *diandehon,* so that, in the event of goods being owned jointly by two persons, one can thus become the sole owner. A joint owner can prevent the transfer of a part of the goods which has taken place without his knowledge, *mangambati.* This right is absolute. The right of first offer is only applicable, however, where a joint owner wants to sell: it does not apply if he wants to give his part away as part of a marriage payment which he has to make, or if it is to be surrendered to a third party for any reason prescribed by *adat,* for instance, in a case of *utang adat.*

The responsibility for goods owned jointly rests on all partners unless damage to, or loss of, the goods can be attributed to one of them. Should the goods cause damage, if for example, a harvest is destroyed by cattle; if a house catches fire and the one next to it is set on fire too, etc., then the first question is, by whom were the goods managed at the time. If the manager is shown to be blameless, if, for instance, a horse unexpectedly kicks a man to death, then the consequences are apportioned between the partners and it does not then solely concern the manager. It is obvious that these few rules do not cover all cases. Justice, the circumstances, and above all the mutual relationship existing between the parties concerned, must be considered by the judge, so that the burden of goods held in joint ownership will be borne fairly.

With regard to the most important items that can be owned jointly and the form of that ownership some particulars will be given here. Cattle can be owned jointly and the basis of this ownership can be very complicated. If, for example, each of two people owns a half, *sambariba,* of a buffalo cow then, when the cow calves, the partners share the increase equally, unless there is another agreement to the contrary. Each can dispose of his own half separately and each can also divide his half again, his part of the animal then being quartered, *haehae,* which four quarters can be disposed of individually: division into

21

eighths, *bola tambirik,* is even possible. The young of the second generation of a buffalo cow can each be divided in the same manner and the parts can be separately disposed of: those of the third generation can be similarly treated, and so on, so that after some years, a great number of people can be owners of parts of a herd of descendants of one cow. Anyone who sells a part, gives it away, uses it as a marriage payment, allots it to his *boru, mangupahon,* etc., must introduce, *padjumola,* the new partner to his existing partner(s) and the new partners then exchange tobacco as a sign that they henceforth accept each other as *dongan ripe-ripean.* If the transfer of the animal has taken place, then it must be tapped all over in the presence of the joint owners, and it is proper that a small whip be handed over: this is a token of the transfer of control. The *Patik dohot Uhum* gives a few examples of trials in cases where these formalities were neglected, the judgements given being conducive to the protection of these really sound formalities. I have already remarked that they are often neglected, and nowadays it is hardly possible to consider whether this observance or the absence of it, are decisive in deciding whether or not there has been a complete transfer. There is a similar neglect of the formalities whereby the increase of the possession should be announced and acknowledged. For example, the partner who manages the cow should inform his co-partners that she has calved and they then should take him the *indahan parmahan* = rice for the manager, sometimes accompanied with fish, or they should take food and drink for the young animal, *gagaton soburon.* Co-owners of cattle can exercise their rights by taking their turn in the management, *masiolatan,* and in this way benefit of the dung, and working the animals in the field can be enjoyed alternately.

The *solu,* the long canoe, 30 feet and upward in length in which marketeers of Samosir and the neighbourhood set out to the markets on the shore of Lake Toba, are mostly jointly owned by men who alternately exercise their right to use the boats over a given period. The marketeers are their own paddlers and pay a small indemnity to the owners of the craft. (These craft are more and more being ousted by small motor boats.) Each manager attends to the daily maintenance himself: the costs of heavy reparations must be borne jointly. If a part-owner becomes difficult because something in the conduct of his partners does not please him, and as a consequence he refuses to meet his part of the costs of maintenance, he is barred from using the craft until he is willing to conform to the *adat parripe-ripean.*

If a house is held in joint ownership, then it is similarly maintained jointly by the partners. If a partner who at the time is a co-inhabitant of the house, refuses to contribute to its maintenance, then he can be evicted. When separate parts of houses or shop buildings in the market are in different hands, they are not held in joint ownership.

CUSTODY AND MAINTENANCE

All goods can be given into the custody of another person. The general term is *palumehon* = to give into custody, *lume*. If land is taken into custody for another person, the term is *mangaramoti*, a form which occurs particularly in respect of absentees and minors.

Custody and maintenance are subject to some general rules. Goods taken into custody from another person remain the property of the owner, and he is responsible for any loss or damage suffered. Nothing more can be required of the custodian than such care for the goods as he would give were they his own property. If he acts accordingly, then the following saying is applicable to him: *ndang tarseat tangan ni paniopi* = the hand of a man who holds a thing must not be cut off, which means that he cannot be held responsible for what befalls the goods. This rule applies not only to long-term custody but also to short-term custody, *maniop*, of goods. Only when a custodian can be blamed for lack of care, can he be held responsible.

Damage caused by the goods is the owner's responsibility if no fault can be found with the custodian. If he is shown not to be blameless, then he is held to be responsible.

Movable goods given into custody are, as a rule, handed over. Land is given into custody by indication either verbally or by special act. When cattle are given into custody, the custodian frequently gives a small sum of money to the owner as a *tobus tali*, or *batahi* = redeemer of rope, or whip, with which he takes over the custodianship of a buffalo, cow, or a horse, because he wants the dung, milk, etc.

A prerequisite of custody and maintenance is the use of the goods and of any fruits thereof. If a custodian manages land he may plant it; if a house, he can live in it; the dung, milk and stud fee of cattle are his though he does not usually have the use of the animals for working his fields. He may also have disposal over the goods to a certain extent, for example, he can give out a rice-field for sharecropping, surrender it to a member of the in-dwelling *marga* under the *parripean*-rules; he can give a gold ornament as a pledge. He must then remember, however, that he must always hold himself in readiness to return the goods to their owner or must be in a position to replace them if the user would

be inconvenienced by their unexpected withdrawal. The first demand
is, naturally, a more forcible one than the second. If land is attached
and the custodian fails to release it, then the principle holds good that
it reverts to the owner, and the third party concerned tails on behind
with his claim. In respect of other and more easily replaced goods, the
original custodian and the man who received the goods from him will
possibly both be held responsible. Nobody may derive benefit from goods
held in custody in such a way as to profit unlawfully: it would then be
a case of the hedge devouring the rice which it encloses, *handang mangan
eme*. Alienation of goods held in custody, *manggadis lume*, is regarded
as a more serious offence than theft.

When goods are restored to their owner after a long period of being
in custody, then the owner can give the custodian an *upa mangaramoti*,
a fee for his faithfull custodianship. This happens particularly when a
man who has been absent for a long time returns to his village and
withdraws from his *uaris* the land left in his charge and the *uaris* returns
it unaltered and without objection. It also happens when a close kinsman
of a deceased person places the land and other things which he has
managed for the young children at their disposal when they have grown
up. The custodian may well have drawn benefit regularly from the
goods, but the fact that he has not mismanaged them, that, for example,
he has desisted from inventing ingenious devices, *manghaliangi*, in order
to appropriate the goods himself (*haliang* = round about) during the
long period which his custodianship lasted, is an inducement to the
owner to reward the custodian when the latter gives him back his goods.

Payment of a reward for custodianship is often ordered by a judge as
a means of reaching a friendly arrangement, or to effect a mediatory
settlement between two people who both lay claim to a property that
has been in the hands of one of them for a long time. Obscurity and
carelessness in entering into contracts; allowing someone the use of
goods for a long time; allowing a following generation to have the use
of goods; and similar circumstances, can often result in property being
in the hands of someone who, in good faith, imagines it is his. Suddenly
he is faced with a strong claim by another. His unwillingness to surrender
the goods and his inclination to pretence, sophistry, *sidalian*, in an
endeavour to keep them, can often be overcome by treating him as a
custodian whose good services should be rewarded. In a legal situation
like this, the maxim regarding the return of goods (see p. 310) naturally
applies. The last line of the maxim can also read: *songon i didjalo*,

songon i ma dipaulak = goods must be returned in the same condition as they were received.

PROFIT-SHARING

Profit-sharing is a form of taking goods into custody. It occurs particularly in respect of cattle from which no daily benefit accrues, pigs, horses at large, etc., and the reward for looking after them must, therefore, consist of a part of their young. The owner of the animal calls this form of custodianship *pamahanhon* = giving out into care, while the custodian calls it *mamahani* = to care for. There are various forms of compensation. I noted the following forms: on Samosir the *pamahan* = profit-sharer, received a quarter, *sanghae,* of every foal of a mare; in Toba (Balige), he received one foal and the owner would take two. On Samosir, if a woman pastures four sheep, she receives a quarter of one of the lambs dropped. The custodian who is at the same time part-owner of a *sanghae* of a pig, receives half the farrow. Local usage and local circumstances provide a variety of forms to the *adat mamahan,* which can also be modified in many ways by mutual agreement.

SHARE-CROPPING

Share-cropping agreements, *mamola-pinang,* literally, to split an areca nut, will be dealt with for preference in this chapter.

In this form of contract, a plot of land, mostly a wet rice-field, but it can also be a benzoin garden, is transferred temporarily and accepted, with the object of cultivating it, maintaining it and planting it and harvesting it, with the proviso that a previously agreed part of the crop be handed over to the owner. The right of a share-cropper, *na mamola-pinang,* does not extend beyond the right to work the land. He cannot hand it over to another on any terms whatsoever, neither on a share-cropping basis, as a pledge, as payment in *sindor* as part of a marriage payment, nor as anything else. He is only entitled to part of the harvest. Kinsmen and affines will, therefore, never object to land being given out to share-cropping, *dibola-pinanghon,* neither will they lay a preferential claim to being share-croppers themselves. In Toba, however, for self-evident reasons, a son-in-law who lives far from the parents-in-law's village will for preference let his parents-in-law or his brothers-in-law use his *pauseang*-fields in the vicinity of their village as share-croppers. Recently it has become common for money-lenders, *parhepeng,* to take a rice-field as pledge against a sum requested as a loan and then to give it out on a share-cropping basis to the *partano* (the owner) with the proviso that the portion of the harvest that must be handed over to them will obtain as the interest. The money-lender then has the right to deal with the land as a *partano* if the debtor defaults in his part of the share-cropping bargain.

The owner of land given out to share-cropping usually supplies the seed and sometimes the draught animals for the ploughing.

The basis of the division of the harvest between the man who provides the land and the share-cropper, is usually one-for-one or one-two. This varies according to the region and it is also dependent on the extent to which there are other opportunities for remunerative work for people who do not have land of their own. Further details will be found in the relevant chapters of Ypes' work.

LOANING AND BORROWING

Borrowing, *mangindjam*, and loaning, *paindjamhon*, of goods must be distinguished from placing in custody by the fact that the use to which the borrower is to put the goods comes to the forefront. It is usually the would-be-borrower who takes the initiative in contracting this legal relationship. *Manarbut* also means 'to borrow' and expresses particularly the benefit and advantage which is expected to accrue from the loan. Agricultural implements and household utensils are loaned between members of a house and of the village on a footing of daily reciprocal help, but more valuable goods are also borrowed, such as buffaloes, for ploughing and pieces of gold for settling debts. Such loans are more in the nature of help in need. The temporary loaning, *pasarbuthon*, of land to a friend and neighbour does occur to a limited extent (in Toba it is called *manoro-noro?*), and confers a right to the harvest and nothing more.

The general rules applicable to custody and maintenance also apply to loan contracts, and in practice both legal forms frequently merge. I have already dealt with borrowing from necessity without first asking. Borrowing valuable objects from kinsmen, affines and friends is a frequent occurrence, the aim being to settle a debt, or to give a pledge for a marriage payment, *manindorhon*.

There is a striking form of borrowing which is termed *maisolat* = to live free of financial obligations in another man's house, which frequently occurs in those villages where the idea of letting houses, or a part of a house, such as is done in the market, has not yet penetrated. It is quite possible in the old-fashioned Batak dwelling where it is the custom to have each of the four corners occupied by individual families. There are a variety of reasons for this form of borrowing: the desire of the village chief and of his lineage to increase the number of co-dwellers; the craving to keep all those born in the village community together; the desire to provide shelter for someone who, because of a death or a sickness, wishes to leave a neighbouring village, etc. The *paisolat* does not necessarily stand in a subordinate relationship to the master of the house; he can be a *dongan sadjabu* = co-dweller, with the same household rights and obligations as the other co-dwellers who are joint-owning partners. Only when he is the co-inhabitant of someone else's corner, which also occurs, is he not a *dongan sadjabu,* with his own house rights in relation to the dwellers in the other living corners. Here again, local usages deviate considerably.

RENDERING SERVICES: PEONS, SLAVES, ARTISANS

In olden times there was considerably less wage-earning than now. The rich and powerful assured the regular services of subordinates by peonage and slavery. A peon, called *parutang ginomgom* = debtor under the control of a person, placed himself, and his family as pledges to the creditor against the large debts he had contracted. If a man was a *djolma mandingding*, he only had to go and live in the creditor's village and had to assist him in important works, such as cultivating land, repairing the village wall, and so on. In his spare time he could try to scrape enough together towards discharging his debt. If, however, a man had incurred a debt that had increased continually, or if he had contracted gambling debts that he could not pay, he became a *djolma mangadop* = a dweller in the house of his creditor, and had to place all his working force at his creditor's disposal without in any way thereby diminishing his debt. Kinsmen and affines could buy such a man out of these kinds of peonage, which fact distinguished a peon from a slave proper, the *hatoban masak*. Peonage in any form was forbidden after the establishment of the Netherlands Indies Government and all traces of its having existed have now been expunged, except in South Tapanuli where the social structure which existed in olden times has, up to now, prevented a complete merging of the freed and the free. In Toba any reference to former peonage or to slavery is regarded as an offence and is punished. The surrendering of young daughters as menial helps in a household, for which service they are given food but no wages, does, however, still occur. Such a girl is called the *parumaen di losung* (see p. 187). She is either surrendered as payment of her father's debt, or against the receipt of cash by her father.

The hiring of labour is increasing at present. For example, since many of the inhabitants of the Silindung Valley have migrated in recent years to the Dairi Country and Angkola, there has been a constant shortage of labour at harvest time in Silindung and this has induced a number of Tobanese to go there during the harvest season to offer their services for remuneration in money or rice. A number of seasonal workers from Toba and Samosir in particular, go to the plantations on Sumatra's East Coast. The money the Administration gets from the buying off of statute labour is for the greater part spent again on wages. Hired labour will continue to rise in importance as the supply of money and its free movement increases. Skilled labourers are now also more frequently being paid in money. Formerly a smith who made and repaired simple agricultural implements, guns and weapons, etc., was rewarded in part with a *djambar* when a beast was slaughtered; it was given to the *pande* = the particularly skilled one, by many a man to whom he had given his services. A contractor-carpenter who provided the wood for building a house and who did that part of the work for which particular skill was necessary, could use this service to find good spouses for his sons and daughters by settling the terms of a marriage payment when the building contract was discussed; or he could look forward to a plot of land being given him permanently, *pate*, as his remuneration. As a member of the in-dwelling *marga* he could hardly hope to obtain land otherwise. But these forms of remuneration are being superseded by payment with money. Modern relationships, such as that between car-owner and chauffeur, are established entirely on a money basis, the example for which is provided by the practices of Westerners and Chinese. The village school teachers of the Christian Mission, who are often also pastors at the religious meetings in the place where they are stationed, however, still frequently receive part of their salary in kind.

BUYING AND SELLING

Buying and selling is primarily the exchange of money against movable goods. To buy is *manuhor*; to sell is *manggadis,* and as far as movable goods are concerned, these terms indicate that the transfer is permanent. Such goods are usually handed over immediately, but even if this is not done, the contract is valid. A bond can be paid when an agreement of sale is concluded.

If a house is to be sold, the fellow members of the villager who is selling it, the *isi ni huta,* have a preferential right above people from elsewhere; they will have assisted more or less in its erection, though formerly more than at present now that there are carpenters to do such work. The seller must inform, *mangalimbehon,* the villagers that he wants to dispose of the house. If a fellow villager offers a reasonable price, then the house cannot be sold to anyone from elsewhere, neither can it be taken away by the owner should he go to live somewhere else. The offer of a fellow villager can be somewhat lower than that from an outsider. If a house is sold to someone from another village, then a small part of the *upa domu-domu* can be given to the co-villagers as an acknowledgement that the sale has taken place. Here and there, it is proper that the seller provides them with the *indahan pamonggar* = the meal of rice, at which the forthcoming removal of the house from their village is made known to them. It is also a warning to the villagers and to their children to get out of the way while the house is being dismantled in case they get hurt.

In Silindung and its environs, it is proper at the sale or removal of a house to hand over a quarter of the value of the house as an *upa radja* to the village chief, where the *huta* members have co-operated in its erection. In respect of houses that were built wholly for wages, a small compensation can be paid to the villagers for the removal of the house from their community. Elsewhere the *upa radja* is also due, but under what circumstances it should be paid and how much it should be are points about which there is some uncertainty. The seller gives the buyer the *balatuk* = ladder, as a token that the house has been transferred. If such a formal transfer has not taken place, then the buyer himself takes away the ladder, by which act he places himself in possession of the house. Once this has been done, then anything that may have been left in the house belongs to the new owner.

Houses which are built in the market, along the wayside, and at cross roads, are not subject in all respects to this *adat gadison djabu* if they are outside the village — many villages nowadays do not have a wall. Many of these houses are built by skilled carpenters, and belong to people whose villages are situated some distance from the house itself. This means that the relationship between the small village community and the sphere of interest of the people who own the house may be lost. In how far such houses must be reckoned as belonging to the village of which their owner is an inhabitant and subject to the rules prevailing there, is dependent upon local usage and on the circumstances. Here again, there is a tendency to individualise.

In a shop building (Mal. *toko*), which consists of *pintu* = separate sections, each *pintu* can have its own owner. A dwelling house outside the village can also be divided up by separating walls or by boarding up doors, and these sections can be let separately and even sold. When someone who owns one of the parts of a building desires to sell it, form ordains that he must first offer it to the owners of the other parts, *mangandehon*. Neglect to so do does not, however, nullify a contract concluded with a third party.

When cattle are sold, they are not subject to the rules which limit freedom of disposal to the same extent as those applying to houses, unless the animal is jointly owned. After a sale of cattle has been concluded and the beasts have been taken away, a part of the *upa domu-domu* is sometimes given to the villagers, but this is not to be understood as an acknowledgement of their preferential right, but only as a gift of notification. This bears on the fact that owning cattle and agreements concerning cattle are village affairs about which the inhabitants desire to be, and should be, properly informed. Cattle in particular, because of their mobility, must be openly disposed of in public so that everyone can know about it. When a small whip, *batahi,* is handed over with the animal, which still happens in Toba, this shows that the control and responsibility have been transferred. I was told that the seller continues to be responsible until a beast has been led a distance of about 300 feet from his village: this seems to me to be an embellishment. As mentioned earlier, the *domu-domu* often act as intermediaries at the sale of cattle, and the contract is often confirmed by the payment of a small sum of money as a bond. This also applies when dogs are sold for hunting or for slaughter. The *domu-domu* are also used when crops, fruit trees and timber are sold. Benzoin from regularly cultivated gardens must be sold openly in public. The reason for this is that the gardens are a long way from the villages and cannot be constantly guarded; they are not clearly separated by individual boundaries; they are not tapped daily but only a couple of times a year; and as a consequence it is easy to steal the benzoin from the tree, *mamorus*. There must, therefore, be mutual confidence, and the public sale gives a measure of mutual control. In the *sidjamapolang* region, where the benzoin gardens form large solid forests, there is even the need for sale-centres, *pangkalan*, where all the benzoin from the area is offered for export. The need for regulating the benzoin trade is clearly shown in Appendix IV. A contract whereby the right to tap a benzoin plantation for a number of successive harvests is transferred against a sum of money, is called 'selling the leaf', *manggadis bulung*.

The term for the sale of human beings, which was formerly done, was *manggadis djau,* of which compound, *djau* means 'stranger'; the second line of the *umpama* mentioned on p. 140 sometimes reads: *na oto tu pardjauan* = the stupid one ends up abroad. *Manggadis djau* thus probably means to hand over a person with the object of taking him a considerable distance away in order to make it practically impossible for his kinsmen to end his slavery by ransoming him, or in any other way.

With regard to land: when it is sold without the right of redemption, *ndang sitobuson be,* the permanence of the transaction is indicated by the term *pate* or *sipate-pate*. One might expect to find the term *manggadis pate* used in this context, but this is not always regarded as being sufficiently definitive of the irrevocable character of the sale and therefore the term *manggadis horbo* is often used. This term is borrowed from the sale of a buffalo and is more definitive. The compound *manggadis pate* must be of as recent an origin as the permanent sale of land, in the sense of alienation against a sum of money, without the right of redemption. The term has predecessors such as *libe sipate-pate,* while *mamatehon* = to transfer permanently (*pate*), a plot of land to another person, refers to the conversion of a pledge relationship into a permanent transfer. There are older terms for the permanent transfer of land in addition to *mangalean* (see p. 318): in Toba there is *manggabehon,* and in Silindung, *marsialabane,* of which the first points to the formalities connected with the transfer, namely, the wishing of good fortune, *gabe,* to the new owner to whose life the land will henceforth be bound, and the second to the distribution of the *sialabane,* the gift of notification, to the co-dwellers of the former owner's village, so that they know what has been removed from their community. In Toba there is also the term *manombahon* which points to the *somba* = reverential homage, with which a plot of land is offered in settlement of a debt which is much greater than the value of the land; and *mangupahon,* which is the allocation of land by the *hula-hula* to the *boru.* In some regions land was not redeemable if it had been alienated in payment of a gambling debt.

When the actual transfer of land is made, it should be attended by buyer and seller setting foot on the land, *mandegehon,* for the purpose of showing the boundary posts and introducing the new owner to the owners of adjoining plots. Further requirements and formalities will be found in Ypes' work.

HIRING

The hiring and letting of land and property, that is, the surrender of the use thereof for a certain period of time for a monetary remuneration, is modern and is still lacking its own definite character. The Batak term for this form of hiring is *mangongkosi*, of which the stem is *ongkos* from the Dutch word *onkosten*, expenses. Its purport is: having the use of something for which one pays with money (rice can also be used in payment in place of money). The term is used in respect of hiring houses in the market, and building plots. The relationship between hirer and letter can be considered as being subject to the general rules applicable to custody and maintenance. The form is still open to typical limitations. I once saw that at first hand when someone wanted to set up a rice-hulling mill driven by motor power on land which appeared to be only in part the man's own *golat*, and for the rest was the joint property of his smaller kinship group; I proposed that he hired the part belonging to his *sisolhot* for a fixed yearly sum so long as he used it, but this idea was not well received by his kinsmen. "This is not done between next of kin", they said.

On such particular questions as to whether buying breaks a contract of hiring, or whether there is a right of preference of *uaris* and neighbours, there is, in my opinion, still no answer to be given. So long as this remains the position, disputes will have to be adjudicated by a reasonable weighing up of the interests of the different persons concerned. The term *sohe*, known in Barus and Silindung, and which, according to van der Tuuk's dictionary, stems from the Malay word *tjukai*, denotes the levy which a man can charge when he has made the use of something available to another, for example, rental due for the use of space in the market, *sohe ni inganan dibagasan onan*; the payment to be made to the leader of an organised gambling party, etc.

MONEY DEBTS: UTANG SINGIR

That money debts were numerous and that they were subject to individual treatment technically, appears from the large vocabulary relating to them. Besides the term *marsali* = borrowing with nothing but the obligation to pay back the value of the object received, there is *manganahi* = interest bearing, and *mangurang*, which means the same thing, the interest being termed *anak* = son, or *hua*; hence the term *manghuai*. The term *mangongkosi* = to 'hire' money, to loan money on an interest bearing basis, is a more recent usage. Borrowing rice with the obligation to increase the amount when it is returned, is called *morlali;* to buy on credit is called *marsambut;* to waive a substantial part of a money claim is called *mangalaplap;* to ask for remission of a balance outstanding is *manelpang.* For immediate payment in hard cash, there are the synonymous terms: *terter, tedjek,* and *deter;* to pay in instalments is termed *manopihi* = to settle in fragments, *topik;* to receive money piece meal is called *manderder;* compensation is termed *tembes,* and cession, *legot.* For security there are several words: *tahan, singkoram, daga-daga (gada-gada).*

Formerly a great part of transactions regarding money were those contracted at gambling parties where special rules supplementing the general rules were sometimes established by the organiser of the party. But other reasons for money transactions were trading in cattle, the marriage settlement, fines, etc., to which must now be added the import and export trade, seasonal work, the cultivation of cash crops and the sale (or hire) of cars.

INTEREST STIPULATIONS

Outsiders who come into contact with the Batak rate of interest, as a rule, find it very high. Compared with elsewhere, 20, 30, 40 per cent. and sometimes more, per annum is indeed high. The position is, however, often misjudged. The Batak who has money does not yet make the most of the opportunities his money presents of getting interest on it. If something is given as a redeemable pledge in payment of a money debt, no interest is calculated when it is redeemed, even if the pledge is a gold ornament, a weapon, or cattle. If a long outstanding debt is finally settled by 'attaching' a still unmarried little daughter, the claim with which the child is burdened will be determined at a fixed amount, irrespective of the length of time before the girl can marry.

If a precursor to the marriage payment and a precursor to the *pauseang* — both of which usually differ considerably in value and productivity — are exchanged at a child betrothal, including a betrothal resulting from a debt relationship, then no interest is calculated even if later a divorce results from quarrels. No interest is calculated on a sum of money, payment of which is ordered by a judicial judgement — though many a European President of a Customary Court often tries to force the issue in the opposite direction — for the period between the day of the judgement and the day of payment, not even if there is a possibility that the debtor will have to delay considerably in paying up. The underlying idea here is, that in the old Batak society, which was not a mass of separate individuals but a community bound together in many ways, money, which was, moreover, scarce and could neither be a general medium of exchange nor a daily basis for a widely extended system of credit, had another sphere of operation than that which it has in modern society. This will continue to be so until the principal features of modern society become operative among the Toba Batak.

Interest was, and is, especially claimed when the aim of borrowing is to use the money for commercial purposes or to gain profit in another way. A man who places his money at the disposal of another for such purposes — though there are few who will offer or be able to do so — asks a high rate of interest. The man who borrows money probably sees there is a chance to use profitably a medium which, because of its scarcity, not many possess. If the borrower fails through no fault of his own, he usually finds that his creditor is prepared to reach a reasonable compromise and to be lenient; or, if his creditor is not helpful, the borrower will place the facts of his distressed circumstances, with a measure of success, before the judge.

It is often stipulated that payment of interest is to be made in rice and not in money. The usual condition is that the interest is to be paid per month, but the interest does not itself become interest bearing if the monthly payment is not made.

There are, however, contracts which are definitely onerous, though they occur rarely, which recall the time when failure to honour them could lead to the debtor becoming a slave if he could not get assistance from his kinsmen and affines. In these contracts interest was reckoned on the basis of, for example, 'three becomes four', *na tolu gabe opat*. Worse still, however, were, and are, the loans of rice because of failure of the harvest, which, in Toba Holbung were, and still are, contracted according to the rule that 'one becomes two'.

If no interest is to be calculated, then the creditor will demand that he is completely safeguarded as regards costs, and that he has security against the trouble which the recovery of the money loaned would entail — a debtor so easily gets himself involved in all kinds of complications. The creditor will then require that the debtor accept any trouble and the costs related to collecting the money, *nasa haboratan laho mandjalo*.

MONEY LOANS

The method of contracting money loans is discussed on p. 298.

If a group of people borrow money, then, in principle, each is responsible for the entire amount. Assigning, *legot*, a claim for a debt is only a legal act if the debtor is previously made known to his new creditor, *padjumola*, and assigning a debt requires the consent of the creditor. Debts recalled by a dying man and his acquainting his heirs regarding them have been dealt with on p. 277. The permanent transfer of a plot of land, *manombahon*, as settlement of a debt, *parsaean ni utang*, is dealt with on p. 312. The pledging of one's own or another man's land, *manindorhon*, will be dealt with shortly. For a man to pay another man's debts without his consent, does not mean that he will derive any advantage from the terms of the debt.

SECURITY AND PLEDGING

Placing oneself as surety in default of payment of a debt; giving movable goods as security, and probably also attaching a still unbetrothed daughter, are to be regarded as being older forms of giving security for a debt, than using land as a redeemable pledge for an already long-standing debt, for a new one or for the pledging of land against an immediate receipt of a sum of money, and also, probably the most recent form: assigning land as security for a debt, but without surrendering the right of usufruct.

Enough has been said about peonage and 'attaching' an unmarried daughter, and I will now discuss placing property, movable and unmovable as security for a debt. Movable and unmovable goods, indicated as security, can remain in the hands of the debtor, the general term then being *tahan ni hepeng* or *singkoram* or *daga-daga* (*gada-gada*). If the goods are placed in the hands of the creditor, then a pledging agreement has come to the fore. The goods are then *sindor* or *gade* (in respect of land there are other terms used). This form of pledging is called *manindorhon* or *manggadehon*, and again, in respect of land other terms are used. Pledging land will be dealt with separately.

Cattle, as far as I know, are not used as security for a debt and they are not pledged for a debt. Objects which act as security are almost always placed in the hands of the creditor. Frequently, they are gold ornaments, if the money debt is somewhat considerable, and, since such objects are generally old things of small commercial value, they are less and less being used as pledges. A pledge can also be a utensil belonging to the debtor, which is of very little value, but of which it is generally known that it is his. This means that the creditor has the desired security because the debtor will pay up quickly since he will not be too anxious that the object remains long in the hands of another. This is probably partly due to the idea that something of the personality of the owner has been communicated to the object and thus gives the creditor power over the debtor. This usage is, however, dying out. If a pledgee needs money, it is not considered proper that he repledges the object to a third party without first giving the original owner of the pledge the opportunity to redeem it, *martobus*: this is often neglected. When a number of transfers of this kind have been effected the pledge sometimes disappears completely from the view of the first contractors, a situation that gives rise to insoluble puzzles. Once I heard the first holder of a gold pledge sentenced to restore its full value, determined on the owner's oath, less the amount of his claim.

If a garden, a house or a *lapo* = small eating house, with its contents, etc., are given as *tahan* = security, then they usually remain in the hands of the debtor. A house in the market can be placed in the hands of a creditor and he then acquires the right to live in it or to let it, so that he can gain some profit from the money he has laid out; it is then also *sindor* = redeemable pledge.

A creditor is exclusively responsible for movable goods placed as *sindor* or *gade* with him. He is held responsible for any damage to them if he fails to prove absence of negligence. The loss of an object through no fault of the holder, must be borne by the owner; the extent to which the holder is responsible will be determined by the circumstances. The *mara* = risk of damage to a house or crops that are in the hands of a creditor, for example, an accidental fire, is not his responsibility; the debtor is responsible and he remains in debt to the creditor. One often finds this expressed in agreements in the statement made by the debtor thus: "The responsibility for this pledge is mine, *mara ni gade i di au do*".

If a money debt is contracted which stipulates interest, and the object handed over brings no profit, for example, a gold pledge, or when the security remains in the hands of the debtor, then neglect to pay the interest will gradually reduce the margin on the pledge. In precisely phrased contracts, therefore, there is usually a time-clause, or the stipulation that the debtor will have defaulted if he gets behind with one or more of the interest payments, and the creditor can then dispose of the pledge. In more slipshod contracts, it is only stipulated that the pledge can be disposed of in the case of 'failure to pay'. Such a broad clause can be disadvantageous for the creditor. Although it is not said in so many words, however, it is generally always the intention that default on the part of the debtor gives the creditor the right to dispose of the pledge. If he holds the object as *gade*, then it is usually said that he can have it valued, *asam*, which means that he can sell it for a reasonable price as assessed by a third party: it is then lost to the debtor.

Of land that remains in the hands of the debtor, for which the term *borok* or *borot* (from Dutch 'borg' = guarantee) is used besides *tahan* and *singkoram*, it is also said that the creditor can take possession if the debtor defaults. The manner in which this is stated varies considerably. In written documents, among others, I found the following: N. is then entitled to sell it or to cultivate it, *N. marhuasa manggadis manang mangula*; N. can take the land as settlement of the debt, *N. boi buatonna bahen garar ni hepeng i*; the field is then to be transferred direct to N., *torus ma hauma i sahat tu N.* In spite of these various but positive ways of expressing the principle, in practice the purport of all of them is, however, that the creditor can reimburse himself in the event of the debtor defaulting, from the land itself either by repledging it to a third party, giving it out on a share-cropping basis to another, or by taking it for his own use, until the debtor redeems it. Permanent transfer, *pate*, of the land to the creditor should the debtor default, is not the intention of a *tahan*-contract. Were such the case, then it would mean a more complete loss of the land, simply for the want of money, than would be the case in the contract of land pledging which creates a closer tie between the money-lender and the land. Fields which one holds in pledge and one's own fields for that matter, are bound by the same formulae. That a debtor is sometimes compelled from sheer necessity to transfer the land permanently in final settlement of a long-standing debt relationship, does not alter the original nature of the contract.

If the creditor has to reimburse himself from the security, then, according to the terms of the agreement and the nature of the contract, a special agreement must be made. Whatever the creditor receives in excess of the debt must be returned to the debtor, and if the proceeds are less, then the debtor has to make good the deficiency. On this point the agreements are usually perfectly clear and, though it is in the nature of a *tahan*-contract that if the debtor is without doubt in default, the creditor can take possession of the security that is not then in his hands, or can dispose of such security as he does hold in order to reimburse himself; nevertheless, a creditor seldom resorts to this. This lenient attitude is partly due to the fact that such a threat is not always meant seriously when people who are related to each other in a variety of ways are involved. It must also partly be attributed to the influence of the

22

Government which has designed that the intervention of the Customary Courts must always be invoked to obtain the right to dispose of a security. I even found some documents containing the clause that a creditor could effect the sale of the security he held without submitting a request to a court, *timbangan ni rapat*, but ... the approval of the Government, *pamarintah*, had to be obtained. The hand that the Government has stretched over the private law of the Batak indeed reaches far.

It is also in the nature of a *tahan*-contract, that a particular object of property, movable or otherwise, shall be placed as security for a particular debt, and, therefore, such a *tahan*-contract creates the privilege for the creditor of reimbursing himself from it, or of being paid out of the goods bound to him before all other creditors. Since debts of some size, when they are contracted in the village, are not usually without security — trading debts will be discussed later — the total of the debts that a man contracts does not usually exceed that of his assets. We have already noted that the village chief should see to it that a debtor does not encumber any item of his property that is already encumbered.

A man can place his land and his property at the disposal of another as security for his debts. There are, as already shown, cases where the approval of a third party is necessary before land is attached, either because the ties binding the land to its former legal owner have not been completely severed, or because the cultivator holds it under the *parripean*-law.

There is no possibility for a debtor, in whose hands the security remains, of selling it with the obligation on the buyer to clear off the debt. The debtor is not free to alienate his mortgaged property, nor can he give it in pledge. Should he do so, then he has committed a fraudulent act or has acted with a flagrant disregard for another man's interests. The man who concludes this last contract becomes the injured party, because he has not ascertained the precise legal position of the goods, unless the earlier contract was not concluded according to *adat, dibagasan adat*.

PLEDGING LAND

For the details of all the aspects of pledging land the reader is referred to Ypes' work.

In this Chapter, I will only endeavour to throw some light on the financial aspects of the contract of which the origin is the pledger's need of ready cash.

First, the terms which are used. In view of the preceding, the term *sindor* should be dealt with first. This term is used particularly when a plot of land is given as a pledge to settle existing financial obligations of one kind or another. If, for example, a marriage payment, a *pangoli ni anak*, is paid partly in cattle or in other goods and if, in addition, the *parboru* is given a wet rice-field as a pledge, as a provisional settlement of the remainder, it is called *manindorhon*. The land is then *sindor ni hepeng* = a pledge for money. The term *sindor* is not, however, applied only to this form and method of pledging.

Manggadehon = to give as a pledge, *gade,* is used in respect of land as well as movable goods. The word *gade* shows its affinity with a foreign word, namely, the Malay word *gadai*.

A genuine Batak term is *dondon,* which like *dokdok* means, weighing heavily on, pressing upon. *Mandondon* = to press heavily on something; *padondonhon* = to press one thing on another, which can be said of objects pressed against each other, but figuratively it can be used in respect of land pledged against money; the money presses on the land. A *hauma dondon* = an encumbered field; *pandondon* = the debt that presses on the field; *padondonhon* = raising money by handing over one's land. The word *dondon* (with its derivates) is not in common use for the *sindor*-form just mentioned.

Neither *sindor* nor *dondon* has derivate forms by which the act of the pledgee receiving the pledge from the pledger can be expressed. The pledgee defines his part in the transaction by saying: *"hudjalo sindor hauma i* = I have acquired this field as *sindor"*, or *"dondon di ahu hauma i* = I hold this field as *dondon"*.

Quite often land, usually a rice-field, is pledged for remarkably small sums of money or is left in pledge, notwithstanding the gradual increase in the value of the land. The harvest is then worth quite a good deal more that the current rate of interest. The reason for this, apart from kinship- and affinal relationships, friendship, etc., is that the pledger prefers not to borrow more on his land than he has need of since he might have difficulty in redeeming it. A pledge cannot be paid off gradually, and neither can a plot of land that has been pledged be redeemed piece-meal. On the other hand, however, if a man needs more money, then the amount of the loan already on the land can be increased, *pabagashon, manggurguri, manggodangi,* to deepen, to increase, to enlarge, respectively. As a rule, the pledgee, who wants to hold on to the land, will lend the pledger the additional money in order to prevent the redeeming and repledging to another person. It can, of course, happen that, because neither his kinsmen nor his affines are disposed to help him, a man gets into much financial difficulty and is finally compelled to surrender the land permanently and unredeemably, *mamatehon*, to the pledgee.

Redemption, *martobus*, cannot be effected before the clods of earth have been turned over twice, *balik bungki*, thus after two years, and must always be done after the harvest. It is then obligatory for the pledgee to surrender the land immediately. A year's respite can, however, be requested and granted, but the pledgee can never ask for an increase of the amount of the original loan because the land has increased in value in the meantime.

If the pledgee wants to have his money back and to return the land, then it is proper that he approaches the pledger first of all and asks him if he will take his land back: the pledger is not obliged to comply with the request. The *Patik dohot Uhum* also says that the pledger is not compelled to take back a rice-field because it has depreciated in value. I do not know of examples to the contrary in Toba, though there was a case in Padang Lawas of a man who wanted a field which he held in pledge to be redeemed because, as a result of an act of another man, no water reached it from the irrigation canals. The pledger turned a deaf ear to the request. However, his own village chief and that of the pledgee reached an agreement to redeem the field and to pledge it to another person. If the pledgee does not find the pledger prepared to redeem for some reason or another, then he has a right to repledge to a third party, for which operation there is no specific term, provided that he does not do so for an amount greater than he laid out originally. This does sometimes happen, but it is a fault, *sala tu adat*, which merits corrective measures.

We have already seen on p. 309 the complications which can result from repledging and the rules then applicable. These rules do not obtain if a chain of repledging has been effected as a result of which the original pledger again takes the land in pledge from the last pledgee: the land is than said to have "reverted to its grandfather, *mulak tu ompuna*".

Pledging for a stipulated period (of long duration) hardly ever occurs. In the one case that I came across, no stipulation had been made as to what was to happen after the time had expired.

I learnt from a datum from Dolok Sanggul the extent to which the tie between the pledger and his land can continue between the time he pledges his land and the time he redeems it. This element does not apply in Toba with its numberless pledgings and repledgings. In Dolok Sanggul when the annual agricultural offering, *mangase bondar* (cp. *asean taon*, p. 68), which in some regions is held regularly, takes place, the pledger, if he was the person who first cleared the land, can take precedence over the pledgee, if he wishes, and can be the *suhut*, the leader of the offering-ceremony which pertains to everything concerning the field in question. I enquired in vain about this on Samosir.

I have already said on p. 271 that a pledged field is regarded as belonging to the estate of a deceased person. The *sisolhot* (*uaris*) of a man who leaves the village, or cluster of villages, to which he belongs and who pledges his land to a third party, always bear in mind that they can discharge the debt, *utang*, that burdens the land. Two people can make an agreement in respect of a field which is held in pledge by a third party, that it will not be redeemed by the pledger but by the third party who will then own the land. The man who has acquired the land as a pledge must bear in mind that it always lies under the threat of redemption, since the original *partano* has not been deprived of his rights: his land is still to him, *haumanghu na marutang* = my land upon which a debt rests.

STANDING SURETY

Placing collateral security is often coupled with a personal guarantee, of which the purpose is not primarily that it will serve to supplement any deficiency in the collateral security, but as a guarantee for the accuracy of the debtor's statements; as an earnest of his intensions; and as a guarantee of the rightness of his later actions. The man who acts as a guarantor is the *pangamai* = the one who will act as 'father' to the debtor and who will keep an eye on him so that he will not do anything wrong. The guarantor is also the *panahani* = the one who stands with his own goods as security for a debt contracted by the debtor, *manahani*, from *tahan*. Other terms that are applicable are: *manghangkungi* and *manaoni*, placing one's own goods as security: the guarantor is called *taon* = the one who shoulders the burden. If the debtor fails to pay, the guarantor will be called upon forthwith to meet the claim. The term *taon* is used mostly when no collateral security besides the personal guarantee is placed — which can also happen — but the terms are interchangeable. The obligation of meeting, if necessary, the debtor's payment is expressed in the following maxim:

ripak-ripak ni saung, aos-aos ni ansuan;
ia olo gabe taon, olo na manggarar utang.

A worn out curtain, a used spade.

Whosoever offers to be a guarantor must also be prepared to pay the debt.

After the guarantor has settled the debt, the debtor is then accountable to him. The guarantor has first preference to be reimbursed out of the collateral security. Sometimes a debtor does not pay his creditor, but pays the guarantor who then pays the creditor and thus clears the commitment. In many cases the guarantor is a kinsman, an affine or the debtor's village chief.

INSOLVENCY

I have already remarked several times that it is not usual in the villages for a man to incur debts of which the total amount exceeds his assets. In his small village he is always surrounded by kinsmen or friends who take care to some extent that he does not kick over the traces and, if necessary, are prepared to stand by him. Repeated failure of the harvest or other disasters, and, especially in olden times, losses at gambling can, however, lead to debts being incurred that are beyond the financial capacity of the debtor. Peonage was the only solution in the *Pidari* time, or the debtor fled the country overnight, *bungkas borngin,* and then his chief took his property and used as much of it to pay the debts as suited his own interests. To quote the relevant maxim:

> *habang lali ndang habang tungko;*
> *habang tungko ndang habang tano;*
> should the kite fly away, the stump on which he perched remains;
> should the stump also fly away, the ground in which it stood still remains.

Such land frequently also comprised the paternal heritage which had already been given to a brother of the man who had fled.

At the present time there is no clearly developed law in respect of regulating an insolvent estate. There is an urgent need for appropriate rules because insolvency is occurring more often as a result of commercial dealings with non-Bataks. One of the difficulties is that the debts which a trader contracts in the villages with his friends and kinsmen are covered in the Batak fashion by pledging and security, while the debts contracted elsewhere, with expatriate trading firms, for a great part rest on confidence, so that the one group of creditors, usually the main one, are in a weaker position than the other if the business miscarries. Another difficulty is that the circle of kinsmen around the debtor, who can maintain some control over commitments that are contracted within the village, often remain completely ignorant of the nature and extent of the obligations contracted elsewhere, and as a result they are but little inclined to be held responsible for the goings-on of a member of their group. They will try to salvage as much as possible for the family if the business venture of a member of a family fails. It is therefore desirable, for the time being at any rate, that trade credit should be limited to small amounts or should be covered in the same way as Batak debts. If, then, the debtor is not able to handle his affairs properly, it will be easier for a judge to reach a settlement between the creditors which will take into account all claims and interests and will give to each a fair part of the assets.

CORPORATIONS AND ASSOCIATIONS

Societies and associations which are independent units with their own objectives, their own legal relationships, their own administration — all of which elements can exist separately or in combination — and sometimes having their own property and their own responsibility, have always been known to the Batak. The genealogical relationships have always predominated. These units work best if they are only composed of kinsmen who form the larger and smaller lineages, *marga*-branches, *marga* and tribal groups as described in Chapter I, A. The tie which binds such a unit is the descent of all the members from a common ancestor who desires to be honoured by his descendants. Each individual belongs, by virtue of his birth to a series of these societies which go back ultimately to the mythical Si Radja Batak. Transfer from one series to another is possible by adoption or, as already mentioned, by admission of a group and by changing *marga*, the one being done as seldom as the other. The specific aims of these kinship groups are defined by the offerings they have to make and the reverence which they pay to the ancestor, and the manner of doing so is differing from one region to another.

Due to the fact that they live together in their own village, cluster of villages, territories and tribal areas, numerous of these genealogical groups have naturally created legal relationships within the villages and within the territory which they occupy, into which they have admitted other people as co-dwellers, but where they are the masters and which they regard as their own. Absentees retain their interest in the wealth which consists of the land, the timber and the water by which their lineages are sustained, and they are always freely admitted to the village of their origin.

Besides these units, there are those that owe their existence to the irrigation of fields by streams, or by irrigation canals, *bondar*. These associations serve the fertility of these fields and protect them and are therefore units with distinct interests of their own, having their own internal organisation, their own administration, and their own legal rules. This is most conspicuous in regions such as Toba where, by much *pauseang* gifts to persons living far off and by much land pledging and other kinds of transfers, the dwelling place of a great number of the cultivators is no longer in or near the irrigated land. In other regions, however, the water interests go together with the other interests of the ruling lineage in village and territory, so much so that sometimes a close and independent unit based upon common water interests is hardly to be discerned, and the administration of the water for a good part coincides with that over land and the people.

The associations with freely chosen aims often seek to affiliate to some extent with existing units. It is even vitally important for them to do so. But if possible, such an association should not comprise too many units if it is to be successful. The Study Foundations of recent years, which aim to bring together as units whole *marga* and half a tribal group of thousands of *dongan,* are not likely to produce tangible results. Those smaller associations which only contain a smaller lineage, and which send the most intelligent boys of the group to school on the joint account, have been more successful. The trading societies, established about fifteen years ago, in which the common men, *na torop,* could participate by taking a few shares, have all rapidly broken down because of the elaborateness of the plans and insufficient organisation of the mutual control. The co-operation of a few financially sound people in small (trading) associations (Mal. *kongsi*) has, on the other hand, yielded fruit. For the time being, therefore, Batak societies and associations will continue to find their main basis in the co-operation of smaller groups living together from of old, or in groups consisting of a few unrelated individuals which set themselves a limited aim. The *parkongsian* — a new term in addition to *hatopan, hadosan, hasaoran,* etc., for associations — have regulations, *patik parpadanan,* which contain such provisions as the following:

the *boru gomgoman,* the in-dwelling *marga* can join, but the *anakhonta* = our own children, have preference (mutual relief fund of a co-dwelling lineage);

the amount that has already been paid out for the study of a boy who has died need not be paid back by the father, since the death concerns us all because we are of one lineage, *ai na rap matean do hita na saompu disi* (study fund of a *marga*-branch);

anyone who leaves our agricultural society of his own accord or anyone who is expelled from it because he has been contrary, receives back unaugmented what he has already put into the venture of laying out gardens. The same applies to those who have lost a father, or a spouse, and who wish to leave the society even though they could easily maintain their contributions; but widows and orphans who are not able to continue their contributions receive their previous payments back, increased by 10 per cent; and in the case of persons who, because of long illness, have had to suspend their co-operation, what is to be done will be decided later (agricultural society of the inhabitants of a small group of related villages);

the association may not become involved in disputes which may arise between its members (funeral society). Some other regulations of these societies are: a member may not sell or give away his part of the property of a society, not even if he moves elsewhere; a son of a member who has been expelled from a society, can be accepted if he so requests.

There are many societies of this kind. They usually have a large chosen board of managers in which the nuances of the group within which the society exists are expressed. High-sounding Dutch titles are usually used for the officers of the Board, the *pangula,* instead of Batak terms that could be used, such as *induk* or *ihutan* for President, *panurat* for Secretary, *simata-matai* for Directors, etc.

The property of the society can consist of cattle, money, land (in pledge), houses, etc. If regular contributions, *guguan,* are required, they can often be paid in rice. The handling of the money and the supervision of the society's property is a matter which has to be learned and is a matter in which the members do not yet fully trust one another. That is why security is demanded from the members of the Board who control the monies and the other parts of the property in case they should commit fraud. It is also for this reason that the limits of responsibility of the society, of the members of the Board and of the other members of the society are still so vague in respect of damage or the insolvency of the society. In my opinion, the underlying idea is that, if it has not otherwise been agreed, and if the members of the Board have acted with property, no one of them is more responsible than the ordinary members for the debts of the society. For all members of these *kongsi* are 'one in loss, one in profit', *sisada hamagoan, sisada pango-moan*. The question of whether a fraud has been committed or whether the managers of the property have been reprehensibly careless, is left to the judge's discretion. He bears in mind that most managements are still conducted rather inefficiently by inexperienced people. This carelessness is usually the reason that the threats and penalties and other measures in the regulations against members who have not properly observed their obligations, are rarely efficacious.

If there is a disagreement arising from the obstinacy of an individual member, then the drastic rule is applied:

> *hata mamundjung hata lalaen;*
> *hata torop sabungan ni hata;*
> the word of the individual is the word of a fool;
> the word of the many is the final word;

of which the purport in general is that, in taking corporate resolutions, agreement by reasonable opinion is striven after. Therefore, a rule concerning the manner in which decisions are reached is usually lacking.

That these societies with freely chosen aims are to be regarded as corporate bodies, is without doubt. In lawsuits their representation by the leader and one or more of the co-members of the Board is accepted as natural by the courts.

The Christian parishes, the *huria*, built up by the Rhenish Mission, are likewise native corporate bodies to which the church and primary school buildings belong. They own money and loan it out, and at present, according to the Church Regulations of 1930, are organised internally and are united in larger associations. Outside the Batak Country there are affiliated and separate Church societies among the Batak living in some of the principal cities of Java and Sumatra, all of which have the same creed as the main Church in the homeland. They are organised on the same basis and adhere to many of the same customs.

RESPONSIBILITY FOR DAMAGE

For damage inflicted by man, an animal or an object, recourse can be had to the person responsible. A father is responsible for any damage caused by his children; the owner of a herd guarded by a herdsman, *parmahan*, is responsible for any damage the herd does because the herdsman is a subordinate, a servant of his, *ai naposona do parmahan*. Formerly, damage done by adult servants (debt-slaves, an *ulubalang* etc.,) was the responsibility of their masters. The close relationship which existed between master and servant made this a natural rule. This cannot now always be said of more modern relationships, such as the car-owner chauffeur relationship, in which so much depends on the capability and sense of responsibility of the chauffeur. Rules regarding the apportionment of damage after an accident have yet to be evolved, or almost so. There is an inclination to absolve the owner from responsibility as soon as it is evident that he has taken good care of the car; has seen that it was not overloaded; and has made sure that the chauffeur has a licence, etc. This question has come to the fore because chauffeurs frequently indulge in wild driving. The interests of the person injured are, however, frequently against such an arrangement of the division of responsibility. It is to be hoped that the courts will move cautiously in the direction of stabilising the position which, in the long run, will be necessary in view of the increase in motor traffic.

Keeping pigs also presents some difficulties. These always occur in villages where the pigs roam freely in the village compound and the small gardens behind the houses must be protected from these animals by the owner. When all villages were heavily walled and when these walls, like the village gate, were well cared for, the rule could be applied that every inhabitant of the village was considered responsible for damage which resulted from his inadequate maintenance of his part of the wall. And a pig which was found outside the village in the rice fields could be killed. Pigs which were particularly wild were provided with a neck yoke, *halung-halung*. At present, however, the walls are less and less well maintained and in newly founded villages are often completely absent and, also at present, the fields lying around the village are used more than formerly by people who are not inhabitants of the village. It is impossible to give every pig a yoke, and it is difficult to keep them in sties all the time. If pig owners are fined and charged with the damage the animals have caused, which has now been the practice for many years on the insistence of the Government, it only sharpens the controversies within the village and sometimes costs the person whose property has been damaged more time and money than the damaged rice is worth. It is a subject which lends itself pre-eminently to treatment according to the views of those directly concerned. This could be effected by giving the small autonomous communities the right to handle these matters as they see fit. If buffaloes or other large domestic animals damage, *manunda*, the harvest, a wet rice-field or an irrigation dyke, etc., then the owner of the beast must make good such damage. But if the owner himself, or his herdsman follows a short time afterwards and explains why the animals strayed and offers apologies (this is called *ihut batangi* = following the small dyke), then a reasonable person abandons his claim for compensation. There is much reciprocity in matters such as these.

If buffaloes or horses belonging to two different people have been fighting and one of the beasts is killed or if one throws the other over a ravine, then the loss must be apportioned between both owners. If a buffalo attacks a horse, the reverse never occurs, then the owner of the buffalo is held responsible. There are more rules of this kind.

If an animal kills a man, then it has to be surrendered as the *boan* for the deceased and further funeral costs can be claimed from the owner. If a man becomes seriously ill because of a dog bite or because a horse has kicked him, then the owner of the animal should visit the sick man and should perform the *mangupa* (*mangari-ari, manulangi* pp. 81, 94) : he must also make good the costs the sick man has incurred in being cured again.

If one of the helpers in the fields or in house-building is injured, then the cost of his treatment must be borne by the person who asked for his help. Formerly this also applied if such a helper fell ill, because it was generally believed that there was a connection between the illness and the sphere within which the work was done.

It is understandable from the rules just given, which could be easily supplemented by a number of other details, that, where particular relationships exist between those concerned, such as those based on kinship, affinity, ownership of adjacent ricefields, joint-ownership of cattle and living in one village, etc., a high price is placed on maintaining friendly relations. Such relationships often play a greater role in determining compensation for damage than the question of the degree of carelessness or negligence.

CHAPTER IX

THE LAW OF OFFENCES

(*Panguhumon tu angka parsala*)

The material presented in the preceding chapters was mainly the result of my observation over a period of some years of the operation of customary law in the social life of the Toba Batak. With regard to judicial practice in respect of offences, I found that the rules of customary law did not operate any longer. It had become the practice of the courts, under the leadership or supervision of the Dutch District Officers, to deal with offences according to the general and uniform East Indies Penal Code, notwithstanding the fact that, according to statute, this Code did not apply to the Toba Batak. The consequence was that the Batak ideas regarding offences and the judicial way of dealing with them were pushed into the background. I could not, therefore, study them in actuality as I had been able to study the 'civil' aspects of the Toba Batak customary law.

It is true that there has been some betterment in this situation, but not to such a degree that at the time of my departure Batak legal concepts had acquired the place in the daily procedure of criminal trials which are their due.

The only way in which I could get the information I required was by asking the older men and in this way I learnt what the position had been previously under the conditions then prevailing. I did obtain much knowledge and data from reading the more recent as well as the older Batak writings and also other works on Indonesian *adat* law, and if among these last, which so much enriched the insight, I single out Mallinckrodt's thesis[21], especially Chapter IV, and Professor van Vollenhoven's *Het Adatrecht van Nederlandsch-Indië*, particularly Chapter XI of the 4th part,[22] it is not only because these two works provide stimulating reading, but because they also helped me in the interpretation of the data which I had obtained.

---

[21] J. Mallinckrodt: *Het Adatrecht van Borneo* (The Adat Law of Borneo), thesis, Leiden, 1928.
[22] "Adat Law of the Netherlands East Indies", Leiden, 1931, II, pp. 731-757.

On the law of offences also I had to search for an appropriate term in the Batak language. I decided on *panguhumon tu angka parsala* which means the law in respect of those who do wrong, their trial and punishment. *Sala* means wrongs, faults, offences; *parsala* = one who has done something wrong, one who commits an offence. The term *parsala* is somewhat broader in its application than the word *pangalaosi* = transgressor, since *mangalaosi* = to transgress, relates to rules and orders which are specifically promulgated as rules that must be observed, whereas the *parsala* can also be guilty of doing something which may not be done, in a more general sense.

I will endeavour to explain how the Batak thought, and still think, on this subject.

CONFESSION OF GUILT AND ATONEMENT

Setting aside for the moment the obstinacy with which a malefactor sometimes pleads that the evidence against him is a pack of lies, he who has done wrong must admit his guilt and must acknowledge that he is deserving of punishment, *manopoti salana*. This means that he subjects himself, *tunduk*, to custom and general judgement; that he has placed himself at the disposal of authority so that he can make such reparation as has been decided or will be decided. He is no longer refractory; recognises the error of his action; admits that he has done wrong; knows denial useless; is perhaps repentant; all of which separately or together, and is prepared for what will be demanded of him. He is prepared to redress his wrongdoing, *pauli uhum,* by personal atonement. The *manopoti salana* is his act of self-abasement; the *pauli uhum* demands that he makes some sacrifice. He must pay for his misdemeanour, *manggarar utang sala,* with which he has burdened himself. He must atone according to the requirements of *adat, manggarar adat*; he must pay the debt incurred because of his wrongdoing, *garar ni utang pipot, dosa ni utang sala.* When a decision has been reached as to his punishment, he is then said to be burdened with the reparation he must make, *marutang,* which is effected by his self-abasement and his observing of the obligation imposed upon him, *panopotion.* This obligation is called the *parpauli* = the form and the means whereby legal redress is achieved, or the *topot-topot* = that which shows his confession of guilt (*topot* also means to visit, to call upon).

The *manopoti salana* and the accompanying redress of injustice is not always a voluntary act. It can be voluntary, but it is usually the outcome of inescapable pressure from outside. In olden times there was always an inherent threat in a decision of being placed outside the protection of the law, *dipaduru diruar ni patik,* or outside the *adat, dibalian ni adat.* In a small cluster of villages or in the lineage within which a malefactor lived, ostracism, *mandurui,* could mean that he was 'shunned', *pasiding-siding,* and that friends and neighbours would withhold their support and interest without which nobody could live. But in a broader context, and in more serious cases, a malefactor could be banished and driven from the village and from the region. Thus of old this compulsion, which was in the background, characterised as a punishment the settlement of the obligation imposed. The obligation which was imposed on an offender and which he had to perform was his punishment, *uhumna,* that which according to the judgement fell upon him only.

That willingness to fulfil the obligation can always play a great part in giving its fulfilment the character of a genuine acknowledgement of guilt, appears from the following maxim which defines the attributes most to be desired in an offender:

> *gala-gala sitellu, tellúk mardagul-dagul;*
> *molo sala pambahenanku lehét huapul-apul.*
> (The first line is untranslatable.)
> If I have done wrong, then I will make it good.

If the offending act takes place wholly within the community in which the offender lives and in which he must spend his future life, then his *panopotion* must be accompanied by a request for forgiveness and a promise that he will refrain from wrongdoing in the future and that he will behave himself, *mandok djora.* This is the situation as it affects the offender.

THE INJURED PARTY

Looking at the offence from the point of view of the injured party, the latter must receive satisfaction for his injured feelings, reparation for the loss he has suffered, and for the violation of his rights. He visits the person responsible and seeks reparation from him because of the wrong to which he has been subjected: this is termed *marlulu.* He wants the existing injury to be expunged and his outraged sense of justice to be redeemed by *daon* = medicine, by a *daon ni sala* = redressor of the existing wrong resulting from the offence. This idea, in respect of two different kinds of injuries, is expressed in the following maxim:

> *sineat ni raut gambir tata daonna;*
> *sineat ni hata djuhut daonna.*

If a knife has caused a wound, fresh gambier is the cure.

If a word has caused an injury, then meat is the cure.

But in actual practice the 'medicine' of redress is not limited to these two forms: the *parboru* demands a *daon ila* after his daughter has been abducted as a 'medicine' against the shame, and a *daon rotak* is due after the land has been polluted by obscene filth. The sense of justice is considered to have been injured because its balance has been disturbed by a shock. Besides this *daon*, reparation must be made for the loss to which a property has been subjected.

THE COMMUNITY

Seen from the point of view of the community, it appears that re-dressing violated rights is one of the principal aspects in the treatment of offences, or as another relevant maxim has it:

pauk-pauk hudali pago-pago tarugi;

na tading niulahan na sega pinauli.

The hoe is brandished, the rib of the sugar-palm is cut.

What has been neglected has still to be performed, what has been broken into fragments must be remade.

This maxim has naturally a broader purport than the bare words suggest: interests and rights have been infringed; susceptibilities have been offended; legal order has been disturbed; harmony and good relation-ships have been disrupted. On all sides order has been rent; the *adat* has been broken, *sega adat*; the established rules have been shattered, *sega patik*. This situation must be rectified, *pinauli*. The offender is as much in breach against the prevailing law and moral order, *sala tu adat*, as in default in respect of authority, *sala tu haradjaon*, the *sahala* of which has been assailed. He is a violator of acknowledged rules, a *sitangko uhum*; he is the one who has brought to naught the rules obtaining, who has obliterated them, *mansoadahon uhum* or *mangapus uhum*. And this is not only in respect of those whose individual rights he has violated, but also in respect of the authority of the community. For example, it can be said of the *pangalangkup* = abductor, that he has not only done the husband a wrong but also the chiefs, *mansoadahon uhum tu parnioli dohot tu radja*. Formerly, if there was a disturbance at a *gondang*-feast which had its own *patik ni gondang* = rules of the *gondang*, or if a serious offence was committed in the market place whereby the peace of the market was disturbed, there would be a sudden stamping and clapping as in a dance on a bamboo floor, *rumiop rumonton songon tortor ni pantar bulu,* and people would stream in a crowd to the assistance of the leader, *suhut*, of the gathering affected. There have been cases where the "drums resounded and the tiger roared", when the whole territory was so distressed that it assembled to express its displeasure; cases where, as the saying in Padang Lawas goes, "the chief's gong was fractured". Hence, in addition to the offended party who has to receive satisfaction, *mandjalo uhum*, the chiefs also must participate when a punishment is carried out where meat and rice are served, *mandjuhuti mangindahani*, and a fine, etc., has to be paid. If the offence is a minor one affecting only the members of the village, then the act of repentance which redresses the violated rights of the village is made to the village chiefs. If more villages are involved, then the chiefs and elders of the villages concerned, or of the whole territory, assemble: this is also done when the whole region has been affronted and defiled and feels its well-being threatened.

THE SUPERNATURAL EFFECT OF THE OFFENCE

An offence frequently produces an unfavourable effect on the person concerned and on his surroundings or, if more than one person is affected by the offence, on the village or the region where the offence was committed. This harmful effect is of a magico-religious character. The offence has brought about a disturbance of the harmony that must necessarily be present in a person and in a territory if desired prosperity is to be achieved. This balance can be upset by 'black magic' being used against a person, a village or a region, *mandabu sipuspus*. But it can also be the result of actions which conflict with law and morals, that violate *adat*, and pollute purity and disrupt the calm and peace. If blood has flowed; if violent and insulting words have been spoken; if fear has been spread abroad; if the purity of a virgin has been defiled; if people have sexual intercourse when such is forbidden between them; if by acts such as these, a person, a village or the land is defiled, *rotak*; if someone is brought under false suspicion; if a great danger threatens a person and so on, then the *tondi* of the person concerned must be strengthened and the supernatural balance must be restored both to the person concerned and to his environment: both he and the region must be purified from stain. This must be done by the person who is responsible for the evil, in a manner determined by the judge and in a way that will bring about the desired counter-effect, namely, to bring to naught the evil consequences of the offence. This "punishment" is imposed either alone or in conjunction with another, according to the seriousness of the offence.

23

PERSONAL VENGEANCE

The person against whom an offence has been committed may, of course, feel a desire for personal vengeance as a means of satisfying his injured feelings. But this aspect should not be emphasised to the extent of giving the law of offences the character of private vengeance. I have intentionally discussed other aspects of the rules for offences before mentioning the thoughts of vengeance which might inspire the injured party, in order to stress the fact that there can be reasons of personal and social interest that definitely demand the offender's being tried for his offence. Certainly a number of phenomena point to the fact that in the *Pidari* time a principal factor in inflicting punishment was to appease the injured party's desire for vengeance: the strongest evidence for this being the killing and eating of perpetrators of grave evils, and other coarse habits. The Batak does not easily forget or forgive a wrong that has been done to him, but the injured party was not, and is not, always by any means the only *parlulu* (or *pangalului*) = seeker after satisfaction, who takes the matter up. When something iniquitous happens in a village, the chief directs the investigation and adjudicates, and he is at the same time the support of his villagers against the outside world.

There were in the past limits to arbitrary action. It must be noted that many *'adat'* sanctions — which are yet to be discussed — have a dual aspect in the sense that, in the society of which both the offender and the injured party form a part, it is to the latter that satisfaction has to be offered, but at the same time the person who is to be punished must be assured of his being able to continue to participate in the life of the community. Many other factors could be mentioned that considerably temper the element of vengeance.

SECURITY; THE RESTORATION OF HARMONY

In olden times the self-preservation of both the individual and society required that the security of land, village and the individual had to be maintained — though in practice imperfectly — and that rules had to be made against criminality. Thus, the incorrigible criminal, *na tartaon sangketa*, against whom neither force of arms nor magical power were effective, became the enemy of all and was outlawed. The homicide who, in his unbridled passion, felled a man to the ground in a public place could be summarily punished by the public. For a number of serious offences it was necessary to have vigorous means of redress. Today, the administrating chiefs are inclined to keep an audacious thief, a notoriously quarrelsome person, a murderer, and any individual who appears

to be dangerous, outside the community where he committed his crime
— and to which he will eventually have to return — as long as possible
by demanding a long term of imprisonment.

On the other side, however, are the tempering factors: a sense of
harmony; a sense of belonging together and of having to get on with
each other in daily life in village, lineage and territory. All these create
an inclination to forgive and to treat wrongs lightly. They make legal
redress possible; allow for reconciliation; for the expunging of rancour
and the restoration of the disturbed balance. It is an attitude without
which no orderly society, and especially Batak society, is conceivable and
it always activates people into seeking possible ways in which offences
that affect a group living together and its prosperity; that have disturbed
the harmony in a kinship circle; or have threatened the peace of a
territory, can be amicably settled.

THE RULES RELATING TO DISCIPLINARY MEASURES

Disciplinary measures play an important part in Batak society. And,
as a result of all kinds of disorderly and unwarranted daily happenings,
they appear repeatedly to be necessary in order to maintain law and
order. The Batak are well aware that they have to rule each other with
a strong hand. This is nowhere more clearly stated than in the last
section of the Regulations of one of the mutual credit societies: "Any
transgression of the rules by any one of the (nine) members of this
partnership will be punished by a judge". Obstinacy, inflexibility and
carelessness, of which I have given many examples, have led Batak
judges to realise that a transgressor requires a hand to rule and discipline
him.

Unwillingness to do what should be done; doing something in a
manner other than that in which it should be done; acting first and
waiting to see what happens; flagrantly neglecting to meet one's
obligations, are all typical attitudes which the Toba Batak know from
experience create disturbance, *guntur*, in their small communities,
provoke anew all kinds of squabbling, *bada*, and which therefore must
so frequently result in authority wielding its rod. And, as will be shown,
the field that rod covers is practically unlimited, both as to the reason
and the manner of its use.

THE MEANS OF LEGAL REDRESS AND OF DEFENCE AGAINST OFFENCES

The observations regarding the need for measures will be confirmed
by the later description of the obligations which the offender has to
perform according to the judge's decision. These are the so-called

adat-punishments, where emphasis is laid on the threat which is always behind a judgement. The *adat*-sanction, as the new technical term defines it, looks more to the relationship between the offender and the means of redress for which the Batak terms are: *uhum, utang, topot-topot, daon, parpauli ni sala,* etc.

PUNISHMENTS HAVING A MAGICO-RELIGIOUS CHARACTER

Foremost of these punishments is the group of which the purport is purification, the restoration of the condition of well-being and the warding off of injurious influences.

The purification, *manguras, mangias, mamangir,* of which the aim, with the help of lemon juice, is to remove a stain, to restore the state of purity, and to cleanse (*ias* = pure = *uras*) is an important means by which an offender appeases the injured feelings of a person whose well-being he has violated. The purification, *pangurasion,* can be demanded after conduct that we should class as 'an offence against morality' such as the violation of a virgin; having sexual intercourse with a member of one's own *marga*; abduction; whoring among young people, and similar delicts. But it can be necessary after other offences, such as the fouling of a spring, creating a disturbance in the village or the market whereby blood flows or abusive language has been used. The cleansing and strengthening effect is not produced exclusively with the lemon juice, it can also result from other acts of which the aim is to remove a supernaturally unfavourable situation. These acts are: offering a meal, a cloth, a sum of money, a plot of land, all of which can be done separately or together, according to the circumstances of the case. All these acts are accompanied by the words appropriate to the occasion and which must express a confession of guilt. Sometimes this is done to the accompaniment of dancing and the music of the *gondang*.

A few words will be devoted to each of these forms. Meat and rice, *djuhut dohot indahan,* are the usual ingredients of the meal, *sipanganon,* during the eating of which a confession of guilt is made, the act of penance is performed and the reconciliation takes place. Anyone who is sentenced to serve such a meal, *mandjuhuti mangindahani,* finds it a very chastening experience since the female members of his immediate family and of related families must participate in its preparation and, if the offence is a serious one, must join in offering the food to the injured party or parties. In minor offences the slaughter of a piglet is adequate (for Mohammedans this is replaced by a young goat), but in serious

offences a cow or even a buffalo, *sisemet imbulu* = the one covered with
thick hair, *sigagat duhut* = the one which eats grass, must be slaughtered. The great care associated with the preparation of the meat of
these animals evokes the idea that 'the cooking pot and the mat and the
ladle must bow, *marsomba hudon, marsomba rere dohot sonduk'*, which
accentuates still further the humiliation which is associated with carrying
out the punishment. It takes place in full view of the community concerned. The meal must be served in the house of the person who has
been offended, in his village compound, or in the neighbourhood of the
place where the offence was committed. The persons directly concerned
partake of the meal as well as their chiefs, kinsmen, affines and the
members of the village community. The effect ascribed to such a meal
has been described in Chapter II and it is only necessary to again
mention that sometimes particular homage must be shown to the *tondi*
and the *sahala*. This is often expressed by the person who has been
offended or insulted, such as a chief, etc., being fed from the hand of the
offender: this is shown in photo IIa where the brother of the offender
performs the act of feeding, *manulangi,* the injured party. The act of
manulangi sometimes gives its name to the whole *panopotion* = propiti-
ation ceremony. Serving a meal is an integral part of any act of discharging guilt. According to the second rule of the aphorism mentioned
on p. 351 the *djuhut* is essential in the case of a verbal insult.

If two or more parties have to effect a reconciliation as an acknowledgement of mutual guilt, for example, when people have created a
general fracas or when there has been a marital quarrel, then all
involved must contribute to the ingredients of the meal. If, for instance,
a married couple are reunited, the man gives a piglet as a *topot-topot*
and the wife gives the rice, and their partaking of the meal together,
mangan indahan sinaor = eating a mixed meal, expunges once and for
all the dispute that existed between them. This offering of a meal,
whether it is termed *mandjuhuti, mambabii,* or *manulangi,* can be an
element of the *mangupa* or *mangari-ari* of the *tondi* of the person
affected. Strengthening, enriching and stabilising the *tondi* of a sick
person, a *tondi* beset by danger, one that has been threatened or harmed
in any way, can be a voluntary act — as we have already seen — but
it can also be done under compulsion: the person responsible for causing
the harm can be ordered by a judicial decision to perform it. Here
again, the *mangupa,* which is the principal element in many a *panopotion,* often gives its name to the purification ceremony. But even if this
term is not specifically used, one of the aims of the whole ritual, the

meal, the address, the gifts, etc., is always the appeasement of the *tondi* of the injured person.

Mangulosi is also connected with it. Except in an affinal relationship, and especially that of the *hula-hula* towards its *boru* — the latter gives money in return — the offering of a woven cloth, *ulos,* can play a role in a *panopotion* which concerns two kinsmen; I heard of it in connection with insulting and injuring a person, assaulting a young girl and adultery committed by a married woman. If I have been correctly informed, it operates mainly in close kinship- and affinal relationships of a couple of *sundut* at the most.

A plot of land can be offered instead of an *ulos.* It appears that the guilty person will do this of his own free will when he attaches much importance to the fact that the harmony, which the offence disturbed, shall be restored. Gifts of money are intended either as a supplement to an act of penance, or as a substitute for it. If they are supplementary, then they are as a rule given in addition to a meal. They are then called the *batu ni sulang-sulang.* Such a supplement is intended purely for the party to whom the meal is offered and its purpose is to mitigate the distress that has been caused. In determining the size of the *batu,* attention is given to the gravity of the offence that has been committed. If only a piglet has to be slaughtered, then the *batu* is not more than a few guilders; if the penalty is a cow or a buffalo, then the amount of the *batu* is always some scores of guilders. The amounts are never fixed. The wealth of the person penalised is also taken into consideration according to the following maxim:

nipis mantat neang, hapal mantat dokdok.

What is thin carries what is light,

what is thick carries what is heavy.

This rule applies in determining what should be borne by the convicted person. Where the *boru* has a penalty imposed on it, over and above a meal, which has to be paid to the *hula-hula,* this can also be called by the more general term of *piso.* In respect of a physical injury, the supplementary gift of money fulfils the role of the *gambir tata* = fresh gambier, referred to in the first rule of the aphorism quoted on p. 351. In my opinion, this is partly to be regarded as the compensation which must be given to the injured person for the medicine he has to buy, *manuhor taoar,* a contribution which at the present time can be considerable now that an injured person is frequently taken to a mission hospital.

Another form of supplementary payment is the *pandjoraan,* the small sum of money which is a payment conferring a promise of good behaviour, *mandok djora*. And there are probably many such typical payments, each of which can throw some light on an aspect of settling offences. The substitution of a penalty was apparently much less common in olden times in the Toba Batak Country than it was in the Dairi Batak Country where a great number of precise contributions in money are mentioned in cases in which, in the Toba Country, meals, cloths, etc., are offered for preference. Money is now offered as a substitute for the lemon juice. The remainder of the ritual, however, is the same.

In one of the few decisions on offences given by the official native courts, which upheld customary ideas, it was laid down that money could not be used as a substitute for the cloth which had to be offered to the injured party and to his affronted kinsmen by the person who had to perform the act of *paulihon*. But the cloth intended for the chiefs who had to witness the execution of the judgement could be replaced by money. In other judgements affected by European influence the necessary elements of a punishment according to *adat*-rules were estimated according to their money value, and the total was deposited in the court's coffers: a materialistic approach that does not seem to harmonise with indigenous concepts.

This substitution of money for the actual act of penance, naturally approaches the modern payment of a fine. However, according to Tobanese ideas, the *dangdang* = fine, is something quite different again, as will be seen presently.

The address which the person who has been penalised must make, is likewise an integral part of the whole affair. Here, too, the word that can do 'evil' and 'good' cannot be dispensed with. This address is spoken at the end of the meal and besides being a confession of guilt, it should contain a request for forgiveness, a promise of better behaviour in the future, and express a desire for reconciliation as the case may be. In many cases the parents or other close relations are also expected to express their acknowledgement of the wrong that their kinsman has done, and to promise that they will exercise control over him. I have translated such an address from the collection of Toba Batak stories called *Torsa-torsa*. This address was given by someone who had unjustly suspected his wife of having a relationship with another man. He had reproached her with his accusation and had hurled all kinds of abuse at her, but, when he had later understood the situation, paid his debt for his mistaken accusation, his *utang sala ni pangkulingna,* by offering a meal, *sipanganon,* to his wife and his father-in-law during the course of which he spoke the following: "I have acted very unjustly, but now I request that you do not charge me with this because I now come humbly before you and confess my great guilt. Everything in which I have been neglectful I will refrain from in the future". At the conclusion of the address, the father-in-law, noting the humble mien of his son-in-law, gave him his blessing, *pasu-pasu,* and then accompanied him to his own house.

When the aim of an act of penance is to strengthen a person's *tondi,* it must always take place to the accompaniment of *gondang,* as is done at the *mangari-ari,* but the *gondang* can be played at the settlement of other offences as well. Besides being used to summon the spirits for their veneration at the sacrificial ceremonies, the *gondang* also has the effect of putting the *tondi* in a favourable mood and, more generally, creates a beneficial atmosphere for men. *Gondang* music is an integral part of the severe punishment called *utang saribu radja, tolu sadalan* = guilt towards a thousand *radja* (?), three at a time, because this punishment consists of:

1) *mamunu horbo sada* = to slaughter a buffalo;
2) *mardongan napuran* = to add betel;
3) *mamalu ogung* = to strike the gongs = to play the *gondang.*

When a ceremonial meal is offered in the grand manner to chiefs and elders of a territory because a serious offence against morality has been committed, the *gondang* and dancing must accompany the other acts attendant upon the meal. It is during the dancing that *ulos* = cloths, or other gifts are offered and then the dancing of the women cannot be omitted.

I have already mentioned that the Church has often objected to the *gondang* ceremony but, where no thought of spirit veneration is connected with the *gondang* music, it is more and more being permitted at *adat* ceremonies. So, for example, in 1929 it was possible in Christian Silindung for a number of *negeri* chiefs to be sentenced to perform a penance, which consisted of a buffalo, the *gondang* and an *ulos,* towards their Assistant Demang (Batak sub-district officer) against whom they had laid a false accusation. See also Appendix II. Many of these originally exclusively magico-religious concepts are gradually being enveloped in the garb of old usage, good custom, old and venerated forms, sacred usages, and have become an expression and a symbol for satisfying the sense of justice. They have, therefore, more and more acquired a neutral secular character and now their legal character, which has come gradually more to the fore, deserves continued consideration.

Finally, mention must be made of the asking of forgiveness. This is done when someone has committed a minor offence against another person and offers him betel, *napuran,* by which act he desires to show that he humbles himself, *paboa naung tunduk ibana.*

COMPENSATION AND FINES

Obligations of a more objective nature are the compensation and fines which can be imposed on a person, each being in addition to the aforementioned acts or separately. Their object is to redress the deficiency resulting from a person's offence and, if the misbehaviour is of a grave character, to compensate for it to a greater degree. They are best defined by the term *dangdang* which term, however, indicates also in a much narrower sense, the compensation for damage caused involuntary, and in a broader sense it can define the total obligation to which a person can be sentenced for an offence. But the common use of this term refers to the monetary penalty and compensation due for committing an offence. Foremost is the compensation for loss resulting from the offender's action. This is the *abul,* which can be the compensation of the value of a man (during the former wars a man killed in battle or one who was murdered) or the compensation for goods damaged by fire or in some other way, and stolen goods. According to the "Rules of Naipospos" this 'weer-geld' for the fallen in war differed according to whether the man was a *radja,* his brother, a *namora boru,* or his brother, a married man, a child, a slave, etc. At the present time there is no question of assessing compensation in money for a man who has been killed. We have, however, already seen that the *boan* or *ola,* the funeral meal which must be provided at the deceased's funeral and the *saput,* the funeral costs, are the responsibility of the person at whose door the death can be laid, which is only fair.

Compensation for goods that have been damaged and the consequent decrease in their value, also comes under this *abul.* In addition, there is the increased compensation which is intended to be a penalty for having committed the offence and which accrues to the injured party. Formerly this was especially applicable in respect of theft when the penalty of the 'sevenfold' compensation, *simamitui,* of the article(s) stolen, could be imposed, according to the *Patik dohot Uhum.* The "Rules of Naipospos", however, contain separate fines for not less than 17 kinds of theft from stealing a buffalo, the worst kind, to stealing a chicken basket. These fines too, had to be paid to the man who had been robbed, but the payment did not have to be associated with any other form of satisfaction. All these penalties have fallen into desuetude now that the thief is sent to prison or fined. However, for petty larceny committed within a village or in the fields around the village, it is still always required by good neighbourliness that the violator of the security of property gives satisfaction to the person who has been robbed, and thereby to the group to which they both belong, by making an addition to the value of the object(s) stolen.

The payments in money, rice or meat which are so often mentioned in the 32nd chapter of the "Rules of Naipospos" for homicide, embezzlement, absconding, arson, destroying crops, etc., are fines in the more strict sense, as is the payment once or more than once the *satimbang badan* = as much as a body, of which the *Patik dohot Uhum* speaks for very serious offences and which I heard equated with 'to the extent of one's possessions'. This fine can be as much as the marriage payment which has been received for a woman who has been murdered, or, if it refers to a man who has been murdered, has been paid by him. These penalties have almost been obliterated by the fines and imprisonment imposed by the Penal Code.

OTHER SANCTIONS

Imprisonment and capital punishment have taken the place of the severe punishments with which the most serious crimes were punished in earlier times. Then, if someone wantonly set a village on fire, his 'heaven and his earth', *langitna dohot tanona,* which meant literally everything he could call his own, his wife, his brother, his children included, were forfeit and were distrained on, *ditaban,* so that such an offence would not be repeated again, *asa unang somal songon i.* Murderers and rapists, common thieves, poisoners, traitors to village and country could be struck down anywhere. Should they sit in the place of honour or should they eat from the consecrated dish, they could be seized, *hundul di pontas pe i mangan di pinggan puti, boi do buaton;* if they went to the river to drink, then it had to be drained, *laho tu aek ingkon arsihon;* if they fled into the forest, then it had to be set on fire, *maporus tu ramba ingkon tutungon.* They were not safe at *gondang* feasts or in the public market, and only if their kinsmen solemnly promised to pay all the compensation, *dangdang,* claimed could their lives be saved. Failure to pay the fines resulted in the convicted person being handed over to the injured party who could sell him as a slave or kill him and let him be eaten. A life for a life, *hosa ali ni hosa,* was a guiding principle in a case of murder or homicide. Fortunately, these corrective measures are now all canalised in the regular administration of justice, operated under the aegis of a more humane thinking Government which has relieved villages and territories of the task of taking action against the more serious forms of crime. This is the more to be valued because in the violent practices of the *Pidari* time, it was often less the measure of guilt than power or weakness that determined how heavy the punishment would or would not be.

The previous practice of putting a person in the block was not a separate punishment: it was either a provisional measure in anticipation of justice being done, or a means whereby the injured party arbitrarily extorted payment of the penalty by the offender's kinsmen before or after the judgement. Thus, if an offender or one of his near kinsmen were put in the block, it was for an unspecified time. For minor offences, administering a reproof could be sufficient correction. Besides the other obligations imposed on a man who had defiled or raped a young virgin, he could be compelled to marry her.

Humiliating punishments, other than cutting off an adulteress's hair, mentioned in the *Patik dohot Uhum,* are not known to me.

The obligations which must be met towards the chiefs who participate in the meals just mentioned and which consist of offering a cloth, or a gift of money, or both, are supplementary to the main punishment. The money gift then serves as *pago-pago* = the "sealing money", which is a remuneration for the judges and also a confirmation that the lawsuit has been definitely concluded. In the south it is also called *ingot-ingot* = remembrance money. In Barus, I heard mention of an *uang boto-boto* = notification money, which was given to the co-inhabitants of a village in which a case of larceny was settled; it was also given to those who had not been present so that they 'would know about it'.

Formerly, another kind of remuneration for the judges was a portion of the sum of money which was a substitute for the obligation imposed, and a portion of the fine imposed which, because the judiciary was not a firmly established organisation, were not always divided in the same way and in respect of which there were, as far as I know, no fixed rules as a consequence.

A specific response against a person who has misbehaved contrary to the standards of *adat* is to 'shun' him or her:

bulung ni bulu diparigat-rigat halak;
ianggo na so maruhum dipasiding-siding halak.
The bamboo leaves are split by men.
Whosoever does not abide by *adat* is 'shunned'.

It is an attitude for the protection of decency, good custom, and good mutual conduct. I recollect once someone was 'shunned' by his kinsmen and friends because he persisted in his refusal to co-operate in seeing that a lone girl, an orphan, whose late father was the last member of a family, was allowed to retain a small amount of capital which would otherwise have to be divided among more than forty heirs. This attitude can (could?) result in the more serious formal exclusion from the group, *pabalihon, paduruhon,* if the person concerned shirks his obligations which he is bound to honour. It is also a form of being shunned when a widow or a permanently sick person, among other things, is not allowed to enter a house that has just been consecrated; when an old childless widow is evicted from the dwelling where she has lived for years because she is 'unlucky'; when a man is 'shunned' if his *huta* has been completely burned down and he is not accepted into another *huta* for a couple of weeks during which time he has to pass the night in the open in the cold and rain so that his *tondi* can mend its ways, *asa djora tondina,* because it is a fire-raiser.

This response to these situations, even though they are not offences, is thus just the same as though the persons concerned had committed a breach of good behaviour.

This leads us to the question of guilt and intent.

INTENT AND GUILT

The question of intent and guilt does not arise in a number of offences, or is hardly taken into consideration with regard to them. This group of delicts are thought to have automatically harmful effects for others. To give an example from the Dairi Country: a woman who gives birth to a child in someone else's rice-field is punished by having to pay a penalty to the owner of the field. This is because there is a magically injurious effect of the event on the land and those who are connected with it.

However, there has always been an awareness of the difference in intent. To do with intent is termed *manuntun,* and a person accused of an offence will say: *so na hutuntun do i* = I did not do it deliberately, it was not my intention. According to the "Rules of Naipospos" a person was only liable to the death penalty if he had killed someone when it was not definitely known that they had quarrelled. He is then a murderer, whose criminal intent is deduced from the circumstances. The writer of the *Patik dohot Uhum,* in enumerating the cases in which the killing of a man is to be reckoned as murder, *todos,* is of the same opinion. Among other things, it was reckoned as murder to kill an enemy who, during a war, was carrying the ritual meal to an affine, which act demonstrated his peaceful intent. It was also murder to kill someone who had placed himself under the protection of a neutral third party; to kill someone on his way to the market, because he was protected by the 'peace of the market'; to kill anyone who was participating in a ceremony and who was thus under the protection of the suspension of hostilities during a festival. The circumstances in and under which the killing took place marked it as a proper murder against which the whole community had to take action. Malice, though it possibly did not have serious results, could be considered as criminal, as could an act of poisoning and treason within the village walls: these acts are on a par with *todos*. On this point a doctrine had already been developed, though it was still in an embryonic stage, which in principle had taken into consideration some necessary distinctions. And on those points which have not been influenced by ideas of a magico-religious nature, there is the realisation that intent to do evil is of itself a crime. This realisation will increase in strength in the course of evolution. However, despite the fact that the Batak could see the relationship between intent and the act itself, his group mentality tended to his laying the blame in more serious cases on others as well as on the actual perpetrator.

RESPONSIBILITY OF PEOPLE OTHER THAN THE OFFENDER

In olden times this responsibility went further than at present. The village which housed thieves had to accept that it would be held responsible as a whole for offences committed by any of its inhabitants. Major offences committed against a stranger could result in the whole territory being held responsible if the perpetrator was not discovered or punished. The law of hospitality ordained that a host was responsible for the safety of his guests and the security of their goods and that he should co-operate in tracing anything that was missing. If a person known to the host had been accompanied by someone unknown to the host and who had made off with the host's goods, then the guest had to make good the loss. Where it was impossible to apprehend a major criminal, his closest kinsmen were held responsible for the *dangdang* which was then due. This situation has changed since the coming of the Dutch administration. The safety of goods and persons is now almost exclusively in the hands of the public authority. The possibility of tracing a criminal has greatly increased and there is no longer inability or unwillingness to punish a known offender or to execute the punishment imposed upon him. Nevertheless, the idea of responsibility for another has not entirely disappeared: a father has to make reparation for the harmful consequences of his children's misdeeds; nearest kinsmen and affines must co-operate in the implementation of *adat* sanctions; if damage is sustained as a result of an outrage and the perpetrator cannot alone make reparation, then his *uaris* must come forward. In minor cases which affect only a village or a small cluster of villages, the old concepts are often still active.

SUMMARY JUSTICE

Taking the law into one's own hands also for the greater part belongs to past history. In olden times, in its worst form, it was admissible to kill summarily an offender in those serious crimes which placed their perpetrators beyond the law. The *partodos* = murderer, the *pangalang-kup* = abductor, the *pargadam* or *parrasun* = poisoner, the *pandobo* = street robber, the *babi di eme* = the man caught in the act of seducing a woman, and such persons, were *parbalian* = persons ostracised, banished, they were *di balian ni saksi* = outside the protection of the law. It was not allowed to escort them or to receive them, *na so djadi iring-iringon do i, na so djadi tomu-tomuon.* They were exposed to any act of summary justice. So also was the thief who had committed any of the grave forms of theft, when he was caught. With regard to the latter, the *Patik dohot Uhum* gives as a limit that the stolen item must be more valuable than a pig. A malefactor discovered at night in or around a village would always have been pursued, with consequent violence. In the cases in which the killing was lawful, the kinsmen of the dead man could not demand any satisfaction, *so djadi morlulu.* If the killing had not taken place at the moment when the miscreant was caught, but if instead he was tied to the slaughtering pole, *taluktuk,* then the right to dispose over him could be redeemed by the payment of the 'loosener from the slaughtering pole, *harhar taluktuk'.* At the present time, there can hardly be any question of summary justice. The diligence of the police has changed the situation in this matter. In cases like those just mentioned, if violence does, however, occur, the judge will doubtless take into account the old law. A reaction on the part of the injured party which at present obtains as entirely lawful, is for him to remove stolen goods found in the possession of another person and to hand over the goods to the competent authority.

IS THERE ALWAYS A PREVIOUS RULE?

Can it always be said that according to Batak law and custom a person can never be punished if it cannot be shown that he has infringed a definite legal rule? In my opinion, the answer must be in the negative. The development of the law of offences has not progressed so far that a complete set of rules has come into being which define without fail when an *adat* sanction operates against an offender. The whole field of law and social life do contain the norms — though not always in a definite form — regarding what may or what may not be done. These norms potentially contain the possibilities of corrective action against one who transgresses them and many of them do have a reasonably fixed form, often with an indication of what may affect a transgressor. A list will be given further on which is capable of extension. The Batak texts already mentioned and especially the "Rules of Nai-pospos", list a multitude of offences, but neither of these texts is exhaustive. Serious crimes against the person and against property such as those regularly committed in the old society, more frequently than they are at present, and of which the main outlines clearly distinguish the one from the other, have often acquired an individual designation which constitute an adequate basis for determining the punishment though admittedly there may sometimes be less differentiation than is desirable at the present time. But, on the other hand, there are qualifications which are vaguely defined and which also apply so broadly, that it is difficult to speak of a rule with a specifically delimited field of application. I have in mind such a qualification as the following: *mambahen na so uhum, mangula na so djadi* = to do what is unlawful, to do what is not allowed, which relates to all kinds of misbehaviour committed by a man towards a woman, and can embrace also everything that is against custom and conflicts with accepted norms. For example, I once heard it used in a judgement concerning the insulting of an official. A qualification such as *ndang mangoloi hata ni radja* = to pay no attention to the order of a chief, can overrule a whole set of bye-laws. In this context there is also the term *sitangko uhum* = the robber of (another man's) rights, which also covers a broad field. Now, in many cases when use is made of qualifications of this sort, a sharper definition is often possible, but it does not alter the fact that the outlines are very vague and that all kinds of behaviour against which no defined specific rule has ever been directed can quite easily be accommodated within this general framework.

The same can be said of the disciplinary rules which are operative as soon as the judge considers that corrective measures are necessary against disorderliness of one kind or another. Sometimes the misdemeanour thereby acquires some definition, but this does not always mean that the qualification is an acknowledged definition of what is generally accepted as an offence. The peculiar attitude of a Batak judge is this: there are a number of known facts which have abused and there is an individual right or a rule of social intercourse that has been infringed, by virtue of which I impose on the perpetrator the obligation which is the most appropriate to the case. The offender, who belongs to our society and is thus able to follow the train of thought, will know precisely why I have arrived at the decision. To an official of the Dutch Administration, however, the judge would have to add: "if you want an explanation of my procedure and decisions, I can give it to you circumstantially and you will realise that I have acted reasonably, but do not ask of me and of the legal system that I operate, that in each case, without exception, I do and can appeal to a pre-existing and formulated rule of penal law which confines each case submitted within narrow bounds. Let me keep these few broadly framed terms which embrace so much and also allow me the possibility of making a decision, where necessary, regarding aspects which they do not take into account. For, am I not the protector of social life, its order and its rules?"

There is, it is true, a danger of arbitrary action by the Batak chiefs and judges, but one has to accept the fact that the Toba Batak justiciaries can be such untractable people, can adopt such surprising attitudes and can defy all reasonableness, so that an orderly communal life would be impossible if they were not governed by a firm hand acting within the confines of the law but without too many formal restrictions.

It is not always necessary that the formulation of a rule of *ius penale* has an attendant threat of punishment, *pangonai* (*hona* = to hit). It is remarkable that in the *negeri* Manalu Dolok, in respect of the rules concerning tapping, planting and disposing of benzoin, etc., (App. IV) the only threat of punishment mentioned for selling and buying benzoin secretly is that the perpetrator shall be punished by a court, *siuhumon ni rapot,* but there is no indication of the character of the punishment or of its extent. It was thought that the judge before whom the particular case would be brought, would be in a better position to judge how the transgressor should be punished than the legislator who had only to draw up the general rule. The punishment to decide upon should depend on the varying facts, *marguru tu pangalahona be anggo i.* Here too, the rule: what is thin carries what is light, what is thick carries what is heavy, (p. 358) is applicable.

SOME OTHER DATA OF A GENERAL CHARACTER

In the light of the foregoing it can easily be understood that in the present situation the possibility of alternative punishment is readily seized upon. In olden times there was always the threat of being banished, *didurui,* and judges whose decisions had been flouted felt that their own honour and prestige had been outraged and sided with the party who had been injured by the offence. But sometimes it was a very difficult task to reach a final decision and the observance of an imposed obligation which was unpalatable was often dependent upon power relationships fortuitously present within the village, territory or region. Many an injury remained unredressed for this reason and many punishments were not executed. Now it is different. Established authority can compel the penalty that is imposed by a judge to be carried out and it now stands behind him by means of the threat of distraining on property or of depriving the recalcitrant one of his freedom. I have already mentioned that imprisonment is also regarded as a means of banishing criminals from society for a prolonged period.

The audacious robber who dares to resist the law and authority was formerly called a *partali-tali haen na niarutna* = one who wore stolen goods as a headcloth. Like murderers and rapists, he was placed outside the law.

A man who is repeatedly caught thieving is long-fingered, *sigandjang tangan,* and merits more serious punishment. Any repetition of the same offence brings the perpetrator into bad repute.

We learn from the "Rules of Naipospos", particularly the 31st chapter in which 17 different kinds of larceny are dealt with individually, that in olden times the punishment could vary according to the gravity of the offence.

Milder forms of otherwise serious offences were called *anggina* = the younger brother thereof, an idea we have already met in the term *anggi ni langkup* = taking to oneself a woman who had not lived in regular marriage with her husband for a long time, which approaches *langkup* = adultery. The *Patik dohot Uhum* contains two examples: *anggi ni todos* and *anggi ni dobo,* between which and real homicide and real robbery, *todos* and *dobo,* respectively, there is only a formal difference. In our discussion of *mangulahon gomos* (see p. 306) we have already mentioned excusable circumstances which can convert an offence

24

into an admissible act. Theft within the family group, *panangkoan ni na saripe,* is either not punishable or is dealt with in a simple way. I found mention of a son-in-law not being punishable if he took away something from his father-in-law which he particularly desired although it had already been refused him. The family group must be viewed in this context as a rather broad group which can include, for example, the perpetrator, whose father's brother is married to the father's sister of the one who has been robbed; or the perpetrator whose brother is the brother-in-law of the injured party's father.

When people plot to commit a crime together, the apportionment of the responsibility is expressed as follows: *dos do sitiop sige dohot sitangko tuak =* the one who holds the ladder is as guilty as he who steals the palm wine, which aphorism means that the *partahi =* those who are in the plot, and the *parsidohot =* those who are accessories, are equally responsible. Or as another *umpama* has it:

sada sidjaringkat, sada sidjarongkat, marsanggul djabi-djabi,
sada ma i parmitmit, luhut partahi-tahi.

A kind of weed, a *djarongkat* crowned with *djabi* leaves.

One man has concocted the plan, but all have had a hand in it. The one who remains behind the scenes is called the *parmitmit.* If there is a principal agent who has others to assist him, for example, friends who have helped in abducting a girl, then the accomplices are called *sipangurupi tahi =* those who have helped to accomplish the plan. Passive acquiesence or suppression of known facts can be called: *sadalan satahi dohot na mangula =* being in agreement with the perpetrator. Secretly helping to spirit away stolen goods is called *marmihim-mihim ugasan na tinangko.* If a *parboru* is an accessory to his married daughter's cohabiting with a man other than her lawful spouse, it has the special name of *palangkuphon.* If women are in a plot or are accessories, they also can be punished. In Toba I once saw a widow punished for *palangkuphon.* Formerly, in cases of *langkup,* the hair of the guilty spouse could be cut off. The aunt who had insulted her niece was sentenced to *mangindahani* and *mangulosi* the injured girl, and once quarrelling women had to *mangan indahan sinaor.* As regards the wife of a thief who unexpectedly brings a pig's head home or who brings home a collection of clothes, I heard that she is never convicted of receiving because it is not presumed that a husband tells his wife the source of everything he brings home. Similarly, a sister or a cousin who receives something from a brother or a male cousin that has been stolen, goes free.

If damage is done to property as a result of an offence, then full restitution must be made, if need be by distraining on the property of the perpetrator and his *uaris*. Stolen goods must be returned by the thief or compensation must be paid for them. If the goods come into the hands of a third party, then he must surrender them and must request compensation from those who gave them to him.

PARTICULAR OFFENCES

For reasons that I have already stated on p. 349 it is not possible to enumerate particular offences in their entirety, any more than it is possible to define indisputably the meaning, extent and purport of the Batak terminology.

VERBAL INSULT

I have said elsewhere that particular attention must be paid in these offences to the magical effect of the words used. There are numerous terms for these offences. In the simplest form of verbal insult, harm can be done by using words which 'go too far', *hata na masalpuhú*. Abuse, *pababa-babahon* (derived from *baba*, a vulgar word for 'mouth'), to open one's mouth and speak with contempt and anger; to address a person in a contemptuous and insulting way is also called *paroa-roahon* or *paleahon,* from *roa* = ugly and *lea* = contemptible, as well as *marhata pasul* = to use rude words. There is no essential difference between all these forms of insult. To falsely accuse someone is expressed as *manggombahon hata na so tutú*. If a prominent person, who is known to be of good repute, is falsely accused, it is said that: the chickens have been let loose and that unrest has been brought to the market place, *palua-lua manuk, paguntur-guntur onan*, which means that a disturbance hase been caused in the region.

The name of the *adat* sanctions to all these forms of verbal insult is *gatip* (or *gansip*) *bibir* = to close the lips with tongs. This is affected by imposing an obligation on the guilty party to pay a penalty that can range from offering some betel to the *utang saribu radja* (p. 360) according to the words used and the rank and position of the person insulted. On this point also, it appears that the imposition of a money fine — destined for the court's coffers — or of imprisonment is not always the best form of restoring a good name and calm to the region.

MORAL TRANSGRESSIONS

This group of offences, which includes *marsumbang, mangabing, manggogoi* and the various forms of *mangalangkup*, marital infidelity and other such moral transgressions, was dealt with in Chapter V.

DISTURBING OF PEACE AND ORDER

Many kinds of *manggunturi* = creating a disturbance, have been mentioned in the previous chapters. The *pangguntur ni halak* = creator of strife among people, is for example, a person who gives someone a wet rice-field and neglects to indicate the boundaries properly to the recipient, from which neglect a dispute arises; the *domu-domu* who does his work as an intermediary badly; the people who contract a marriage and who make incorrect statements of the payments to the keeper of the register; the holder of a *pauseang*-field who attaches it for a debt without informing the donor, and so on. There are also other misdemeanours for which there are no special terms but which likewise fall in this category of disturbers of the peace between individuals, which so often means that public order is also disturbed. For example, to give a woman in marriage a second time when she has not been freed from the ties of her first marriage; the failure of the chief of the one party to a transaction to inform the other party to it what the position is regarding his subordinate's possessions; and *mangose,* failure to keep to the terms of an agreement or of an accepted obligation. Such a *pangguntur ni halak* always has to take a chance that corrective measures will be taken against him.

The more deliberate disturbing of the peace by fighting, using invective, etc., also comes under *manggunturi,* as does usually taking justice into one's own hands, *padjolo gogo papudi uhum.* I once saw in a judgement a general commotion which had been created by provoking disputatious rows in village and territory described as 'making such a noise that the waringin tree of the territory's chief trembled, *manorong-norong pola tarhutur baringin ni radja'.* A more serious form of disturbance is that created in the market place, *paguntur-guntur onan,* as is also the disturbing of the peace at a feast or a ceremony. These forms can be punished by the mandate to slaughter a buffalo for the chiefs of the territory and the other *suhut* = principal persons, concerned. Anyone who violates the peace of a house or of another man's village is a *pangarompak,* and must give satisfaction to the inhabitants of house or village.

INFRINGING AUTHORITY

Infringing authority consists primarily of violating the *sahala* of the holders of authority in whose *tondi* the ruling power which must be honoured and respected, is embodied. Insulting a *radja* is more serious than insulting an ordinary man, as is also fighting with or manhandling a chief. If a man neglects to invite a chief to a festival to which he is entitled to be invited, he is said to be *tois tu radja* = ill-mannered towards the chief. This also applies to withholding from a chief the portion of the *djambar* = share, of the slaughtered feast-animal to which he is entitled. Such offences as fighting, using invective and misbehaving in the presence of a chief or at an assembly of chiefs, are an outrage. Conduct of this kind is called *ndang marpaho didjolo ni radja* = showing no manners in the presence of the chief. It is an assault on the chief's *hasangapon* = honour and prestige. Once a dispute or a quarrel is brought before a chief, the persons concerned cannot again fall to fighting or squabbling. If they do, they are guilty of disturbing the armistice brought about by the chief(s), *mangalaosi pongpang ni radja*, which in olden times naturally had still more significance than at the present day (this will be discussed further in Chapter X under the heading 'Respect for the Court'). If the chief officially summons someone, then it is unlawful not to give heed to this summons, *mandjua djou-djou ni radja*. The more general term is *so mangoloi hata ni radja* = to pay no attention to the chief's summons. This principle, naturally, also holds good for the judicial courts, *parriaan ni radja*, which can give such orders as are necessary for the good administration of justice, such as ordering witnesses to be brought up, parties to appear personally, etc., which orders have to be obeyed. The decisions of the courts are also assured by the general authority against any unwillingness to comply with their judgements, as is the actual execution in that the recalcitrant one can, in fact, be compelled to carry them out — at present by a fine or imprisonment, but formerly judges could resort to force. The relevant orders of public authority which are rooted in law and custom, likewise lie for the great part in the field of measures with the absence of pre-existing definite rules. In the long run, however, they will acquire more consistency. Sedition or resistance to the authority of village or territory resulted in olden times in expulsion, fettering or being put in the block, and possibly worse. Anyone expelled for these reasons was not readmitted later, *ndang pinamasuk aili dibagasan ni huta* = one does not allow wild pigs to come into the village.

Treason against the village or the territory committed by the *pordjehe* = traitor, resulted in the severest punishment, from which there was no pardon.

VIOLATION OF THE GENERAL WELFARE

In former times arson, *manurbu*, which resulted in the destruction of a whole *huta* was avenged by driving the incendiary from the land or even by burning him to death. A man who carelessly causes a fire is under an obligation to make compensation for the damage and he may possibly be ordered to offer a meal to the injured or frightened party to appease and reassure him. It is also possible that the perpetrator be shunned.

It is an offence not to be willing to co-operate in executing the regulations obtaining in a village or territory, as is also the refusal to give a helping hand in cases of acute danger, such as fire and when a canal is breached.

In many regions in olden times the chief of a territory or the offering priest, the *parbaringin,* gave the sign to start the cultivation of the fields after the end of the dry monsoon and anyone who paid no attention to it had to offer a meal as his *panopotion* to the leaders.

Tampering with merchandise, *mangalansum,* was classed in olden times as a serious offence. It was established in the market and was punished by the chiefs directly concerned with the market. It is unlawful to pollute wells, springs and ponds, *sirotahi mual,* in a way that makes the water unfit for human or animal consumption.

Bribery, *mangondong* or *mangalehon sisip,* is an old offence which was resorted to in wartime when a neutral third party was persuaded to injure the enemy secretly by word and deed; hiring a fighter to take the enemy by surprise, *ulubalang na so mangua,* came under this heading. Judges before whom a matter was awaiting a decision could also be given a *sisip* or *upa* so that they would abandon their impartiality. This prac- tice was so widespread that it was hardly regarded as punishable. The attitude to it has already begun to change.

In this category of violating the general welfare can also be placed transgressing a prohibition which was instituted in the interest of the community and which could be attendant upon acts of a supernatural purport, such as the *robu*-prohibition of former times after the cere- monial rice-offering and other ritual acts, and the *hapantangan,* the prohibition orders which related to the ceremonies performed by the *datu.* Violation of any of these prohibitions naturally had to be made good by magical means.

OFFENCES AGAINST THE PERSON

Intent and guilt in such offences have already been dealt with. Severe manhandling, *pasiak-siakhon* is at present punished with the offender's being imprisoned, unless the matter is one between kinsmen and affines.

Kidnapping, *mamangus,* no longer takes place.

In the former periods of war, killing someone who was under the protection of a neutral third party was akin to murder, *iring-iring so djadi mago (sitompas iring-iring),* as was also the killing of a guest of a neutral host. The market and an authorised *gondang*-feast also offered the participants protection. In actual warfare it was permitted to kill by stealth, *marbadjo*: such violence is, of course, forbidden now.

The poisoner, *sibahen rasun,* is a vicious criminal as is the *pargadam =* one who uses poison to produce skin eruptions. This applies to a lesser degree to anyone who administers the *dorma*, the magical means resorted to by young lovers, since this also may result in disturbing the natural faculties, or in abortion.

If someone heightens the danger in which a person already stands, he is said to be *sidabu djolma dibibir ni lombang, situndjang na rugút, sidegehon na ompás =* one who causes another to fall from the brink into the abyss, one who kicks another who is already falling down.

To strike someone with the hand is termed *mangonai tangan.*

OFFENCES AGAINST PROPERTY

In this group are primarily to be reckoned a number of offences which have been mentioned already and which come under the rule of corrective measures, such as repledging a field for an amount in excess of the original pledge, which is an improper act and can lead to quarrels and to difficulties for a court; carelessly or in bad faith crossing the boundaries of land, woods, roads (*manuruk andor, mangalangkai abor*); burdening an already attached girl. Any of these forms can take the worse form of *manghaliangi =* stealthy appropriation, adroit pilfering (*haliang =* round about), such as for example, appropriating the property of a minor by a custodian, *manghaliangi ugasan ni anak na metmet,* which can be deduced from the circumstances in which the management of the property has been conducted. Akin to this offence is that of *mangangati =* benefiting at the cost of another by cunning means, *angat.* The element of trickery is also present in the offence termed *mamogo =* keeping or using for oneself that which is definitely intended for another purpose, for example, goods on commission, money which should be passed to another. Actions such as these are usually defended with sophisticated arguments which neither the evidence nor reason support. If, in addition, goods on commission or money held for another are disposed of, one form of which is termed *manggadis lume =*

selling goods placed in custody, then the offence assumes a more serious aspect. In olden times, if a judge ordered a penalty he had imposed to be paid over through a particular intermediary, the *sisampe dangdang,* the latter sometimes kept it. At least, according to the *Patik dohot Uhum* and the "Rules of Naipospos". *Mamogo* is for that matter by no means unknown at the present time.

Appropriation of goods which are found by the wayside, *na dapot di tonga ni dalan* is punishable if no mention is made of finding the objects to the village chief and, if they are valuable, to the chief of the cluster of villages and the territory.

Larceny, *manangko,* is known under many names according to the goods stolen and the manner of the theft: *mamorus* = to steal the produce of the fields; *manarus* = to steal palm wine; *mandobo* = to pillage; *manamun* = to rob a traveller; *mambarobo* = to rob fish nets in lakes or rivers; *mangarut* = burglary; *mangemur* = to steal in the market place.

Receiving stolen goods is termed *marmihim-mihim ugasan na tinangko* = the secret spiriting away of goods known to have been stolen. It is also regarded as larceny to accept goods the origin of which is unknown but suspect, *ugasan na djinalo soada hatorangan.*

CHAPTER X

SETTLING DISPUTES
(*Ruhut ni parhataon*)

A wide variety of things can be the subject of a lawsuit, for which the term is *hata* or *sihataon*, the matter that is to be discussed. When a woman is the subject of a dispute, be it over a betrothal, a marriage, or the conduct of a wife or a daughter, the term used is *hata boru*; when it is over land, the term is *hata tano*; over damage caused by fire, or over arson, it is *hata surbu*; over the destruction of the harvest by cattle, *hata gagat-gagat*; over breaking off a betrothal, or a divorce, *hata sirang*; over debts, *hata singir,* and so on. The case itself is called *parhataon,* and the course of the suit is termed *ruhut ni parhataon.*

In discussing the course of the case, attention will only be given to the procedure followed in early times in accordance with the conditions then prevailing as far as it is necessary for a proper understanding of the relevant rules and usages operative at present.

According to the Batak texts to which I have frequently referred, the principal features that distinguished the old manner of conducting a case from that of the present day were: the general absence of an established judicial structure; the great importance that was attached to supernatural means in reaching a decision; the use of the oath to arrive at a decision; and in many cases the parties in a dispute had to agree with the judgement because there was no special power for ensuring that it was carried out.

ORIGIN OF DISPUTES

I have already mentioned the careless usages in the matter of contracts. The many *sidalian* = evasions, the sophistries which are so readily resorted to, and the inclination to take the law into one's own hands, are some of the causes of the numerous conflicts that play a part in the life of the Batak and which in olden times gave rise to many wars. It is a singular trait of a Batak's character to think that he is always in the right and as a consequence he will make an issue over the merest trifle, fighting over swallows' feathers, *manggulut imput ni leang-leang,* it is called. He is also particularly desirous of gaining the victory in a lawsuit as being the most sagacious party: he suffers a corresponding shame if he loses it.

Disputes are fostered by the mutual friction inevitable between kinsmen who live together and are further heightened by the unmannerliness in mutual intercourse and the vehemence and rudeness which are characteristic of the Tobanese in general. As the Tobanese well know, insolence is the beginning of a quarrel, *tois mula ni gora*, and there is more that could be said that would explain why quarrels are constantly brewing among these people.

There are a great number of terms by which the causes and forms of quarrelling are defined, and it should be noted that most of them make a charge of mutual unfairness: *mandjoha* = to make a false claim about something; *masidjohaan* or *masitodoan* = mutually to lay claim to the same goods; *masironsangan* = to desire mutually to cultivate the same plot of land; *masituho-tuhoan* = mutual accusation; *masitorpaan* = to quarrel over mutual debts; *masituhasan* = mutual suspicion; *manggomak* or *mangalahangi* = to bring something arbitrarily under one's own authority; *masilindian* = to make mutual counter-claims; *mandaho* = to make a false complaint. This list suggests that these offences are of very frequent occurrence.

TRACING AND PREVENTING OFFENCES

Formerly, divination was often used in tracing unknown criminals, especially thieves. Winkler describes a *mangarambu* = divination, which the *datu* performed with the help of a calendar that was counted out while he counted out on his fingers at the same time. From this performance it was deduced what kind of person it was who had stolen the lost property. The ordeals resorted to formerly, such as chewing uncooked rice, trial by molten lead or iron, which are described in 'Adatrechtbundel' 35 pp. 77 and 148, had the same aim. The *patindang gana mangaliat* = summoning together for a communal oath-taking, is something still applied to the inhabitants of a village or a cluster of villages, for example, when the person who has been robbed administers the oath of purgation to all the inhabitants who must thus make known that they have no knowledge of the missing objects. Anyone who evades in any way participating in this general swearing is suspected of the theft. Not so long ago, on Samosir, a father whose son was found dead in a field close to the village gate, made use of this procedure in order to discover the murderer. At present, and formerly, when a man finds some of his goods are missing, he gives a little rice, *dahanon parnungnung*, or another present, to all the members of the village with the object of inducing them to restore the stolen goods, *manganungnung,* as though they were goods that had been found, *na djumpang.* All these means of tracing offenders had to be performed under the supervision and direction of the village chief concerned, who, if necessary, could act as guarantor for his co-villagers and could take the oath on behalf of all of them, *mangampu gana.* This chief also stood by the injured party in the prosecution and also when claims were made for reparation, *marlulu,* from the known offender.

Formerly, there were no persons who were entrusted, either exclusively or in the main, with the task of tracing offenders or of preventing offences. As far as the security of the village was concerned, the closing of the village gate each evening was the duty of the inhabitant whose house was hard by it. In times of unrest when there was danger of an attack, the men took it in turns at night to watch on the walls. This could go on for months on end. When there was a war, even the women had to lend a hand.

A person caught *in flagrante delicto,* the thief, the murderer, the seducer, etc., was arrested in anticipation of the investigation. These major criminals were fettered, *diihot,* put in the block, *dibeanghon,* or, in the more serious cases, were dragged immediately to the slaughtering pole, *taluktuk,* from which a prisoner could be ransomed by his kinsmen: after that his trial could commence.

MASITOLONAN = ADMINISTERING THE OATH MUTUALLY

When two people wish to settle a dispute of minor importance, they can mutually swear the oath — a frequent occurrence in former times. Only the barest formalities are observed. If it is the boundaries of a rice-field which are at issue, then only the owners of adjoining fields have to be present; when the dispute concerns the amount of, or the payment of, a debt, only a co-villager or a good friend has to be there. When the oath is administered mutually, it is immaterial which man asks the other to swear:

dos do sanggar dohot tolong;
dos na marmangmang dohot na manolon.
Sanggar grass is similar to *tolong* grass.

The one who imposes the oath is similar to the one who swears it. This rule deliberately enjoins the parties concerned neither to take nor to administer a false oath. A true oath is harmless to either party. This *masitolonan* is the complement of the mutual accusation. It is used, for example, in the first stages of the annual work on a wet rice-field if the owner of that field accuses his neighbour of having shifted the small boundary dykes and this neighbour makes the counter accusation that the owner of the field is laying the complaint in order to acquire an extra strip of land. Since neither party has conclusive proof of this *masidjohaan*, they must resort to the oath.

THE MANGUDJI; PROOF BY COMPETITION

The *mangudji,* which was common in olden times, is a similar idea to the *masitolonan.* Each party hung up a cloth or put up a length of banana stem and each shot at the target the other had set up. The outcome of this shooting match determined where right and truth lay and where wrongdoing and lies. This proceeding could take place with or without the collaboration of a judge, but for the maintenance of good order, the chiefs saw to it that everything was fairly done. The more serious form of *mangudji* occurred less frequently. This consisted of both parties engaging in a formal duel during which they shot at each other over a measured distance. It only took place in quarrels which had reached such a pitch that no judge had been able to effect a settlement. Before the commencement of the shooting, both parties addressed their *tonggo* = prayers, to the gods and to the spirits for their help in the contest beween right and wrong.

MARMUSU = GOING TO WAR

War was also considered as a judgement by the gods and the spirits on the contentions and acts of the parties. War could follow on an unsuccessful or an unfulfilled mediation, on the non-acceptance or non-observance of a judicial decision, or after acts of violence had taken place. If a man went to war because he thought he had been unjustly treated, then he said of it that:

> *bodil manungkun* = the rifle asks;
> *hudjur manise* = the spear inquires;
> *tali manahut* = the rope stirs.

The commencement of hostilities was also often preceded by the saying of prayers, *martonggo.* Magical means of fighting were frequently used for forcing the fortunes of battle, the *pangulubalang* (p. 100) being particularly regarded as a formidable weapon if the battle was between the larger genealogical groups. A number of rules, not always faithfully observed, of which some are mentioned in the Batak texts already quoted, regulated the law for these wars between man and man, village and village, clan and clan. The war usually ended because the one party had driven the other out of house, village or fields, *mamuhar,* or because both parties got tired of it, *lodja,* or because friendly or affinal chiefs offered to intervene. This they might do when a war, which had originally begun as a small war, had so extended that it had become a war involving the many, or in those areas where the super-magician Singamangaradja was all-powerful, his aid was sometimes enlisted to put an end to the public calamity by uttering a powerful interdiction. Sometimes, however, small wars were continued indefinitely and the offshoots are to be found to the present day in endless lawsuits. The right of the victor to pillage, *martaban,* differed according to the region. After the Dutch began to govern the country, the *status quo* in respect of villages and fields which had been captured in a former war was upheld everywhere unless the victor had voluntarily returned them to their rightful owners. There are places, however, where up to the present the people have not been able to adjust themselves to this *status quo* and sometimes the old submerged desire for disputation rises up again, especially over land, and with it the desire to settle the quarrel with cudgels and knives. There are also those who await a suitable opportunity to unearth the hatchet should the central authority weaken. Should that happen, then quarrels may again grow into wars between lineage and lineage, *marga* and *marga,* and perhaps between tribal group and tribal group.

MEDIATOR & JUDGE

In olden times it would appear that there was not a distinct dividing line between the mediator, the *pangulu* (also called *pande-pande*), the arbitrator, *panolai,* the one whose help one could enlist, and the chiefs, *radja,* whose intercession one could invoke as judges, *radja paruhum* = those who gave judgement, and whose support was then sought in the implementation of their verdict. And furthermore, each case was not dealt with in the same manner, it was not brought before the same kind of chiefs or persons, nor did it always pass through the hands of a definite sequence of authorities. There was so much variation in the local power relationships, so many nuances in the organisation of the chiefs' authority, that it is hardly practicable to describe the variety of ways in which a dispute could be dealt with.

If the dispute took place within a more or less confined group, as, for example, between the inhabitants of one village or a cluster of villages of one lineage, then the chiefs of that group desired that it was brought before them, and they exerted themselves to effect a solution in order to prevent the chiefs from outside becoming involved in their affairs. But only the fear of the disfavour of his own chiefs restrained a person who had no confidence in them and their administration of justice, from submitting his case to others.

If someone had something to settle with a person from a remote village, then he could go there himself and approach the opposing party, or his village chief, or he could go with his own village chief, and perhaps with even one or more friendly or related chiefs, *radja na pulik*, to visit the village chief or one of the higher chiefs of the opposing party in an endeavour to settle the dispute. But it was also possible for him to send a third party as his mediator, *pangulu*, with a formulated mandate. Both the parties could avail themselves of the services of this mediator until agreement was reached, or until it was apparent that the gulf between the standpoints of both parties was unbridgeable. Such a mediator, naturally, should not become partisan, *panolai gabe sangkan*. Another way was to bring the matter before the chiefs each of whom sat in his territory's own corner, *parampangan*, of the *onan* of the *marga* or *bius*. They were there to discuss the affairs of the land and to deal with complaints brought before them. The defendant could be summoned before them, or some of the chiefs, acting as *pangulu*, could convey to him the plaintiff's claims and learn his reply: consultation or war.

If a protracted war had already been going on between persons or between villages belonging to different village clusters or territories, and if it was the desire of both parties that agreement should be reached, then each party, seconded by his own chiefs and some chiefs from the neighbourhood whose assistance had been requested, drew themselves up opposite each other, *mardompak*, on a neutral piece of ground, *holang-holang* (this could be a small market place that had been declared neutral territory, an arid strip of heath land, or an arbitrarily chosen spot) and kept arguing, *masipollungan*, until a decision was reached, or weapons were taken up again. If one or more of the chiefs were of the opinion that a war had gone on long enough and that their intercession could be fruitful, it was also possible for them to intervene either during the actual fighting, as *pamonari* = those who could bring about a suspension, *bonar*, of hostilities, by waving an *ulos*, or, during a lull in the fighting, they could persuade the contestants to lay down their arms, *pongpang* = truce, and after that the matter at issue could be submitted for judicial consideration.

Where more stability existed in the organisation of the chieftaincy of the territories, the more serious offences as well as the important disputes that could not be settled in the villages or clusters of villages, could be brought before the *parluhutan, parriaan, harungguan,* the assembly under the direction of a prominent chief, the *ompu ni saksi,* the *radja doli* or the *radja partahi,* or the *loloan na godang* = great council, which could assemble in the market or at other fixed places, *toguan,* of the territory.

Whether any of these forms of enlisting intervention could lead to a decision or to mediation, depended to a great extent on the *hasangapon* = respect in which the parties concerned were held and that accorded to the persons who acted as arbitrators in their affairs. The ordinary man, *na torop,* had to go before the chiefs and he had to await their decision. For him, the chiefs, particularly the mightiest of them, were the judges who could bring a lawsuit to a conclusion, *paudjunghon sihataon;* those who could *pasaehon* = bring a dispute to an end, *sae hata,* who could end a suit, *pasauthon.* They could pronounce judgement, *mandabu uhum* (or *uhuman*) in an ordinary man's case. To flout their pronouncement was termed, *so mangoloi hata ni radja* = unwillingness to comply with the orders of a chief, which was a motive for the *radja,* whose honour and prestige had been affronted, to place his powerful help at the disposal of the party opposing the obdurate one. The sanctions behind these judgements were compulsion, or expulsion. But, if the parties were of some consequence, if they had a substantial clan behind them, so that they did not have to regard the judges as being a power far above them and did not feel compelled to respect them, then, although they submitted their disputes to the judgement of an assembly of chiefs, they nevertheless retained complete freedom to revert to force of arms. What the judge then had to seek was less a decision to be maintained by compulsion, than a solution which would satisfy both parties and avert a great war.

Naturally, great changes took place in all this after the arrival of the Netherlands Indies Government. After the formation of the native authorities, *hundulan,* started in 1883, and later the *negeri,* about 1918, the opportunity presented itself of establishing courts of the chiefs of the territories, which courts, under the leadership of the *djaihutan* (since 1918, the *negeri* chiefs) could administer justice in respect of disputes over land, women, money, etc., and in the less serious criminal offences committed within their communities. These new kind of law courts had the higher authority of the State behind them, so that they could effect a judgement or mediate as they thought fit without being influenced by the social position of the parties before them. Mediation still has its uses and there is room for it, also outside the scope of the organised judiciary.

THE ADMINISTRATION OF JUSTICE AND THE AFFINAL RELATIONSHIPS

It will already have become apparent that the affinal relationship is of great importance in the juridical life of the Batak. The especial task of this remarkable and typically Batak phenomenon in respect of the administration of justice, was discussed in Chapter I. Nevertheless, there are still some peculiarities which I will discuss here.

The influence that an affine can exercise on a pair of kinsmen who are carrying on a dispute, is not commonly given expression in formal legal proceedings. His intercession in the affair is usually voluntary and even if he is invited to intercede, he does not have to put on the formal clothes of a judge in order to have authority. If he is of the *hula-hula* then, as the *tunggane* or the *tulang* in the smaller groups, and as the *radja hula-hula* in the larger groups, he has a natural ascendancy over the disputants on account of his affinal relationship with them.

Conversely, the *boru* who intercedes in the dispute of his *hula-hula* possesses the moral authority of the one who is by nature non-partisan. An affine can be active in a way that is hardly noticeable, since his activities are conducted completely outside the instituted administration of justice. But, neither the extent of his activities nor his influence should be underestimated. He can prevent cases accumulating before the judge and frequently enables disputes to be settled which a judge has already dealt with but has not resolved yet.

In some regions, in olden times, the affines functioned more or less regularly in the administration of justice in village and territory. This could be the case especially where representatives of the in-dwelling *marga* had acquired a somewhat firm footing in the ruling of the village or territory, such as occurred most frequently in the south-western part of the Toba Country (also in South Tapanuli). An influential *namora boru* who coupled a powerful personality and a sagacity of judgement with the authority resulting from his prosperity, was, in the village in which he was an in-dweller, the principal support of the village chief in controlling the latter's sometimes somewhat difficult-to-handle kinsmen. Such a *boru* could make the village renowned as a place where the law was cared for and well-maintained. He assisted a co-villager who had a claim on someone from a neighbouring village or territory, by bringing the claim forward and defending it, and sometimes, in conjunction with the *namora* of the defendant, decided what was to obtain as the law in a dispute between parties who belonged to the same ruling *marga*. If a *sihataon* = dispute, had arisen between persons of different territories, then members of the *boru na godjong* of both parties, as the representatives of the oldest in-dwelling *marga,* appeared as the negotiators, or they conducted the lawsuit for both parties before the council of chiefs in the great market of the region. The discussions were then held in a spirit of complete disinterestedness and service to the law. The *boru na godjong* could also be charged by the judge with the further settling of a case in which the decision had been taken in principle and its main lines drawn.

This representative of the oldest *marga boru* also had the influence of the neutral in the assembly of chiefs of the territory. He endeavoured to see that the law was honoured and tried to ensure that peace was preserved between those who had power in his *hula-hula.* In many a case he could, therefore, work for the maintenance of peace and could make sure that no injustice was done and that no misuse of power prevailed over the law within the community. Consequently, in quarrels his voice was often of decisive importance.

It was not everywhere the case, however, that the representatives of the in-dwelling *marga* regularly functioned in the administration of justice in village and territory. Sagacity and eloquence, which were prerequisites for active participation, mediation and assistance in the administration of justice, were not always coupled with a man's being an elder of the *marga boru* or a direct descendant of a companion of the village's founder. One can probably attribute the Government's failure to devote any thought to the co-operation of the affines in organising native justice, to the fact that, at first, few prominent figures came to the forefront, and later, to the fact that the need for it did not become apparent. Moreover, the *marga boru* itself scarcely expressed a noticeable desire regarding its participation in local government and the official administration of justice.

INTRODUCTORY GIFTS

Formerly it was often the custom to enlist the judges' intercession by offering them food and drink or a money gift. The object of the food and drink was to testify to one's respect for the judge as well as to bring him to the right frame of mind necessary for him to arrive at a just decision. In some regions it was the custom for the plaintiff to

25

pour out palm wine, *tumahu tuak,* into small beakers and to offer it to the chiefs when they were assembled in the market place. The plaintiff set the wine before them by way of introducing his complaint. The chiefs then asked him in *umpama*-form: *"Dia nangkatna, dia ultopna, dia hatana, dia nidokna* = How are the darts, how is the blow-pipe, what is there to discuss, how should it be worded?" Elsewhere the chiefs were offered a piece of roasted meat, *longit.* If a man summoned one or more mediators to his house, then he set a meal before them; this is still done.

In some areas the plaintiff in a lawsuit paid a small sum of money to the judge as an 'opener' of the case, *sibuha hata,* or the judges themselves demanded a small sum from one or both parties. This was called *ginagat ni harungguan* = what was eaten by the gathering, or *parrait ni parrapotan ni radja* = the 'tie beams' of the assembly of chiefs; there were also other terms for it. This sum was an advance on the much larger sealing money, *pago-pago,* that was paid when the case was concluded. This will be discussed later. At the present time, because many small problems are settled in the coffee houses, *lapo,* one sometimes speaks of coffee-money, *pasikopi.* In this connection it must be mentioned that such introductory gifts, in addition to the technical designation current in a region, can always be called *ulos* or *piso* when the inhabitants of a village make them to their own chiefs. In that case the villagers are therefore the *hula-hula* or the *boru* of their chief, or are regarded by him as such.

In making these introductory gifts, it was not the purpose of the parties to place themselves under an obligation to accept the judgement. Many times I heard of the gifts being returned if the case could not be concluded. From this it follows, that the offering of such a gift signified, provisionally, a willingness to accept the judge's intervention, without a promise to abide by the decision; it was also possibly a provisional remuneration of the judges.

RESPECT FOR THE COURT

In olden times it was unlawful for hostilities to continue during the period that a dispute was being formally dealt with. The parties had to accept the judge as a representative of a higher authority:

> *disí sirungguk disí sitatá;*
> *ia disí hita hundul, disí ompunta Debatá.*

Where the *sirungguk* sways there will always be the wild banana.
Where we, the chiefs, are seated, the Deity is also present.

The principle that the adjudicating chiefs were the dwelling place of the Deity and the revered spirits, *sorangan ni Debatá, sorangan ni sombaon,* was, in fact, one of the basic fundamentals of the society. It ensured, provided it was rigidly upheld, that at least during the legal hearing of a dispute, peace and order prevailed, without which any regular settlement would have been impossible among these quick-tempered people. As soon as the parties were prepared either to suspend hostilities, *pongpang,* if they were fighting, or to refrain from starting to fight, the knife of the adjudication, *raut marhata,* or *tintin marang-kupan* = the rings that coincide, was demanded from each of them and by handing them over the contestants bound themselves to desist from engaging in mutual hostilities any further. Then the rifle was slung on the back, *tu tangkingan bodil,* the lance was hung on the cord, *tu rompuan hudjur,* because for the time being the war had been turned into peace, *parbadaan nunga menak.* The chiefs could deliberate in peace and the consultations were conducted in a peaceful atmosphere, *menak radja marhata, menak pinahatana.* Violation of such an armistice supervised by the chiefs, *mansoadahon pongpang ni radja,* by a breaker of faith, *pangose,* was regarded as one of the most serious of offences; as a crime against the judicially arranged truce. It was a dire insult to all the chiefs concerned. However, if a man would not accept a given judgement, or a recommended solution, he could claim the return of his surrendered peace pledges. And, after a stipulated period, which was determined by knots, *pudun,* tied in a piece of rope that was given to both parties, he could resort to arms again.

During the truce it was likewise forbidden to contravene certain orders, *hata siunang,* such as, for example, tilling a piece of land over which there was a dispute. And it was absolutely forbidden during the hearing to indulge in physical violence or to create a disturbance in any way:

> *hite bulu diparhite paronan;*
> *ugus pe tanggurung, ndang djadi masihaoran;*
> the bamboo bridge is used by the marketeer;
> even if their backs do rub against each other, people may not importune each other;

as the saying goes, and in West Humbáng I heard the following maxim for disturbing the peace at a hearing under the direction of the *ompu ni saksi:*

> *pinggol ni andjing puti lepe-lepe tu toru;*
> *utang sisegai saksi saratus pitu pulu manang horbo simate mangolu.*

The ear of the white dog hangs.

The punishment for the breaker of the truce is 170, *viz.* a slaughtered buffalo and a live one.

The question of whether the judge could summon a person about whom a complaint was laid before him, was likewise mainly decided by the power relationships. Where a powerful authority ruled, the common man could not flout a *djou-djou ni radja* = summons from the chief, with impunity. We have already seen, however, that the chiefs before whom a complaint was brought in the market, could also regard themselves as mediators who passed on to the accused the plaintiff's complaint.

Under the present system, in which the judge is by no means lacking power, the introductory gift has lost its real importance, the peace during the hearing is not less guaranteed than formerly, and the accused is not free voluntarily to absent himself from the hearing to which he has been summoned. The Batak judge who knows his people, deems discipline a first requisite and always bears in mind the possibility that he will have to take definite steps against actions that hinder the regular administration of justice, for example, the deliberate failure of a summoned witness to appear; the use of offensive language at the hearing; the blatant lying of a party or of a witness; the refusal to provide witnesses; all of which acts constitute 'contempt of court' and their perpetrators can be subjected to discipline because their conduct 'tires the court', *mangalodjai rapot,* causes it to assemble needlessly and hold up the proceedings, or because it makes a fool of the judge, *paoto-oto radja, paruhum,* etc.

THE ATTRIBUTES OF A JUDGE

Unfortunately, the Batak do not in general possess in their chiefs judges who are unselfish, impartial and incorruptible. Many a time a chief is easily angered when someone has deliberately, or accidentally, offended him by word or deed. Thereafter, as I have seen many times, he is no longer in a position to give an unprejudiced judgement. Moreover, he does not always remain neutral during the course of the lawsuit; while the investigation is still in progress he is sometimes carried away in defending the viewpoint that he had decided initially was the right one. He is so susceptible to bribery — especially in Toba — that, taking into consideration the quantity of disputes, it must be regarded as the scourge of the country. He is seldom capable of being completely impartial if one of the parties is a somewhat close kinsman or affine of his. He has little interest in matters that take place outside his known surroundings, and often looks up to the wealthy and the powerful, and as a consequence does injustice to the ordinary man.

This is not a favourable testimonial, either for the judges or for the people as a whole. But disclosing a sore point can be more advantageous than concealing it. Fortunately, on the other hand, there is many a capable, honourable and clever chief who desires to co-operate in an investigation and in the search for a just solution. And one and all are filled with a real love for their country and for their *adat*.

THE HEARING IN PUBLIC

No more powerful antidote is to be found against the evils just mentioned than the public hearing of the suit from beginning to end. Excluding the public from the proceedings, as was done in later years when cases were heard behind closed doors guarded by courtmessengers, is completely un-Batak. The main reason for this action was the fear that a listener might provoke the losing party. There were many *radja* who shunned the criticism of the public and always pleaded for its exclusion. The cost of this hearing in secret was the loss of confidence of the people in their own judiciary. It is true, that the presence of well-paid officials standing outside and above the parties and the judges, provided some guarantee of honesty, but if such officials are Europeans, who are masters of neither the language nor of customary law, then they can be more easily misled than a sizeable public will be.

A public hearing, however, has little meaning when it is held outside the group of people directly involved in the case, for then nobody puts in an appearance.

When hearings are held in public, there is always an opportunity of following up a hint which someone present might give unexpectedly and which might produce fruitful results, for example, when the investigation concerns a difficult case or one which has reached a deadlock. This I witnessed on more than one occasion.

The public character of the hearing is, moreover, of great advantage in that, as in former times, the people are kept fully in touch with the case as it proceeds, can keep abreast of their law and can form an opinion regarding the weak places in it and can exercise their influence on the proper maintenance of their law and custom.

PARTIES: REPRESENTATION AND ASSISTANCE

Parties as a rule appear for themselves. Large groups, such as a lineage, are represented by the persons most suitable to act for them; associations, by one or more of their officers; a Church society, by one or more of the Elders of the Church Council or the pastor, *pandita*. Persons who are not in their own region are naturally represented by their relatives whose competency is determined by their mutual relationship (a father is fully committed on behalf of his son; a *boru* takes on itself all the obligations of its *tunggane*, etc.). The mother acts for male minors without a father, but an uncle or a village chief can also act for them. As a rule, in these cases they do not need to have special powers. The circumstances are the determining factors as to whether or not the persons acting are qualified to represent a plaintiff or a defendant. If the judge is in doubt, he will seek enlightenment from those qualified to give it. Anyone who appears to have interfered in what does not concern him can be punished on the grounds of '*mangantoi na so ulaonna*', or perhaps even as one who extended a quarrel, *siparagat parbadaan*. The judge can of his own accord summon third parties in the case; he can look after their interests or can force a provisional or permanent obligation on them as circumstances require.

If a person does not put in an appearance when he knows that a case in which he is involved is pending, he will be ignored: *pitu gadja nilapa, molo soada na mangido ndang adóng na malá* = though not less than seven elephants are skinned, when no one comes to request a portion, nothing is given away.

The village chief is naturally the one to give legal aid, he is the *pangondian,* and *parsinabul,* spokesman, for his subjects. He is alive to their interests and even appears for them in a case where their claims are legally doubtful: his intercession is then termed *marbulu suhar* = tearing out a bamboo stalk against the grain from its stool. If a person feels that he is insufficiently skilled to conduct his own case alone, then he will often allow a sagacious kinsman or an affine to assist him.

COMPLAINT AND DEFENCE: THE JUDGES' ATTITUDE

In olden times, and even today, the frequent precursor to a dispute was a verbal argument, *pollung*. Before the plaintiff, *na mangalu,* takes a matter to court he bears in mind the saying:

sise mula ni uhum;

topot mula ni hata.

To ask for an explanation is the beginning of the administration of justice.

A visit [to elicit an explanation] is the beginning of a lawsuit.

He will already have communicated with his opponent, *alona,* in order to receive satisfaction from him. The latter will reply to his request, *mangalusi,* and will take particular care to do so in the appropriate terms. This arguing between the two parties, *masipollungan,* can afterwards be continued in front of the judge, who grants the parties the freedom to do so, since it will sometimes enable him to sift lies from truth at an early stage of the case. As a rule, however, each party in the suit endeavours to place himself in a favourable light and his opponent in the darkest one by the clever way in which he presents his complaint, *alu-alu,* and the quick-wittedness of his defence, *alus,* to achieve which each party communicates precisely as many of the facts as he deems necessary. Each then endeavours to build up an advantageous position in the suit by an adroit coupling of the facts with the relevant arguments. This frequently necessitates the Batak judge adopting the attitude which his colleague in a European lawsuit does: he acts according to the facts the parties have chosen to place before him, and bases his final decision thereon. He will adopt this method if, for example, the two parties are well matched, or if it is known to him that prospective disputes exist between them which it appears useless to unravel for the time being, or if further penetration into the case would extend its proportions excessively by bringing large groups, among which there are slumbering feuds, around the parties into action against each other. But he need not refrain from acting otherwise, if he sees fit. He is free to investigate what appears to be obscure to him, to lay bare a concealed kernel; to uncover the background of the case:

> *aek na litok tingkiron tu djulu;*
> *hori ni rundut bahenon tu tapean.*

If the water is turbid, then one must go upstream.
Flax that is tangled, must be unravelled.

And, if the judge wishes to do this, it will often have to be done in the face of the pretences and sophistries of the one party who, because of his greater ability, has been able to establish a position in the dispute behind which the true facts of the case are concealed. In such a case, the party's opponent, for particular reasons, may often not be in a position to adduce sufficient factual evidence — he may be an orphan who has reached adulthood, or it may be a woman, or it may be a person who has returned after a long absence — or the man may be awkward in defending his own case, so that he can only hope that the judge will be zealous, have good insight and good judgement. If the

plaintiff, *pangalu*, is such a one, he will request the judge to restore the
right he considers to have been violated. If it is the defendant, *na
nialuhon*, then he will appeal to the judge in order to get to the bottom
of the injustice of the complaint. In the event of the investigation, which
the judge can then initiate, the onus of proof will sometimes lay on the
one party and sometimes on the other, but this does not deter the judge
from proceeding even though the party concerned objects. And also in
a case where each of the parties has contributed to circumscribing the
boundaries and to establishing the foundations, the one by a well-founded
and well-authenticated claim, the other by a well-prepared defence, the
judge has the authority to extend his investigation outside these limits.
To this, the parties who act in good faith are usually quite ready to
agree, as they are to accept a solution or a judgement which deviates
from the one they had hoped for, or is more broadly based, as being
the better one given according to the elders' knowledge of *adat*. The
freedom of the judge to take an independent stand in a lawsuit is sometimes quite remarkable. This freedom also exists in respect of judging
the importance of the facts that are brought forward and disputed. In
disputes over facts, of the kind which are especially so common in Toba
and of which the treatment there is so much hindered by bribing witnesses, it is, in the main, a question of the truth or the untruth of the
allegations, and if once it is established what must be upheld as true,
the legal question is usually easy to solve. The judge himself can determine which facts to take into consideration and which are irrelevant.

Similarly, the decision whether a counter-claim against the original
claim can be admitted and dealt with at the same time, rests with him.
Here he demonstrates the strong, the markedly strong, tendency to
refuse to deal with them jointly. The rule that everybody should claim
the debts due to him and pay his own debts, *masitunggu singirna be,
masigarar utangna be,* which is opposed to the coupling of claims, has
significance in legal procedure and restrains the admittance of counter-
claims. Only in a definite connection, for example, claims made together
in respect of *sinamot* and *pauseang,* in the event of a divorce, or if
there is a lawsuit over a rice-field and over its harvest which has been
unlawfully appropriated, and so on, are there no objections to coupling
the claims. If there is no question of the claim or the counter-claim
being genuinely related, or if the nature of the obligations is completely
different, *utang adat ingkon digarar dibagasan adat* = debts incurred
according to law and custom must be paid according to law and custom,
in contrast to debts arising from casual circumstances, then the judge

prefers to treat the claims separately. To give an example: if it was agreed mutually during the discussions on a divorce that some of the property would be returned with the wife, and if, after some time, the *parboru* lays a complaint that the ex-husband has not handed it over, then the latter might bring a counter-claim concerning the unfulfillment of the money debt which the *parboru* had contracted at a totally different transaction. When this counter-claim is disputed, the ex-husband would be advised to make his claim separately; even though it concerns a divorce with complete termination of the affinal relationship, *sirang laos tos partondongan.*

A judge will make short shrift if a wrong person is summoned and will bear in mind the saying on p. 308 *ansimun na martagan,* etc.

THE PROOF OF THE FACTS

Though formerly, when an allegation or an indictment was denied by one of the contending parties, the judge could always demand proof, it was not always thought necessary to obtain a complete and clear picture of the events and of the facts of importance for the case. The idea of full verification was not developed until the Batak came into contact with modern legal procedures. The normal procedure was much associated with a sphere in which people had a tendency to resort to judgement by supernatural powers and to the invoking of the powers of disaster in order to find out a truth or an untruth. Taking the oath in order to cleanse oneself of suspicion, or as a means of deciding a dispute, made it sometimes unnecessary to require proof in respect of a fact to be furnished or the truth of an allegation to be substantiated, because its purpose was to transfer the judgement to a supernatural power. Taking the oath could be applied at every stage of the case and the satisfaction it provided could give the opposing party, as well as the judges, a reason for obviating the need to lay bare all the events or to provide complete and reliable evidence for the disputed facts. No use was made by either party of written evidence, and to my knowledge, written records of contracts were unknown. There was but little room for the evidence of witnesses, reasoning and presumption playing a prominent role. A rather great measure of carelessness in respect of substantiating proof was possible without its being a hindrance to the progress of the case.

The imported rationalised procedure under European direction in which, for want originally of written documents as evidence, the principal role was assigned to the evidence of witnesses, and the oath was treated in a totally different manner, was consequently a reform of great significance. Up to the present day, many parties in a lawsuit and their witnesses, and even the more old fashioned Batak judges, feel somewhat out of their depth when confronted with the tendency of every European court President always to demand concrete evidence for all the disputed facts submitted to the court.

The parties are willingly allowed to argue backwards and forwards, the judges interrupt with questions, and the oath is quickly resorted to:

timbang daon ni na tutú;

gana daon ni na so tutú.

Deliberation is best when the facts are known.

The oath is the solution when the facts are not known.

To this situation must be attributed the absence of precise rules regarding the onus of proof. The language, rich though it is in legal maxims, does not contain, as far as I know, the equivalent of our definite "Whosoever makes an allegation must prove it". More than once I saw the defendant compelled to bear the full burden of giving an explanation of his attitude, of clarifying his assertion or of providing proof of the facts he had adduced — sometimes this resulted in exposing the falseness of the defendant's standpoint — though neither statement nor proof was demanded from the plaintiff. In respect of the onus of proof, it can therefore only be said in very general terms that in most cases each of the parties must substantiate his allegation. Sometimes more weight is attached to the plausible but not adequately substantiated assertion than to the apparently substantiated but improbable explanation. This is partly due to the evil of bribing witnesses.

Neither are there definite rules stating what is required so that evidence can be considered complete. In a case where the decision is not reached by means of the oath, the conviction as to what is true or untrue, right or wrong, is deduced rationally from all the material produced at the hearing and that known from other sources. Neither is it always necessary that the judgement must be determined solely according to the facts which have been proved beyond doubt. If sufficient indications are obtained to make it possible to get an overall picture of the case and thus to reach a satisfactory solution, then even though mutual contradictions may have arisen and may continue on some points, further argument is abandoned, including instruction to swear the oath. The latter is required only if the judgement for the greater part will depend on the truth or untruth of one or more of the allegations.

In the light of all this, the judge, nevertheless, takes a stronger stand against careless evidence than one would expect. The motive of order speaks with a powerful voice. And the judge regards secretiveness as harmful because it creates above all unrest, *guntur,* and makes him tired, *lodja,* without any need.

INFORMATION AND ADVICE

In many cases, because of the limited significance of the part played by the evidence, the judge is inclined to make inquiries outside the parties, since he is free to investigate beyond what is claimed and what is defended. There is naturally no need for him to do so when the case he is hearing is one within his own limited group about which he knows as much as anybody else. If he chooses to listen to the relatives of the parties, it is because he wants to profit by their good counsel in his search for a solution. But when the parties are more or less far removed from his own group, the necessity for inquiry and advice then becomes stronger. He then turns to the chiefs of the parties or to the elders. If the parties are close relatives, then their affines will usually be able and willing to provide some important facts regarding the background of the dispute. These people, who are able to add many a useful hint to their information regarding the direction in which the dispute might be settled, often go of their own accord to the court where their presence can be taken as an indication that they have already tried to mediate, though unsuccessfully; they hope the judge will be more successful. Fortunately, the disputes are numerous that only need an authoritative and interested neutral third party in order to be brought to a satisfactory conclusion in due course. And to this end, these informants are an unmistakable support. They call themselves *hatorangan* = the evidence, a word which, like *saksi* = witness, is a recent loan from Malay, though the idea is Batak. When they are officially summoned by the judge, they consider themselves not simply as witnesses who will speak on behalf of the parties they represent, but as informants who are outside the parties and who will provide the judge with their non-partisan information regarding the circumstances relating to the pending case. Whatever their information turns out to be, they are always outside taking the oath, which may finally have to be resorted to. They do not contribute directly to providing evidence: it is their task to increase the judge's knowledge and insight into the case and its background. These incidental informants, who do not belong to any court organisation and who come from quite unexpected places, are an important factor in the Batak administration of justice.

In addition to furnishing information regarding the facts of a dispute already before the judge, they can also be of service to the judge in acquainting him with the local features of *adat* law which play a part in the suit, and which naturally are not all known to him when he does not come from the region in question.

WITNESSES

The witnesses, *na umbegesa* = those who heard, or *sibege hata* or *padan* = those who heard what was agreed upon, or *na umbotosa* = those who know what has taken place, are generally men. Women never act by design as witnesses in legal matters. They can only appear as witnesses before a judge as a result of their being unintentionally involved in a case; mostly offence cases. Occasionally a person who is on his deathbed, if his conscience is troubled, passes on evidence to those around him, or if he thinks it desirable that important information should not be lost, such evidence is then regarded as *tona ni na mate* (see p. 283). Here and there one finds an heir of someone who was summoned many times in legal proceedings during his life and was concerned in numerous cases and who, before his death, had passed on much data regarding third parties to his sagacious son so that the law would continue to prevail. That the information regarding the legal facts of their property and fields that a father has communicated to his sons sometimes constitutes their main evidence, *tona ni natorashu* = the explanation left us by our father, is understandable in the absence of written documents. And it is underestimating the value of such evidence to stamp it as heresay.

The worth of witnesses differs according to the mutual relationship of the persons concerned. A man who owns a neighbouring field or who has cultivated it over a long period, is more deserving of belief than others. He can know the ins and outs better than another and only becomes involved in the dispute by virtue of the accidental situation of his land. He is usually present when the bamboo boundary poles are driven in. The mediators, *domu-domu,* when an agreement is concluded, are, or should be, the chief witnesses in a lawsuit over the agreement. The village chief who assists in concluding a contract must be regarded as the one person who can tell the judge the true situation and as a completely trustworthy and reliable witness, even though he may represent the interests of his co-villagers. A man whose knowledge of a transaction is of a casual kind, is of less value as a witness than one who was present or who was invited to give his approval to it, *mangolopi*. Witnesses derive their value from their thorough knowledge of the transaction that has taken place:

> *madekdek gandar bulu tu bulung ni ampapaga;*
> *unang be hamu pagulut nunga adóng sibege hata;*
> a small bamboo stalk falls on the leaf of the *ampapaga* plant;
> do not quarrel any longer for there are witnesses;

or, expressed in another way:

> *molo sega na ginaduan, panggadui djouon,*
> If the dyked (field) is damaged, then the dyke-builders must be summoned.

This means that if an agreement is concluded with the co-operation of a number of persons and if discord arises concerning it, the knowledge of those who have co-operated must be sought.

Anyone who bears witness against a son, a grandson, a cousin or other related kinsman or affine usually deserves to be believed. Anyone who speaks for them is often regarded as valueless as a witness. The question of admissibility or inadmissibility of witnesses is not posed. The only question that arises, is whether it is reasonable and of value to hear a certain witness. There are many cases where the persons concerned are nearly all close kinsmen and affines, so that their evidence is indispensable, for example, when a dying man has given his final commands regarding his property, or when simple transactions are concluded within a *huta*.

That the question of admissibility does not arise especially bears on the taking of the oath. For years it was the practice in the officially organised judiciary for all admitted witnesses to swear the oath before making their statements, a practice since discontinued. This was not a Batak custom. It does not encourage reliability and undermines the force of the oath. Witnesses are not sworn if there statements are irrelevant or if they are hardly worth considering; if they are quite clearly partisan; if they cannot be believed; if the other party has been ordered to take the decisive oath; if their evidence has placed the matter beyond all doubt (for example, grandfather against grandson); if there are no contradictions worth mentioning between the parties, and so on. Witnesses can be sworn together with the party for whom they are testifying when their evidence is the same as that of their party. The latter is then ordered by the judge to swear the decisive oath. The judge can, however, also let the witnesses alone be sworn if he realises that their statements clinch the matter. A separate swearing of witnesses, besides

the party concerned, takes place when their statements stand by themselves. All this is determined wholly by the circumstances and con-
siderations resulting from the proceedings. Close kinsmen and affines
are so clearly related to a party involved in a suit, that it would be
superfluous for them to be sworn as well as the principal person, the
suhut, concerned: what concerns the *suhut* likewise concerns them.

If women are in a position where they could bear witness against their
husbands, father or mother against their sons, sisters against their
brothers, etc., they usually ask to be exempted from this obligation. It
conflicts with Batak susceptibilities and reason.

Any witness who patently lies, is disciplined by the judge, since he
will not permit a *paoto-otohon*, to make mock of him. The disciplinary
measures chosen are the stronger if the witness is a *saksi ginadis* =
bought witness, or one who has been instructed, *diadjarhon*.

DOCUMENTS

I have already mentioned that written contracts are a recent innovation. In the *Pidari* time, the *datu* were the only ones who commanded
the art of writing, one of their titles being *pormangsi di lopian* = those
who write in ink on tree bark, but they confined themselves to using
their art in the service of their learning by writing books on divination
to pass their knowledge on to their pupils. Writing first came into greater
use after the Mission introduced schools. It was initially especially the
teachers in the small dispersed Mission Schools to whom the rural
population turned when they wanted their agreements written down.
These teachers thus acted as the notaries of the village and the region,
noting in their deeds what the parties had agreed to. They often kept
these documents, which were sometimes written in school exercise books,
at home, and they frequently passed them on to their successors. As
education spread, naturally, the writing of village documents took place
more and more without the co-operation of the teachers. But it is still
the rule, though there are, of course, exceptions, that these documents
are drawn up by a writer, *panurat*, who, while he belongs to the region
where the disputants live, is an outsider as far as their contract is concerned. This *panurat* identifies himself as such at the end of the
document. He is the confidential agent of the parties in respect of the
agreement between them and, in my opinion, he seldom if ever abuses
this confidence. He appends the names of the parties and of the witnesses
who cannot write to the document or leaves a blank space in which they
put either a cross or the imprint of their thumbs. Or, he himself puts the

crosses on the document after extending to each of the signatories the tip of the pen. Even people who can write their names are often quite satisfied with simply touching the pen. They apparently consider this a sufficient indication that they have made an agreement or have witnessed a document. Though the object of the document is primarily to establish proof of what has been agreed upon in the event of its later being necessary, in this Batak world which is still so much influenced by magico-religious ideas it is thought that something of the personality of the signatory is transferred to his 'mark'.

People have quickly come to realise that the written document is an important means of preventing the difficulties that can arise if one of the parties to a contract denies its existence or its contents. In a written document people have what is often called a *parningotan* = document of recollection, which confirms the fact that a contract has been made and which helps the mind to recollect its contents. It is a means by which evidence is provided and the legal security increased of both the parties concerned or of the person who holds the document.

If the document contains a unilateral obligation, then, naturally, it remains in the hands of the party with whom the obligation has been incurred, as in many debt contracts, for example. But in a bilateral obligation also, of which pledging a wet rice-field is the principal form, only one document is usually drawn up and this remains in the hands of the pledgee. It makes no difference at all to the land rights of the pledger, but it does provide the pledgee with evidence of the monetary loan he made and safeguards him against the intervention of a third party. The pledger, *partano,* does not, as a rule, feel it necessary that he, too, has a copy of the contract for the protection of his legal rights. He reasons, often to his detriment, that the legal history of the land is known; that it is common knowledge that it belongs to him; that people were present when he pledged it; whereas, for the pledgee to commit a breach of good faith, he would have to invent the facts and bribe his witnesses, and besides that, the situation of the land, his dwelling place or his genealogical position in the region would argue against him. In the case of an exchange, each of the parties receives a copy of the contract. In a permanent sale of land, or when land is given as a gift, the document, which must clearly state that the transfer is intended to be permanent, is retained by the recipient of the land. In addition, the document is important because it states who were the witnesses and who were the other people who collaborated in the transaction and states the amount of the *pago-pago* (*ingot-ingot*) = 'sealing money' and that it has been paid. The contents often leave much to be desired, a fact usually attributable to the inexperience of the person who draws it up. For example, the exposition of what has been agreed will be badly stated; the legal terms may be incorrectly used — one must realise that the *panurat* = writer, may have been a schoolboy — sometimes some of the 'signatures' are missing, on occasions that of the parties; there may be no date on the document; and there are other deficiencies that the educated Batak regards as faults, but which, nevertheless, do not make the document entirely valueless.

One must never expect in a document more than the main items of the contract. Its specific aim is to establish that a contract has been made and what its kernel is. The details and their observance are readily left to good faith. A written document is therefore easily overtaken by the course of events. It often turns out that after it was drawn up, many things happened that have not been recorded therein but which give a wholly different aspect to the relationship of the parties than one would judge to be the case from perusing the document. This situation not only applies in such daily affairs as settling debts but also to the more important events as, for example, a child betrothal, when a document is drawn up stating what precursors to the marriage payment as well as to the *pauseang* have been exchanged, but silent as regards later mutual gifts. In cases relating to the settlement of debts, if a written document is produced it must often be regarded simply as representing a casual incident of a particular moment in the creditor-debtor relationship. In each case, therefore, the judge must use his discretion and prudence in assessing the value and significance of a document. He sees it as a more or less important core of the evidence of the person who invokes it, which substantiates his allegations, but which, by virtue of the nature of the case submitted to him, requires all the additional information and corroboration necessary when the other party contradicts the allegations.

It must also be borne in mind that, more important than the existence of a document, is the question of whether the people who should have been informed were informed, especially in land transactions, whether they were present and which of them were consulted and had given their consent.

CIRCUMSTANTIAL EVIDENCE: PRESUMPTION OF FACT

Both the judge and the parties in a Batak lawsuit readily make use of circumstantial evidence and presumption of fact and make their

deductions from them. The judge sometimes does so rather too exten-
sively and, since he, too, readily accepts the general application of a
phenomenon that is known to him, neglects as a consequence to hold
the controlling investigation that could give him more certainty. To cite
an actual case: a party in support of its right of ownership of a plot of
land, invoked the fact that thereon was a *homban* = small spring,
belonging to his *marga* or lineage. The judge, who had had experience
of one or two such cases, was highly inclined as a consequence to come
to the conclusion that the party's ancestor had cleared the land, but
had he broadened the scope of his investigation, he would have been
able to find cases where springs of the one *marga* lay in the *golat* of
another. However, there are, in fact, various circumstances from which
it is admissible to make deductions. For instance, on Samosir, where
each of the component *marga* of a *bius* association was assigned its own
land area, *talian*, when a new area was occupied, the situation of a
disputed field in the *golat* of a *marga,* provides, in many regions, clear
evidence in a dispute between members of different *marga* regarding the
right of ownership of the land. And, if it is generally known that on
entering a land transaction, the nature of which is disputed, a meal
was eaten, then that ceremony, called *panggabei,* or *parhorasan* = the
accompaniment of the wish of good fortune, may give rise to the
assumption that a permanent transfer of the land was intended. Such
a ceremony is never performed in land pledging, sharecropping, *libe
gogo,* etc.

   If cattle exchange hands by the wayside, *di pinggol ni dalan,* i.e., outside the village circle or not on a market day, then there is ground for
the supposition that the cattle so disposed of had been stolen. A finder
is regarded as a thief if he does not announce his find, *na djumpang
gabe na tangko molo so dipaboa.* A perpetrator of an offence will often
betray himself by his actions:

   dapot do imbo dibahen soarana;
   djala dapot ursa dibahen bogasna.
   The ape is caught by its voice.
   The deer by its spoor.

Whether these actions will furnish sufficient proof to effect the giving
of a verdict on an accused, will depend entirely upon the circumstances
under which they occurred. But if they establish his guilt beyond doubt,
it is said that:

   hunsi do hunsi-hunsi ransang do ransang-ransang;
   tiningkir lubang-lubang, sangkot do rambang-rambang,

26

tung ise na mambahen i, ia so ho?
The key is a small key, the bolt is a little bolt.
Into whichever hole it is placed, there are cobwebs everywhere.
Who else but you could have done it?
The negative way of reasoning is also very popular:
ndang heá diahut halak hubang tu bohina;
no one smears ash on his own face.
This expression is used when someone is injured and blames someone else.

THE TANDA

I seldom encountered *tanda* = tokens, as evidence. There was, how-ever, one instance when officials of the Public Works Department had damaged some land and its standing crop and a number of people complained about it to the Resident taking with them as evidence bundles of the torn up paddy. The same idea obtains when a man finds another man's cattle grazing on his fields and he drives them off to the dwelling of the village chief, sometimes taking with him some of the stubble. When a girl is raped, she will endeavour to seize some object belonging to her assailant as evidence in support of her accusation.

The *tanda* as a bond token, be it an object or a sum of money, is primarily the outward sign that the one party gives to the other at the time of the concluding of the contract between them to indicate that he has, in fact, really concluded such an agreement. Such a token can be produced later before a judge as proof.

THE OATH

For a Batak to take the oath, the *gana* or *uari,* is to curse himself. Anyone who takes it invokes a judgement on himself if his allegation is false. Swearing the oath is often a negation, but it can be positive. The judgement invoked by the oath is a judgement by a higher power, i.e., of the gods and the spirits, while the magical character of the objects used as media for the oath-taking, as well as the procedure itself, indicate that evil is invoked in the case of lies.

The swearing, *manolon,* is effected with the help of an object which acts as a medium for the oath, *panolonan* or *gana.* The medium is subjected to some action, the idea being that the oath-taker will be similarly affected if he has sworn a false oath. For instance: if rice is the medium, it will be strewn about; if tobacco is used, it will be cut up; if the oath is sworn on a small dyke, it will be levelled and if a small metal figure is used, it will be thrown to the ground. The same idea applies when a wooden or a stone image with a contorted face and a twisted body is used as a medium. The oath-taker who commits perjury will become so disfigured.

All this force has to be invoked and summoned up, *dimangmang,* by the person who directs the oath, the *parmangmang,* who pronounces the swearing formula, *mangmang,* or the *panonai* = invoking formula. He coaches the oath-taker as to what he has to utter and how. Meanwhile he performs the actions just mentioned. To give an example: when the oath called *gadu-gadu tinaktak* = the washed out dyke, has to be sworn in litigation over a rice-field, the *parmangmang* hacks at the dyke a few times with a chopper and says the following:

> *Songon gadu-gadu na tinaktak on, duhut-duhut sirahar, aek sibaor-baor, ditaktak Ompunta Martua Debatá ma ho, borúm dohot anakmu djala sirang ma hosám sian dagingmu, mabaor sibukmu sian holi-holím alé Si N.* (raising his voice): *so nda tutú tohó (hurimba hauma on,* etc.)*
>
> As this dyke is hacked away so that the vegetation on the field will wither away and the water flow away from it, so shall Our Holy God hack you, your sons and daughters and separate the breath from your body; so shall your flesh wither from your bones, O friend, Si N., if it is not true (that I have cultivated this rice-field, etc.)

The person who directs the oath, can be the opposite party in the dispute, or the judge, who orders it to be taken (*na patolonhon*). The formula is altered according to the purpose for which the medium is used. A swearer can invoke evil against himself or upon those close to him. The narrower oath formula which contains the statement to be sworn, always begins with: "*So nda tutú,* or *so tohó (hulehon,* etc.), if it is not the truth (that I gave, etc.)", or with "*sapiri (hutangko,* etc.), if it is true (that I have stolen, etc.)."

The objects that can be used to '*manolon*' (on Samosir I heard it called *martonggo* = to invoke with reverence), are very numerous. The Batak legal sources I have quoted list many *gana panolonan,* without exhausting them. Ypes gives some photographs in his work of a couple of small images, with descriptions, which are used at oath-taking. Some of these forms of oath-taking are only indigenous in particular areas and they often there have a certain standard value, but they are unknown elsewhere. A very generally distributed oath is that using the large and small stone. This form is much feared where it is used. The sympathetic magic exists in the homonymous words in the lines of the accepted swearing formula spoken as one stone is tapped against the other:

batu na balga, batu na metmet, paradian ni sitapi-tapi;
mate na balga, mate na metmet, unang adóng tinggal siombus api.
A large stone, a small stone, the resting place of the *sitapi-tapi* bird.
The great die, the insignificant die, and no one is left to stoke the
fire.

The distribution of the frog oath has been curious. On Samosir, in
addition to other forms of the oath, one is sworn with a frog which has
to be crushed, *bodjak siranggang* (as this frog is crushed, so I, etc.).
The frog is sometimes adorned with flowers, *asa djumorbut*, so that it
will appear to be more frightening. This oath was probably taken to
South Tapanuli by the Lontung *marga* which migrated there. It was
there regarded by the Government as *the* "Batak Oath". Later, in the
eighties, it was introduced into Silindung, Humbáng and Toba when
these areas were annexed. Until then it had not been known there, but
from thence onwards it was used for many years in the Government
offices where the dried up little beastie, hung on a small piece of cane,
was always ready for use. It was only about half a century later that it
was discovered that no pagan Batak outside Samosir believed in it.

A particular way of taking the oath is on the *batu somong* = the oath
stone, which in many regions lies in the central market place of a
tribal group or *marga* or in the ancestral village of a large lineage. Many
important oaths were sworn and promises affirmed on this stone. It is
a large stone purported to be the dwelling place of the spirits of the
ancestors who are invoked by playing the *gondang*. It is also thought
to possess of itself great supernatural power which is released when the
gondang are played. A token of homage and an offering is made to the
spirits by feeding the stone from the hand, *manulangi*. Such homage
can also be made to other objects used in oath-taking in the same way
in order to strengthen them.

Different oaths are known for lawsuits relating, for instance, to rice-
fields and trade, etc., but many of them have now fallen into desuetude.
They are, and were, not the only oaths that can be used in those
particular cases. The oath by the large and small stone and by the frog,
etc., is used in all kinds of cases. For preference, the oath is taken near
the object in dispute. For Christians, the oath on the Bible is substituted
for the old Batak oaths. One end of he Bible is held by the person who
is to be sworn while the person directing the oath holds the other end
and pronounces a formula roughly as follows:

„*Nampuna hata na tarsurat di buku on na ra maminsang ahu*
molo margabus ahu di djolo ni paruhum on: so tutú (hulean, etc.),

If I lie before this court, may I be punished by the One whose word is written in this Book. If it is not true (that I gave, etc.).

To this the oath-taker replies: *"Olo"*, "Yes".

There have been many complaints that this oath is not sufficiently feared by Christians. If, however, the use of this oath were to be adapted so that it conformed more to the Batak judicial rules and concepts, then its value would possibly increase. That there can be a danger of superstition in using the Bible, seems unquestionable.

Oath-taking is avoided in some cases. If, for example, a pregnant woman should have to be sworn, the supernatural force that is invoked by the swearing is regarded as being harmful to her, and her husband also prefers not to swear an oath during his wife's pregnancy. Similarly, when the case is between very close kinsmen, people endeavour to avoid swearing the oath since it is detrimental to the good relationship existing between them. In olden times, according to the *Patik dohot Uhum*, a 'repeal' of the oath, *handit gana,* was demanded of an accused person who was under grave suspicion, and upon whom the judge did not dare to lay an order to take the oath of purgation for fear of perjury. Even now, when for some reason an oath has to be sworn in a lawsuit, a similar fear can cause a judge, if necessary, first to hand over the person to be sworn to his village chief, in order to privately warn him, *mangunung,* and so that stress can be laid on the importance of the oath. The oath is then administered on the following day, unless the person concerned recoils from taking it, as I once saw happen.

Swearing on behalf of and as a substitute for another person, *mangampu gana,* can be done by a village chief who stands as guarantor for the members of his village; by the principal dweller of a house who swears for all his co-dwellers; by a father who swears for his young son; etc. Swearing for a kinsman who cannot himself be present, is permissible. Formerly a person who had once been sentenced and who could not be trusted was not allowed to take the oath of purgation, though a *pangampu,* for example, his father or brother-in-law, could take the oath for him and then became his guarantor except when the suspect was a habitual criminal, *na tartaon sangketa,* who did not care what the charge might be and who was capable of accepting a false oath irrespective of who swore it. If a person represents the interests of a large group in a lawsuit, then he can swear in the name of all of them.

The oath serves different aims: to confirm a given promise, including a promise to improve after committing an offence, *pandjoraan,* but the promises especially concerned are those of mutual alliance and loyalty, like those which in earlier times were made when entering agreements of a political character, *parbulanan* (these oaths, which are not judicial, will not be dealt with any further); to trace an unknown offender, when a general oath is administered to a circle to which he could belong; to terminate a dispute; to purge oneself of the suspicion of having committed a misdeed, *paiashon diri*; and the oath is sometimes taken to strengthen an accusation that cannot be substantiated by other evidence.

The person who has to be sworn is called *na mangalehon gana* = the one who offers to take the oath, also called *mangalehon sapiri*; the person who accepts the oath is called *na mandjalo gana,* and he is also called *na patolonhon* = the one who causes another to swear. The judge decides who has to swear. If the parties agree before the judge on the question of who is to swear and what to be sworn, then the principle obtains that the one who imposes the oath is affected in the same way as the person who takes it. If the parties cannot reach agreement then, in general, the judge will allow himself to be guided by his common sense in deciding the question of whether the oath is to be taken, which party must swear and whether the witnesses must be sworn. If the main facts are sufficiently established or, conversely, if no grain of truth is adducible, then naturally, neither party is sworn. In specific circumstances, however, the judge must be guided by certain rules.

One such rule is that a man may not take the oath if, by so doing, he would increase his quarter of the buffalo, *pabalga hae-hae ni horbona,* which means that he must not be placed in the position of benefitting from an accrual as a result of his being sworn. For this reason, if the subject of a lawsuit is money that was borrowed, it is not the person to whom it must be paid who must swear but the person who has to pay it back, thus the *parutang* = debtor; where the case concerns a divorce and the refunding of the marriage payment, then it is the *parboru* who swears, while the *paranak* in his turn swears to the counter-presents received on the marriage from the side of the *parboru*; the *partano,* the pledger of a rice field and who wants to redeem it, is the one who swears regarding the amount of money involved. It is not the person who states that he has loaned money who is sworn, but the person who denies having received it, if there is no pressing reason that decides otherwise; it is not the person who denies he has been paid who is sworn, but the person who asserts that he has paid. I was even present when a person who had been robbed by a street robber, *panamun,* was not permitted to swear to his own statement because the amount the thief admitted he had stolen was less than that given in the statement.

Another rule is, that in a suit over land, it is the person who uses the land who must be sworn if the evidence is weak. He takes the oath called *gana ni na hundul di gadu* = the oath of the one who sits on the dyke, or *djongdjong di porlak* = the one who stands in the garden. I observed that this rule, more than the others, has an ancilliary character and is used as an expedient when the judge is doubtful about the choice of the person to be sworn.

If an accusation of misbehaviour cannot be adequately substantiated, it cannot, generally speaking, be strengthened by the deciding oath. It is the accused who denies the charge who takes the oath of purgation and thus invokes a higher judgement on himself:

hinurpas dingding sinigat oma;

molo ro tuhas uari daonna;

the door will be knocked upon, the grass will be searched;

when suspicion is aroused, the oath gives satisfaction;

so reads the universally known maxim. The accused swears that the suspicion is unfounded, that he is *lias* or *ias* = pure. The swearing of the oath of purgation is a *paiashon diri,* or *goar,* a swearing that one is not guilty of the suspicion resting upon one, a cleansing of one's name, *goar,* among people. The oath of purgation counter-balances the absence of rules regarding the minimum of proof. It gives the judge and the accuser the satisfaction they need where proof of guilt is weak. But, if the accusation is sufficiently substantiated according to the judge's opinion, or if, conversely, there is no proof at all, then there is no need for the oath of purgation. And, as soon as a case is in the judge's hands, it is he who decides whether or not the oath is to be sworn.

In some very special circumstances, where the evidence is incomplete, the oath is not administered to the accused. Instead, the accuser swears to strengthen his accusation. This is done, for example, when a man denies a young girl's accusation that he has raped her when she has no witnesses and if she had not been able to snatch a token, *tanda,* from him by which to identify him. This oath then acquires the same decisive character as the oath in a lawsuit and the oath of purgation.

The oath to confirm an accusation that is sufficiently substantiated by the evidence, was, as far as I know, not known in the old procedure, nor were the oaths of witnesses in such a case required to confirm their testimony. Administering the oath only at the end of the court's investigation, and regarding it as a decisive oath leading to the accused's being punished, does not, however, appear to conflict with the Batak rules regarding the oath.

As soon as it has been decided to administer the oath, it is then established precisely what has to be sworn. When witnesses had to be sworn before the official customary courts before making their statements, they were taking the oath on whatever they would eventually say, *sipaboaonna*, which is not a Batak idea. They should make a definite statement and this should be put before them. This is related to the decisive character of all oaths. The statement should, for example, read: "If it is not true that I formerly cultivated the field before I moved to S., *so nda tutú diula iba hauma i djolo asa bungkas tu S.*" Among the many factors that either a party concerned or a witness adduces, this is the element that motivates the judge in his final judgement.

It also bears on the decisive nature of the oath that, when it is taken in a lawsuit, the Batak regards a dispute or an accusation as being absolutely settled, *nunga sae hata i,* or *sun hata,* or *naung marudjung.* The suit cannot then be re-opened, not even in the event of the oath later being shown to have been a false one. For example, if a buffalo was stolen and the accused swears that he was not the thief, that is the end of the matter, even if he is seen later herding that same buffalo, *horbo pe ditangko, molo dung ditolon, sae do i agia diparmahan muse tinangkona i, tung sura.* This idea apparently bears upon the fact that the act of swearing transfers the matter to a higher power and also on the magical character ascribed to ritual oath-taking. The injurious force aroused thereby is thought to act automatically on anyone who speaks an untruth, though the effect is probably not immediately apparent. Anyone who swears a false oath, *siallang gana,* also called *sibondut gana,* or *siata gana,* all of which terms mean 'to swallow' the oath — and strangely enough, *manolon* = to swear, also means 'to swallow' — must reckon on a wretched fate either forthwith or later:

> *tinaba ni tangke martumbur;*
> *tinaba ni gana ndang martumbur;*
> what is cut down with an axe will still sprout,
> but, what is struck by an oath, never;

so people believe. The idea is particularly applicable to childlessness. Instances are told of people, who had apparently taken a false oath and had begun to languish shortly afterwards. If it is known that an oath is false, then the perjurer is never again allowed to take the oath; but in former times he was not punished.

If all the witnesses in a lawsuit (civil or criminal) are always sworn before their statements are taken, it is obvious that prosecution for perjury is inevitable.

THE RESULT OF THE LAWSUIT

Though at the present day there is no longer a political aspect to the question of whether the judge will mediate or whether he will give a compulsory judgement, nevertheless, there is still much that requires that he directs his efforts to searching for a solution acceptable to both parties, the amicable settlement; or to reach a decision that though it may not be entirely acceptable to both parties, takes into consideration the interests of both of them as well as the importance of their mutual relationship, the mediatory judgement. The one merges into the other. The party who refuses his consent to an amicable settlement can, nevertheless, indicate his approval to a mediatory judgement by his silent acceptance and by refraining from opposing it. Many a decision can only be given, and interpreted, within the framework of definite group-relationships and for this reason its content is different from a decision applicable to separate individuals. Often, as I learnt from experience, an endeavour to reach an amicable settlement, that is obstinately opposed by one of the parties, can and must be forthwith changed into a mediatory decision as being the best possible solution of the dispute. What is of particular importance here, is the kinship or affinal connection in which the Batak parties so often stand to each other. There are a tremendous number of disputes between people who are closely related, such as brothers, half-brothers, grandsons of one grandfather, brothers and sisters, widows and brothers-in-law, etc.; among those who belong to small kinship or affinal groups, such as members of one lineage, and among persons between whom there is a rather close *hula-hula* and *boru* relationship. The disputes in which these people become involved, are of the kind that arise between inhabitants of one village or a cluster of villages. All these *perkara* (Mal. = cases) are rampant in a system of relationships of which the orderly, and if possible, peaceful continuance is, as a rule, more important than the accurate delimitation of right and wrong, truth and untruth that so often brings dissension and discord to the people who are compelled to live together in the milieu in which they were born. In these circumstances, searching for co-ordinating factors, grinding down the sharp edges, passing over incidental small quarrels, sometimes even scamping over important points, can be conducive to the restoration of harmony between the disputants. The law within the kinship group is

not so sharply delineated on all points as is the law that operates between strangers, while the basis of the relationship in which affines stand
to each other, is in the main different from a rigidly juridical one. The
judge, therefore, so often has no option than to take the course of
mediation, of seeking intermediate solutions in which neither party wins
or loses. This is especially the case when he himself belongs to the same
group as the litigants. He will then seek the more diligently for a
solution by which they can continue to live peaceably together.

But the possibilities are, here again, limited, because there are so
many grievances slumbering or just moving to the surface. Many a man
has a grievance against other members of the various groups among
which he lives, so that a dispute that does come to the surface is often
only one of a series, a link in a chain, so that the best attitude a judge
can take, indeed frequently the only one he can take, is to give his
decision in a formal judicial manner. The better the judge's knowledge
is of the sphere within which the case that is brought before him
occurred, the better will he be able to decide what he has to do.

THE AMICABLE SETTLEMENT: PARDAMEAN or PARDENGGANAN

When two or more parties reach an amicable settlement that puts
matters right again and restores the concord between hem, it is called
mardenggan (*denggan* = good) or *mardame* (*dame* = peace). The
activities of the chiefs or of the intermediaries who have brought about
the reconciliation, are termed *padengganhon* or *padamehon*. The most
striking element of the amicable settlement is the payment of the *pago-
pago* which seals the agreement that has been reached. This is the same
pago-pago which, under the name *ingot-ingot,* is also paid to all those
chiefs and notables who have participated in concluding a contract and
by whose assistance and co-operation it has been effected. When an
amicable settlement terminates a dispute, the irrevocable character of
the agreement becomes clear by the handing over of the *pago-pago*. It is
a *tanda ni hata sun* = a token that a case is finished; that it has ended.
The last word in the dispute has been spoken as soon as the *pago-pago*
has been paid:

    ndang tarungkap batang batu;
    ndang tarharhar pudun mate;
    a stone chest cannot be opened,
    a tight knot cannot be undone;

so reads an *umpama* that has already been quoted and which is relevant
here. Anyone who later says or acts to the contrary is a *siuba hata,* and

anyone who deliberately refuses to fulfil the obligations imposed on him
by the terms of the agreement, is a *pangose* = lawbreaker. Both are
guilty of a very serious form of bad faith, which is not only committed
against the opposite party and the chiefs concerned in the settlement
but towards the community that, in olden times more than now, is
interested in maintaining in a pure form this kind of legal administration of which the efficiency is always threatened by perverseness and
rudeness, and similar typical attitudes which undermine the social order:

> *mambahen tata naung masak djala*
> *marimbulu naung tinutungan;*
> *mangangkat naung tinanggoan.*
> to make unripe what has already ripened, and
> to let hair grow on what has already been singed;
> to let jump what has already been cut in pieces.

The *pago-pago* gives the amicable settlement the validity of a judgement
entered.

The rule is that both or all parties pay the *pago-pago* and that each
of the chiefs and notables who contributed to effecting it receives a
share. There are occasions, however, where only one party pays it. In
that case, the one who pays it is quite aware that in doing so he confirms the agreement and accepts the obligation stated therein. The
amount of *pago-pago* that each party has to pay does not have to be
the same in each case. Here also the rule applies:

> *nipis mantat neang, hapal mantat dokdok;*
> what is thin carries what is light, what is thick carries what is
> heavy;

thus the principle of payment according to one's financial ability to pay,
whereby less is demanded from a poor person and more from a wealthy
one. It is, however, affected by the proportional principle laid down in
a well-known *umpama*:

> *molo balgá binanga, balgá dengkena;*
> *molo metmét binanga, metmét dengkena;*
> if the stream is large, then the fish will be large;
> if the stream is small, then the fish will be small;

according to which rule, the remuneration is dependent upon the value
of the issue in dispute. I also did note repeatedly that the amount that
had to be contributed to the *pago-pago* depended upon the interest a
party had in the settlement of the dispute. If, for instance, a third party
demanded that a recently concluded agreement about pledging a rice-
field should be dissolved, then the pledgee, who in reality stood outside

the dispute, only contributed a few pennies against the plaintiff's few guilders. Taking into consideration the standard of living and of wages, the amount that the parties pay as *pago-pago* is sometimes remarkably high. The Batak who is more or less comfortably off, is accustomed to rewarding royally his chiefs and notables for their legal mediation.

If one of the parties declines to accept the settlement offered or recommended, not infrequently a village chief or a close kinsman or an affine accepts it for him and pays the *pago-pago,* partly in the belief that the settlement is the best in the circumstances and partly in the belief that the unreasonable and obdurate one will respond to persuasion. In such a case, the *boru* particularly has great influence. But it depends upon the persons concerned and their mutual relationship whether the chiefs will accept such an offer. A settlement is sometimes made so carelessly that not all the persons who have co-operated therein and who profit by the *pago-pago* comprehend what has been effected. This sort of carelessness is mischievous, hinders justice, sometimes results in lawsuits, and many times I heard people ordered to return the *pago-pago* they had received. This is a humiliating command. Even the chiefs who effected the agreement can be ordered to return it because they knew, or should have known, that they could not do so without the co-operation and approval of those kinsmen and affines whose consent was necessary.

The sealing-money can also be called *ulos ni radja* and *piso ni radja* where there is an affinal relationship between the party concerned and the chiefs. The part of the *pago-pago* that is destined for the *boru na godjong* is called *ulos partompi* = a scarf in which one carries a burden on one's back. Other names are also in use. If the settlement is of a permanent character, such as land being sold for good, *pate,* etc., then the term also used is *upa manggabei,* since wishes of good fortune, *gabe,* customarily accompany such a settlement. Written statements of settlements are frequent.

THE JUDGEMENT: UHUM

In olden times, the *pago-pago* was also demanded after the pronouncement of judgement, even in offence cases, from those who had to fulfil an obligation or a punishment. Failure to pay it was a sign that the judgement was not considered satisfactory and that the case would be settled by war. The judges, who were the chiefs, allowed the parties to resort to war if they felt themselves powerless to prevent it. But, if possible, when they had given a clear and definite judgement, they brought such strong pressure to bear on the obstinate one that he might then feel that he had no choice but to submit to it. If fighting did break out, then the influence of the kinsmen of the parties and who might possibly find themselves involved, was naturally great in getting them to accept a judgement that was not really unjust. A man who was put under restraint, or who was put in the block because of debts or because of an offence, was naturally entirely in the power of the judges and had little choice but to accept their decision.

In this way, formerly, the judges received the formal approval of both parties, and an appeal or a re-opening of the case was excluded. At present the demanding of the *pago-pago* by the judges as proof of acceptance of a decisive judgement, is no longer possible. Those concerned, knowing the power of the Government to enforce a judgement, do not feel themselves obliged to make a *pago-pago* payment. Undoubtedly, this has accentuated the onesidedness of judgements. The term *mamutus,* from Malay *putus* = broken, has thus come into use. In 1927, when the *Rapat na godang* = highest official customary court, at Tarutung, after many years, again gave a mediatory judgement, the interested spectators referred to it as a *pardengganan.* The judgement in question did not simply divide a disputed field in half between the parties, as was often done, but made use of methods that were typically Batak: the one party was allowed to keep the field but had to give a *piso*-gift to the other party who was of his *hula-hula.*

Formerly, the men who acted as judges at the hearing of a lawsuit — the *harungguan* = 'court', did not have a fixed composition — did not especially strive to reach a unanimous agreement. The weight in the balance was the judgement of the chiefs who were the most respected, *na sumangap.* A chief who was clearly a powerful one and who directed the hearing was the central figure of law and deliberation, *pandapotan ni uhum, pandapotan ni tahi,* and it was he who made the final decision.

CONTENT OF THE JUDGEMENT

It is by no means necessary that the judgement that is given will represent an evaluation of all the disputed facts that have been adduced. Facts of minor importance can be left out and, if need be, even the main facts of the dispute can be wholly set aside in order to find a solution that is intended to satisfy the parties fully. A good example of this is the judgement of which a summary appears in my Report of the Native Administration of Justice (Verslag omtrent de inheemsche rechtspraak) [23]: everything that had been agreed about the field in dispute over a period of 30 years was passed over — there was no certainty about the facts — and a decision was given on a completely new basis which took into account the fact that both parties were of one and the same *marga* and that one of them had already lived for a long time in the territory of his opponent. Naturally, judgements of this character do not occur every day. Usually, because the facts and claims are more or less established, they provide the material for the mediatory judgement, which in the main is based on the principal point at issue. The sharpness of the decision is then softened by additional stipulations.

A judgement of this kind can be reached in many ways. In a matter between affines an exchange of *piso-* and *ulos*-gifts is always the first solution taken into consideration and the object in dispute can then be a part of the present or the counter-present. The appropriate forms were mentioned on pp. 64, 306. Some more examples from daily life may throw some more light on the matter. A rice-field which was the subject of a dispute between the son of a brother and the son of a sister (as in-laws they are *marlae*) had to be allocated to the son of the brother, because without doubt it was quite clear that it was only in the hands of his *boru* on a basis of temporary use, *mangindjam*. The judges, however, enjoined him to be mindful of the duties that a member of a *hula-hula* has to a member of its *boru*, if according to *adat*, his in-law should request that the field be given to him permanently. Two members of a village who were each other's affines, each owned a benzoin garden. Separating these gardens was a strip of forest which was regarded by each of them as his *duru* = land to which he had a preferential right. Due to the hilly nature of the area, a good decision was difficult. The solution was that the party who was the *boru* of the other received most of what he wanted, but had to pay a few score of guilders as *piso,* as a gift of homage to his *hula-hula.* In a dispute regarding the pledging of a rice-field between affines, the main point at issue was whether the pledging took place before or after the *Porang Tangga Batu* (the war of 1883 at a place called Tangga Batu) for claims for redemption of fields that had been pledged previously could not be accepted any longer. On the evidence, the court came to the conclusion that the field was redeemable. It thus instructed the one party to allow it to be redeemed. The other party, however, was ordered to offer a meal which had to be carried on their heads and to offer an *ulos* = cloth,

---

[23] See p. 148 of the publication mentioned in note 1.

manghunti sipanganon dohot mamboan ulos. A person belonging to the
in-dwelling *marga* of a village who accidentally caused a forest fire that
destroyed a number of gardens of the *marga radja,* was ordered to offer
his *hula-hula,* which had suffered damage, a meal accompanied by a
money gift as *piso,* and to ask its forgiveness.

Between kinsmen it will often be a question of dividing in half, or in
other parts, an object in dispute. But among them, too, there is sometimes the chance to exchange gifts of money which are then called
sulang-sulang or sometimes *ulos* and *piso.* To give an example: a son
of a man who had died claims that a rice-field in the hands of his late
father's brother, should accrue to him. The uncle says that his brother
had pledged it to him. If proof is not forthcoming from either side in
support of their contentions, the judge can order the son to ask for the
return of the field by offering a meal and a *batu ni sulang-sulang*
approaching the amount of the pledge as stated by his uncle, so that the
uncle cannot very well refuse to surrender the land.

The following case is characteristic of a Batak relationship: a man
died without male issue and a quarrel arose among some of his male
relatives over a rice-field which had been pledged to a close *boru* of the
deceased. It was allocated to one of the disputants, with the instruction,
however, that if he wanted to redeem it he would have to add to the
redemption money a sum as an *ulos-ulos* for the affine-pledgee who was
otherwise outside the case.

Particularly in land cases, and as much between kinsmen as affines,
it often happens that the judge instructs that a payment of an *upa
mangaramoti* or an *upa mangingani* must be made as a fee for managing
and maintaining the land. There is then usually a small claim made
by the one which is superseded by the obvious right of the other. In
cases of debt or in settling up a burdened estate, mediation by way of
judgement is often possible in respect of change of principal, rate of
interest, or manner of payment, etc.

In the light of much of the foregoing, it is obvious that behind the
instruction to serve a meal or the obligation to performs some other
act, there is now the sanction of loss of right or possibly even of a fine
or imprisonment.

Many judgements, which, according to their nature, are mediatory,
contain a rule for the future relationship which is to exist between
the parties and in some cases even between those who are not parties
in the narrower sense. Settlements for the future can be made in
many ways. To give a few examples: a dispute arose over some item

which belonged to a man who had died and it appeared that there were still many questions to be settled regarding his estate. The judge took the dividing up of the estate entirely into his own hands. In Silindung, it was uncertain whether, or how, the rights to the rice-fields of the members of the in-dwelling *marga* were regulated when a new village was founded and those members moved there. As a result of a dispute arising over one of these *parripean*-fields, the legal position of all the other fields affected was at the same time defined. On one occasion, a fight started in connection with the building of a house in a village in which there had been factions for a long time. The judge who dealt with the case also settled how building was to be done in the future.

Not all judges dare or desire to go so far. Some are work-shy, others lack authority and spirit. A judgement which does not settle a matter definitely, thereby providing a motive for new quarrels, is in general regarded as unsound and men say of it:

sae di djolo potpot di pudi

songon pamoluson ni gadja.

Opened in front and closed up again behind

as is the case after the passage of elephants.

During the hearing of a case, the judge can take into consideration anything that happens during the course of it or anything that comes out of his investigation and can deal with it together with the main case as he thinks fit. If the one party insults the other or is disrespectful towards the judge, if guile and artifice are in conflict with good faith in a case of debt, if a witness lies blatantly, if the *ingot-ingot* that was paid to the chiefs who led the discussions when an agreement was concluded appears to have been quite unfairly divided, if in a dispute over a field force and not the law has been resorted to, *padjolo gogo, papudi uhum,* if a chief has interfered in matters that lie outside his jurisdiction and that concern another chief, then, in all such cases, the judge can take such corrective measures, including imposing punishment, as he deems necessary. From this and the many examples I have given, it follows that civil law and criminal law are interwoven. If one and the same action embraces both spheres, or if there is a marked connection between both types of action, the idea does not occur to the Batak judge to try each case separately according to the difference in the legal subject matter. If he does try them separately, then his motive is the same as that which makes him averse to mixing cases.

It is true, he believes in separating the different grievances and claims that can exist in the mutual intercourse between people. But to treat a case, such as the building of a house on another man's land without permission, first as a civil case and then as a criminal case is time-wasting and paper-consuming, since all the statements at the civil hearing are repeated at the criminal hearing. Some of the examples cited also lie in the field of administrative law. It is, in fact, inevitable that the Batak administration of justice, if it wants to work according to its nature, will frequently occupy itself with points that concern the legal rights of the village, the chief and the territory.

THE ADMINISTRATION OF JUSTICE BY THE CHIEFS and CUSTOMARY LAW

The administration of justice is the chief's duty. He is the authority for enforcing the law and he has the responsibility for caring for the law. Therefore, coupling the adjudication of issues of municipal law with those cases of civil and criminal law with which they coincide, is a natural operation against which dogmatic prohibitions can only act as a spoke in the wheel, while transferring the right of decision to a staff of civil servants means dismantling the social structure. There have been complaints about the quality of the chiefs and the fact that people have little confidence in them, but the mutual control and the criticism of public opinion, supported by the guidance of the judiciary and general supervision by the Administration, must be a force by which this part of the chiefs' activities can also be kept on the right path. The maintenance of the authority of the *adat* by giving them the mandatory right of adjudication, will naturally result in customary law being upheld by the judiciary. When, during the course of my investigation, the chiefs from all kinds of areas so frequently requested that the administration of justice be restored to them, one of their motives was always that in recent times there was much that had become unsettled and that people often acted as they thought fit. What they wanted was that, at least within the circle which they themselves could survey, and within which they lived, they should be made responsible for law, order and morals, by having their authority restored to them, so that they could counteract disorder and could regulate or restore the norms by which the life of the group should be lived. This desire is understandable in view of the many-sided character of Batak society.

To make rules by legislation which are applicable to everybody and in all cases is an idea that does not suit the chiefs. What really suits them is to determine by adjudication what is the law. This is what they are accustomed to from of old. The feeling for the concrete, the importance

27

of the individual case in relationship to the milieu in which it occurred, gives the chiefs a preference for a way of administering the law that is not founded on case law. Seldom, if ever, did I encounter an appeal to a previous judgement. To establish what is the law in each individual case is a means by which a Batak chief keeps the judicial life on its proper course. The judgements he gives contain for all the inhabitants the norms for their social life, norms which they understand and which are applicable in their circle as it is and as it will develop. This social life is not static and the judiciary must never lose sight of that fact and must take it into consideration.

The question arises as to whether the judge does not apply rules of law that are already established, pre-existing rules of law when he administers justice. Certainly he upholds rules, but few are the lawsuits which can be terminated by the simple application of a rule of customary law that is definitive in all its provisions, and in its operation. Those rules, as they stand, are but rarely suitable for direct application to lawsuits. They often leave much to chance. This can be attributed frequently to the manner in which they came into being. Sometimes they are too broad, or too vague, or too comprehensive, or they show too little differentiation and are thus not always suitable for strict application in a concrete case. But, conversely, they can be too specific and only applicable to a given situation, so that each application outside that can become a disputable extension. This must have already become clear from the preceding chapters. It is for this reason that the rules that lie behind all judgements (or are incorporated in them) are more to be regarded as lines along which the lawsuit has been adjudicated than as a basis upon which the judgements have been founded. From this it follows that the judgement given along such lines establishes the law for the case at issue and does to a great extent create the law specifically for that case. The law and the facts are interwoven; the facts help to give form to the law in a special case. From the foregoing it should be clear that it is hardly conceivable that a judgement cannot be given just because there is no rule upon which to base it. Even in a somewhat unusual case, a competent judge can always find, within the framework of *adat* law, a basis for a solution, and a valid rule.

THE LONG-NEGLECTED COMPLAINT

If a man does not take his case before the judge for a long time, or if he delays making his claim without good reason, then he stands in danger of the judge dismissing his claim with the following reproach:

agoan asu na hurang doda;
agoan uhum na hurang turut.
One loses one's dog if one does not call it often enough.
One loses one's right if one does not claim it.

This does not apply to those contract relationships which, by their nature, have no specified time limit, such as pledging a rice-field where no time is fixed for redemption, nor to arrangements relating to specific circumstances, such as, for instance, the right of usufruct of a *parripe,* of land belonging to the ruling *marga* of the village in which he is an in-dweller, which continues so long as he and his descendants remain in the village. But it does affect claims which in normal life should have been made long before, but which the complainant has neglected. To give an example: a man had promised his sister on her marriage some years previously that as his counter-present, *ulos-ulos,* to the *todoan* he had received, he would give her an *ulos pinunsaan,* a certain kind of over-garment. He did not immediately hand over this present but provisionally gave her a rice-field as a pledge, *sindor,* for it. It was only after the woman had been married for a long time and had had children and had become a grandmother, that he provided the promised cloth, requesting at the same time that the field be returned to him. The judge rejected his claim on the grounds that, after so many years, the field must be regarded as having become the permanent *ulos-ulos* of the woman and her family. In this decision, the judge quoted the saying above. Another example: a man claimed that twenty years earlier he had made a *toto* = preferential mark, on a piece of forest land and that about eight years later he had planted benzoin trees on it. He did not complain that his right had been violated by another man until the latter had already had his trees planted on the same piece of land for ten years. In less striking cases, I often heard the rule included in the maxim used as an auxiliary consideration in cases in which the complaint was badly expounded, inadequately supported by the evidence and clearly had been neglected too long, so that there were many reasons for its subsequent rejection.

THE PORANG TANGGA BATU LIMITATION

Shortly after the establishment of Dutch authority in the Toba Country, a rule was introduced that the official administration of justice would not deal with any claims which appeared to be older than the famous *Porang Tangga Batu* which was fought in 1883 against Ompu Badia in the neighbourhood of Balige. Such claims would be *perkara lama* (Malay) = claims that were too old. At present, there is a degree of uncertainty with regard to the scope and the sphere of this limitation rule. So far as it concerns Uluan, Habinsaran, Samosir and the Dairi Country, which were annexed in 1908, it is said that the date of the annexation feast is accepted as having the same meaning as the year 1883 has for Silindung, the Plateau and Toba Holbung. But officially, and privately, it is not accepted and is hardly ever applied. In 1915, a change was decided upon and the Resident issued a Circular — fortunately forgotten — in which it was laid down that henceforth no claims wuld be accepted that were older than two years. A later attempt to introduce a limitation period of ten years foundered because the people objected to it.

One observation should be made. The rules of limitation were primarily meant for cases concerning pledged rice-fields. A number of land cases are, however, closely related to the mutual relationship of the *marga,* thus with the right of disposal over land belonging to the villages and territories, which does not permit of the application of an automatically operating limitation. In Silindung and elsewhere, for example, it is impossible for the right to land cultivated for more than half a century by a *parripe* under the *parripean*-rule, and after his death worked by his sons who continued to dwell in the village, to be converted into something else by the mere passing of time. Even the *boru na godjong,* though it may have founded villages in the territory of its *hula-hula,* and may have been given its own *talian* = land for free cultivation and may use its fields as *pangoli ni anak pangias ni boru,* must always bear in mind that if it leaves the territory it will lose this land, despite the fact that its members have used it for centuries. The Batak, therefore, will always raise objections to a limitation rule which affects these relationships and those of a similar kind.

And little approval will be found for new forms of such a rule for pledged fields, opposed as the people always are to the loss of land for the lineage who cleared it and who desire to keep it. A new kind of *Porang Tangga Batu* rule can probably embrace little more than simply debt cases. After what has been said about oath-taking and the too-long-neglected claim, one would have one's doubts that it will be necessary for such a purpose.

Finally, claims based on the former laws regarding slaves, the law of war, the law of booty and peonage, to which must be added the law of gambling debts, can no longer be heard in these modern times.

IMPLEMENTATION

In respect of the implementation of the judgement he gives, the judge adopts a very realistic attitude. If a man has to surrender land and will not hand it over, then his land is not assessed in terms of money nor are his goods distrained on, but he is evicted from the land and if he returns and continues to act as its owner, he is guilty of overruling the judge's decision, *mangalaosi hata ni radja,* and he will be punished. If a village is founded without authorisation, it is demolished. If a co-dweller in a house will not contribute to its restoration, he is evicted. In olden times a man who could not pay his debts as ordered in a judgement, became a peon or was put in the block. If a *pangido-idoan* = water right levy, (in Toba), is not paid to the person who is entitled to it, then he is permitted to take as much of the harvest as is necessary to balance the levy. If a gold pledge must be handed over and the person who has to hand it over is unwilling to do so, then he can be put under restraint until he complies with the order. If a man is ordered to offer a meal, either with or without a *batu ni sulang-sulang,* and he fails to carry out the order, then he can be threatened with imprisonment.

Did the judge in olden times place importance on the observance of a judgement and could he intervene to see that it was carried out? Yes. Though he often delegated the trouble of seeing that it was implemented to others. We have already seen what happened in the case of offences that were regarded as offences against the community. Interference in the enforcement of a judgement was considered as a usual extension of the court's activities.

A *pangose* who shirked doing what he had agreed to do before the judge, was dealt with by the chiefs whose chiefly honour and respect were at stake. If a debt case was disposed of or if a penalty was imposed, the day and place when payment had to be made could be fixed; the chiefs were sometimes present and the *pago-pago* was usually settled then. I noted a solemn concluding formula, in *umpama* form, which covers the end of the lawsuit on such an occasion:

"sahat-sahat ni solu tu bontean, sahat ni haroan di tonga djabu; dibahen hupapungu pe hamu radja, nunga sae utangku.

The *solu* is drawn up into the boathouse, a little feast is held in the middle of the dwelling.

I have asked you, honourable chiefs, to come to this assembly so that you shall know that I have paid my debts."

To this the judges replied:

"tapor pansadian ni gondang, tula hasohotan ni gora

ba lean pudun di amanta pangulu, pago-pago di amanta radja.
When an instrument breaks the music must cease, separation ends
a fight.

So, now hand over your knot (as a token of the agreement) to the
honoured mediators, the sealing-money to the honourable chiefs.''
The responsibility of seeing that the judgement is carried out can be
delegated to another person. Formerly this was often done in a case
where a woman was divorced while she was still burdened with a debt,
i.e., part of the marriage payment. She then became the *boru ni radja* =
woman under the control of a chief, which chief could take receipt of
the marriage payment for her second marriage and could settle the debt
out of it. And in the case of a judgement to pay a fine, *dangdang*, or
compensation, a person was sometimes designated as an intermediary,
sisampe dangdang. The sum was handed over to him and he then had
to give it to the person entitled to receive it. The arbitrator in a case
could also assume the function of the *sisampe dangdang.* Frequently
the actual implementation of what both parties had agreed upon in
general terms, for example, the dividing up of a field into half, was
left to the common *boru* of the parties or to the two *boru* affines of both
parties. The *boru namora* of the village or the *boru na godjong* of the
territory could also be called upon.

Distraining on the possessions of a man who is unwilling to observe
a judgement to pay a sum of money, has only become the practice of
later years. The threat of attaching land and thereafter selling it publicy,
is often sufficient, because the kinsmen will not willingly see plots of
their *golat*-land offered for sale to anyone else.

If land is attached, then all Batak desire that no non-Batak will
come into permanent possession of a slice of Batak soil by buying it at
a public sale. A married woman will object to the attachment and sale
of her *bangunan*-field or the *indahan arian*-field which her small son
or daughter was given when they were born, and her own kinsmen are
opposed to her *pauseang*-field, which they gave her on her marriage,
being made available without their knowledge for the discharge of her
husband's debts, trading or otherwise, while the village chief objects to
the attachment of a *parripean*-field belonging to one of his *parripe* and
to its being sold other than by public sale as a pledged field, *lelang
dondon.* Moreover, the chiefs of the territories want to receive the *pago-
pago* and *sialabane* to which they are entitled when the *golat*-land of a
marga member is sold to a non-member. The pledgee of a pledged rice-
field that is attached, wants the *balik bungki* = time during which the

pledge cannot be redeemed (a minimum period of two years) to be upheld, or he desires that the period agreed with the pledger is not affected, and in any case that his right as a pledgee in respect of the land is safeguarded and that his right to the standing harvest is assured. The kinsmen insist that land should not be sold when they are ignorant that it has been attached or have not had ample opportunity to think it over. The chiefs of the village and the territory object because only people like clerks and such who have absolutely no interest in the territory or in matters concerning its land, are employed as witnesses, so that the chances are that the attachment gives rise to some secret scheme.

If a house in a village is distrained on, then the village chief and the inhabitants desire that they are given preferential right and that the *adat gadison djabu* will also be taken into consideration. If a part of something held in joint ownership is distrained on, then the part owners similarly want to protect their right of preference when the item is to be sold.

I mention these things, which I noted during the time I was a court President, to show that the institution of judicial distraint, which in itself can be useful, should in the course of time, acquire its own Batak character and deserves more attention than it has been given up to the present.

APPENDIX I (see pp. 31, 49, 160)

THE FEAST: MEMBERS ATTENDING AND USAGES

(From a report I have received)

M. of the marga Lumban Tobing, which is established in the Silindung Valley, belongs to the lineage of Ompu Tuan Nahoda, of which the position in the *marga* connections is indicated in the following genealogical tree:

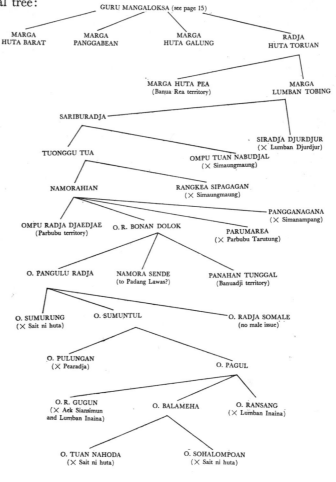

GURU MANGALOKSA (see page 15)

MARGA HUTA BARAT

MARGA PANGGABEAN

MARGA HUTA GALUNG

RADJA HUTA TORUAN

MARGA HUTA PEA (Banua Rea territory)

MARGA LUMBAN TOBING

SARIBURADJA

SIRADJA DJURDJUR (× Lumban Djurdjur)

TUONGGU TUA

OMPU TUAN NABUDJAL (× Simaungmaung)

NAMORAHIAN

RANGKEA SIPAGAGAN (× Simaungmaung)

PANGGANAGANA (× Simanampang)

OMPU RADJA DJAEDJAE (Parbubu territory)

O. R. BONAN DOLOK

PARUMAREA (× Parbubu Tarutung)

O. PANGULU RADJA

NAMORA SENDE (to Padang Lawas?)

PANAHAN TUNGGAL (Banuadji territory)

O. SUMURUNG (× Sait ni huta)

O. SUMUNTUL

O. RADJA SOMALE (no male issue)

O. PULUNGAN (× Pearadja)

O. PAGUL

O. R. GUGUN (× Aek Siansimun and Lumban Inaina)

O. BALAMEHA

O. RANSANG (× Lumban Inaina)

O. TUAN NAHODA (× Sait ni huta)

O. SOHALOMPOAN (× Sait ni huta)

× Groups of *huta*, i.e. small territories, in the Huta Toruan territory.

The position of M. in the lineage of Ompu Tuan Nahoda is indicated in the following genealogical tree in which, for the sake of simplicity, numbers and letters are substituted for the names:

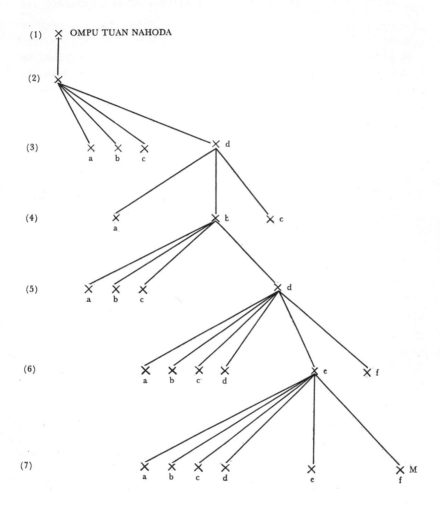

M. had built a new house and was appointed *kampung* chief. In 1927, for the ceremonial consecration of the new dwelling, *mangompoi djabu,* and also to celebrate the welcome appointment, he invited his kinsmen, affines and friends to a great four-day feast in order to receive their *pasu-pasu* and their benedictory addresses.

M. was the *suhut,* the giver of the feast, and, together with his five brothers, formed a *hasuhuton* = feast-giving group.

The first day was the day for the *pardongan-sabutuhaon* = members of the lineage, *marga* and tribal group. The *hasuhuton* and their wives opened the ceremony as a group and danced to the music of the *gondang.* The melody played was called *gondang haroan* = opening melody. Then all the male descendants of Ompu Tuan Nahoda who were present, 44 in all, danced, with their wives. Each person held his *sampe tua* = good fortune bringing gift, in his outstretched fingers while he danced. Such a gift is given when a new house is consecrated. In this instance it consisted of sums of money of varying amounts. As the *suhut* received his gifts, he noted down the name of the donor and the amount, so that he would have a reminder of the presents he would have to give in the future.

When the descendants of Ompu Tuan Nahoda had concluded their dance, the following people danced in their turn, (see genealogical tree I):

the present male descendants of:

Ompu Sohalompoan,

Ompu Radja Gugun,

Ompu Ransang,

Ompu Pulungan,

Ompu Sumurung,

Panahan Tunggal,

Ompu Radja Djaedjae, Parumarea and Pangganagana,

Rangkea Sipagagan,

Ompu Tuan Nabudjal,

Siradja Djurdjur,

and also the representatives of the *marga* Huta Pea, Huta Galung, Huta Barat and Panggabean. All gave money gifts.

The second day was the day for the *parhula-hulaon* (*na nialap*). These men danced with their wives to the melody called *somba-somba* = reverential invocation, and during the dance they made their benedictory gestures with their fingers.

They were: a representative of the *hula-hula* group, *marga* Simandjuntak, from which Ompu Tuan Nahoda had taken his wife; a representative of the *hula-hula* group, *marga* Huta Barat, from which the *suhut*'s forefather, 3d in genealogical tree II, had taken his wife; a representative of the *marga* Huta Barat, from which great-grandfather 4b had taken his wife; a representative of the *marga* Manik, from which originated the wife of grandfather 5d; a *tulang,* mother's brother, *marga* Manik; and a brother-in-law, the *suhut*'s wife's brother, *marga* Huta Galung. All these dancers gave their *sampe tua,* consisting of woven cloths, *ulos,* to the *suhut.* Some of them also gave a sum of money, or rice, the latter being represented by a bag held in their hands.

Then the members of the *suhut*'s brothers' *hula-hula,* their brothers-in-law, danced. Each gave his *sampe tua,* which consisted of woven cloths, and a sum of money to his own brother-in-law, and a smaller gift, *tampe-tampe,* to the *suhut.* The total sum received by the *hasuhuton* from their *parhula-hulaon* was upward of 600 guilders.

The third day was the day for the *parboruon* (*parianakhonon*) of the lineage of Ompu Tuan Nahoda, as well as for the friends and distant affines of the *suhut.* The men of the *parboruon* danced first, with their wives, to the melody called *parmeme* = the rice chewer, (p. 58). During the dance they made the gestures with their fingers requesting benediction. Those of the wives who were barren pointed to their stomachs and pressed them in to show their emptiness. A score of people from different *marga,* Sihombing, Manik, Huta Galung, Sitompul, Pohan, Simamora and others, who had either taken as wives the daughters of the *suhut*'s forefathers or who were descended from these daughters in the male line, participated in the dancing. As their *sampe tua* they gave the *suhut* a money gift totalling 350 guilders, and they also gave a small sum of money, *tampe-tampe,* to be divided among the rest of the descendants of Ompu Tuan Nahoda.

Then the friends and distant affines of the *suhut,* among whom were many chiefs from the surrounding areas, danced and gave their *sampe tua* consisting of small sums of money.

On the fourth day, all the descendants of Ompu Tuan Nahoda again joined together in the dancing and danced to the melody called *panggompuli* which announced the end of the ceremonies. They were joined by all their affines on both sides, and then all the chiefs and elders of the territory Huta Toruan joined under the leadership of the *negeri* chief.

The dancing concluded, they then divided the *djambar,* the portions of the slaughtered buffaloes, to which those participating at the feast were entitled according to their genealogical position. The divisions were as follows: the *hula-hula* received a rib, *somba-somba,* for each group represented at the feast; members of the lineage, *marga* and tribal group received a piece of the thigh, *soit,* for each of the groups that had participated in the first day of the feast; the *boru* received its usual part, the *rungkung* = neckpiece.

The rest of those present received the *sitoho-toho* = remainder of the meat. The distribution, *manarima*, of these *djambar* is done by a kinsman of the *suhut* who is expert in knowing which portion should be given to each person. The man who does the distribution stands on a raised platform, calls the name of each person at the top of his voice and turns the piece of meat around so that everyone can see clearly the part the recipient is getting. He then throws the meat onto a mat = *sosar*, and from there the guest collects it.

At the conclusion, the melody called *gondang hasahatan* = the concluding melody, was played, and some of those present addressed the *suhut* with their good wishes, *marhata sigabe-gabe*. When that had been done, the *negeri* chief gave a Christian thanksgiving.

THE RESTORATION OF CONCORD AND PEACE IN THE MARGA SILITONGA OF THE SIPAHUTAR TERRITORY, EAST HUMBANG

(Translated from an article in 'Suara Batak' 12th and 19th July, 1930)

The *marga* Silitonga occupies the Sipahutar territory (*luat*) and lies like an island in the middle of some other *marga*, which, like it, stem from Sibagot ni Pohan, i.e., Pandjaitan, Simandjuntak, Tampubolon, Napitupulu and others. One can, however, say that the *marga* Silitonga is rather exclusively established in the Sipahutar territory because this region has for a long time been divided, *marbagian-bagian,* between the different *marga.* There is a *haradjaon* = autonomous community here, and another there, and that of Sipahutar is occupied by the Silitonga. This *marga* is smaller than the surrounding *marga.* Still, it has never been driven out, *dipaoto-oto* = (literally) made a fool of, of this territory by the other *marga,* neither during the previous warring period, nor at the present day.

When Christianity penetrated into Sipahutar, the population of the territory consisted of some 90 immediate families. At present, there are about 250 families and there are also approximately 15 families of the in-dwelling *marga, boru gomgoman.* The first missionary was received cordially by all and Sipahutar became the centre of the parish, *huria,* Sabungan, (which contains some chieftaincies). [This comment is Vergouwen's.]

When the Government began to regulate the chieftaincy, a *Radja Ihutan* (= *Djaihutan*), one Ompu Sodunggaron, was immediately appointed to the *marga* Silitonga. He was succeeded on his death by his son, the present *negeri* chief.

So long as Ompu Sodunggaron was alive, he led, *manguluhon,* the *marga* forcefully towards God's Word. But in 1923, the Evil One penetrated into the territory and stirred up widespread discord among the Silitonga. It began over the question of the division of the *djambar.* This produced general dissension which assumed extraordinary proportions. The Silitonga divided into two camps each of which went its own way in respect of marrying off daughters, *parmuli ni boru,* and sons, *pangolion ni anak.* The two factions were completely at loggerheads in their mutual juridical life, *uhum,* and in the promoting of their general interests, *siluluan.*

Once camp consisted of the *negeri* chief, certain of the *kampung* chiefs and some of the elders, *panungganei.* The other embraced the rest of the *kampung* chiefs and the elders. Their leader was Radja N. Among the rank and file, *na torop,* of the Silitonga, there were those who, though they were very close kinsmen of the one party, yet sided with the other. And so the Evil One pursued his vicious way.

If two men who were bound for the same destination met, they did not greet each other, *masisungkunan.* Even in church the two factions sat separately. And, as far as carrying out the Government's regulations was concerned, if anyone did something wrong in error, there was always someone ready to take advantage of it. Further strife was also stirred up by some individuals from the neighbouring territories (*hombar balok*).

The quarrel had reached such a pitch, that at one time the *hula-hula* of the Silitonga of Sipahutar, i.e., Radja Kilian Sihombing, the *negeri* chief of Lintong ni Huta (West Humbáng) visited with a great number of people the territory in an endeavour to settle it. That was in 1927, when about 1,000 people of our *hula-hula* came to visit us, *marebat-ebat.* But, because there was no unanimity of opinion as to how the guests should be received according to *adat, mangalusi, mangadati,* only the *negeri* chief and his party performed the various ceremonies and nothing came of the attempt to settle the quarrel. Later on, Radja Kilian came once again with a number of companions, bringing with them a cow of which the slaughter was to serve to bring us together again. But this time, too, people remained obdurate. The wedge had been driven too deeply into the *marga.* The Controleur (= Dutch District Officer) himself was even asked to intervene in the matter, but nothing came of it.

So affairs stood in 1929, when a younger brother of Radja N., the leader of one of the factions, who was an official, was pensioned off and returned to the village where he was born. He speedily made it known to the villagers that the quarrel which had arisen during his absence had made a deep impression on him and that he was desirous of bringing it to an end. He had only been in the village for three months when he made up his mind to see the *negeri* chief to discuss a reconciliation, *pordomuan.* Previously, he had prayed to God that He would make the *radja*'s heart susceptible to his well-chosen and well-meant words, *mandok hata na uli djala na lehet*. The *negeri* chief lent a willing ear to what his visitor had to say and viewed the plan very favourably. The upshot of their discussion was that the *negeri* chief invited all the *kampung* chiefs and the elders who belonged to his faction to come to his office on a particular day. At the same time, the leader of the other faction made an appeal to his own party to attend the gathering.

When all the elders of both parties had assembled, the proposer of the meeting addressed them as follows: "For a long time I have had the desire that we Silitonga should again be united in peace and harmony, *marlehet mardame,* and that there should be concord in the territory if Sipahutar which we who are the descendants of Siradja Silitonga and who are of one family, *na saripe,* occupy". Thereupon all present expressed the wish that peace should be restored. And, since it had also become apparent that the Holy Ghost had entered into them, they agreed that they should slaughter a buffalo to confirm the peace settlement and also to strengthen people's determination to live in harmony and good-will in the future. All that had previously happened and all that had been said previously would be regarded as being over and done with. It would be as though God Himself had expunged it all.

It was then decided that 15th October, 1929, would be the day for the festival gathering. All were agreed that the *gondang* must be played as an expression of joy at their restored unity.

The same day that they made this decision, a written request to be allowed to play he *gondang* was sent to the Ephorus (= Head of the Batak Church) at Pearadja, a request which was granted since the Church Council at Sipahutar had declared that it had no objection because there was no question of a pagan ritual.

At the same time, it was decided that the place where the feast should be held would be in the *huta* of the *negeri* chief, because he is our foremost elder, *situa-tuanta,* and because his house, built in the old Batak style, is a suitable place for the *gondang* to be played.

The Assistant Demang of Pangaribuan who was the Batak sub-district officer, the missionary of the province, the Batak pastor, *pandita,* the mission teachers of the elementary schools and others were invited to the feast.

On the appointed day, a small dais for the speech-makers was erected in the front of the *negeri* chief's house and adorned with beautiful flowers; the village-gate and the chief's house were hung with palm leaves. The arrival of the missionary was awaited but he did not put in an appearance, neither did the Batak *pandita* nor the school teachers. In the meantime, the rest of the people who had arrived by then crowded into the broad village square.

The festivities began with the dance of the married women, *inanta soripada,* for which one or two women from each of the 23 villages represented were selected. After this dance, the *negeri* chief and his principal adversary mounted the dais. The former then gave the reason for the gathering, in *umpama* form:

"The bamboos are growing on the village wall.

The *nangka* tree begins to bear fruit.

We are now gathered in this village by our God.

The very desirable concord again binds us together."

At the conclusion of this speech, all present shouted *horas!* = hail, three times. Then the leader of the other faction spoke, and he, too, enlarged upon the reason for the assembly and then he led the prayers. After that, all the women present danced under the direction of the *negeri* chief's wife. They formed two long rows standing opposite each other and stretching from one end of the village square to the other. They presented a lively spectacle. When the dancing was finished, the *kampung* chief N., and two church-elders proceeded to the dais from which the chief made a brief speech in *umpama*-form and after that one of the elders made an edifying speech and another said the prayers.

Then all the women of the *marga* Silitonga danced under direction of the *negeri* chief who gave them lively encouragement and even began to lead his dancing *iboto* = sisters, i.e., the female members of his *marga* around, with the result that there was great merriment and much happy confusion. People danced and laughed and could hardly find their way out from among the crowd. When finally order was more or less restored, such a clamour broke out that it was barely possible to hear the music. One or two of the older *marga* members spoke and then the old people danced behind each other in rows.

Following them, the members of the in-dwelling *marga, boru gom-goman,* and the members of our common *boru,* the *boru hatopannami,* who had come in from the other territories, danced together in a group. After this, two of them, Radja N. and Elder N. both from the *marga* Pardede which can be regarded as the oldest in-dwelling *marga,* the *boru na godjong,* took their places on the dais. The former then spoke the following in *umpama* form:

"In this land, scandal-mongers have created suspicions, in this Sipahutar territory which is of the *marga* Silitonga, *marga Silitonga do nampunasa*. In the past, we have quarrelled very very much. But from now on we are of one mind. Let us, therefore, praise God's goodness."

The Elder them made an edifying and very moving speech that was telling because he was so familiar with all that had happened.

When these speakers had finished, every man of the Silitonga living in the Sipahutar territory danced, everybody kissed everybody else and many hopped about to express their joy. And, even though perspiration was running down the *negeri* chief's face, no one failed to kiss him. The ground shook with the stamping of their feet. The members of the *hula-hula* were visibly participating in the general enjoyment which they expressed by giving money to the dancers.

Some little time later, the Assistant Demang gave his good wishes and then two of the chiefs of the affinal neighbouring territories spoke:

"The kinds of rice called *sitalitoba* and *purbatua*.

Now peace has been restored among you who belong to one *marga, na marsabutuha*.

May we, the *boru,* prosper as well as you, our *hula-hula*."

"The waves are breaking on Silangge, the rice grains are rolling.

Now that you, our affines, are in concord again, we, too, are joyful."

At the conclusion of these speeches, the Assistant Demang and the two chiefs danced, and did it quite well. It was by then evening and the people started homewards.

The following day, people again assembled to slaughter the peace-buffalo. Each family had brought rice. The meal proceeded in a very orderly way, many speeches were made and prayers of thanksgiving were said expressing the gratitude of the people that they were again united after so much discord.

28

THE VISIT OF THE HULA-HULA

(From "Palito Batak", 5th July, 1928)

Some time ago, the *marga* Pakpahan which lives at Pangaribuan, again made a visit, *marebat-ebat,* to the *marga* Panggabean at Silindung. That Lontung *marga* is the *hula-hula* of the Panggabean. The affinity relationship is a very old one because the ancestor of the Pakpahan, Radja Datu Ronggur, who left Samosir and went to live at Pangaribuan, married off his daughter, Si Boru Purnama, to a Panggabean, and, since then similar marriages have been repeatedly concluded. Both *marga* have prospered, *rap gabe,* for which reason they have frequently visited each other, *masiebat-ebatan.* But on this occasion the visit was on a grander scale than any previous one, for literally all the descendants, *pomparan,* of Radja Datu Ronggur, old and young, with their wives, made the journey.

They were welcomed with great joy by the Panggabean. Very skilled musicians played the *gondang* and the wind instruments. The visitors were entertained in the small Pansur na pitu territory where they danced, and they were also entertained in the Lumban Siagian territory about 3 miles further on by the *marga* branch living there. And, only when darkness fell on the first day did the people sit down to eat.

Many beautiful addresses were delivered, *marhata marsilehet-lehet,* after the meal.

The following morning, the cow which the Pakpahan had brought with them and which the Panggabean were to eat, was slaughtered. Addresses were again delivered after this meal and there was more music. And what a dance there was! The ground in front of the *negeri* chief's dwelling was packed tight. There were no less than 300 people dancing, all in rows; the men danced behind the men, while the Pakpahan women faced the Panggabean women. The dancing went on and on.

After the dancing, the Pakpahan offered their gifts which consisted of six over-garments, *ulos,* one for each of the five lineages of the Panggabean *marga* which are the *boru* of the Pakpahan and one for the *boru*-group which had originated from Boru Purnama.

RESOLUTION of the elected *radja* of the *negeri* Manalu Dolok who have discussed the manner in which the earnings of their subjects can be improved; how to counter the theft of harvests and of benzoin; and how to increase prosperity.

(1) In respect of benzoin, *hamindjon,* in the forests, the following applies: the first tapping, *sigi,* must be done by making at the most three, at the least two, lengthwise cuts in the tree. The cuts must be made over five times a man's height. The trees must be cleansed of parasitic plants, *sarindan.* Once in three years there must be a replanting to replace old trees. In this way the benzoin farmer will remain prosperous.

(2) In respect of the collecting of benzoin, the following applies: the village chief's permission must be obtained and the collecting must be done four times a year; first the *sidungkapi* (grade I), then the *barbar,* then the second *barbar,* and finally the *tahir,* scrapings. In this way the trees will last.

(3) The collected benzoin must be sold at trading places, indicated for the purpose by the *radja,* as central points, *pangkalan.*

(4) The trade centres are at: Lumban Tobing, Sisoding, Tor Nauli, Lumban Hariara, Parratusan, and Sihopong.

(5) The punishment, *pangonai,* is as follows: anyone who buys or sells benzoin secretly, *di na buni,* will be punished by the court, *siuhumon ni rapot* and an informer, *na paboahon,* will receive a reward.

(6) Each household must lay out a sweet potato garden, of one *bau* (= ± two acres).

(7) Each household must keep a sow, *babi kasin,* so that taxes and the redemption money from statute labour can be paid.

(8) Each household must lay out a variety of gardens for its sustenance.

(9) When there is a suitable place in an area for the cultivation of rice, *parhaumaan,* each household must lay out a ricefield. If it is necessary to dig an irrigation ditch, and if this is beyond the capacity of the village, then it may ask the Government to help.

(10) According to the rule, *patik,* now given by us, the *radja,* there may in future be no gambling within our *haradjaon* under one *kepala*

negeri = negeri chief, of which the boundaries are: with **Ranggitgit** the region Tano Perak pangengge-enggean; with Sigulok, the river Aek Bontar; with Sibuntuon the river Aek Bundong; with Huta Tua, from Adian Bolak to Tulpang; with Parmonangan, the river Aek Bulu Boltak; with Huta Djulu, from Adian Rihit to Adian Matutung; so that all the inhabitants of this territory, *pangisi ni luat i,* will prosper and will diligently cultivate their gardens.

(11) If gambling is reported in the area under the jurisdiction of a *kampung* chief, then he is obliged to take action and he must bring the gamblers before the district officer. Gambling gives rise to thieving and lying and it hinders the regular cultivation of the fields.

(12) Two honest people, *na burdju marroha,* have been chosen by the assembled *radja* to supervise the carrying out of these rules.

AGREEMENT between the entire inhabitants of a group of *huta* in selecting one of their number as a *kampung* chief (1929).

"Hami angka na martanda tangan di toru ni surat on, i ma angka *parripe* ni lungguk Gompar Sipaet na *morhuta di* Gompar Sipaet I, Gompar Sipaet II, Gompar Sipaet III, Lumban Binanga I, Lumban Binanga II, dohot di Lumban Mual Dolok Gandjang, negeri Sitiotio, district Porsea Toba, naung mangaku do hami marhite-hite hasadaon ni rohanami padjolohon si Friderich Marpaung on (*pahompu* ni Kepala Kampung Ompu Simangimpalan nahinan) asa ibana gabe *kepala kampongnami.*"

"We the undersigned, the inhabitants of the group Gompar Sipaet and living in the villages Gompar Sipaet I, II, and III, Lumban Binanga I and II and Lumban Mual Dolok Gandjang in the negeri Sitiotio, district Porsea Toba, hereby declare that we unanimously recommend Friderich Marpaung, grandson of the deceased *Kampung* chief Ompu Si Mangimpalan, to be appointed as our *Kampong* chief."

"Asa manang andigan pe tingki *mamillit* radja di hami sandok olat ari pardjandjian on, hot do ibana todoonnami, ndang pola marhite verkiezing."

"So that, when the time comes for us to *elect* a chief, we will abide by the preference stated in this agreement and no further election will be necessary."

"Aut sura masa pe parsalisian manang aı ı ni aha di hami di pudi ni ari pardjandjian on, tung na so boi be pauł ıonnami *pardjandjiannami* on."

"And should disagreement arise after the date of this *agreement* for some reason or other, we shall, nevertheless, stand by it."

"Asa i ma na hutandatangani hami di toru ni on.

Angka on ma goarnami na martanda tangan:"

"And to this agreement we append our signatures.

Which are as follows":

1 Ama ni Hantor Marpaung
2 Ama ni Anda   „
3 Hiskia   „
4 Thomas   „
5 Ompu Situngkot Tampubolon
6 Aman Tungkot   „

and so on for the remainder of the 26 signatories.

INDEX OF BATAK WORDS

The words are listed under their stems, as in Van der Tuuk's and Warneck's dictionaries.

Numbers in bold face indicate the most important references.

haanon 226, 284, morsahala 84.

sahat 312, 337, sahat mara 312, na so sahat 198, pasahathon 205, 312, dipasahat di tondi ni na mandjalo 317, gondang hasahatan 428, sisada hasahatan 72, tanda hasahatan 72.

saksi 144, 387, saksi ni djudji 145, saksi ni gade 294, saksi ni onan 144, ama ni saksi 145, di balian ni saksi 366, bona ni saksi 125, ompu ni saksi 125, 145, 201, 383, 387.

saksi (Mal.) 395, saksi ginadis 398.

sala 162, 350, 351, 356, pl. II, sala tu adat 170, 340, 352, sala tu haradjaon 352, daon ni sala 351, utang sala 350, 359, upa sala-sala 313, hasala-salaan 55, parsala 349, 350.

sali, marsali 295, 332.

salpu, hata na masalpuhú 371.

sambar, marsambar 171, masisambaran 318, pasambarhon 318.

samboli, panamboli 72, 90.

sambut, marsambut 333.

samot, ulos pansamot 174, 180, pansamotan 171, sinamot 171, 172, 174, 176, 196, 198-200, 205, 271, 392, marhata sinamot 171, 172, 174, 176, 193, 199, bohi ni sinamot 175, 190, 203, 262, 263, 271, 279, boli ni sinamot 171, 174, patudjolo ni sinamot 191, 262, ulos ni sinamot 60, 174, sisada sinamot 43, 149, parsinamot 171.

sampang, onan sampang 120.

sampe, sisampe dangdang 376, 422, sampe tua 99, 305, 317, 426, 427.

sampur, indahan sampur 182, pasampurhon 182-184.

samun, manamun 376, panamun 406.

sangap 61, 83, 204, hasangapon 49, 62, 77, 83, 131, 135, 288, 383, sisada hasangapon 43, na sumangap 89, 288, 413.

sanggar 379.

sangge, parsangge talak 225.

sanggul 101, parsanggul baringin 77, parsanggulan 91.

sangkan 382.

sangketa 354, 405.

sangkot, manangkothon hohosna 244, manangkothon simata 190.

sanihe 212.

santi, hordja santi 57, santi rea 36, 44,

71, parsantian 36, ruma parsantian 72, 100, 121.

saor, indahan sinaor 93, 150, 357, 370, hasaoran 344, parsaoran 228.

sapata 84, 86, 95, 227, pl. III.

sapiri 403, 406.

saput 274, 361.

sarbut, manarbut 326, pasarbuthon 326.

sarindan 435.

sarune, parsarune 90.

sasap 90.

saudara tu bohi 97, na marsaudara 88.

saur, saur matua 62, dengke saur 91, 182.

saut 146, 302, 303, pudun-saut 175, pasauthon 383, parsaut ni sipanganon 96, 97, 179.

seang, pauseang 52, 60, 61, 123, 142, 153, 174, 181, 190, 198, 200, 202, 203-210, 215, 217, 223, 226, 227, 239, 241, 242, 246, 250, 259, 271, 273, 280, 282, 283, 287, 318, 325, 333, 344, 372, 392, 400, 422.

seat, sineat ni bibir djuhut daonna 95, ndang tarseat tangan ni paniopi 323.

sega adat 352, sega patik 352, sisegai saksi 387.

sĕmbarur (Dairi) 122.

semet, sisemet imbulu 357.

serak, marserak 23, 121, parserahan 23, 121.

sere (Mand.) 172.

siak, pasiak-siakhon 374.

sial 99.

siala, sialabane 180, 302, 331, 422, marsialabane 331.

siat, parhata siat 65.

sibaso 70, sibaso na bolon 72, parsibasoan 73.

sibuk ni djuhut 90.

siding, pasiding-siding 351, 363.

sigi 435.

sihol, daon sihol 65, 286, pardaon siholan 286, parsiholan 286.

sila 178.

silaon, boru silaon 20, 51.

sili, porsili 69, 85, 95.

silua 305, 318.

simata, manangkothon simata 190.

simbora, porsimboraan 69.

simen 71.

sinabul, parsinabul 390.

sindor 114, 154, 197, 200, 207, 277,

LEGAL MAXIMS AND APHORISMS

aek na litok tingkiron tu djulu 391.
agoan asu na hurang doda 187, 419.
anak sipanunda ndang digadis 214, 227.
ansimun na martagan ama ni mandulo 308, 309, 393.
ansimun sada holbung dohot pege sangkarimpang 265.
baris-baris ni gadja di rura Pangaloan 131.
batu na balga, batu na metmet, paradian ni sitapi-tapi 404.
bodil manungkun, hudjur manise, tali manahut 380.
bulung ni bulu diparigat-rigat halak 363.
butar-butar mataktak butar-butar maningkii 243.
dangka do dumpang, amak rere 63.
dapot do imbo dibahen soarana; djala dapot ursa dibahen bogasna 401.
dia nangkatna, dia ultopna 386.
disí sirungguk disí sitatá 386.
disi tano niinganhon, disi solup pinarsuhathon 141.
djodjor bona songon boras ni taem 40.
djolo mulak sian topot asa djumadihon parbadaan 314.
dos do sanggar dohot tolong 379.
dos do sitiop sige dohot sitangko tuak 370.
dung sansimu marsambola 33.
gala-gala na sabotohon 150.
gala-gala sitellu, tellúk mardagul-dagul 351.
gandjang abor ndang djadi suruhon 139.
gokhon sipaimaon, djou-djou sialusan 97, 298.
habang lali ndang habang tungko 342.
hata mamundjung hata lalaen 79, 346.
hata na torop sabungan ni hata 79, 346.
hinurpas dingding sinigat oma 407.
hite bulu diparhite paronan 387.
hori ihot ni doton 307.
hori na rundut bahenon tu tapean 391.
hunsi do hunsi-hunsi ransang do ransang-ransang 401.
idjuk di para-para, hotang di parlabean 140, 331.
inggir-inggir na mapipil, lombu-lombu na tartading na so sidohon-dohonon 301.
lata nidanggurhon tu porlak ni deba, nampuna porlak nampunasa 267.
lili ma di gindjang, hodong ma di toru 98.
madekdek gandar bulu tu bulung ni ampapaga 397.
mallandja pallandja, pallandja ni radja 134.
mambahen tata naung masak 411.
mandurung pandurung, pandurung ni radja 134.
manggulut imput ni leang-leang 377.
mangkuling taguk-taguk diatas ni arirang 146.
mangula pangula, pangula ni radja 134.
manuan bulu di lapang-lapang ni babi 164, 265.
manuk-manuk hulabu ompan-ompan ni soru 251.

tapor pansadian ni gondang, tula hasohotan ni gora 421.
timbang daon ni na tutú; gana daon ni na so tutú 394.
tinaba ni tangke martumbur; tinaba ni gana ndang martumbur 408.
tinapu salaon, salaon ni situa-tua 62.
tiniptip sanggar bahen huru-huruan 21.
togú urat ni bulu, toguán urat ni padang 142.
topot mula ni uhum, sungkun mula ni hata 314.
tungkap marmeme anak, tungkap marmeme boru 58.
tutú ninna anduhur, tió ma ninna lote 98.
ugasan ripe-ripe ndang tarbahen panghimpalan 285, 320.
unang pabalga hae-hae ni horbóm 199.

ERRATUM

Page 306, line 22 and line 30 *mangasahan*, read: *mangasahon*.

KONINKLIJK INSTITUUT
VOOR TAAL-, LAND EN VOLKENKUNDE

Translation Series

1. W. F. STUTTERHEIM, Studies in Indonesian Archaeology. 1956. xx, 158 pp.

2. G. J. HELD, The Papuas of Waropen. 1958. xv, 384 pp.

3. W. H. RASSERS, Pañji, the Cultural Hero. A Structural Study of Religion in Java. 1959. ix, 304 pp.

4. TH. G. TH. PIGEAUD, Java in the Fourteenth Century. A Study in Cultural History. The Nāgara-kĕrtāgama by Rakawi Prapañca of Majapahit, 1365 A.D.

   I. Javanese Texts in Transcription. 1960. xvi, 125 pp.

  II. Notes on the Texts and Translations. 1960. xvi, 153 pp.

 III. Translations. 1960. xiii, 177 pp.

 IV. Commentaries and Recapitulation. 1962. x, 552 pp.

  V. Glossary, General Index. 1963. viii, 451 pp.

5. F. D. K. BOSCH, Selected Studies in Indonesian Archaeology. 1961. 203 pp.

6. H. SCHÄRER, Ngaju Religion. The Conception of God among a South Borneo People. 1963. xv, 229 pp.

MARTINUS NIJHOFF · THE HAGUE